Emotions, Imagination, and Moral Reasoning

Emotions, Imagination, and Moral Reasoning

edited by
Robyn Langdon &
Catriona Mackenzie

Psychology Press
Taylor & Francis Group

New York   London

Psychology Press
Taylor & Francis Group
711 Third Avenue
New York, NY 10017

Psychology Press
Taylor & Francis Group
27 Church Road
Hove, East Sussex BN3 2FA

© 2012 by Taylor & Francis Group, LLC
Psychology Press is an imprint of Taylor & Francis Group, an Informa business

Printed in the United States of America on acid-free paper
Version Date: 2011922

International Standard Book Number: 978-1-84872-900-1 (Hardback)

Library of Congress Cataloging-in-Publication Data

Emotions, imagination, and moral reasoning / editors, Robyn Langdon, Catriona Mackenzie.
    p. cm. -- (Macquarie monographs in cognitive science)
    Includes bibliographical references and index.
    ISBN 978-1-84872-900-1 (hardcover : alk. paper)
    1. Emotions. 2. Imagination. 3. Reasoning. 4. Cognitive psychology. I. Langdon, Robyn. II. Mackenzie, Catriona.
    BF511.E465 2012
    155.2'5--dc23
    2011036768

Visit the Taylor & Francis Web site at
http://www.taylorandfrancis.com

and the Psychology Press Web site at
http://www.psypress.com

Contents

Acknowledgments

The chapters in this volume all stem from an international, interdisciplinary workshop on "Emotions, Imagination, and Moral Reasoning" held at Macquarie University in Sydney, Australia, September 5–7, 2008, and the subsequent collaborative discussions that were prompted by that meeting. We wish to thank the Macquarie Centre for Cognitive Science and the Research Centre for Agency, Values, and Ethics in the Faculty of Arts, Macquarie University, for providing financial support for the interdisciplinary workshop that culminated in this volume. We also thank the administrative staff of the Macquarie Centre for Cognitive Science for their assistance with the organization of that workshop. The chapters in this volume have all been subject to peer review. We would like to thank a number of anonymous reviewers as well as several of the contributors to this volume for their assistance with the review process. Finally, we are particularly grateful to Paul Keil for his invaluable editorial assistance with collating the contributions for this volume.

About the Editors

Robyn Langdon is an associate professor of the Macquarie Centre of Cognitive Science and a senior research fellow of the Australian Research Council (ARC) Centre of Excellence for Cognition and Its Disorders. Her research interests lie within the field of cognitive neuropsychiatry; she uses this approach to better understand the disturbances of normal information processing associated with specific psychiatric symptoms such as poor social functioning in schizophrenia and other psychopathologies. In her current research, she is extending her investigations into the relations between poor social cognition and poor social functioning to better understand violent tendencies in people with schizophrenia and amoral behavior in psychopathically inclined individuals. She has been a guest editor of the journal *Cognitive Neuropsychiatry*, and regularly publishes in journals such as the *Annual Review of Psychology*, *Schizophrenia Bulletin*, *Psychological Medicine*, and *Cognitive Neuropsychiatry*.

Catriona Mackenzie is a professor of philosophy and the director of the Research Centre for Agency, Values, and Ethics at Macquarie University in Sydney, Australia. Her areas of research specialization include ethics, philosophical moral psychology, social and political philosophy, and applied ethics. She is a coeditor of *Relational Autonomy: Feminist Perspectives on Autonomy, Agency, and the Social Self* (Oxford University Press, 2000) and *Practical Identity and Narrative Agency* (Routledge, 2008). Mackenzie has published articles in journals such as *Australasian Journal of Philosophy*, *Hypatia*, *Journal of Applied Philosophy*, *Journal of Social Philosophy*, *Philosophical Papers*, and *Philosophical Explorations* as well as book chapters in numerous edited volumes. She was awarded the 2007 Australian Museum Eureka Prize for Research in Ethics.

Contributors

Avi Aronstan
Department of Psychology
Macquarie University
Sydney, New South Wales, Australia

Eleni Caldis
Department of Psychology
Macquarie University
Sydney, New South Wales, Australia

Trevor Case
Department of Psychology
Macquarie University
Sydney, New South Wales, Australia

Wayne Christensen
Konrad Lorenz Institute for Evolution
    and Cognition Research (KLI)
Vienna, Austria

Fred Cicchini
Department of Psychology
Macquarie University
Sydney, New South Wales, Australia

Mark R. Dadds
School of Psychology
University of New South Wales
Sydney, New South Wales, Australia

Ricardo de Oliveira-Souza
D'Or Institute for Research and
    Education
and
Federal University of the State of Rio
    de Janeiro
Rio de Janeiro, Brazil

Marc de Rosnay
ERIC Working Group
School of Psychology
University of Sydney
Sydney, New South Wales, Australia

Kristy Delmas
School of Psychiatry
University of New South Wales
Sydney, New South Wales, Australia

Jess Evans
Department of Psychology
Macquarie University
Sydney, New South Wales, Australia

Elian Fink
ERIC Working Group
School of Psychology
University of Sydney
Sydney, New South Wales, Australia

Chloë FitzGerald
Centre de Recherche en Éthique de
    l'Université de Montréal
Montréal, Québec, Canada

Kristina Fritz
ERIC Working Group
School of Psychology
University of Sydney
Sydney, New South Wales, Australia

Peter Goldie
Philosophy Department
University of Manchester
Manchester, United Kingdom

Steve Guglielmo
Department of Cognitive, Linguistic, and Psychological Sciences
Brown University
Providence, Rhode Island

David J. Hawes
School of Psychology
University of Sydney
Sydney, New South Wales, Australia

Jeanette Kennett
Philosophy Department
Macquarie University
Sydney, New South Wales, Australia

Robyn Langdon
ARC Centre for Excellence in Cognition and Its Disorders
and
Macquarie Centre for Cognitive Science
Macquarie University
Sydney, New South Wales, Australia

Neil Levy
Florey Neuroscience Institutes
The University of Melbourne
Melbourne, Victoria, Australia

Catriona Mackenzie
Philosophy Department
Macquarie University
Sydney, New South Wales, Australia

Bertram F. Malle
Department of Cognitive, Linguistic, and Psychological Sciences
Brown University
Providence, Rhode Island

Victoria McGeer
University Center for Human Values
Princeton University
Princeton, New Jersey

Jonathan McGuire
ARC Centre for Excellence in Cognition and Its Disorders
and
Macquarie Centre for Cognitive Science
Macquarie University
Sydney, New South Wales, Australia

Doris McIllwain
Department of Psychology
Macquarie University
Sydney, New South Wales, Australia

Jorge Moll
D'Or Institute for Research and Education
and
Federal University of the State of Rio de Janeiro
Rio de Janeiro, Brazil

Megan J. Oaten
Department of Psychology
Macquarie University
Sydney, New South Wales, Australia

Ian Ravenscroft
Philosophy Department
Flinders University
Adelaide, Australia

Richard J. Stevenson
Department of Psychology
Macquarie University
Sydney, New South Wales, Australia

John Sutton
Macquarie Centre for Cognitive Science
Macquarie University
Sydney, New South Wales, Australia

Alan Taylor
Department of Psychology
Macquarie University
Sydney, New South Wales, Australia

Adam Wright
Department of Psychology
Macquarie University
Sydney, New South Wales, Australia

1

Introduction
Philosophical and Psychological Perspectives on Moral Cognition

ROBYN LANGDON and CATRIONA MACKENZIE

Macquarie University

This volume brings together philosophical perspectives on the role of emotions and imagination in moral cognition with psychological findings from the neurosciences, cognitive sciences, social psychology, personality theory, and developmental psychology. Among the issues and the questions examined are the following: What can we learn about the importance of empathic responsiveness in moral cognition by studying typically developing young children, young children and adolescents with callous-unemotional traits, and adults from the general community with psychopathic tendencies? What are the theoretical implications for moral philosophy of recent experimental research on emotions and moral reasoning in the neurosciences, cognitive science, and social psychology? Conversely, do the existing theoretical frameworks and experimental methodologies in empirical moral psychology do justice to the normative dimensions of moral discourse and to the complexity of everyday moral reflection? How might these theoretical frameworks and experimental methodologies be improved, with collaborative input from researchers across the various disciplines involved in moral cognition research?

INTRODUCTION

O ver the last decade there has been a resurgence of interest in moral cognition among psychologists of varying theoretical perspectives. At the same time, there has been increasing interest among philosophers in the empirical findings from this new research in experimental moral psychology.[1] This convergence of interest in moral cognition creates both opportunities for cross-disciplinary collaboration and risks of cross-disciplinary misunderstanding. The aim of this volume, and the workshop from which it arose, is to promote cross-disciplinary dialogue—to reduce mutual misunderstandings, clarify theoretical conceptions, discuss underlying assumptions and methodological limitations, and highlight new directions for future research. We thank all our workshop participants and, in particular, the contributors to this volume for their willingness to step beyond their own disciplinary safety nets, their openness to novel perspectives, and their enthusiasm for advancing cross-disciplinary understanding of moral cognition. Our aim in this introductory chapter is to briefly discuss some of the themes that emerge in subsequent chapters while leaving more detailed reflections to Christensen and Sutton in their concluding chapter.

The specific focus of the volume is to investigate the relations among emotions, imagination, and reasoning in moral cognition. Dominant traditions within both psychology and philosophy conceptualize the emotions as in conflict with, and subversive of, moral reasoning.[2] Within psychology these traditions are being challenged by research on normal and abnormal moral development and moral competence in several subdisciplinary fields, including developmental psychology (see, e.g., Eisenberg, Spinrad, & Sadovsky, 2006; Hoffman, 2000), cognitive neuroscience (see, e.g., Damasio, 1995; Tranel, 1994), and personality theory (see, e.g., Paulhus & Williams, 2002). This research provides evidence that capacities for emotion processing and empathic responsiveness play a crucial role in the development of moral cognition in young children and the sustaining of moral competencies in healthy adults. Traditional views of the emotions as solely in conflict with moral reasoning are thus grossly inadequate and do a disservice to the positive force of emotions in healthy moral agency. The chapters in the first part of the volume investigate the relations between empathy and moral competence from different psychological perspectives. In doing so, they highlight the multifaceted nature of empathy.

MORALITY, EMPATHETIC RESPONSIVENESS, AND THE MULTIFACETED NATURE OF EMPATHY

A recurring theme in many chapters is the role of empathy in healthy moral development and in curbing callous manipulative behavior in adults. In Chapter 2, de Rosnay and Fink provide a developmental psychological perspective on the relations between empathy and moral understanding. Their findings highlight the critical importance of typically developing young children's experience of empathic responsiveness toward others' feelings in the longitudinal development of a moral self-concept at 5 to 6 years of age. Their introductory review also alerts us to potentially different ways of "knowing" right from wrong and of the disconnections that might occur between rule-based and emotional moral understanding in young children's moral development. An example here is the literature on happy victimizer expectancy, which describes the phenomenon of young children, at around 6 years of age, being able to consistently judge moral transgressions as wrong while appearing unable to demonstrate a full appreciation of the moral emotional consequences for transgressors (i.e., young children will typically report a transgressor as feeling happy, rather than guilty, that a desired goal has been achieved via amoral means). While de Rosnay and Fink's empirical findings raise questions about what precisely happy victimizer expectancy has to tell us about young children's awareness of moral emotions, the suggestion that conceptual and empathic ways of knowing right from wrong might dissociate recurs in subsequent chapters, albeit in slightly different ways.

These different ways reflect, in part, the different terminological usages of *empathy* that appear throughout the volume; some authors use the term empathy more narrowly to refer to an emotional or affective responsiveness toward others that is more in keeping with the others' feelings than with one's own (e.g., de Rosnay & Fink, Chapter 2; Ravenscroft, Chapter 4), while others use empathy more generally to encompass both conceptual (or cold) and emotive (or hot) ways of appreciating what another person might think or feel (e.g., Hawes & Dadds, Chapter 3; McIlwain et al., Chapter 6). Regardless of these terminological differences, the findings discussed in these chapters all illustrate the importance of these distinctions. For example, de Rosnay and Fink report that empathic (or affective) responsiveness toward others, rather than a conceptual understanding of others' mental lives (also termed psychological perspective-taking or theory of mind) is more critical in the longitudinal development of moral conscience in typically developing young children.

Hawes and Dadds (Chapter 3) touch on a similar distinction when they discuss the possibility of different developmental routes to antisocial behavior in young children and adolescents. They use the term empathy more broadly to distinguish between cognitive and affective facets of empathy, a usage that is more in accord with the literature on psychopathy in adult criminals (see, e.g., Blair, 2005). After discussing various methodological issues with regard to operationalizing this distinction, Hawes and Dadds then review empirical findings that suggest the developmental pathways to "callous-unemotional" (or psychopathic) traits may differ for boys and girls; for example, their data suggest that only boys show the characteristic association between deficits of affective empathy and callous-unemotional traits that is reported in adult criminal psychopaths—most often, male criminal offenders. Their findings also indicate that cognitive empathy (perspective-taking/theory of mind) may be more impaired in younger antisocial boys than has previously been thought. These findings on cognitive empathy are surprising for a number of reasons. First, adults with psychopathic tendencies show evidence of dissociation between intact cognitive empathy and impaired affective empathy (see, e.g., Blair, 2005). Second, higher-order capacities for cognitive empathy, in particular, theory of mind, are thought to develop first around 4 to 5 years of age in typically developing young children. Third, it is the intact cognitive empathy in psychopathically inclined individuals, alongside their lack of affective empathy, that purportedly facilitates the psychopath's tendencies toward self-interested and uncaring manipulation of others' wants and needs. The implications of Hawes and Dadds's findings include that cognitive empathy may be acquired via different developmental processes in individuals with psychopathic compared with nonpsychopathic tendencies and more slowly in the former individuals, only maturing in the later pubertal years in psychopathically inclined male adolescents.

Ravenscroft (Chapter 4) continues the theme of empathy and its role in moral development, focusing on the impact on young children's moral development from exposure to different fictional worlds. The idea that fiction can enhance the development and exercise of moral capacities has a long philosophical history, dating back to Aristotle. More recently, this idea has been developed by Nussbaum (1995, 1997) who claims that literary imagination develops both children's and adults' capacities for compassion and, via this route, for moral understanding. In his chapter, Ravenscroft assesses Nussbaum's claims in light of work by psychologists Oatley (1999, 2008) and Mar (2004, 2009) on the role of fiction in enabling first-person "simulation-based" understanding of others' subjective worlds, and empirical research on imagination and imitation. Ravenscroft argues that just as motor imagery can enhance motor performance by providing opportunities for rehearsal and practice, so too can fiction scaffold and extend our imaginative capacities to empathize with others, thereby enhancing our capacities for empathic responsiveness. In the case of children, Ravenscroft cites evidence indicating that capacities for imitation are central to moral development; he suggests that some kinds of fiction recruit imitative capacities in the service of empathy, so providing young children with opportunities to practice (emotionally) empathetic responses and in turn facilitating the development of prosocial moral agency. However, he also cites empirical evidence reporting increases in aggressive behavior in young children who are exposed to violent fictional media—albeit with some dissenting voices in the literature about the significance of these findings—proposing that violent action-based fictions promote increased aggression via the recruitment of action-oriented, imitative mechanisms. Ravenscroft concludes by pointing to the pressing need for further research to better identify those properties of fictions that facilitate prosocial empathetic development and those that promote antisocial aggressive behaviors.

The chapters from Langdon and Delmas (Chapter 5) and McIlwain and colleagues (Chapter 6) take up issues first raised in the chapter by Hawes and Dadds concerning the impact of callous-unemotional traits on moral cognition. These chapters examine the relations between empathy and moral competence in nonincarcerated adults with varying levels of psychopathic tendencies. Both chapters argue for the importance of shifting the focus away from adult criminal psychopaths to successful psychopathically inclined adults in the general community to better understand the empathy deficit that purportedly lies at the core of psychopathic behavior.

Langdon and Delmas (Chapter 5) take as their starting point the influential study from Blair (1995), who reported that psychopathic inmates failed to make the moral-conventional distinction when judging the "right" or "wrong" and seriousness of moral and conventional transgressions. Langdon and Delmas caution that, while some philosophers interpret Blair's (1995) data as showing that psychopaths treat moral transgressions as if they are merely conventional and use that interpretation to support a sentimentalist approach to moral reasoning (see, e.g., Prinz, 2006), Blair's (1995) actual data show that psychopathic and nonpsychopathic inmates treat moral transgressions equally seriously. Where the two groups differed was that the psychopathic inmates treated the conventional transgressions as more like moral transgressions and not the other way round. Langdon and Delmas argue that Blair's data are just as consistent with the claim that the psychopathic inmates genuinely distinguished between moral and conventional transgressions and obscured this distinction by manipulatively inflating their ratings to impress authority figures. Since the behavioral responses of manipulative psychopathic individuals who are incarcerated need to be treated with great caution, Langdon and Delmas argue for a greater focus on moral reasoning in nonincarcerated adults with psychopathic tendencies. In their own study, they report no evidence of a relation between psychopathic tendencies in nonclinical, nonincarcerated adults and the capacities to distinguish between moral and conventional transgressions. They do find, however, that more psychopathically inclined individuals are more likely to endorse emotionally aversive acts of personally harming others in moral dilemma scenarios. They attribute this dissociation to a distinction between third-person (conceptual) and first-person (empathic) understanding of moral violations and the consequences for victims, picking up a theme first raised in Ravenscroft's chapter concerning the connections between first-person and third-person moral understanding. Compromise of first-person (empathic) understanding, they suggest, associates with an attenuated automatic emotional curb on behavior when psychopathically inclined people contemplate causing personal harm to another. But what of more controlled, deliberative empathic responses? This is a question that McIlwain and colleagues (Chapter 6) take up more directly.

McIlwain and colleagues investigate the distinction between automatic and strategic empathic processes when they go beyond a solitary focus on psychopathically inclined people in the general community to also consider people with Machiavellian personality traits. While psychopathically inclined people seem to have specific deficits in discerning and responding to the emotions of others, in particular, others' distress and fear, Machiavellian personalities seem to have more across-the-board, and perhaps strategic, affective distance. McIlwain and colleagues begin by reviewing psychometric approaches that measure these personality traits in the general community using self-report inventories. They then introduce their "cascading constraints" model, whereby early deficits (e.g., in emotion processing) have knock-on consequences in later development; early deficits constrain certain developmental opportunities while making other developmental pathways more likely. In their attempts to better specify these different developmental pathways in psychopathic and Machiavellian personalities, McIlwain and colleagues find that both personality styles share callous-unemotionality and a strategic capacity to control and use one's own emotional responses when it suits, alongside a reduced capacity for automatic empathy. Where the two personality styles differ is that the compromise of automatic empathy may be more strongly associated with callous-unemotionality in psychopathically inclined people. Their chapter also goes beyond quantitative research to explore not only the decisions made by psychopathically inclined and Machiavellian people when presented with moral dilemmas but also the differing rationales they provide for these decisions. These qualitative analyses reveal other subtle differences in the moral reasoning styles of psychopathic and Machiavellian personalities.

Overall, we think there are two important take-home messages from the five chapters on empathy. First, there seems to be strong evidence in support of the view that capacities for empathic responsiveness are central to moral cognition, even if there is as of yet no general consensus about how the concept of empathy, and the relationship between empathy and moral reasoning, should be understood. In particular, the three chapters on psychopathology from Hawes and Dadds, Langdon and Delmas, and McIlwain and colleagues highlight the negative impact of attenuated or impaired empathic capacities on the moral competence of psychopathically inclined adults and callous-unemotional adolescents—and the social cost of this impact. Second, if, as the evidence suggests, intuitive empathic responsiveness, and moral emotions more generally, plays a crucial role in healthy moral cognition, then we need to develop more sophisticated theoretical frameworks for understanding this role, drawing on evidence from a range of subdisciplinary psychological perspectives and from philosophical moral psychology to develop a more integrative rather than conflictual account of the relationship between emotions and moral reasoning.

The chapter by de Oliviera-Souza and Moll (Chapter 7) reinforces these two messages from a neuroscientific perspective. In contrast to experimental moral psychologists such as Greene and colleagues (see, e.g., Greene & Haidt, 2002; Greene, Nystrom, Engell, Darley, & Cohen, 2004; Greene, Sommerville, Nystrom, Darley, & Cohen, 2001), who conceptualize intuitive emotional processing as a primitive, biologically hard-wired response and posit a conflict between emotional processing and controlled moral reasoning, they argue against reductionist, conflict-based approaches. In their chapter on the "Neurology of Morality," de Oliviera-Souza and Moll describe the evolution of a complex integrative system of neural interconnectedness for human morality—one that sustains contributions from intuitive and controlled emotion processing, imaginative processes, semantic and motivational facets of moral cognition, as well as interactions with a social knowledge base that becomes more and more nuanced as young children develop into adulthood. Their main aim is to provide a comprehensive overview of the neuroimaging findings concerning moral reasoning and moral sensitivities in healthy adults and patients with acquired brain damage. Their phenomenological descriptions of these patients illustrate the real-world consequences on moral cognition of different types of brain damage within the complex, yet tightly integrated, neural architecture that sustains fully functional human morality.

The chapters in the second part of the volume take up, in different ways, the second message about the need for more sophisticated, integrative theoretical frameworks for understanding moral cognition. These chapters engage explicitly with influential empirical findings from recent experimental moral psychology, for example, by Haidt and colleagues (see, e.g., Haidt, 2001) and Greene and colleagues (see, e.g., Greene et al., 2004), and their underpinning theoretical frameworks, identifying both methodological and theoretical limitations with this research.

METHODOLOGICAL AND PHILOSOPHICAL REFLECTIONS ON EXPERIMENTAL MORAL PSYCHOLOGY

The first two chapters in this section of the volume, by Levy and McGuire (Chapter 8) and Case, Oaten, and Stevenson (Chapter 9), raise important questions concerning the methodological possibilities and limitations of experimental research on moral cognition. In their chapter, Levy, an empirically informed philosopher, and McGuire, a philosophically informed experimental moral psychologist, report on findings from their collaborative study in experimental philosophy. The aim of so-called experimental philosophy is to design empirical experiments, as opposed to thought experiments (which are a standard philosophical methodology), to test philosophical hypotheses. Levy and McGuire's study was designed to empirically test a philosophical hypothesis inspired by Haidt's work on moral intuitions: that opposition to cognitive enhancement is driven, in part, by intuitive dualism. We leave it to Levy and McGuire to define their terminology, flesh out their hypothesis, and report on their findings in more detail in their own chapter. For our purposes in this introductory chapter, we want to raise two methodological issues raised by their discussion.

The first is the question of what distinguishes experimental philosophy from experimental psychology. Levy and McGuire suggest that philosophers have started doing experimental research because experimental psychologists do not always address the issues that specifically concern philosophers. Nevertheless, we think this question requires further examination given that experimental philosophy appears simply to replicate the methodologies of experimental psychology. This issue is discussed in considerable detail in Christensen and Sutton's concluding chapter (Chapter 15). Second, we wish to discuss some points related to Levy and McGuire's reporting of generally null findings—an outcome that is not at all uncommon in experimental psychology. The first point is that null findings are rarely accepted for publication in peer-reviewed journals, making it imperative that theorists avoid relying too heavily on a single study with results that have not been replicated in subsequent studies and, preferably, across labs. This is a point that Langdon and Delmas (Chapter 5) also make in relation to forensic/clinical studies of the moral-conventional distinction in psychopathically inclined people. These authors are concerned that philosophers and cognitive scientists have too readily accepted claims relating to a purported lack of moral knowledge in psychopathically inclined people, even though these claims are not always commensurate with the cumulative data across forensic and nonforensic studies. Case, Oaten, and Stevenson (Chapter 9) raise similar concerns in relation to influential theories of the role of intuitive disgust experiences in moral judgment (as we discuss below). The second point that we want to emphasize about the Levy and McGuire chapter is that null results do not rule out a hypothesis; they only fail to provide support for that hypothesis. True, the hypothesis might be incorrect; it might be informed by a theory that is not so robustly supported by replicable unconfounded experimental findings. But the hypothesis might also be perfectly correct, in which case the failure to find supportive evidence is most likely due to methodological limitations (e.g., a sample with insufficient range of scores or a relatively insensitive experimental paradigm—of course, one never knows that a paradigm is potentially insensitive before actually conducting the research). In the latter case, the null findings are nevertheless constructive with regard to formulating future research directions, some of which Levy and McGuire discuss in their conclusions.

In Chapter 9, Case and colleagues take up the issue of needing to evaluate theories in light of experimental findings that are unconfounded and reliably replicated across labs. They focus on the claim that intuitive disgust responses contribute to moral judgments (see, e.g., Wheatley & Haidt, 2005). They begin by comprehensively reviewing different empirical approaches to testing this claim, with an eye on methodological limitations, and conclude that most studies to date fail to include appropriate control conditions that would allow critical evaluation of competing explanations of the findings. They then go on to describe three of their own experiments in which they induce disgust and examine the effects on moral and other judgments. Their general conclusion is that support for a direct causal link between basic disgust responses (or "core disgust" experiences) and moral judgments is tenuous. They suggest, instead, that the processing of core disgust cues has been driven primarily by evolutionary forces that promote disease avoidance (Oaten, Stevenson, & Case, 2009), and that core disgust is quite distinct from "moral disgust." Moral violation scenarios, they suggest, trigger feelings of core disgust only to the extent that the eliciting stimuli have been confounded by cues of core disgust (e.g., when a movie scene depicts a morally reprehensible drug addict scrabbling through a heavily soiled toilet—an elicitor of core disgust associated with disease avoidance—to find his drugs). Their alternate suggestion is that disgust descriptors of moral violations might be used only metaphorically to convey complex reactions rather than gut reactions of core disgust.

The following chapter by FitzGerald and Goldie (Chapter 10) echoes some of the concerns raised by Case and colleagues about the descriptors and experimental paradigms that are used in empirical moral psychology to study moral reasoning in adults. They argue that everyday moral discourse and reflection abounds with "thick" moral concepts, such as shameful, kind, courageous, brutal, or generous. Thick concepts are descriptively fine-grained, evaluative, and connected to complex social emotions and to social norms concerning appropriate behavior. The evaluations bound up in our everyday use of thick concepts are not solely moral but involve overlapping spheres of moral, aesthetic, and prudential discourse and judgment—the concept of disgust provides a good example of this overlap, as Case and colleagues' findings also suggest. FitzGerald and Goldie's concern with the methodology of empirical moral psychology is that its experimental paradigms use only "thin" moral descriptors, such as good, bad, right, or wrong. This is problematic for several reasons. One is that it leads to a narrowing of the sphere of the moral, oversimplifying the complex overlapping of moral, aesthetic, and prudential evaluation in everyday discourse. FitzGerald and Goldie cite the moral-conventional distinction as an example of this kind of narrowing, arguing that the boundary between moral and conventional judgments is not as clear-cut as the experimental literature suggests. Another reason is that it leads to an oversimple conception of emotions as intuitive, irrational gut feelings, overlooking the normative dimensions of the emotions. They cite dual-process accounts of moral judgment as exemplifying this kind of simplistic understanding of the emotions. In contrast, a focus on thick concepts suggests that *system 1* and *system 2* (in dual-process theory) are both involved, in complex and integrated ways, in moral emotions. The upshot of their chapter is that experimental moral psychologists need to devise experimental paradigms that adequately capture the role of thick concepts in moral discourse, rather than paradigms that exclude them from the data set.

FitzGerald and Goldie's focus on the complexity of everyday moral judgment and reflection is developed in Chapters 11 (Mackenzie) and 12 (Kennett). Mackenzie's chapter takes up the concern, raised first in the chapter by de Oliviera-Souza and Moll and subsequently by FitzGerald and Goldie, about the way that emotions are conceptualized in some of the empirical literature in moral psychology. Mackenzie's chapter responds specifically to the work of Haidt and colleagues (see, e.g., Haidt, 2001) and Greene and colleagues (see, e.g., Greene, 2008; Greene et al., 2001, 2004). Like FitzGerald and Goldie, she argues that dual-process accounts of moral judgment operate with a reductive conception of emotions as hard-wired, biologically driven gut feelings that fails to account for the social and normative dimensions of the moral emotions. She also argues that moral psychologists such as Greene and colleagues tend to promote an oppositional view of the relationship between emotions and reasoning in moral cognition, one that conflates intuitive processing with the emotions and controlled processing with rational moral thinking. Kennett raises similar concerns in her chapter (Chapter 12). Mackenzie cautions that characterizing moral reasoning as conscious and effortful thinking about moral principles ignores the reflective emotional processes that also contribute to moral reflection and moral agency. She also raises concerns about the reliance in experimental moral psychology on participants' one-off, time-limited judgments about hypothetical, often rare, moral dilemma scenarios, which, she cautions, are so unlike the temporally extended moral reflections that characterize everyday moral decision making. In the final section of her chapter, Mackenzie proposes that an evaluative appraisal approach to the emotions yields a richer, more complex understanding of the interaction between emotions and reasoning in everyday moral reflection and judgment.

Taking Haidt's (2001) social intuitionist model of moral judgment as the main focus for her discussion, Kennett (Chapter 12) also cautions of the methodological limitations of relying too heavily on highly unusual hypothetical scenarios (e.g., versions of the Trolley Problem) and relatively rare, extreme acts (e.g., sex with animals, consensual incest between adult siblings, cannibalism) in moral psychology research. As Kennett argues, these are not the sorts of moral dilemmas that typically confront adults in the real world. In addition, the once-off moral judgments that participants in moral psychology experiments are typically asked to make in response to hypothetical vignettes are not at all like the temporally extended moral reflections that characterize everyday life. Kennett argues that real-world moral decisions are inevitably contextualized; they involve the exercise of complex, controlled agential capacities involving memory and prospective imagination; and they have their own unique histories and consequences—people in the real world must live with the aftermath of the moral choices they make and their effects on other people. There are therefore good reasons, she argues, to be wary of the data elicited by such experiments: because they sever the connections between third-person and first-person moral judgment and reflection; and because participants are likely to be cognitively resistant to the experimental scenarios but may not feel confident to express this resistance to the experimenters. The possible experimenter effects raised by Kennett hark back to de Rosnay and Fink's developmental psychology chapter (Chapter 2); in particular, de Rosnay and Fink found that young children's reflections on the emotional consequences of transgressions vary depending on whether those children are responding to an adult experimenter or discussing their responses with their peers. In the latter case, the children's reflections are much more emotionally sophisticated. There is one other point from Kennett's chapter that we want to emphasize. Many experimental paradigms in moral psychology take the form of a two-response, forced-choice format (e.g., Is the act "okay" or "not okay"?) or require participants to make a single rating on a unidimensional rating scale ranging, for example, from "intentional" to "not intentional." Such methodological constraints will inevitably shape the pattern of research findings, as Malle and Guglielmo nicely illustrate in Chapter 13 on intentionality judgments and morality.

Malle and Guglielmo (Chapter 13) set out to test the claim, advanced in the recent literature in experimental philosophy (see, e.g., Knobe, 2003a, 2003b), that judgments of intentionality are driven by intuitive moral judgments rather than grounding such judgments. This claim is based on recent experimental results that suggest that if a behavior is described as morally bad, people judge the behavior as intentional even when critical facets of intentionality (e.g., an intention or skill) are missing. In contrast, when the same behavior is described in a morally neutral way, nobody judges it to be intentional. Such findings appear to fly in the face of a traditional conception of intentionality judgments as grounded in inferences of an agent's beliefs and desires. So, Malle and Guglielmo set out to review the evidence for these claims and to report their own novel findings. They conclude that previous research on this issue has methodological limitations (e.g., critical pieces of information are often not held constant across the bad and neutral behavior conditions). Moreover, and in accord with Kennett's (Chapter 12) concerns about the reliance on two-response, forced-choice format, they find that, when their experimental participants are offered a variety of response descriptions of an act, they will least often choose the intentional description. Finally, they present their own novel experimental work on the timing of blame versus intentionality judgments, and on response priming, and report findings that further challenge the proposal that intuitive moral judgments underpin intentionality judgments.

Intentionality judgments and connected judgments and practices of blame or praise are central to attributions of responsibility. In Chapter 14, McGeer focuses on the social practices of holding agents responsible for their actions. McGeer's chapter has two main aims. First, she provides a detailed analysis of the concept of *reactive attitudes,* originally articulated by philosopher P. F. Strawson (1974).

Reactive attitudes, such as gratitude and resentment, shame and guilt, remorse and forgiveness, are a subset of the moral emotions. They are also a species of thick moral concept; just as FitzGerald and Goldie emphasize the normative dimensions of the emotions bound up with thick concepts, so McGeer stresses that reactive attitudes embody a fundamentally normative demand: to be treated with good will and respect by others. In much of the philosophical literature on moral responsibility, it is assumed that moral responsibility requires a capacity for libertarian free will. Libertarians claim that moral agents do possess this capacity; determinists argue that we do not. McGeer argues that Strawson's analysis of reactive attitudes sidesteps this metaphysical debate and locates responsible agency in the capacity for "co-reactivity": the capacity to be sensitive and responsive to the reactive attitudes of others; to be open to reshaping one's emotional and evaluative responses in the light of ongoing reactive exchange with others. McGeer's analysis of co-reactivity thus recapitulates a central theme that emerges from this volume, which is that moral cognition is a socially mediated and socially scaffolded process.

The second aim of McGeer's chapter is to critically appraise, from a Strawsonian (1974) perspective, two recent contributions to debates about moral responsibility and legal culpability by cognitive neuroscientists (Goodenough, 2004; Greene & Cohen, 2004). Greene and Cohen, and Goodenough assume that libertarian free will is a necessary condition for moral responsibility, an assumption that Strawson's notion of reactive attitudes aims to bypass (McGeer refers to this as Strawson's "metaphysical noncommitment thesis"). Greene and Cohen think that recent findings in the cognitive neurosciences show that the idea of libertarian free will is an illusion, that our reactive attitudes are misguided, and hence that legal practices underpinned by ordinary notions of moral responsibility are unfair and counterproductive. So they advocate radical law reform, guided by consequentialist principles. Goodenough agrees that neuroscience and evolutionary psychology provide evidence that libertarian free will is an illusion, but he argues that it is still a useful fiction that undergirds necessary social practices of retributivist punishment. McGeer argues that for all their appeal to neuroscientific evidence, neither proposal makes a genuine contribution to law reform, recycling long-standing theories. She concludes her chapter with a discussion of the kind of progressive legal reform that she thinks is supported by the Strawsonian position: restorative justice approaches to punishment and sentencing.

Christensen's and Sutton's concluding chapter (Chapter 15) offers some higher-order reflections on the other contributions in this volume. They begin by discussing three possible approaches to the evolving relation between philosophical and psychological perspectives on moral cognition: separatism, replacement, and engagement. In the separatism model, philosophy has fundamentally different aims and methods to the empirical sciences and will continue to operate autonomously. Christensen and Sutton do not think that this model can work since philosophy needs to be informed by the results of empirical research. In the replacement model, moral philosophy will be subsumed by empirical psychology. Christensen and Sutton do not think this model can work either since the drive for methodological rigor in the empirical sciences can be at the cost of good theory construction and the questioning of fundamental assumptions—both of which are strengths of philosophy. So Christensen and Sutton advocate for an engagement model and the development of a common conceptual framework for multidisciplinary moral cognition research that might help mitigate cross-disciplinary misunderstandings. In pursuit of this framework, they identify a number of core issues arising from the volume that might be the focus for future cross-disciplinary research, such as clarifying the relations between descriptive and normative approaches to moral cognition, and between moral cognition and broader theories of cognitive architecture. They also discuss the need to clarify moral taxonomies to reach a better understanding of core moral phenomena, including the domain of the moral (and its relation to conventional, aesthetic, and prudential evaluations); the relations between rule-based and contextual understandings of moral judgment; and the moral emotions. In general, they argue for multilevel theorizing that approaches specific topics in moral cognition research with an explicit awareness of how these topics are embedded within a broader, cross-disciplinary picture of moral cognition as a whole and, in turn, of cognition as a whole.

We endorse Christensen and Sutton's appeal for a consensus multidisciplinary agenda that will promote and engage reciprocal interaction between psychological and philosophical researchers of moral cognition. We hope that the contributions to this volume go some way to laying the groundwork for future engagement of this type.

REFERENCES

Blair, R. J. R. (2005). Responding to the emotions of others: Dissociating forms of empathy through the study of typical and psychiatric populations. *Consciousness and Cognition, 14,* 698–718.

Damasio, A. R. (1995). *Descartes' error: Emotion, reason, and the human brain.* New York: Avon Books.

Eisenberg, N., Spinrad, T. L., & Sadovsky, A. (2006). Empathy-related responding in children. In M. Killen & J. Smetana (Eds.), *Handbook of moral development* (pp. 517–549). Mahwah, NJ: Lawrence Erlbaum Associates Publishers.

Goodenough, O. R. (2004). Responsibility and punishment: whose mind? A response. *Philosophical Transactions of the Royal Society B: Biological Sciences, 359,* 1805–1809.

Greene, J. D. (2008). The secret joke of Kant's soul. In W. Sinnott-Armstrong (Ed.), *Moral psychology, volume 3: The neuroscience of morality: Emotion, brain disorders, and development* (pp. 35–79). Cambridge MA: MIT Press.

Greene, J., & Cohen, J. (2004). For the law, neuroscience changes nothing and everything. *Philosophical Transactions of the Royal Society of London. Series B, Biological Sciences, 359,* 1775–1785.

Greene, J., & Haidt, J. (2002). How (and where) does moral judgment work? *Trends in Cognitive Sciences, 6,* 517–523.

Greene, J. D., Nystrom, L. E., Engell, A. D., Darley, J. M., & Cohen, J. D. (2004). The neural bases of cognitive conflict and control in moral judgment. *Neuron, 44,* 389–400.

Greene, J. D., Sommerville, R. B., Nystrom, L. E., Darley, J. M., & Cohen, J. D. (2001). An fMRI investigation of emotional engagement in moral judgment. *Science, 293,* 2105–2108.

Haidt, J. (2001). The emotional dog and its rational tail: A social intuitionist approach to moral judgment. *Psychological Review, 108,* 814–834.

Hoffman, M. L. (2000). *Empathy and moral development: Implications for caring and justice*. Cambridge, UK: Cambridge University Press.

Kant, I. (1785/1998). *Groundwork of the metaphysics of morals* (M. Gregor, Trans., Ed.) Cambridge, UK: Cambridge University Press.

Knobe, J. (2003a). Intentional action and side effects in ordinary language. *Analysis, 63,* 190–193.

Knobe, J. (2003b). Intentional action in folk psychology: An experimental investigation. *Philosophical Psychology, 16,* 309–324.

Kohlberg, L. (1971). From is to ought: How to commit the naturalistic fallacy and get away with it in the study of moral development. In T. Mischel (Ed.), *Cognitive development and epistemology* (pp. 151–235). New York: Academic Press.

Kohlberg, L. (1984). *The psychology of moral development: Essays on moral development.* *Vol. 2*. San Francisco: Harper & Row.

Mar, R. (2004). The neuropsychology of narrative: Story comprehension, story production and their interrelation. *Neuropsychologia, 42,* 1414–1434.

Mar, R. (2009). Empirical research on reading and watching narrative fiction. In D. Schram (Ed.), *Reading and watching: What does the written word have that images don't?* (pp. 53–61). Delft: Eburon Academic.

Nussbaum, M. (1995). *Poetic justice: The literary imagination and public life* Boston: Beacon Press.

Nussbaum, M. (1997). *Cultivating humanity: A classical defense of reform in liberal education.* Cambridge, MA: Harvard University Press.

Oaten, M. J., Stevenson, R. J., & Case T. I. (2009). Disgust as a disease-avoidance mechanism. *Psychological Bulletin, 135,* 303–321.

Oatley, K. (1999). Why fiction may be twice as true as fact: Fiction as cognitive and emotional simulation. *Review of General Psychology, 3,* 101–117.

Oatley, K. (2008, June 28). The science of fiction. *New Scientist,* 42–43.

Paulhus, D. L., & Williams, K.M. (2002). The dark triad of personality: Narcissism, Machiavellianism, and psychopathy. *Journal of Research in Personality, 36,* 556–563.

Prinz, J. (2006). The emotional basis of moral judgments. *Philosophical Explorations, 9,* 29–43.

Sinnott-Armstrong, W. (Ed.). (2008). *Moral psychology* (3 volumes). Cambridge, MA: MIT Press.

Strawson, P. (1974). *Freedom and resentment and other essays.* London: Methuen.

Tranel, D. (1994). "Acquired sociopathy": The development of sociopathic behavior following focal brain damage. *Progress in Experimental Personality and Psychopathology Research, 17,* 285–311.

Wheatley, T., & Haidt, J. (2005). Hypnotic disgust makes moral judgments more severe. *Psychological Science, 16,* 780–784.

ENDNOTES

1. See, for example, the three volumes of Sinnott-Armstrong (2008), which include chapters from some of the most important researchers in experimental moral psychology, as well as from some of the leading philosophers engaging with this experimental work.
2. Within psychology this tradition is associated with more cognitivist approaches to moral cognition, such as the work of Kohlberg (1971, 1984); in philosophy with Kantian moral philosophy (see, e.g., Kant, 1785/1998).

Section *I*

Morality, Empathetic Responsiveness, and the Multifaceted Nature of Empathy

2

The Development of Moral Motivation at 6 Years of Age

MARC DE ROSNAY and ELIAN FINK

University of Sydney

This chapter considers the development of children's moral motivation at approximately 6 years of age, a time when children understand that certain transgressions (e.g., stealing) are "wrong" in a moral sense (Smetana, 1993, 2006) but are unable to engage in the kind of reasoning that is characteristic of mature moral deliberation (Rest, 1983). Two perspectives on children's moral motivation—happy victimizer expectancy and conscience development—are presented and contrasted to better understand why children choose actions that they consider moral. In Study 1, we explore the developmental predictors and behavioral correlates of moral motivation using a longitudinal study of 115 children between kindergarten and year 1. In particular, we focus on children's psychological perspective-taking and their empathy as predictors of moral motivation, and we explore how moral motivation relates to children's social competence and behavior. In Study 2, we examine happy victimizer expectancy and ask, by way of observing child–child interactions, whether so-called happy victimizers really fail to understand the emotional consequences of moral transgressions or whether they simply fail to report such emotional consequences to researchers. Our findings suggest that children's conscience but not happy victimizer expectancy is closely linked to their empathy and positive social conduct.

INTRODUCTION

*T*his chapter is concerned with the development of children's moral motivation in the context of transgression at approximately 6 years of age. Moral motivation centers on the reasons people choose actions that they consider moral, especially in contexts where such a decision involves enduring a personal sacrifice (Nunner-Winkler, 1993; Rest, 1983). We focus on children at 6 years of age because we feel that this age group speaks to a transition in the awareness and understanding of moral concerns and, in particular, the emotional consequences of moral transgression (e.g., is the child able to conceptualize or contemplate the fact that the wrongness of an action should have moral emotional consequences for a transgressor?). Indeed, 6-year-old children fall precisely between two highly productive and well-established research traditions focused on moral development. Starting with the cognitive developmental framework outlined by Piaget (1932/1997), moral stage theorists have focused on children's moral reasoning from about 7 or 8 years of age. Before this time the child's ability to reason about morality is viewed as very limited and is better characterized, in Piaget's words, as a morality of constraint determined by adult prescriptions and proscriptions (see Eisenberg & Mussen, 1989; Lapsley, 2006; Rest, 1983). In contrast, social-cognitive domain theorists, starting with Turiel (1983), have sought to view children's moral awareness as one strand of their developing social knowledge, which is derived from reciprocal individual–environment interactions and, thereby, evident long before children can reason through moral dilemmas (Smetana, 2006; Turiel, 1983). Somewhere between the developments outlined within these contrasting traditions, however, it seems that children begin to grasp the emotionally binding nature of moral transgression, and it is this development to which we turn our attention.

We begin by contrasting two influential ways of conceptualizing children's moral motivation at 6 years of age: children's transition from happy victimizer expectancy and their conscience development. Happy victimizer expectancy concerns the well-documented cognitive developmental finding that while virtually all 6-year-olds are able to judge moral transgressions appropriately as wrong or bad, many are still unable to conceptualize the (moral) emotional consequences for the transgressor (e.g., guilt, contrition: Arsenio, Gold, & Adams, 2006; Nunner-Winkler & Sodian, 1988). Conscience development is concerned instead with the extent to which children identify moral and empathic emotions in themselves—their *moral self-concept* (Kochanska, Gross, Lin, & Nichols, 2002). Following this discussion of moral motivation, we provide a selective summary of the literature indicating that specific child factors—psychological perspective-taking, empathy, and social behavior—are likely to support children's moral development. Finally, we review two new studies that capitalize on individual differences in children's moral sensibilities to clarify the nature of moral motivation at 6 years of age and child characteristics contributing to such development (de Rosnay, Fink, Kurukulasuriya, Wall, & Fritz, 2010; Fritz, Percy, & de Rosnay, 2010).

MORAL MOTIVATION AT 6 YEARS OF AGE

Are Young Children Happy Victimizers?

An influential proposal of childhood moral development is that somewhere between 4 and 8 years of age children come to understand that certain social rules or prohibitions—against stealing, hurting, and teasing—are not merely wrong or bad but are also personally binding. That is, transgressing these prohibitions should have emotional consequences for the transgressor: The act of theft, for example, should result in feelings of shame or guilt, and refraining from such an action, particularly when it conflicts with one's desires, should result in feelings of pride. Prior to the realization that moral rules are personally binding in this way, it appears that children understand moral dilemmas that pitch desires against prohibitions in two ways that are, to an adult mind at least, inconsistent. Thus, younger children will evaluate the emotional consequences of a transgression (for the transgressor) on the basis of desire fulfillment while at the same time bringing an apparently moral orientation to the evaluation of the transgression itself. The most persuasive and persistent demonstration of this is the so-called happy victimizer phenomenon, whereby young children reliably judge that it is wrong or bad to steal but nonetheless judge that a thief will feel good or happy if the theft has resulted in the fulfillment of a desire (Nunner-Winkler & Sodian, 1988). It is also encouraging to note that (1) Nunner-Winkler and Sodian's findings have been replicated by independent research groups (Arsenio, 1988; Arsenio & Ford, 1985; Keller, Lourenco, Malti, & Saalbach, 2003; Lourenco, 1997); (2) there is evidence of a high degree of stability in children's happy victimizer status between 5 and 6 years of age (Dunn, Brown, & Maguire, 1995); and (3) there is some validation of the claim that children's attribution (and appropriate justification) of moral emotions (e.g., guilt and pride) to story transgressors is meaningfully related to their prosocial behavior (Asendorpf & Nunner-Winkler, 1992; Malti, Gasser, & Buchmann, 2009).

While some of those working in the domain of moral development have given fine-grained attention specifically to the happy victimizer phenomenon because of its potential significance for understanding children's moral motivation (Arsenio et al., 2006), others have attempted to situate the phenomenon within the broader context of the development of children's social cognitive understanding (Lagattuta, 2005; Yuill, Perner, Pearson, Peerbhoy, & van den Ende, 1996). This latter approach has yielded some very valuable insights about young children's abilities to understand situations in which desires and rules conflict while also incorporating a focus on children's ability to evaluate an actor's intent. So, for example, Yuill and colleagues found that when children between 5 and 7 years of age were directed to a transgressor's wish (e.g., to cause harm) they subsequently attributed more intensely positive emotions to the protagonist's successful action (e.g., hurting another child) compared with when they were first directed to a moral evaluation of the act itself and then asked to make the emotion attribution. Both Yuill et al. and Lagattuta also provide evidence that children under 7 years of age have a very strong tendency to base emotional outcomes on desire fulfillment–frustration rather than rule transgression–adherence, not only in situations of moral rule violation but also in the context of prudential rules, rules about living routines (i.e., health and nutrition), and rules about privacy and ownership.

Despite the robustness of the happy victimizer phenomenon and its generalization to other nonmoral domains, the central position it has occupied with respect to children's moral motivation has not always sat comfortably with other research groups, and the straightforward nature of the developmental transition outlined by Nunner-Winkler and Sodian (1988) has been contested in various ways (see Arsenio et al., 2006). Thus, Murgatroyd and Robinson (1993, 1997) pointed out that even 10-year-old children and adults sometimes attribute positive emotions to transgressors in the first instance. Conversely, Arsenio and Kramer (1992) showed that 6- and 8-year-old children who spontaneously demonstrate happy victimizer expectancy can, by way of further questioning, also identify a negative emotional outcome experienced by the transgressor. Furthermore, Keller and her colleagues (Keller, Lourenco, Malti, & Saalbach, 2003; Malti, Gummerum, Keller, & Buchmann, 2009) argued that children's performance on happy victimizer–style tasks is strongly influenced by directing their attention to subjective and deontic aspects of the task concerning obligations, for example. Thus, fewer children attribute positive emotions in the context of a transgression if they are asked how they themselves would feel as transgressor (self-attribution).

Our own reading of this literature is that, despite over 20 years of concerted, fine-grained examination, the meaning of children's happy victimizer expectancy is not yet well understood, especially insofar as it can provide a window on children's moral motivation. Furthermore, the happy victimizer expectancy paradigm offers a somewhat constrained framework within which to explore children's moral motivation (Arsenio et al., 2006). In light of these issues, we consider a different literature on the development of children's conscience.

Conscience in Early Childhood

There is a rich and long-standing research tradition concerning the development of children's conscience within the context of family socialization. For the most part, this research has proceeded in isolation from cognitive developmental concerns about the nature of children's moral understanding, focusing instead on the influence of parenting practices and behaviors on children's internalization or adoption of standards of (moral) conduct (Grusec, 2006; Grusec & Goodnow, 1994). Despite these differing historical foci, however, the empirical investigation of children's conscience is directly concerned with how children conduct themselves in contexts that elicit "good/right" or "bad/wrong" behavior, such as following rules, resisting prohibited temptations, and causing harm. As such, the study of conscience development has particular relevance for understanding children's moral motivation.

Conscience in childhood has been construed in terms of (1) the child's adherence to parental and other societal requirements; (2) the child's emotional response in the context of failures to adhere to requirements or transgression, with a particular focus on guilt; (3) confession and attempted reparation in the face of failures of adherence or transgressions; and (4) adherence to parental and societal requirements in the absence of surveillance by authority figures such as parents, teachers, and experimenters (Grusec, 2006; Kochanska & Aksan, 2006). Although conscience construed in these terms implies a high degree of autonomous inner guidance whereby children assume responsibility for their actions, the very nature of this research tradition acknowledges that such inner guidance is hard won in early childhood and can be manifest in various ways, and with varying success, at different ages and in different individuals (Kochanska & Aksan, 2006).

There are several empirical approaches to the study of conscience development that speak to the coherence of the construct over the period of early childhood. Of particular note is the longitudinal continuity in how individual children behave—including their actions and emotions—in situations that should elicit feelings of guilt (e.g., breaking something precious or not adhering to parental prohibitions) from 2 to 4 years of age (Aksan & Kochanska, 2005; Kochanska, 2002; Kochanska et al., 2002). Furthermore, and encouragingly, aspects of children's behavior that reflect the influence of conscience, such as independently complying with parental requests or prohibitions and seeking to make reparation after transgression, are robustly associated with parenting socialization practices that should on theoretical grounds (Grusec, 2006) promote the development of conscience in early childhood (e.g., Kochanska & Aksan, 2006; Kochanska, Aksan, Prisco, & Adams, 2008; Kochanska et al., 2002; Laible, 2004; Laible & Thompson, 2000).

Our focus in this chapter is on the extent to which children self-identify moral sentiments at 6 years of age, a time at which they should be able to not only evince guilt, for example, but also identify and articulate the feelings of badness that come with it. In a novel paradigm to assess children's conscience, Kochanska and her colleagues (Kochanska, DeVet, Goldman, Murray, & Putnam, 1994; Kochanska, Murray, & Coy, 1997) presented children with an interactive assessment of moral self-concept (or conscience) in which 37 bipolar moral sentiments were expressed by two puppets (e.g., "I tell someone if I break something" vs. "I don't tell someone if I break something"; "When I do something bad, I don't get upset" vs. "When I do something bad, I get really upset"). Upon hearing each contrasting view expressed by the puppets, children were asked to endorse one of them. Surprisingly, even at 56 months, children's responses on the puppet interview were very reliable and meaningfully related with independent measures of conscience, both concurrently and longitudinally. Thus, Kochanska et al. (2002) showed that behavioral measures of children's guilt at 22 and 45 months predicted higher moral self-concept scores at 56 months, while Kochanska (2002) found that children's independent compliance with parental requests or prohibitions (both concurrent and at an earlier time period) were related to moral self-concept, at least in boys. In sum, even at 4 years of age, it seems that children may be able to provide an accurate assessment of their own moral sentiments. We now consider specific child factors that are likely to underpin and promote children's moral development.

Characteristics of the Child Related to Moral Motivation at 6 Years of Age

What characteristics of the child should we expect to relate to their moral motivation at 6 years of age? Two prominent candidates are children's psychological perspective-taking abilities and their empathy (Eisenberg, Spinrad, & Sadovsky, 2006; Rest, 1983). While many contemporary accounts of children's empathy in fact subsume psychological perspective-taking, we believe it is important to try to tease apart these factors to offer a satisfactory account of the development of children's moral motivation. Therefore, in the following subsections we provide a rationale for considering psychological perspective-taking, empathy, and social behavior in relation to children's moral motivation.

Psychological Perspective-Taking (Emotion Understanding and Theory of Mind)

There are several reasons to expect that children's psychological perspective-taking will be related to their moral motivation. If, as Nunner-Winkler and Sodian (1988) argued, happy victimizer expectancy results from a conceptual failure to understand the emotional perspective of the transgressor or a persistent fixation on immediate outcomes over intentions and future outcomes (e.g., Lagattuta, 2005), then it would seem to follow that moral emotion attribution is yet another manifestation of the child's burgeoning understanding of mind and emotion (Pons, Harris, & de Rosnay, 2004). Furthermore, given the longitudinal stability of individual differences in children's emotion understanding (e.g., Brown & Dunn, 1996; Pons & Harris, 2005), it also seems reasonable to expect that children with more advanced emotion understanding at 5 years of age should also be better able to understand moral emotions at 6 years of age.

In support of the previously proposed relations, Dunn, Brown, and Maguire (1995) documented longitudinal continuity between understanding of emotion and young children's moral orientation, including the self-attribution of moral sentiments. Similarly, there is some suggestion that children with more advanced "theory of mind" are more adept liars, which suggests that they may also be more morally astute—if not more moral (Talwar & Lee, 2008).

Beyond any general relationships between individual differences in psychological perspective-taking and moral motivation, it is also important to assess whether specific emotion understanding skills are playing a role in children's moral motivation. A likely candidate here is the comprehension of mixed or ambivalent feelings, for it is certainly the case that the moral emotions already discussed entail some kind of conflict or clash between the emotions that arise from what is desired and what course ought to be pursued. In support of this view, Dunn and colleagues (1995) offered some evidence that higher levels of mixed emotion understanding correspond to a greater moral orientation and discomfort with transgression at 6 years of age.

Empathy

For some, the independent assessment of empathy and psychological perspective-taking may seem superficially misguided. For example, both Hoffman (2000) and Eisenberg (2000; Eisenberg et al., 2006) argued strongly and convincingly that empathic responding to others' distress inherently involves perspective-taking. Our view is that a psychological capacity to take on the intentional stance of the other person (whether rudimentary or sophisticated) need not always be drawn upon or result in empathic feelings toward that other person. Indeed, the developmental literature is replete with illustrations of variation in children's responding to distress in others—only some of which is empathic—well before the ages at which typical children all possess the necessary perspective-taking abilities to understand the other person's plight: The proclivity to respond empathically, therefore, cannot turn solely on psychological perspective-taking abilities. We will therefore maintain a distinction between psychological perspective-taking and empathic feelings. Moreover, we will allow that empathy, as we use the term, can be manifest in two potentially independent ways, both of which can be held apart, to some extent at least, from conventional notions of psychological perspective-taking, including theory of mind. First, in keeping with the empathy elicitation paradigms widely used with young children, we think that children's empathic proclivities can be manifest as experienced emotions, typically sadness or concern for another. Second, we think that children vary in the extent to which they are inclined or willing to take on the emotional stance of a victim (Strayer, 1993; Strayer & Roberts, 1997). This last aspect of empathy, which we refer to as *empathic role-taking*, has received relatively little attention and should, we think, be distinguished from psychological perspective-taking abilities.

There are both empirical and long-standing theoretical grounds (see Blasi, 1999; Pizarro, 2000) to explore continuities between children's empathy, as described already, and moral motivation. For example, it has long been known that children's empathic concern for others associates with their prosocial behavior and altruism (Eisenberg & Mussen, 1989; Eisenberg et al., 2006; Underwood & Moore, 1982). More direct evidence for the influence of empathic concern on moral motivation comes from various sources (e.g., Aksan & Kochanska, 2005; Miller, Eisenberg, Fabes, & Shell, 1996; Thompson & Hoffman, 1980). In particular, Aksan and Kochanska (2005) showed a close contemporaneous and longitudinal correspondence between observational measures of children's spontaneous expressions of empathic concern and moral guilt in structured situations between 33 and 45 months of age. A striking feature of this study, however, is that empathic concern predicted guilt longitudinally but the reverse relation did not entail, suggesting a causal pathway from empathic concern to the experience of moral motivation, in the form of guilt.

Social Behavior and Conduct

There are various reasons to expect that children's moral motivation should be related to their social conduct. The simplest manifestation of this relationship is contemporaneous—that is, one would expect a relation between higher levels of moral motivation and higher levels of prosocial or altruistic behavior. Indeed, a few studies using different methodologies have confirmed this basic correspondence (see Asendorpf & Nunner-Winkler, 1992; Eisenberg & Mussen, 1989; Janssens & Dekovic, 1997; Malti, Gummerum, et al., 2009; Underwood & Moore, 1982). Similarly, one might expect that low levels of moral motivation are more likely to be associated with behavior problems with peers, and specifically aggression (see Arsenio et al., 2006; Blair, Monson, & Frederickson, 2001; Malti, Gasser, & Buchmann, 2009). The investigation of these relations is important for two reasons: First, it offers some validation of the measurement of moral motivation by grounding these measures in social conduct, and, second, it provides us with a richer description of the child as a social agent.

In addition to such contemporaneous measures, it is also possible to investigate longitudinal relations between moral motivation and earlier social behavior and conduct. For Piaget (1932/1997) and Kohlberg (1971, 1984), and for those who have built upon their basic framework, the experience that children gain through social interaction is critical for their later development of moral and ethical understanding. Piaget characterized the younger child's heteronomous morality as one of constraint and realism and the older child's autonomous morality as one of cooperation. So whereas young children accept unquestioningly the moral prescriptions and proscriptions of adults, they are simultaneously acquiring an understanding of social rules via their social encounters and negotiations with other children.

In this section we have outlined three aspects of child characteristics that are likely to be related to the development of their moral motivation: psychological perspective-taking (including emotion understanding and theory of mind); empathy (including empathic responsiveness and empathic role-taking); and social behavior and conduct. Relations between these child characteristics and moral motivation are examined in Study 1.

STUDY 1: THE PREDICTORS AND CORRELATES OF MORAL MOTIVATION AT 6 YEARS OF AGE

This study[1] concerns the development of children's moral motivation at 6 years of age. Participants were 115 children (56 girls), aged 5 years and 7 months on average (SD = 5.0 months) who were assessed at two time periods: in kindergarten at time 1 (T1) and then 12 months later at time 2 (T2), at which time nine subjects were lost from the study. The sample was predominantly middle class and comprised a diverse cultural background representative of the wider Sydney population. At each time point (T1 and T2), children were tested over two sessions, approximately 6 weeks apart.

Children's Moral Motivation at 6 Years of Age (T2)

As reviewed in the introduction, we considered two ways of assessing the moral motivations of young children at 6 years of age: (1) their transition from *happy victimizer expectancy*, which is when the child might understand that a transgression is morally wrong but at the same time fails to attribute negative moral emotions to the transgressor; and (2) the young child's self-identified moral self-concept.

Assessing Happy Victimizer Expectancy at 6 Years of Age

In light of the complex literature surrounding the happy victimizer phenomenon, we decided to adhere to a classical formulation of the moral emotion attribution dilemma, as articulated by Nunner-Winkler and Sodian (1988). Thus, children were first asked to judge the wrongness of an act (e.g., theft), and the experimenter emphasized the fact that the rule was indeed violated; all children judged that it was wrong to violate the rule. Children were then asked to make an emotion attribution on behalf of the story transgressor; to evaluate the reliability with which children showed happy victimizer expectancy, we assessed children's performance on two standard happy victimizer tasks—one at each T2 testing session, using very similar stories presented in a counterbalanced order (an example happy victimizer task is presented in Appendix 2.1). Also, in keeping with the approach adopted by Arsenio and Kramer (1992), children were given further probes to ascertain whether they knew, but withheld, information about a victimizer's moral emotional response to the transgression. However, unlike Arsenio and Kramer, we did not ask children about the victim's emotional response to being wronged before using additional probes. Thus, children were not directed to the emotional consequences of the transgression for the victim before being asked if happy victimizers felt anything other than positive emotions as this seemed something of a confound.

Results showed that 52 children (49%) succeeded on both happy victimizer tasks by attributing a negative moral emotion to both protagonists, and there was a very strong relation between tasks ($p < .001$), which was independent of order of presentation. Also, children's performance did not improve from session 1 to session 2. When questioned further on their responses, less than 2% of children changed their emotion choice, confirming the robustness of their happy victimizer status.

Assessing Moral Self-Concept at 6 Years of Age

We also used the moral self-concept scale developed by de Rosnay et al. (2010) to assess self-identified moral sentiments (see Appendix 2.2). This scale had been adapted from Kochanska and colleagues (Kochanska et al., 1994, 1997), who used the puppet interview technique originally developed by Eder (1990) to assess psychological self-concept. In the original puppet interview, young children identified which of the two puppets making bipolar self-attributions (e.g., "I cry when I get upset" vs. "I don't cry when I get upset") is more like them. As well as including moral self-concept items, de Rosnay and colleagues also included items from Bryant's (1982) Empathy Index to develop a 23-item scale, from which separate scores are calculated for moral self-concept and empathic sadness. The moral self-concept score can be further subdivided into subscale scores for confession, reparation, internalized conduct, concern about others' wrongdoing, guilt and affective discomfort after transgressions (which will be of particular interest in this chapter), and concern about good feelings with parents (see Appendix 2.2). In the de Rosnay et al. (2010) study, 132 children (64 girls), distributed across three school grade levels—kindergarten (n = 53, M_{age} = 5 years 6 months, SD = 4.3 months); year 1 (n = 41, M_{age} = 6 years 6 months, SD = 4.6 months); and year 2 (n = 38, M_{age} = 7 years 5 months, SD = 5.0 months)—were tested at two sessions approximately 2 weeks apart and received the moral self-concept/empathy puppet interview of 23 items at one session and the Eder puppet interview to assess psychological self-concept at the other session. The order of the interviews was randomized. Children were presented with prerecorded videos that the experimenter could pause while children made their selection for each item. The moral self-concept and empathic sadness subscales were found to have good reliability (Cronbach α's of .77 and .69, respectively). Standardized scores from that 2010 study (including results from the Eder scales) are displayed in Figure 2.1 by school grade. Higher scores for moral self-concept and empathic sadness were

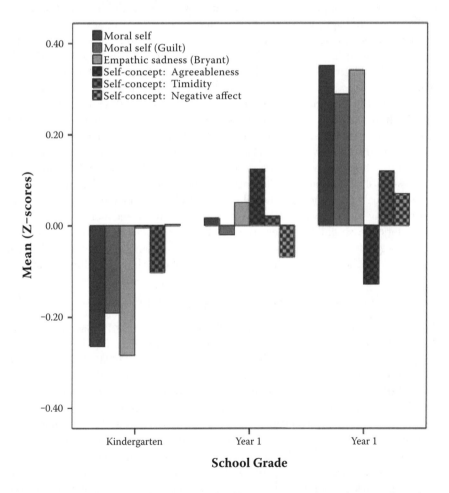

Figure 2.1 Children's self-identified moral self-concept, empathic sadness, and psychological self-concept (agreeableness, timidity, and negative affect) by school grade (N = 132).

associated with increasing age. There was no relation, however, between age and children's psychological self-concept (as assessed on the Eder scales; see Brown, Mangelsdorf, Agathen, & Ho, 2008).

For the current study of a different group of 115 children, Cronbach α's were again calculated to assess reliability. The moral self-concept (α = .81) and empathic sadness (α = .74) scales had good reliability. The six-item guilt subscale, when considered in isolation, also had acceptable reliability (α = .61).

The Interrelationship of Happy Victimizer Expectancy and Moral Self-Concept at 6 Years of Age

Children succeeding on both happy victimizer tasks were scored "pass" and children failing both or one task were scored "fail." Notably, Study 1 found no significant relations between pass/fail on the happy victimizer tasks and either the children's self-identified moral self-concept or their empathic sadness. In contrast, the moral self-concept score and the moral guilt subscore correlated strongly with children's empathic sadness (r's > .55; p's < .001). The two purported domains of moral motivation—self-identified moral sentiments (moral self-concept) and transition from happy victimizer expectancy—were thus entirely independent.

CHILD CORRELATES OF MORAL MOTIVATION

The measures of child characteristics that we considered in Study 1 are briefly described before examining findings for the relations between these factors and moral motivation. Children's verbal abilities were also measured as a global index of cognitive development and because of robust relations documented between psychological perspective-taking and linguistic ability (de Rosnay & Hughes, 2006).

T2 Mixed Emotion Understanding (Mixed EU)

Since we were interested in the relations between mixed emotion understanding in young children at 6 years of age and their moral motivation, children were given five standard assessments of their understanding of mixed emotion at T2 (Harris, 1989; Meerum Terwogt, Koops, Oosterhoff, & Olthof, 1986). To pass, children had to show an appreciation of the story protagonist's mixed or conflicting emotions for each story. The mean score was 1.6 (SD = 1.07) and the internal reliability was modest (α = .56), in keeping with the difficulty children have understanding mixed or ambivalent feelings at this age.

T1 Measures

Since we were also interested in possible precursors of moral motivation, we had assessed the following measures at T1 (i.e., 12 months before T2):

1. Verbal ability. Children were given a standardized assessment of linguistic development (TELD-3; Hresko, Reid, & Hammill, 1999). Children's raw scores were used.

2. Theory of mind (ToM). Children were given six standard false belief tasks that have been widely used in the literature (Wellman, Cross, & Watson, 2001). In each story, a protagonist held a false expectation about the true state of the world and the child either had to predict the protagonist's action on the basis of the false belief or state explicitly what the protagonist thought. Children received a point for each correct response. The mean score was 4.2 (SD = 1.88), and the internal reliability was good (α = .72).

3. Emotion understanding (EU). Children were given a battery of emotion understanding tasks assessing their knowledge of four emotion domains:
   a. Emotions based on diverse desires (two items)
   b. Emotions based on ignorance (four items)
   c. Emotions based on false belief (two items)
   d. Hidden emotion (four items)

   All tasks were pass/fail. With the exception of one item (hidden emotion), which we decided to omit, there was acceptable reliability for children's emotion understanding (α =.60). The mean score was 6.0 (SD = 2.27).

4. Empathic responding and empathic role-taking. Both children's empathic responses and their self-reported empathic role-taking in response to emotionally evocative vignettes were measured. Detailed procedures can be found in de Rosnay et al. (2010). Children were shown a series of videos depicting real children in emotionally challenging situations. Videos were used to elicit a range of emotional responses in children (e.g., "First Day" depicted a child becoming very upset on his first day at school) including expressions of empathy in response to a protagonist's distress. Children's emotional expressions during the videos were used to determine the presence (or absence) of empathic responses.

In the empathy literature, some researchers conceptualize empathic responses as a match between the emotion expressed by the child and the emotion experienced by a protagonist, which is typically a sad expression (e.g., Strayer, 1993). Other researchers regard children's facial expressions of concern to be indicative of empathic responses (e.g., Hastings, Zahn-Waxler, Usher, Robinson, & Bridges, 2000; Zahn-Waxler, Radke-Yarrow, Wagner, & Chapman, 1992), or at least sympathetic responses provoked by an initial empathic response (e.g., Eisenberg et al., 1988). This apparent inconsistency in the literature is further complicated by the fact that children's responses to emotionally evocative vignettes (stories, movies, or simulations) have been shown to be highly context dependent (e.g., Miller et al., 1996) and probably age dependent as well (Thompson, 1994). Nonetheless, despite such complications in the conceptualization and measurement of empathic responses, facial displays of both concerned attention and sadness in children when viewing emotionally evocative events have been shown to relate positively to prosocial behavior and social competence (Eisenberg & Fabes, 1990, 1995; Fabes, Eisenberg, & Miller, 1990; Miller et al., 1996; Roberts & Strayer, 1996). Thus, both sad responses and concerned attention (including interest and worry) are of theoretical interest when exploring the correlates of children's developing social competences.[2] We also considered both, as follows.

Some researchers will use overall frequency or intensity of specific emotional expressions during defined epochs as a measure of empathic response (e.g., Fabes, Eisenberg, & Eisenbud, 1993; Miller et al., 1996), whereas other researchers will use emotional expressions to categorically differentiate children based on the nature of their response (e.g., Cole, Zahn-Waxler, Fox, Usher, & Welsh, 1996; Strayer & Roberts, 1997). We favored the second approach. Children were therefore categorized into one of three groups according to their empathic responsiveness: *inexpressive, concerned,* and *sad*. A second experienced coder blind to the other study variables scored 50 videos. The interrater reliability was very good ($\kappa = .92$), and disagreements were resolved by conference. There were 45 inexpressive, 34 concerned, and 34 sad children.

To measure empathic role-taking, the children were interviewed about four of the videos following Strayer and Roberts's (2004) Empathy Continuum protocol. The four vignettes included themes of peer argument, social exclusion, fear, and distress. When children finished watching the videos, they were cued by a still image and asked how they felt while watching the vignette and, if unable to answer, asked, "Did you feel happy or sad, angry or scared?" Children were then asked to justify their emotional response, "Why do you think you felt that way?" Having discussed their own emotional response, children were asked to nominate an emotional response for the story protagonist in the same manner as previously outlined for self-nominations. Children who did not indicate feeling an emotion after prompting were still asked to nominate an emotion for the protagonist. All children were able to nominate an emotion for the protagonists in the videos.

Responses were scored on the basis of both the match between the child and the protagonist and children's attribution for their own emotional response (Strayer, 1993), with scores ranging between 0 and 19 (for detailed scoring, see Strayer & Roberts, 2004). Empathic responses were those in which children reported feeling emotions that matched the protagonist coupled with a justification that took the protagonists' point of view. Scores from the four vignettes were then combined to create a total empathic role-taking score (possible range: 0–76). This final empathic role-taking score had good internal reliability ($\alpha = .71$).

Results Concerning Child Correlates of Moral Motivation

First we considered the relations between child characteristics; there was a strong positive correlation between T1 theory of mind and T1 emotion understanding ($r = .52$, $p < .001$), so these scores were summed to create a T1 psychological perspective-taking total. Children's verbal abilities were positively related to both T1 perspective-taking and T2 mixed emotion understanding ($p < .001$), but there were no other significant relations between child characteristics or sex. In particular, perspective-taking, empathic responses, and empathic role-taking at T1 were entirely independent in the current study.

We turn now to consider the relations between child characteristics and children's moral motivation at 6 years of age. Table 2.1 shows correlations for child characteristics and moral motivation excluding the child characteristic of empathetic responsiveness, which was a categorical variable. Of particular note is that none of the child characteristics predicted happy victimizer expectancy at T2. By contrast, T1 empathic role-taking and T2 mixed emotion understanding were both modestly but consistently related to moral self-concept and empathic sadness at T2. With regard to gender differences, girls self-identified more guilt on the moral self-concept scale and more empathic sadness as well as more negative affect than boys. Intriguingly, there was a very specific relation between T1 perspective-taking and children's T2 self-identified moral guilt such that higher levels of T1 perspective-taking predicted less guilt at T2. While this finding may seem irregular, it is noteworthy that higher levels of T1 perspective-taking also predicted T2 negative affect (taken from the Eder scale). Insofar as guilt is a negative emotion, albeit a moral one, there is remarkable longitudinal specificity here that deserves close consideration; we will come back to this later in the summary. Finally, we examined whether empathic responsiveness during videos predicted

TABLE 2.1

| Variable | T2 HV status | T2 Moral self-concept | | T2 Empathic sadness | T2 Self-concept (Eder) | |
		Global	(Guilt)		Timidity	Negative affect
Sex (boy, girl)	-.04	.19	.26°°	.25°	.16	.26°°
T2 Mixed-EU	.15	.26°°	.27°°	.24°	-.02	.00
T2 Social maturity	.04	.32°°	.21°	.26°°	.26°°	-.14
T2 Social skills	-.09	.24°	.20a	.17	.19	-.08
T2 Problem behavior	.12	-.27°°	-.21°	-.17	-.24°	.13
T1 Verbal ability	.08	.06	-.05	-.01	-.04	-.14
T1 Perspective-taking[1]	.08	-.06	-.23°	.02	-.01	-.29°°
T1 Empathic role-taking	.01	.23°	.27°°	.21°	-.01	.14
T1 Social maturity	.13	.17	.12	.23°	.05	-.20°
T1 Social skills	.04	.17	.14	.32°°	-.02	-.24°
T1 Problem behavior	.02	-.10	-.10	-.22°	-.09	.11

[1] T1 emotion understanding + T1 false belief understanding; ° $p < .05$; °° $p < .01$; °°°$p < .001$
Bivariate correlations for child characteristics and teacher-rated social behavior and conduct by children's moral motivation variables, empathic sadness, and psychological self-concept (Eder, 1990).

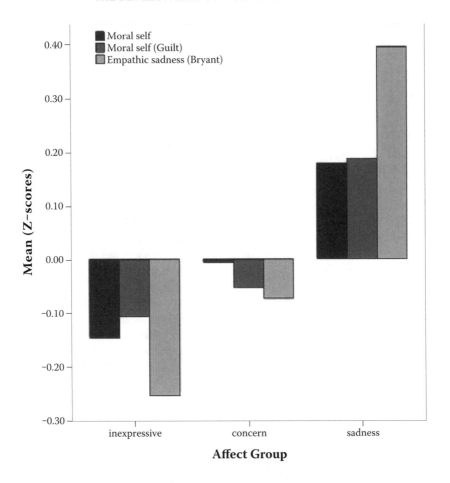

Figure 2.2   Children's self-identified moral self-concept and empathic sadness at 6 years by affective empathy grouping at five years (*N* = 102).

children's moral self-concept and self-identified empathic sadness at T2. Figure 2.2 shows how the different groups at T1 (inexpressive, concerned, and sad) scored on the puppet interview at T2 (generating the moral self-concept and empathic sadness scores) and suggests that the sad group, in particular, self-identified more empathic sadness.

To establish whether there were specific relations between child characteristics and moral motivation, we constructed reciprocal hierarchical linear regression models. The most interesting results concern self-identified guilt (from the moral self-concept puppet interview) and also empathic sadness. The best overall model predicting T2 guilt comprised T1 perspective-taking (β = −.27, p < .01), T1 empathic role-taking (β = .21, p < .05), and T2 mixed emotion understanding (β = .19, p < .05), each of which was a significant independent predictor of children's T2 guilt over and above any relation between empathic sadness at T2 and guilt. (It should be noted that these relationships remained unaffected when T2 negative affect was also entered into the model.) The best overall model predicting T2 empathic sadness comprised T1 empathic responsiveness ($\beta_{\text{inexpressive}} = -.26, p < .05$) over and above any relation between guilt and empathic sadness. That is to say, children in the sad group at T1 self-identified more empathic sadness at T2 than children in the inexpressive group.

Children's Social Behavior and Conduct

Table 2.1 also provides results concerning teacher ratings of children's social behavior and conduct at T1 and T2 and their self-identified moral self-concept and empathic sadness at T2. Two questionnaires were completed by teachers at both time points, the Social Maturity Rating Scale (Peterson, Slaughter, & Paynter, 2007) and the Social Skills Rating System (SSRS; Gresham & Elliott, 1990). Whereas the former provides a window on children's social maturity relative to peers, the SSRS covers a broad range of behaviors including the child's use of social etiquette, prosocial behavior, self-assertion, and the existence of various problem behaviors.

Two aspects of these data are striking. First, there was no relation whatsoever between any index of children's social behavior or conduct and their happy victimizer expectancy. Second, moral self-concept and empathic sadness showed distinctive patterns of association with children's social behavior or conduct. So, whereas T1 social maturity, T1 social skills, and T1 problem behaviors all had a longitudinal impact on children's self-identified empathic sadness at T2, only T2 social maturity had a contemporaneous association with empathic sadness at T2. Moral self-concept, however, showed the reverse pattern. So, whereas T2 social maturity, T2 social skills, and T2 problems behaviors were all concurrently associated with children's moral self-concept at T2, none of these aspects of social behavior or conduct at T1 predicted moral self-concept at T2. In fact, closer scrutiny of these patterns of association showed that children's moral self-concept accounted for significant variance in both T2 social maturity and T2 problem behaviors, over and above longitudinal continuity in each domain, and controlling for sex and T1 verbal ability.

Summary

The longitudinal study presented here sheds light on various aspects of children's moral motivation, both in relation to their empathy and psychological perspective-taking and in relation to their social competence. One of the main findings to emerge from this study is a null finding; Happy victimizer expectancy shows no systematic relation to any of the child characteristics or social and behavioral variables measured in this study. Perhaps more surprising, there was no relationship between happy victimizer expectancy and children's self-identified moral sentiments (i.e., their moral self-concept) or empathic sadness.

In contrast, measurement of children's self-identified moral sentiments and their empathic sadness appeared to open a window on their moral motivation and its relation to closely related constructs. To put some order on these findings, it is instructive to first consider children's self-identified empathic sadness at T2.

Remarkably, there was continuity over a 12-month period between sad patterns of responding in the empathy elicitation video paradigm, which is based on behavioral observation, and children's self-identified feelings of sadness on account of the distress experienced by others a year later. Similarly, children who were more socially mature and skilled at T1, and who also showed fewer behavioral problems at T1, also self-identified more empathic sadness at T2. It appears, therefore, that there are some grounds to assert that children's social experience has direct implications for their developing sense of self-identified empathic sadness.

Despite a strong pattern of association between empathic sadness and moral self-concept, including guilt, there were systematic differences in patterns of relations with other variables that suggest the two domains cleave in important ways. In particular, once shared variance between empathic sadness and guilt was accounted for, only guilt at T2 was predicted by children's T1 empathic role-taking and their T2 understanding of mixed emotions. On the face of it, such findings support the long-held view that moral conscience is closely tied to psychological structures that support the proclivity to take on another person's perspective and that help children figure out what the person might be thinking (see Rest, 1983). The somewhat surprising finding that higher levels of perspective-taking at T1 promote lower levels of self-identified guilt at T2 can, we think, be explained by reference to the more robust association between T1 perspective-taking and negative affect. That is, children who are relatively good at psychological perspective-taking at 5 years of age appear less likely to be preoccupied with negative feelings, including guilt, a year later. The positive relation between T2 understanding of mixed emotions and higher levels of self-identified guilt, by contrast, speaks to the shared cognitive underpinnings of these domains.

Finally, children who self-identify more moral sentiments at 6 years of age are also more socially mature and have fewer behavioral problems with peers. On the basis of our data, such contemporaneous relations between these domains suggest that moral self-concept (as an index of children's conscience and moral motivation) is a salient construct for 6-year-old children. But our data do not offer direct support to the assertion, set out earlier in this chapter, that children's social experience is a primary driving force behind their burgeoning moral understanding. However, caution is needed when interpreting these findings for various reasons. First, our measure of social behavior and conduct, the teacher report, was relatively crude and allowed no qualitative assessment of children's actual social interactions (see Dunn et al., 1995). Second, both children's emotion understanding and their empathic role-taking are directly influenced by distinctive socialization practices (see de Rosnay & Hughes, 2006; Eisenberg et al., 2006), so while we assessed only child characteristics, there is adequate evidence in the research literature that the characteristics in question are strongly influenced by the child's social experience.

The following section describes a final study that aimed to clarify whether the happy victimizer phenomenon yields any psychologically meaningful information about children; in particular, we reexamined this phenomenon in the context of child–child interactions.

STUDY 2: DO CHILDREN SHOW A HAPPY VICTIMIZER EXPECTANCY WHEN INTERACTING WITH PEERS?

In this final study (Fritz et al., 2010), we adopted a different approach to try to understand the significance of happy victimizer expectancy for 6-year-old children. The approach of this study was very simple. Given that we found impressive continuity in children's happy victimizer expectancy—see Study 1 and also Dunn et al. (1995)—we reasoned that this was likely to have one of two sources. First, it could genuinely reflect a conceptual or developmentally driven limitation of the child's moral understanding. To some extent this is consistent with the work of Yuill et al. (1996) and Lagattuta (2005).[3] Alternatively, in keeping with the critiques of Arsenio et al. (2006) and others (e.g., Keller et al., 2003), it might be that the nature of the testing situation or the task itself is structuring children's responding in a manner that does not accurately tap the child's awareness of moral emotion. Therefore, we adopted an entirely novel approach whereby children were given exactly the same happy victimizer style tasks but were asked to solve them in the company of another child, not an experimenter. Furthermore, we pretested children and grouped them according to their happy victimizer expectancy. There were three groupings of children based on the pretest: (1) happy victimizers (HV), who attributed a positive emotion to the transgressor; (2) advanced (AD), who attributed a negative moral emotion to the transgressor; and (3) transitional (TR), who attributed a negative emotion based on fear of retribution (e.g., scared or worried).

A total of 110 children were initially tested using the Nunner-Winkler and Sodian (1988) task. Based on their moral emotion attributions (HV, AD, or TR), children were classified and paired to form five dyad combinations (see below). All children were gender-matched and paired with another child in their same grade (83%) or one grade above or below (17%). All TR children were retained for the final sample because there were relatively few of them. After the formation of dyads, 80 children between 5 and 9 years of age (age $M = 6.70$ years, $SD = 1.07$ years, 65% female) formed the final sample, on which all the reported data are based. Children were from Catholic elementary schools in Sydney, Australia.

There were 10 dyads each with two HV children (HV–HV), 10 dyads each with two AD children (AD–AD), and 10 dyads with one of each (HV–AD). There were also four HV–TR dyads and six TR–AD dyads, making a grand total of 40 dyads. A couple of weeks after the dyads were determined, the researchers returned to the schools. Dyads were put together in a quiet room and presented with a classical happy victimizer style task (see Appendix 2.2). Children were asked to determine how the transgressor felt. They were encouraged to reach a consensus but were also told that this was not necessary, and indeed sometimes children differed in their views. When the dyads made their decisions, they called the research assistant back and explained their choice. Their conversational interactions were discretely filmed, and their reasons and justifications to one another were scored. A little later the same day, children were individually tested on another, novel happy victimizer task.

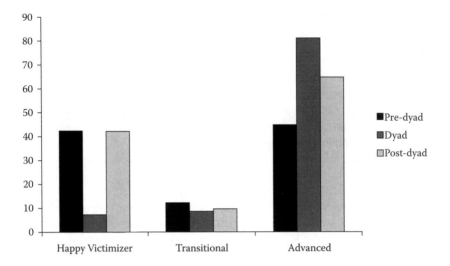

Figure 2.3   Percentage of children within each classification for moral emotion attribution across three sessions.

Two aspects of the results are important for the current discussion. First, as can be seen in Figure 2.3, in the context of dyadic interaction virtually all the children agreed on an advanced response—that is, they attributed a moral emotion and, in fact, often discussed the transgressor's mixed or ambivalent feelings. Second, dyad type (e.g., HV–HV, AD–AD) made no difference to children's moral emotion attributions in the dyadic context. So even if a dyad consisted of two HV children, they were equally likely to make an advance moral emotion attribution as an AD–AD dyad, or any other combination, and were also equally likely to provide a suitable justification for their decision.

The findings of this simple study are compelling: Irrespective of children's predyad classifications, the mere context of the child–child interaction brought out equal moral emotion sophistication in all dyads, and to some extent this carried over to postdyad performance. In short, when children are in the context of their peers, their happy victimizer expectancy has very little to tell us about their moral motivation, at least at 6 years of age. Further, when seen in light of the other null findings presented in this chapter and the substantial critiques that have already been formulated regarding the happy victimizer phenomenon (see Arsenio et al., 2006), it is hard to see what such tasks can usefully tell us about children's moral motivation.

CONCLUSIONS

In this chapter we have explored children's moral motivation at 6 years of age. This developmental window was chosen because it appears to represent a time at which children have considerable social knowledge of moral rules, which is well differentiated from other forms or domains of social knowledge, but they are not yet very able to reason through moral dilemmas (see Rest, 1983; Smetana, 2006).

In keeping with this overall view, there has been a concerted effort to determine whether children at this stage of development understand how moral emotions result from transgression (Arsenio et al., 2006; Nunner-Winkler, 2007). Indeed, on the basis of the extant literature, it seems that there is a tension at this age between children's understanding that transgressing moral rules is wrong or bad and their judgment that the transgressor will feel good or happy having transgressed. The classical happy victimizer task (Nunner-Winkler & Sodian, 1988) nicely embodies this tension: Younger children maintain that the protagonist knows that it is wrong to steal but nonetheless feels happy having obtained the desired object, whereas older children similarly judge the theft to be wrong but maintain that the protagonist will feel bad.

In our view, the robustness of the happy victimizer effect is not really in question; It has been repeatedly replicated, and, importantly, the nature of children's reasoning in such tasks extends to emotion attributions in other rule domains that do not involve morals (see Lagattuta, 2005). In sum, social cognitive understanding tasks show that younger children make emotional attributions in the context of rule violation based on desire fulfillment–frustration rather than rule transgression–adherence. Older children, on the other hand, bring a different psychological orientation to these kinds of tasks; they are more concerned with future and anticipated outcomes for current emotions, and, relatedly, their mind-set is increasingly deontic. The critical issue for us, however, is what this developmental transition means for children's moral motivation; how does it inform their actions?

Contrary to the views of Nunner-Winkler (1993, 2007; Nunner-Winkler & Sodian, 1988), our own findings suggest that at 6 years of age children's happy victimizer expectancy has very little to tell us about their moral motivation. Happy victimizer expectancy does not appear to be related to children's social conduct or empathy, and it bears little relation to the extent to which children self-identify moral and empathic feelings. It is our view that the structure of the happy victimizer task, which essentially asks children to reflect on moral emotion, reveals true differences in how children think. Thus, older children, like adults, tend to be more prescriptive and focused on deontic concerns (the transgressor *should* feel bad), and they probably also have a greater sensitivity to what is expected of them in such a task (how one should answer). This is valuable social knowledge, to be sure, but we do not think that it is inherently related to the child's sense that moral transgression and victimization is connected to emotion. Thus, as Nunner-Winkler (2007) pointed out, children are judging the importance of "two facts that are simultaneously true of a wrongdoer—that s/he transgressed a moral norm and satisfied a personal desire" (p. 403), but their evaluation of which fact is more important apparently tells us little, at 6 years of age, about how emotions affect moral choices.

In stark contrast to our findings with the happy victimizer paradigm, our attempt to tap children's conscience, their self-identified moral sentiments, as an index of moral motivation was fruitful. In keeping with the overall conceptualization of conscience as an inner-guidance system, children's earlier empathic role-taking and their concurrent self-identified empathic sadness predicted higher levels of self-identified moral sentiments on the de Rosnay et al. (2010) moral self-concept puppet interview. Furthermore, higher levels of moral self-concept were associated in predictable ways with prosocial and more mature social conduct. We have discussed the nature of the previous results, so here we simply reflect on three features of these findings.

First, the difference between asking children how a story protagonist feels in a happy victimizer–style task and asking them how they themselves would feel if they transgressed appears to have different implications for what children reveal about their moral sensibilities (Keller et al., 2003; Malti, Gummerum, et al., 2009). One possibility is that asking children to make an *agentive identification* makes the task somehow more salient and thereby allows children to reveal what they actually know about the correspondence between moral transgression and emotional consequences; the task becomes more relevant to them. In a similar vein, although by different mechanisms, Study 2 appears to put children in a context where it becomes easier to reveal their knowledge about the emotional consequences of moral transgressions. A second possibility is that by asking children about their own feelings, one is actually tapping their conscience more directly; children are providing a window on whether they self-identify a moral emotional consequence for the transgression. In the current studies we did not closely examine these two possibilities. In fact, we avoided tapping the extent of children's agentive identification in happy victimizer–style tasks because it seemed to confound conscience with reasoning. Of course, these two domains are unlikely to be entirely independent, and it remains to be seen how the contrast between self- and other-as-victimizer maps onto children's moral conscience (Keller et al., 2003).

Second, our findings offer some helpful insights into the relation between empathy, specifically empathic concern for others' distress, and moral motivation. Of particular note, children's observed feelings of sadness in response to a video of a distressed child at 5 years of age mapped onto their own self-identified empathic sadness in the puppet interview at 6 years of age. Children, it seems, have quite good self-knowledge when it comes to the correspondence between what they actually feel and how they think they would feel in a similar empathy-inducing situation. However, despite the close relation between self-identified empathic sadness and moral self-concept (or conscience), the latter was, longitudinally speaking, more closely linked with children's empathic role-taking—that is, their tendency or proclivity to make an emotional identification with the other person. We suspect that this latter dimension of empathy is more closely tied to socialization and, specifically, to parenting practices that encourage children to engage in role-taking and empathic identification (see Smetana, 2006; Thompson, Meyer, & McGinley, 2006). It is well known that similar socialization practices also promote children's psychological perspective-taking (see de Rosnay & Hughes, 2006), but, importantly, emotion understanding and theory of mind were not longitudinally associated with a higher level of moral self-concept. Far from it, higher levels of psychological perspective-taking at 5 years of age were associated with lower levels of moral guilt and negative affect at 6 years of age. This finding, to some extent, justifies the separate treatment of psychological perspective-taking and empathic role-taking advocated in this chapter; an elaborate but global index of children's psychological perspective-taking at 5 years of age did not, as might be predicted, correspond with higher levels of moral motivation at 6 years of age.

However, there was a contemporaneous association between children's moral self-concept scores and their understanding of mixed emotions. This finding is intriguing because it can be interpreted in two quite distinct ways. First, it can be seen as evidence that psychological perspective-taking promotes children's moral motivation. But consider how few children were able to accurately identify the existence of mixed emotions in the story protagonists; the mean score was 1.6 from a possible score of 5. Perhaps, therefore, the relation between these two factors is actually reversed—that is, children who more often feel moral emotions, which are inherently tinged with ambivalence, are more likely to develop a preconscious understanding of mixed and ambivalent feelings in other, nonmoral circumstances. We cannot distinguish between these two interpretations, but we think the latter more likely.

Finally, we were struck by how readily children engaged with the moral self-concept puppet interview and how much they were prepared to reveal about their moral and empathic feelings. Furthermore, they did this in a reliable fashion that showed a gradual, predictable development. Our findings, therefore, suggest that children at 6 years of age speak truthfully. If you want to know about their moral motivation, it is perhaps best just to ask them.

REFERENCES

Aksan, N., & Kochanska, G. (2005). Conscience in childhood: Old questions, new answers. *Developmental Psychology, 41*, 506–516.

Arsenio, W. F. (1988). Children's conceptions of the situational affective consequences of sociomoral events. *Child Development, 59*, 1611–1622.

Arsenio, W. F., & Ford, M. E. (1985). The role of affective information in social-cognitive development: Children's differentiation of moral and conventional events. *Merrill Palmer Quarterly: Journal of Developmental Psychology, 31*, 1–17.

Arsenio, W. F., Gold, J., & Adams, E. (2006). Children's conceptions and displays of moral emotions. In M. Killen & J. Smetana (Eds.), *Handbook of Moral Development* (pp. 581–608). Mahwah, NJ: Lawrence Erlbaum Associates Publishers.

Arsenio, W. F., & Kramer, R. (1992). Victimizers and their victims: Children's conceptions of the mixed emotional consequences of moral transgressions. *Child Development, 63*, 915–927.

Asendorpf, J. B., & Nunner-Winkler, G. (1992). Children's moral motive strength and temperamental inhibition reduce their immoral behavior in real moral conflicts. *Child Development, 63*, 1223–1235.

Blair, R. J. R., Monson, J., & Frederickson, N. (2001). Moral reasoning and conduct problems in children with emotional and behavioural difficulties. *Personality and Individual Differences, 31*, 799–811.

Blasi, A. (1999). Emotions and moral motivation. *Journal for the Theory of Social Behaviour, 29*, 1–19.

Brown, G. L., Mangelsdorf, S. C., Agathen, J. M., & Ho, M.-H. (2008). Young children's psychological selves: Convergence with maternal reports of child personality. *Social Development, 17*, 161–182.

Brown, J. R., & Dunn, J. (1996). Continuities in emotion understanding from 3-6 years. *Child Development, 67*, 789–802.

Bryant, B. K. (1982). An index of empathy for children and adolescents. *Child Development, 53,* 413–425.

Cole, P. M., Zahn-Waxler, C., Fox, N. A., Usher, B. A., & Welsh, J. D. (1996). Individual differences in emotion regulation and behavior problems in preschool children. *Journal of Abnormal Psychology, 105,* 518–529.

de Rosnay, M., Fink, E., Kurukulasuriya, N., Wall, B., & Fritz, K. (2010). *Emotional determinants of children's developing moral sensibilities: A longitudinal study from kindergarten to year 1.* Manuscript submitted for publication.

de Rosnay, M., & Hughes, C. (2006). Conversation and theory of mind: Do children talk their way to socio-cognitive understanding? *British Journal of Developmental Psychology, 24,* 7–37.

de Wied, M., Maas, C., van Goozen, S., Vermande, M., Engels, R., Meeus, W., et al. (2007). Bryant's Empathy Index: A closer examination of its internal structure. *European Journal of Psychological Assessment, 23,* 99–104.

Dunn, J., Brown, J. R., & Maguire, M. (1995). The development of children's moral sensibility: Individual differences and emotion understanding. *Developmental Psychology, 31,* 649–659.

Eder, R. A. (1990). Uncovering young children's psychological selves: Individual and developmental differences. *Child Development, 61,* 849–863.

Eisenberg, N. (2000). Empathy and sympathy. In M. Lewis & J. M. Haviland-Jones (Eds.), *Handbook of emotions* (2d ed., pp. 677–691). New York: Guilford Press.

Eisenberg, N., & Fabes, R. A. (1990). Empathy: Conceptualization, measurement, and relation to prosocial behavior. *Motivation and Emotion, 14,* 131–149.

Eisenberg, N., & Fabes, R. A. (1995). The relation of young children's vicarious emotional responding to social competence, regulation, and emotionality. *Cognition and Emotion, 9,* 203–228.

Eisenberg, N., Fabes, R. A., Bustamante, D., Mathy, R. M., Miller, P. A., & Lindholm, E. (1988). Differentiation of vicariously induced emotional reactions in children. *Developmental Psychology, 24,* 237–246.

Eisenberg, N., & Mussen, P. H. (1989). *The roots of prosocial behavior in children.* New York: Cambridge University Press.

Eisenberg, N., Spinrad, T. L., & Sadovsky, A. (2006). *Empathy-related responding in children.* Mahwah, NJ: Lawrence Erlbaum Associates Publishers.

Fabes, R. A., Eisenberg, N., & Eisenbud, L. (1993). Behavioral and physiological correlates of children's reactions to others in distress. *Developmental Psychology, 29,* 655–663.

Fabes, R. A., Eisenberg, N., & Miller, P. A. (1990). Maternal correlates of children's vicarious emotional responsiveness. *Developmental Psychology, 26,* 639–648.

Fritz, K., Percy, S., & de Rosnay, M. (2010). *Not so happy victimizers: Child-child interactions reveal precocious sensitivity to the emotional impact of moral transgression.* Manuscript submitted for publication.

Gresham, F. M., & Elliott, S. N. (1990). *Social Skills Rating System (SSRS).* Bloomington, MN: Pearson Assessments.

Grusec, J. E. (2006). *The development of moral behavior and conscience from a socialization perspective.* Mahwah, NJ: Lawrence Erlbaum Associates Publishers.

Grusec, J. E., & Goodnow, J. J. (1994). Impact of parental discipline methods on the child's internalization of values: A reconceptualization of current points of view. *Developmental Psychology, 30,* 4–19.

Harris, P. L. (1989). *Children and emotion: The development of psychological understanding.* Oxford, UK: Basil Blackwell.

Hastings, P. D., Zahn-Waxler, C., Usher, B., Robinson, J., & Bridges, D. (2000). The development of concern for others in children with behavior problems. *Developmental Psychology, 36,* 531–546.

Hoffman, M. L. (2000). *Empathy and moral development: Implications for caring and justice*. Cambridge, UK: Cambridge University Press.

Hresko, W. P., Reid, D. K., & Hammill, D. D. (1999). *Test of early language development*, 3d ed. Austin, TX: Pro-Ed.

Iannotti, R. J. (1985). Naturalistic and structured assessments of prosocial behavior in preschool children: The influence of empathy and perspective taking. *Developmental Psychology, 21,* 46–55.

Janssens, J. M., & Dekovic, M. (1997). Child rearing, prosocial moral reasoning, and prosocial behaviour. *International Journal of Behavioral Development, 20,* 509–527.

Keller, M., Lourenco, O., Malti, T., & Saalbach, H. (2003). The multifaceted phenomenon of "happy victimizers": A cross-cultural comparison of moral emotions. *British Journal of Developmental Psychology, 21,* 1–18.

Kochanska, G. (2002). Committed compliance, moral self, and internalization: A mediational model. *Developmental Psychology, 38,* 339–351.

Kochanska, G., & Aksan, N. (2006). Children's conscience and self-regulation. *Journal of Personality, 74,* 1587–1618.

Kochanska, G., Aksan, N., Prisco, T. R., & Adams, E. E. (2008). Mother–child and father–child mutually responsive orientation in the first 2 years and children's outcomes at preschool age: Mechanisms of influence. *Child Development, 79,* 30–44.

Kochanska, G., DeVet, K., Goldman, M., Murray, K., & Putnam, S. P. (1994). Maternal reports of conscience development and temperament in young children. *Child Development, 65,* 852–868.

Kochanska, G., Gross, J. N., Lin, M.-H., & Nichols, K. E. (2002). Guilt in young children: Development, determinants, and relations with a broader system of standards. *Child Development, 73,* 461–482.

Kochanska, G., Murray, K., & Coy, K. C. (1997). Inhibitory control as a contributor to conscience in childhood: From toddler to early school age. *Child Development, 68,* 263–277.

Kohlberg, L. (1971). From is to ought: How to commit the naturalistic fallacy and get away with it in the study of moral development. In T. Mischel (Ed.), *Cognitive development and epistemology* (pp. 151–235). New York: Academic Press.

Kohlberg, L. (1984). *The psychology of moral development: Essays on moral development*, vol. 2. San Francisco: Harper & Row.

Lagattuta, K. H. (2005). When you shouldn't do what you want to do: Young children's understanding of desires, rules, and emotions. *Child Development, 76,* 713–733.

Laible, D. J. (2004). Mother-child discourse surrounding a child's past behavior at 30 months: Links to emotional understanding and early conscience development at 36 months. *Merrill-Palmer Quarterly: Journal of Developmental Psychology, 50,* 159–180.

Laible, D. J., & Thompson, R. A. (2000). Mother-child discourse, attachment security, shared positive affect, and early conscience development. *Child Development, 71,* 1424–1440.

Lapsley, D. K. (2006). *Moral stage theory*. Mahwah, NJ: Lawrence Erlbaum Associates Publishers.

Lourenco, O. (1997). Children's attributions of moral emotions to victimizers: Some data, doubts and suggestions. *British Journal of Developmental Psychology, 15,* 425–438.

Malti, T., Gasser, L., & Buchmann, M. (2009). Aggressive and prosocial children's emotion attributions and moral reasoning. *Aggressive Behavior, 35,* 90–102.

Malti, T., Gummerum, M., Keller, M., & Buchmann, M. (2009). Children's moral motivation, sympathy, and prosocial behavior. *Child Development, 80,* 442–460.

Meerum Terwogt, M., Koops, W., Oosterhoff, T., & Olthof, T. (1986). Development in processing of multiple emotional situations. *Journal of General Psychology, 113,* 109–119.

Miller, P. A., Eisenberg, N., Fabes, R. A., & Shell, R. (1996). Relations of moral reasoning and vicarious emotion to young children's prosocial behaviour toward peers and adults. *Developmental Psychology, 32*, 210–219.

Monin, B., Pizarro, D. A., & Beer, J. S. (2007). Deciding versus reacting: Conceptions of moral judgment and the reason-affect debate. *Review of General Psychology, 11*, 99–111.

Murgatroyd, S., & Robinson, E. (1993). Children's judgments of emotion following moral transgression. *International Journal of Behavioral Development, 16*, 93–111.

Murgatroyd, S., & Robinson, E. (1997). Children's and adult's attributions of emotion to a wrongdoer: The influence of the onlooker's reaction. *Cognition and Emotion, 11*, 83–101.

Nunner-Winkler, G. (1993). The growth of moral motivation. In G. G. Noam & T. E. Wren (Eds.), *The moral self* (pp. 269–291). Cambridge, MA: MIT Press.

Nunner-Winkler, G. (2007). Development of moral motivation from childhood to early adulthood. *Journal of Moral Education, 36*, 399–414.

Nunner-Winkler, G., & Sodian, B. (1988). Children's understanding of moral emotions. *Child Development, 59*, 1323–1338.

Peterson, C. C., Slaughter, V., & Paynter, J. (2007). Social maturity and theory of mind in typically developing children and those on the autism spectrum. *Journal of Child Psychology and Psychiatry, 48*, 1243–1250.

Piaget, J. (1932/1997). *The moral judgment of the child*. Oxford, UK: Harcourt, Brace.

Pizarro, D. (2000). Nothing more than feelings? The role of emotions in moral judgment. *Journal for the Theory of Social Behaviour, 30*, 355–375.

Pons, F., & Harris, P. L. (2005). Longitudinal change and longitundinal stability of individual differences in children's emotion understanding. *Cognition and Emotion, 19*, 1158–1174.

Pons, F., Harris, P. L., & de Rosnay, M. (2004). Emotion comprehension between 3 and 11 years: Developmental periods and hierarchical organization. *European Journal of Developmental Psychology, 1*, 127–152.

Rest, J. R. (1983). Morality. In P. H. Mussen (Ed.), *Handbook of child psychology*, 4th ed., vol. 3 (pp. 556–629). Toronto, Canada: John Wiley & Sons.

Roberts, W., & Strayer, J. (1996). Empathy, emotional expressiveness, and prosocial behavior. *Child Development, 67*, 449–470.

Smetana, J. G. (1993), Understanding of social rules. In M. Bennett (Ed.), *The child as psychologist: An introduction to the development of social cognition* (pp. 111–114). New York: Harvester WheatSheaf.

Smetana, J. G. (2006). *Social-cognitive domain theory: Consistencies and variations in children's moral and social judgments*. Mahwah, NJ: Lawrence Erlbaum Associates Publishers.

Strayer, J. (1993). Children's concordant emotions and cognitions in response to observed emotions. *Child Development, 64*, 188–201.

Strayer, J., & Roberts, W. (1997). Facial and verbal measures of children's emotions and empathy. *International Journal of Behavioral Development, 20*, 627–649.

Strayer, J., & Roberts, W. L. (2004). *The Empathy Continuum Scoring Manual*. Unpublished manuscript.

Talwar, V., & Lee, K. (2008). Social and cognitive correlates of children's lying behavior. *Child Development, 79*, 866–881.

Thompson, R. A. (1994). Emotion regulation: A theme in search of definition. *Monographs of the Society for Research in Child Development, 59*, 25–52.

Thompson, R. A., & Hoffman, M. L. (1980). Empathy and the development of guilt in children. *Developmental Psychology, 16*, 155–156.

Thompson, R. A., Meyer, S., & McGinley, M. (2006). *Understanding values in relationships: The development of conscience*. Mahwah, NJ: Lawrence Erlbaum Associates Publishers.

Turiel, E. (1983). *The development of social knowledge: Morality and convention.* Cambridge, UK: Cambridge University Press.

Underwood, B., & Moore, B. (1982). Perspective-taking and altruism. *Psychological Bulletin, 91,* 143–173.

Wellman, H. M., Cross, D., & Watson, J. (2001). Meta-analysis of theory-of-mind development: The truth about false belief. *Child Development, 72,* 655–684.

Yuill, N., Perner, J., Pearson, A., Peerbhoy, D., & van den Ende, J. (1996). Children's changing understanding of wicked desires: From objective to subjective and moral. *British Journal of Developmental Psychology, 14,* 457–475.

Zahn-Waxler, C., Radke-Yarrow, M., Wagner, E., & Chapman, M. (1992). Development of concern for others. *Developmental Psychology, 28,* 126–136.

APPENDIX 2.1. EXAMPLE OF HAPPY VICTIMIZER TASK (PRESENTED WITH PICTURES)

EPISODE 1

This is Julia and this is another girl in Julia's class. They're putting their hats away in their schoolbags. Now this girl takes a doll out of her bag and shows it to Julia. This girl says, "Look at my doll. My aunty gave me this doll for my birthday." Julia likes the doll very much. She thinks it's really pretty.

EPISODE 2

Later on, Julia is back in the hallway and she's all by herself. She sees the other girl's doll on the floor.
  Control question: Do you think Julia wants to have the other girl's doll?

EPISODE 3

That's right, Julia does want to have the doll. Now Julia picks up the doll.
  Moral rule question: Do you think Julia is allowed to keep the doll or is she not allowed to keep the doll?

EPISODE 4

That's right, She's not allowed to keep the doll. Now, here is Julia and she has picked up the doll.

EPISODE 5

Julia puts the doll into her own schoolbag. She likes this doll a lot and thinks it's really pretty. Nobody has seen her.

EPISODE 6

Julia goes home with the doll in her bag.
> Test Question (moral emotional attribution): How does Julia feel inside?

APPENDIX 2.2. MORAL SELF-CONCEPT

CONFESSION

6. I tell someone if I break something.
   I hide it if I break something.
23. When I do something wrong, I tell someone.
   When I do something wrong, I keep it a secret.

REPARATION

8. If I spill something on the floor, I clean it up.
   If I spill something on the floor, I don't clean it up.
17. If I broke a friend's toy, I would give them one of mine.
   If I broke a friend's toy, I wouldn't give them one of mine.

INTERNALIZED CONDUCT

14. If my parents tell me not to do something, I still sometimes do it.
   If my parents tell me not to do something, I won't do it.
20. I usually follow the rules even if my mum can't see me.
   I sometimes break the rules when my mum can't see me.

CONCERN ABOUT OTHERS' WRONGDOING

5. It upsets me when other people do something wrong.
   I don't mind when other people do something wrong.
18. I try to stop other kids from getting in trouble.
   I don't care if other kids get in trouble.

GUILT AND AFFECTIVE DISCOMFORT AFTER TRANSGRESSIONS

4. I usually feel bad when I break something or spill something.
   I don't feel bad when I break something or spill something.
9. When I do something bad, I worry about it for a long time.
   When I do something bad, I don't really worry that much.
11. It upsets me when someone tells me I make a mistake.
   It doesn't really bother me when someone tells me I make a mistake.

12. When I remember a time I got in trouble for doing something wrong, I don't feel bad anymore.
    When I remember a time I got in trouble for doing something wrong, I feel bad all over again.
13. When I do something bad, I get really upset.
    I don't care when I do something bad.
16. When I do something wrong, sometimes I get a funny feeling in my tummy.
    When I do something wrong, I don't get a funny feeling in my tummy.

CONCERN ABOUT GOOD FEELINGS WITH PARENTS

10. If my mum is mad at me because I did something wrong, I hate it.
    If my mum is mad at me because I did something wrong, I don't really care.
15. When I do something bad and my mum is upset, I really want us to make up.
    When I do something bad and my mum is upset, I don't mind.

EMPATHIC SADNESS

1. It makes me sad to see a boy who can't find anyone to play with.
   It doesn't make me sad to see a boy who can't find anyone to play with.
2. I get upset when I see a boy being hurt.
   I don't get upset when I see a boy being hurt.
3. When I see a boy who is crying, it makes me feel like crying.
   When I see a boy who is crying, it doesn't make me feel like crying.
7. When I see a girl who is crying, it makes me feel like crying.
   When I see a girl who is crying, it doesn't make me feel like crying.
19. It makes me sad to see a girl who can't find anyone to play with.
    It doesn't make me sad to see a girl who can't find anyone to play with.
21. Some songs make me so sad I feel like crying.
    I don't ever feel like crying when I hear a song.
22. I get upset when I see a girl being hurt.
    I don't get upset when I see a girl being hurt.

ENDNOTES

1. Study 1 presents the key findings of the program of research presented in this chapter. As it is an ambitious longitudinal study, only certain aspects of the findings are presented here. For further details see de Rosnay et al. (2010).
2. It seems that the critical issue is not whether children appear sad or concerned, but rather whether they express personal distress or not (Eisenberg, 2000). In fact, it was our impression on scoring the videos that concerned attention generally had more qualities of worry and distress in this particular paradigm.
3. Although, see Lagattuta (2005) for an alternative account.

3

Revisiting the Role of Empathy in Childhood Pathways to Antisocial Behavior

DAVID J. HAWES

University of Sydney

MARK R. DADDS

University of New South Wales

Deficits in empathy have long featured in clinical descriptions of antisocial behavior in children; however, these deficits and their contribution to antisocial behavior have proven difficult to characterize empirically. We argue that the construct of psychopathy—most commonly applied to adult populations of antisocial offenders—provides a useful framework with which to reexamine the construct of empathy as it relates to conduct problems in childhood. Drawing on a program of research by the authors, we examine issues of measurement relevant to this line of research and discuss recent data on the relationships between distinct components of empathy (cognitive and affective) and callous-unemotional (or psychopathic) traits across the child and adolescent years. Findings suggest that males with high levels of antisocial behavior and callous-unemotional traits show consistent deficits in affective empathy across childhood and adolescence, while females show no such relationship. Findings also suggest that cognitive empathy may be more impaired in these males than previously thought, albeit at younger ages only; by early adolescence this deficit appears to be largely overcome. It seems then that the characteristic disconnect between cognitive and affective empathy seen in adult males with psychopathy may crystallize during the pubertal years.

INTRODUCTION

S ome of the earliest clinical descriptions of children with antisocial behavior suggested that a lack of empathy could be found among the core features of the presentation. Redl and Wineman (1951), known for their seminal therapeutic work with "wayward boys" in residential facilities, characterized these children as deficient in "the skill of figuring out how another person may feel about us" (p. 122). This view has often been echoed since, with the current *Diagnostic and Statistical Manual of Mental Disorders*, 4th ed., text revision (*DSM-IV-TR*; APA, 2000) description of conduct disorder noting that such children "may have little empathy and little concern for the feelings, wishes, and well-being of others" (p. 95). However, despite considerable investigation, evidence of reduced empathy in children with antisocial behavior has been equivocal (Lovett & Sheffield, 2007). As such, the precise nature of such deficits, and their contribution to the development of antisocial behavior, remains poorly understood.

In this paper we examine empathy in the context of emerging developmental models of antisocial behavior, which in recent years have drawn increasingly on evidence from adult populations to characterize children at risk for chronic antisocial trajectories. It is such a perspective that we think is essential to understanding the divergent evidence reported in previous studies of empathy in children with antisocial behavior and to formulating new questions in this line of research. Specifically, we argue that the construct of psychopathy—most commonly applied to adult populations of antisocial offenders—provides a framework with which to reexamine the construct of empathy as it relates to antisocial behavior in childhood and risk for chronic antisocial outcomes.

We begin with a brief overview of current conceptualizations of empathy and its development, followed by a review of evidence for empathic dysfunction in adults and children with antisocial behavior. We examine the importance of the psychopathy construct to models of this dysfunction in adult offenders and review emerging evidence supporting the application of the construct in childhood. Drawing on findings from a program of research conducted by the authors, we examine key measurement issues in empathy research with children and discuss recent data on the relationship of distinct components of empathy (cognitive and affective) to psychopathic traits across the child and adolescent years.

DEFINING EMPATHY

The construct of empathy has been of enduring interest to a range of academic fields and is often illuminated by competing theoretical positions within them. This makes use of the term *empathy* at times problematic and places considerable importance on issues of conceptualization and the clarification of terminology. Unlike some other perspectives, the conceptualization of the construct that has most directly informed the work presented here emphasizes a distinction among dissociable subcomponents of empathy. Of particular importance is the basic distinction between cognitive and affective forms of empathy, which—in research examining the neural mechanisms of social cognition (e.g., Adolphs, 2003; Blair, 2005; Decety & Jackson, 2004; Singer, 2006)—has received compelling support.

Affective empathy typically refers to the sharing of another's emotional state, with widely cited definitions describing an affective response more appropriate to (Hoffman, 1984) or congruent with (Eisenberg & Fabes, 1990) someone else's situation than to one's own situation. The term *emotional contagion*—used by some authors (e.g., Vreeke & van der Mark, 2003)—captures the involuntary nature by which the affective expressions of others may induce a corresponding feeling state in ourselves. As Vreeke and van der Mark (2003) put it, when someone smiles at us we smile back automatically, "catching" a warm feeling in the process. It should be noted that what we refer to here as affective empathy, and emphasize as only one specific form of empathy, most closely matches the more classic definition of empathy as an emotional response, and indeed reflects the primary (and at times exclusive) focus of many studies in the literature on empathy.

Cognitive empathy, as we will use the term in this paper, involves the explicit understanding of another's mental state and reflects the capacity to represent the internal states of others. For example, cognitive empathy has been defined as the ability to intellectually take the role or perspective of another person (Gladstein, 1983) and involves the decoding and labeling of emotions and their situational cues. Some definitions of cognitive empathy also encompass the "mentalizing" abilities associated with "theory of mind"—those abilities underlying the attribution of propositional attitudes (such as beliefs and intentions) to another person (see, e.g., Blair, 2005).

Beyond the affective and cognitive processing referred to already, it is often argued that fully developed empathy also includes the urge to act on such responses by providing comfort and support to a victim when appropriate. These behavioral responses may be seen as a third component of empathy and are included in more comprehensive conceptualizations of the construct. From this perspective, affective and cognitive empathy may or may not be transformed into prosocial actions intended to alleviate distress in another (e.g., Hoffman, 2000; Roberts & Strayer, 1996). As such, many current conceptualizations of empathy emphasize both the differentiation and interplay of affective and cognitive empathetic processing and behavioral responses.

THE DEVELOPMENT OF EMPATHY

There is neuroimaging evidence to suggest that cognitive and affective empathy may reflect partially dissociable neurocognitive systems that putatively share a common neural foundation—the superior temporal cortex—while also relying on unique neural architectures (see, e.g., Blair, 2005). Such research has provided growing support for the differentiation of facets of cognitive and affective empathy while also informing developmental theories of the interconnectedness of these components.

The *perception–action model* of empathy proposed by Preston and de Waal (2002) suggests that the observation or imagination of a particular emotional state in another automatically activates a representation of that state in the observer, along with its associated autonomic and somatic responses. Such responses are said to be automatic, in that they do not require conscious or effortful processing, but can nevertheless be inhibited or controlled. The neural basis for automatic responses of this kind may involve mirror neurons that are also thought to underlie motor empathy, including the tendency to automatically mimic and synchronize facial expressions, vocalizations, postures, and movements with those of another person (Hatfield, Cacioppo, & Rapson, 1994).

The role of the mirroring of others in empathy is supported by evidence that both the experience of emotions and the observation of the same emotions in others are associated with overlapping patterns of brain activation. For example, Wicker, Keysers, Plailly, Royet, Gallese, and Rizzolatti (2003) found that participants observing photographs of disgusted faces exhibited increased activation in the anterior insula cortex, the same brain region that is also activated when the participants smelled disgusting odors themselves. Likewise, in a paradigm involving the administration of painful stimulation to couples, the knowledge that a loved one was in physical pain activated the same affective pain circuits as activated by the actual experience of pain (Singer, Seymour, O'Doherty, Kaube, Dolan, & Frith, 2004). While this mirroring facet of affective empathy is thought to be largely automatic, it is less apparent what processes underlying cognitive empathy, if any, are automatic in nature. Likewise, while it is clear what cues automatically activate affective empathy (e.g., cues of facial or vocal expressions), little is known about the stimulus conditions capable of automatically eliciting cognitive empathy (Blair, 2005). Such differences between cognitive and affective empathy may stem from the unique neural architectures underlying each.

Facets of affective empathy appear to rely upon the superior temporal cortex via limbic structures that underpin processing of distinct clusters of emotions. As such, the specific patterns of brain activation associated with affective empathy vary according to whether the individual is responding to fearful/sad/happy (amygdala), disgust (insula), or angry (ventrolateral frontal cortex) cues of others' emotional states (Blair, 2005). These limbic and paralimbic structures constitute what has variously been referred to as the *emotional brain* (Dolan, 2002; LeDoux, 1998) or parts of the *social brain* (Adolphs, 2003). Cognitive empathy, on the other hand, is thought to rely more on the integrated neural responding of temporo-parietal regions, temporal pole, and the paracingulate cortex (see, e.g., Frith, 2001).

Current developmental models of empathy suggest that cognitive and affective empathy may follow distinct ontogenetic trajectories that reflect the differential maturation of these respective brain structures. Broadly speaking, it appears that the structures underlying the automatic ability to share emotions were not only early to evolve phylogenetically but are also early to develop in ontogeny. In contrast, the structures underlying the capacity to reflectively understand mental states emerged late in phylogeny and are also among those to mature latest in ontogeny (Singer, 2006). However, while current perspectives highlight the distinct developmental trajectories of cognitive and affective empathy, they also emphasize functional interactions between these trajectories. Therein the capacities underlying one form of empathy are seen to contribute to the development and quality of another.

Typical developmental trajectories for cognitive and affective empathy differ most saliently in terms of the ages at which different facets emerge, with the abilities underlying reflective cognitive empathy developing considerably later than those associated with automatic affective empathy. Indeed, the beginnings of affective empathy appear to be demonstrated soon after birth when newborn infants selectively respond to the cries of other infants by crying themselves (e.g., Martin & Clark, 1982). This "empathic crying"—apparent well before infants demonstrate self-awareness and the capacity to distinguish self and others—is seen as an elementary form of affect sharing and is often regarded as the foundation for the increasingly complex forms of empathy that follow (e.g., Hoffman, 2000; Vreeke & van der Mark, 2003).

It is only toward the end of the first year that infants demonstrate a more active response to peer distress; however, at this time children act to reduce their own empathic distress rather than that of the victim. For example, the child who observes a friend fall down and cry may cry in response and engage in self-soothing behaviors such as thumb sucking. By 13 or 14 months infants may no longer exhibit signs of their own distress but show the first steps toward prosocial actions—approaching, touching, and patting the distressed individual. It is only once the capacities for self-awareness and the distinction between self and other develop, beginning at around 18 months, that classic prosocial behavior is demonstrated (Decety & Jackson, 2004). At this time children may respond to a distressed individual by bringing objects to him or her, making suggestions about what to do, expressing sympathy in words, seeking help from a third party, or even attempting to protect the distressed other (Harris, 1989).

Just as the development of automatic affective empathy precedes that of reflective cognitive empathy, the implicit attribution of intentions and other mental states to others also precedes explicit forms of emotion understanding and mentalizing. These implicit processes include the ability of infants to direct their attention or gaze toward the attentional focus of their mother (joint attention), which develops at around the age of 12–18 months or even earlier. It is only later that explicit forms of cognitive empathy emerge, which are thought to coincide with the emergence of conscious representations of one's own mental states, allowing for statements such as, "I feel sad or jealous" (Singer, 2006).

The beginnings of that facet of cognitive empathy termed theory of mind appear at around age 4 with a capacity to represent first-order beliefs (attributing a belief to oneself or another person, "I believe 'x'"), while the capacity for second-order beliefs (attributing a belief about another person's belief) is not established until between the ages of 6 and 10. This developmental course appears to reflect maturation in prefrontal and temporal structures; this maturation is also thought to continue across childhood and adolescence and support the subsequent differentiation and increasing complexity of explicit mentalizing abilities.

EMPATHY AND ANTISOCIAL BEHAVIOR IN CHILDREN

Empirical investigation of the association between facets of empathy and antisocial behavior in children has employed a range of methodologies. Miller and Eisenberg (1988) grouped the measures of empathy traditionally used in this research into four categories. The most common of these has been picture and story methods such as Feshbach and Roe's (1968) Affective Situations Test for Empathy. Here, children are presented with narratives and visual stimuli depicting an emotionally provocative scenario and are asked to report on the emotional responses of the fictional protagonist. A second category involves experimental paradigms designed to induce empathy in participants, by means such as encouraging them to imagine how another individual feels or to objectively observe them (e.g., Feshbach, 1978). A third category of assessment strategy—developed in part to offset the problem of requiring young children to report on their emotions verbally—involves the coding of children's facial affect and gestural reactions to the emotions of others depicted in films or picture or story stimuli (e.g., Marcus, Roke, & Bruner, 1985). The fourth category includes self-report questionnaires, the most commonly used of which are Bryant's (1982) Empathy Index (BEI) and Litvack-Miller, McDougall, and Romney's (1997) Interpersonal Reactivity Index for children. Both of these represent child adaptations of adult measures.

BEI was developed by adapting Mehrabian and Epstein's (1972) scale of emotional tendency—a widely used measure of adult affective empathy—for self-report in children aged 6 years and older. The 22 items of the BEI contribute to a total score that captures a range of empathic responses and processes, including susceptibility to emotional contagion, understanding of the feelings of familiar or unfamiliar people, emotional responsiveness to others' emotions, and sympathetic feelings toward others. More recently, the original Interpersonal Reactivity Index (IRI; Davis, 1983) was adapted for use with children by Litvack-Miller et al. (1997). Factor analysis of the resultant 22-item measure was employed to identify items that tend to group together and supported a factor structure comparable to the same four relatively independent subscales of the original IRI: perspective-taking, empathic concern, personal distress, and fantasy.

Despite the variety of ways empathy has been operationalized in this line of research, the relationship between empathy and antisocial behavior in children has proven difficult to characterize. The findings have been subject to two major reviews (Lovett & Sheffield, 2007; Miller & Eisenberg, 1988), both of which have emphasized inconsistencies in the evidence base. In support of the anecdotal lack of empathy often described in the clinical literature, a number of studies have found a negative relationship between a lack of empathy and greater antisocial behavior (Burke, 2001; Cohen & Strayer, 1996; de Wied, Goudena, & Matthys, 2005; Endresen & Olweus, 2001; LeSure-Lester, 2000; Strayer & Roberts, 2004). Other studies, however, have reported no evidence of such a relationship (Gonzalez, Field, Lasko, LaGreca, & Lahey, 1996; Lee & Prentice, 1988; MacQuiddy, Maise, & Hamilton, 1987; Marcus, Roke, & Bruner, 1985), while other research has even found support for some positive relationships (e.g., Gill & Calkins, 2003). These researchers examined empathy in 2-year-olds, as coded in two behavioral paradigms (involving child responses to the sound of a toddler crying, and the apparent distress of the experimenter over a hurt finger). Compared with toddlers with low levels of aggression, those identified as highly aggressive responded more quickly to the distress of others, showed more affective concern facially, and inquired more into the victim's distress (Gill & Calkins, 2003).

Explanations for these divergent findings have centered on two issues. First, it has been recognized that decades of research in the area have been hampered by measurement difficulties associated with a lack of valid instruments. On the basis of this conclusion, Lovett and Sheffield (2007) proposed that a first step toward progress should be the development of standardized measures in large representative samples. Second, inconsistencies in this evidence may be accounted for by developmental processes. Given that characteristics associated with both empathy and antisocial behavior are known to transform across development, it is feasible that the relationship between these constructs may in turn be transformed and therefore show different relationships in samples of differently aged children.

Trends in previous findings appear consistent with this assumption, with support for a negative relationship between a lack of empathy and greater antisocial behavior found more consistently in studies of adolescents than in those of younger children (Lovett & Sheffield, 2007). This interpretation, however, is complicated by the first issue—that is, studies of adolescents versus younger children have largely differed in their means of measuring empathy and have generally relied on methods subject to limited psychometric scrutiny. Furthermore, most studies have either operationalized empathy as a global unitary construct—as it is measured by instruments such as the BEI—or have focused exclusively on specific facets of empathy. As such, little is known about the unique associations between antisocial behavior and distinct components of affective and cognitive empathy and even less about how these associations develop over time.

KEY MEASUREMENT ISSUES

The successful early detection and remediation of problems in the development of empathy depends on the accurate measurement of the construct early in life and in the context of other problems. The task of assessing empathy in young children presents unique challenges, as does the assessment of empathy in children with antisocial behavior. Laboratory-based coding systems are often considered the gold standard in the measurement of developmental constructs such as empathy but are expensive and not suited to large cohort studies or many clinical settings. The common alternative to such methods has been self-report checklists.

Youth self-reports of empathy have facilitated research into the construct in populations of older children. At the same time, the psychometric integrity of such measures has often appeared questionable. Youth self-reports of affective empathy and their scores on picture or story indices do not converge with their prosocial behavior (Eisenberg & Fabes, 1990) and are heavily affected by demand characteristics—for example, participants' perceptions of what the experimenter wants (Eisenberg-Berg & Hand, 1979) or other factors such as the gender of the experimenter (Eisenberg & Lennon, 1983). Furthermore, in younger children—those most likely to be the focus of early intervention efforts—developmental considerations preclude their use. Children below the age of about 8 years lack the cognitive or verbal abilities to reliably report on internal states, and the use of self-reports is widely advised against in this age group. While a small number of studies have incorporated teacher reports (e.g., Barnett, Howard, Melton, & Dino, 1982), until recently little was available in the form of parent report measures.

In response to this problem, Dadds, Hawes, et al. (2008) adapted and validated a parent report measure of child empathy in a large representative sample. The BEI was selected as the basis for this new instrument—the Griffith Empathy Measure (GEM). Item content from the BEI was adapted for parent report by rewording questions from the first- to third-person format. For example the original BEI item "I get upset when I see an animal being hurt" was changed to "My child gets upset when he/she sees an animal being hurt." The GEM retains the original nine-point rating scale used in the original adult version of the Empathy Index (Mehrabian & Epstein, 1972) rather than the yes–no format designed for use with children in Bryant's (1982) version. As such, the scale's 23 items are answered on a nine-point scale ranging from strongly disagree (–4) to strongly agree (+4).

Before discussing our use of the GEM in research examining correlates of childhood empathy, it is relevant to recognize the contentious issues that a measure tool of this kind raises. As already noted, the dimensions of empathy emphasized in current conceptualizations of the construct relate largely to internal states and representations that are not directly accessible to others. As such, reports on the GEM reflect the observable signs of empathy rather than levels of empathy per se. Furthermore, it is likely that such observable signs of empathy also reflect a range of other intrapersonal and contextual variables and as such may map only loosely onto the underlying dimensions identified in current conceptualizations of the construct. Due to these potential limitations, the GEM was subject to a rigorous validation process. This process formed the groundwork for our subsequent research relating empathy to developmental pathways toward antisocial behavior and is included here accordingly as part of a comprehensive background to that research.

The measurement properties of the GEM were evaluated in a large representative sample of typically developing children and smaller subsamples of clinic-referred children. These children ($n = 2,612$) ranged from 4 to 17 years of age and were recruited from primary and secondary schools as part of a larger program of research examining the development, prevention, and treatment of child psychopathology. Of initial interest was the convergence between the GEM and the original BEI. Total scores on the parent report GEM and the child report BEI showed moderate correlation ($r = .412$, $p < .01$), with separate correlations for males and females showing similar results. It should be noted that the strength of this association is consistent with that generally seen between parents' reports of their child's behavioral and emotional adjustment and their child's own reports on these domains using well-established measures of child psychopathology.

Factor analysis of the 23 items of the GEM provided support for the utility of the measure in capturing an overall dimension of empathy as well as two independent subscales of affective and cognitive empathy. Specifically, we found that the scale, although based on items primarily designed to capture the affective aspect of empathy, contained three distinct item sets: a subscale of primarily affective items, a subscale of primarily cognitive items, and a set of "interim" items that loaded fairly equally on both facets of cognitive and affective empathy. Consistent with the conceptualization of cognitive and affective forms of empathy as distinct domains, the two factors corresponding to these different domains were found to be unrelated. Confirmatory factor analysis was then used to examine how well the overall two-factor structure found for the entire sample would fit across age and gender groups. Results showed that the GEM can be used with a wide range of ages and both genders, as a single scale using the 23 items (internal reliability or α = .81), or alternatively scored into a cognitive empathy subscale (α = .62, 6 items) and an affective empathy subscale (α = .83, 9 items), after omitting items that load on both subscales. The internal reliability for the cognitive subscale is lower than optimally desirable for a subscale; however, the alpha value of .62 is comparable to that found for the original Bryant scale, which has shown good convergence with criterion measures such as observational indices of emotional responding to evocative vignettes (e.g., Roberts & Strayer, 1996).

These cognitive and affective subscales also demonstrated stable measurement over brief (1-week) and extended (6-month) test–retest intervals. Given that some items on both subscales require the parent to make an inference about the perspective of the child (e.g., "My child doesn't understand why other people get upset"), the convergence across informants was also of particular interest. Consistent with findings for the total GEM scores, mothers' ratings on the cognitive and affective subscales converged well with their child's own ratings on the corresponding items of the BEI (r = .401, p < .01, and r = .381, p < .01, respectively). Likewise, correlations between concurrent mother and father reports (r = .41 − .69) were consistently at the high end of convergence for what is usually achieved for interparental ratings. Support for the integrity of these subscales was further provided by evidence that scores were not confounded by demographic or parent health factors (i.e., depression, stress, anxiety, family income, level of education) that have the potential to bias parent reports of child characteristics.

Finally, there was further evidence that these GEM subscales were discriminative with regard to their distinct relations with verbal intelligence and that they showed good construct validity in relation to direct observation measures of empathic behavior. For example, in a subsample of children (n = 70; 58% male; aged 5–8 years), verbal intelligence was found to be positively associated with cognitive empathy subscale scores (r = .30, p < .05) while showing no relationship with affective empathy subscale scores. Construct validity for the GEM was demonstrated in two paradigms. In the first, children were observed interacting with pet mice in a controlled experimental setting. This paradigm was based on previous research showing that children openly display nurturing versus cruel behavior toward pets when observed in small groups and that these behaviors show good convergence with parental and child reports of an aggressive versus empathic disposition toward subordinates (Dadds et al., 2004; Dadds, Whiting, & Hawes, 2006). In groups of three, children (n = 30; aged 6–12 years) interacted with a mouse in three conditions: (1) free play using a Runabout Ball, (2) training the mouse to run a maze, and (3) feeding the mouse. Child behavior was coded from videotapes on dimensions reflecting *nurturance* (i.e., caring, empathic, gentle behavior), *cruel* (i.e., care-less or aggressive behavior with potential to distress animal), and *engaging* (i.e., active verbal or nonverbal involvement with the animal) dimensions. As predicted, GEM total empathy scores were unrelated to simple engagement but correlated positively with observed nurturance and negatively with cruelty. Furthermore, the GEM subscales were somewhat differentially related to these behavioral dimen-sions, with affective empathy subscale scores showing the strongest association with observations of empathic responses.

The second test of convergence with a direct observational measure used a novel computer-based task that simulates interpersonal responses to a distressed peer. The Interpersonal Reward Task (IRT; Dadds & Hawes, 2004) was developed by the authors as a measure of reward–dominance in children. The participant plays a ball-throwing game with two virtual children (represented by photographs of children's faces) and must continually choose which of these children to throw the ball to. These virtual players react to the behavior of the participant, smiling when the ball is thrown to them and becoming increasingly sad when excluded. Both of these players throw money to the participant when they are thrown the ball; however, one soon runs out of money. The participant is free to ignore this player and focus on the one still rewarding his or her interaction or to continue to interact with this player, thereby actively minimizing the negative affect displayed by the player. Recorded data include the number of times the participant throws the ball to the *distressed* player, the mean and maximum level of distress that the participant allows that player to reach, and reaction time in selecting the target player to which the ball will be thrown. Thus, the IRT measures the extent to which the participant ignores a distressed peer to obtain personal reward and the speed with which this response is implemented.

A subsample of clinically referred children with mixed presentations was assessed with the GEM the IRT. *Maximum distress allowed* correlated positively with GEM total empathy scores ($r = .38$) and cognitive ($r = .56$) and affective ($r = .30$) subscales scores such that lower empathy scores were associated with the participant children allowing the computerized peer to become increasingly distressed to receive a reward for themselves. Reaction times were highly corre-lated with the GEM total ($r = .56$) and affective empathy subscale ($r = .57$) scores, respectively, but not with the cognitive empathy subscale score ($r = .15$), such that higher affective empathy scores were associated with more time spent deciding which peer to throw the ball to. As such, in both of these paradigms scores on the GEM were associated with observations of empathic responses to subordinates or peers. Consistent with current conceptualizations of empathy, these prosocial responses were differentially associated with cognitive versus affective dimensions of empathy, as measured by the two subscales of the GEM.

As outlined here, psychometric evaluation of the parent report GEM (Dadds, Hawes, et al., 2008) found it to be a valid and reliable measure of two largely independent (cognitive and affective) components consistent with current concep-tualizations of dissociable facets of empathy. Convergence between different for-mats of measurement (e.g., direct observations and self-report) has been rare in the psychometrics of empathy (Lovett & Sheffield, 2007). As such, the association we found between maternal ratings of child empathy and independent observations of children's behavior was very promising. Furthermore, no evidence was found that the GEM is prone to reporting error from social adversity or poor parent functioning, which have been shown to contaminate parents' reports on widely used measures of child psychopathology such as the Child Behavior Checklist (Youngstrom, Loeber, & Stouthamer-Loeber, 2000). As such, the GEM appears well suited to developmental studies of empathy and pathways to antisocial behavior in large cohorts of children. We next turn to the conceptual model that underpins our own research in this area, before discussing the findings from one such study.

EMPATHY AND PSYCHOPATHY IN ADULT POPULATIONS

Research into the association between empathy and antisocial behavior in adult populations has been focused largely on the construct of psychopathy. The most empirically supported conceptualization of psychopathy is Hare's (1991) two-factor model, comprising a *behavioral* component describing an impulsive or irresponsible, antisocial or deviant lifestyle, and an *interpersonal* component consisting of low levels of guilt, a lack of empathy, and the callous or manipulative use of others. It is this interpersonal component that is held to distinguish the high-risk psychopathic subgroup of antisocial offenders from nonpsychopathic offenders. This subgroup has been estimated to comprise approximately 25% of individuals who meet criteria for antisocial personality disorder—the majority of whom are free of these specific interpersonal deficits. The psychopathic subgroup demonstrates particularly high frequency and versatility in their criminal behavior, which compared with nonpsychopathic offenders is also more likely to be violent and premeditated (Hart & Hare, 1997). High levels of psychopathy have also been associated with a particularly chronic pattern of antisocial behavior and risk for relapse following release from prison (Hemphill, Hare, & Wong, 1998).

The neurocognitive correlates of psychopathy have been characterized by considerable experimental research with adult antisocial offenders. Early studies in this area related primarily to automatic affective empathy, examining participants' autonomic arousal to stimuli associated with the distress of others. In one paradigm, participants observed confederates whom they thought were receiving electric shocks while their own skin conductance responses were recorded. Offenders with high levels of psychopathy were found to show reduced autonomic arousal when witnessing the distress of these confederates compared with those without psychopathic traits (Aniskiewicz, 1979; House & Milligan, 1976). This reduced autonomic arousal has also been demonstrated in response to images of sad facial expressions (e.g., Blair, Jones, Clark, & Smith, 1997).

Studies of explicit emotion processing have also shown that offenders with psychopathy exhibit poor accuracy in their recognition of emotional states in others. This impairment, however, appears to be somewhat specific to the emotion of fear, as demonstrated in paradigms involving images of emotional faces and vocal emotional expressions (Blair et al., 2004; Marsh & Blair, 2008). Beyond this deficit in the recognition of fearful stimuli, psychopathy does not appear to be associated with poor recognition for other emotions. Studies using theory of mind paradigms have also reported no evidence of impairment in this aspect of cognitive empathy in psychopathically inclined individuals (Blair et al., 1996; Richell, Mitchell, Newman, Leonard, Baron-Cohen, & Blair, 2003; Widom, 1978), just as there appear to be no deficits in this aspect of cognitive empathy among general antisocial populations (Blair, 2005).

Psychopathy is therefore associated primarily with a lack of automatic affective empathy for others' distress rather than a global lack of empathy. Individuals with psychopathy do tend to recognize others' emotions with the exception of fear, yet their capacity for forms of cognitive empathy such as theory of mind appears to be intact. Growing evidence also indicates that the selective deficits exhibited by this subgroup are associated with amygdala-related dysfunction (Blair, 2008). In adult offenders with psychopathy the amygdala shows reduced activation during automatic affective processing tasks (Birbaumer et al., 2005; Kiehl, 2006), and, as we shall discuss, analogous evidence is emerging regarding children and adolescents with psychopathic attributes.

EMPATHY AND CHILDHOOD CALLOUS-UNEMOTIONAL TRAITS

Models of antisocial behavior in recent years have placed increasing emphasis on the childhood origins of chronic antisocial pathways. The application of the psychopathy construct to childhood, while relatively new, is consistent with this trend and has greatly informed emerging developmental models. Research with child samples has supported the same two-factor model of psychopathy seen in the adult literature: (1) distinguishing, a behavioral component comprising impulsive conduct problems; and (2) an interpersonal component that has been relabeled callous-unemotional traits (lack of guilt, absence of empathy, and callous use of others).

The most established measure of these two components of psychopathy in children—the Antisocial Process Screening Device (APSD; Frick & Hare, 2001)—is a self-report instrument originally adapted from the Psychopathy Checklist-Revised (Hare, 1991) and comprises subscales for impulsive conduct problems and callous-unemotional traits, respectively. Measurement research has found that the dimensions captured by these two subscales can be considered relatively distinct while also overlapping to some degree. For example, in a factor analytic study with a large representative sample of children ($n = 1,359$) aged 4–9 years, callous-unemotional traits were positively associated with severity of conduct problems while at the same time predicting prospective growth in conduct problems independent of baseline severity in such problems (Dadds, Fraser, Frost, & Hawes, 2005). This study also found that items on the callous-unemotional subscale loaded (negatively) onto the same factor as items from the prosocial behavior subscale of Strengths and Difficulties Questionnaire. This suggests that callous-unemotional traits can be operationalized, to some extent, by observing very low levels of prosocial behavior.

As a dimensional construct, callous-unemotional traits can therefore be seen to represent the extreme end of a continuum that ranges from caring, prosocial behavior driven by the needs of others at one end to cruel, manipulative behavior driven by one's own needs at the other end. On the other hand, general antiso-cial behavior represents one extreme pole on a continuum ranging from rule con-formity to behavior that is aggressive and violates rules and the rights of others; motivations for this behavior can be wide-ranging, (e.g., peer pressure, poor par-enting, impulsivity, learning and language difficulties). Compared with antisocial children with high levels of impulsive conduct problems alone, those who are also characterized by high levels of callous-unemotional traits exhibit a particularly severe (Christian, Frick, Hill, Tyler, & Frazer, 1997) and chronic (Frick, Stickle, Dandreaux, Farrell, & Kimonis, 2005) pattern of antisocial behavior that is more likely to feature proactive and instrumental aggression (i.e., motivated for gain) as well as reactive aggression (i.e., in response to perceived provocation; see, e.g., Frick, Cornell, Barry, Bodin, & Dane, 2003; Kruh, Frick, & Clements, 2005). These children also appear to benefit less from well-established clinical interven-tions for "externalizing problems" (Hawes & Dadds, 2005; Waschbusch, Carrey, Willoughby, King, & Andrade, 2007), where externalizing problems refer to non-compliance, disruptive and oppositional behavior, and aggression.

In addition to representing a particularly high-risk subgroup, antisocial chil-dren with callous-unemotional traits also share a number of distinct behavioral, psychophysiological, and neural correlates in common with adults with psycho-pathic traits. For example, evidence indicates that children with callous-unemo-tional traits are characterized by a fearless temperament (Frick & Morris, 2004) and are less sensitive to punishment cues (Fisher & Blair, 1998; O'Brien & Frick, 1996; Pardini, Lochman, & Frick, 2003). They are also more likely than their noncallous peers to expect positive outcomes to result from aggression (Pardini, Lochman, & Wells, 2004). Furthermore, this subgroup appears less likely to suffer from the deficits in verbal intelligence that have been associated with antisocial behavior in children more generally (Loney, Frick, Ellis, & McCoy, 1998; Salekin, Neumann, Leistico, & Zalot, 2004). Children with high levels of callous-unemo-tional traits exhibit reduced electrodermal responses to distress (e.g., a crying face) and threatening (e.g., a pointed gun) cues compared with those with low levels of such traits, while these two groups do not differ in their electrodermal responses to neutral stimuli (Blair, 1999).

When viewing an emotionally provocative film featuring a fearful child, such callous-unemotional children have also been found to show lower magnitude change in heart rate than those without callous-unemotional traits (Anastassiou-Hadjicharalambous & Warden, 2008). Likewise, callous-unemotional children exhibit reduced attentional orienting responses to distressing pictorial stimuli (Kimonis, Frick, Fazekas, & Loney, 2006) and report lower subjective arousal to such images (Sharp, Van Goozen, & Goodyer, 2006). They also exhibit dimin-ished reactivity to negative emotional words, as indexed by recognition time for emotional words in a lexical decision paradigm (Loney, Frick, Clements, Ellis, & Kerlin, 2003).

The demonstration of similar effects across callous-unemotional children and psychopathic adults in studies using emotional faces and vocal expressions are also of note. Callous-unemotional traits in children have been associated with poor emotion recognition when viewing faces showing fear, and to a lesser extent, sadness, but not other emotions (Blair & Coles, 2000; Blair, Colledge, Murray, & Mitchell, 2001; Dadds, Perry, et al., 2006; Stevens, Charman & Blair, 2001; Woodworth & Waschbusch, 2008). Similarly, callous-unemotional children demonstrate poor recognition of fear and sadness in emotional vocal tones (Blair, Budhani, Colledge, & Scott, 2005; Stevens et al., 2001). As studies in this area have often focused exclusively on males, gender differences for these effects remain somewhat unclear. There is some evidence, however, that this association between poor recognition of some emotions and callous-unemotional traits may apply more to males than females (e.g., Dadds, Perry, et al., 2006).

Research has also begun to examine the mechanisms through which callous-unemotional traits operate to disrupt the recognition of fear cues in the visual processing of emotional faces. Dadds, Perry, et al. (2006) found that, while callous-unemotional males exhibited poor recognition of fear faces, this deficit disappeared when these individuals were instructed to look at the eye region of the stimulus faces. Alternatively, instructing participants to look at the mouths of the stimulus faces reinstated their previously poor emotion recognition performance. The role of attentional mechanisms suggested by this finding was examined more directly in a follow-up study of visual scanning patterns. Dadds, El Masry, Wimalaweera, and Guastella (2008) presented boys aged 8–15 years (*n* = 100) with images of emotional faces and recorded "eye fixations" on various regions of the face using an eye-tracker paradigm. Compared with their peers with low levels of callous-unemotional traits, boys with high levels of such traits took longer to initially look at the eye regions of these faces, and when they did look at the eyes it was less frequently and for less time. These effects were unique to the eye region, with levels of callous-unemotional traits unrelated to participants' fixations on the mouths of the faces. On the basis of this evidence, the authors speculated that children with high levels of callous-unemotional traits have problems with the allocation of attention to emotionally salient aspects of the environment.

There is growing evidence that the fear-recognition deficit and associated pattern of visual scanning characteristic of antisocial children with callous-unemotional traits may stem from dysfunction related to the amygdala—the limbic structure chiefly responsible for the processing of threat stimuli. Marsh et al. (2008) recently reported the first brain imaging study of amygdala function in children and adolescents with callous-unemotional traits (aged 10–17 years). Consistent with brain-imaging data from adult samples, children with conduct problems and callous-unemotional traits were found to show reduced amygdala activation while processing fearful faces (but not angry/neutral faces), relative to a control group with attention deficit/hyperactivity disorder (ADHD) and a normal comparison group. Relative to these groups, children with callous-unemotional traits also demonstrated reduced functional connectivity between the amygdala and ventromedial prefrontal cortex regions (see de Oliveira-Souza & Moll, Chapter 7, this volume, for a review of these cerebral systems). Furthermore, among children with callous-unemotional traits, extent of reduced connectivity was significantly associated with conduct problem severity. These findings have since been replicated (Jones, Laurens, Herba, Barker, & Viding, 2009).

The emotion-processing deficits that characterize antisocial children with callous-unemotional traits are particularly striking when compared with those that have been associated with antisocial behavior in children more generally. Specifically, there is extensive evidence relating childhood conduct problems and aggression to emotion regulation deficits—primarily those involving high levels of negative emotional reactivity (Eisenberg et al., 2001; Frick, Cornell, Bodin, et al., 2003; Frick, Lilienfeld, Ellis, Loney, & Silverthorn, 1999; Hubbard et al., 2002; Loney, Frick, Clements, Ellis, & Kerlin, 2003; Shields & Cicchetti, 1998). This includes, for example, prospective research that has demonstrated predictive links between susceptibility to anger and hostility in infancy and early childhood and antisocial behavior and delinquency later in adolescence and young adulthood (Caspi, 2000; Pulkkinen & Hamalainen, 1995).

One of the mechanisms through which these high levels of negative emotional reactivity may confer risk for antisocial behavior is via the disruption to social information processing. Intense emotional arousal is thought to impair a child's ability to attend to, and encode, cues in social interactions as well as negatively influencing the interpretation of these cues and the subsequent access to, and evaluation of, potential behavioral responses. Children with impulsive, reactive aggression have been found to demonstrate deficits of this type (Crick & Dodge, 1996; Dodge & Pettit, 2003); specifically, they have been found to attend selectively to hostile cues in peer interactions (Dodge, Pettit, McClaskey, & Brown, 1986) and to attribute hostile intent to ambiguous peer behaviors and emotional cues (Dodge, Lochman, Harnish, Bates, & Pettit, 1997; Waldman, 1996).

EMPATHY AND SUBTYPES OF ANTISOCIAL BEHAVIOR

The subtyping of childhood antisocial behavior based on high versus low levels of callous-unemotional traits has received growing recognition in recent years, as has the notion that the problems exhibited by these two groups develop through somewhat distinct causal processes (Frick & White, 2008). As evident from literature reviewed, some of the factors that most distinguish these putative subgroups relate to the processing of emotional stimuli. Antisocial children with high levels of callous-unemotional traits represent a particularly high-risk subgroup that can be distinguished from the majority of antisocial children by a fearless temperament and a range of behavioral, psychophysiological, and neural correlates associated with reduced sensitivity to (and recognition of) cues of fear or distress and threat. Conversely, children whose antisocial behavior occurs in the absence of callous-unemotional traits appear more likely to exhibit an overarousal to negative emotional cues and oversensitivity to potential cues of hostility and threat.

Based on this model it would appear that the inconsistent findings that have characterized research into the association between childhood antisocial behavior and empathy may reflect the heterogeneity of antisocial behavior as well as the heterogeneity of the empathy construct. As indicated already, many of the deficits found in antisocial children appear to covary specifically with callous-unemotional traits. In contrast, deficits in language development and verbal intelligence are commonly comorbid in children diagnosed with oppositional defiant disorder or conduct disorder while being relatively absent in antisocial children with high levels of callous-unemotional traits (Salekin, Neumann, Leistico, & Zalot, 2004). As these linguistic and intellectual abilities may contribute more to cognitive empathy, it seems possible that antisocial children with low levels of callous-unemotional traits are at greater risk for the impairment of cognitive empathy. Furthermore, disruptions to cognitive empathy may also result from the oversensitivity to emotional stimuli that have been associated with antisocial behavior in this group. Specifically, it seems that in these antisocial children with low levels of callous-unemotional traits, representations of emotional states are frequently activated by inappropriate (ambiguous) emotional cues, resulting in the mislabeling of these cues (e.g., a peer's benign expression is attributed to anger). At the same time, however, this inappropriate arousal to emotional stimuli suggests some degree of intact capacity for affective empathy. This profile describes a child who has difficulty verbalizing the nuances of emotion and thought in others (poor cognitive empathy) yet experiences frequent and intense, perhaps even heightened, automatic emotional contagion (intact affective empathy).

For antisocial children with high levels of callous-unemotional traits, on the other hand, the underarousal to cues of distress and threat that characterize this subgroup suggests a primary deficit in automatic affective empathy. Conversely, the relatively normal development of verbal abilities in these children would be expected to facilitate the development of their cognitive empathy. Consistent with this, the emotion recognition deficits apparent in this group are largely localized to fear. This profile describes a child who explicitly understands the emotional states and thoughts of others (intact cognitive empathy) but is unmoved by this understanding (poor affective empathy).

Preliminary support for these predictions was found in the mixed-gender sample of children studied by Dadds, Hawes, et al. (2008). These authors examined correlations between the cognitive and affective subscales of the mother-rated GEM and dimensions of behavioral–emotional adjustment measured by the Strengths and Difficulties Questionnaire (SDQ; Goodman, 1997). Boys with greater features of behavioral conduct problems according to the SDQ showed significantly lower GEM scores for cognitive empathy, as did boys with more emotional problems and those with lower levels of prosocial behavior. In contrast, affective empathy subscale scores from the GEM were associated only with prosocial behavior, being rated as significantly lower in the boys with lower levels of prosocial behavior.

While the distinct associations seen for cognitive and affective empathy subscale scores were largely as predicted, the analyses conducted did not allow for the modeling of more unique associations among these variables. Furthermore, this study identified some surprising gender differences related to affective empathy, as indexed by the GEM. Among females, affective empathy subscale scores were positively and consistently associated with all indices of behavioral and emotional problems, such that girls who were rated with more affective empathy exhibited more problems with anxiety, ADHD, and conduct problems. While it is difficult to account for this finding in the current model, evidence of gender-specific correlates is common in the literature on developmental trajectories of antisocial behavior, and seemingly analogous findings have been reported previously. For example, in a mixed-gender sample of preschoolers, Zahn-Waxler, Cole, Richardson, and Friedman (1994) found that the social problem-solving of aggressive girls (tested using interpersonal conflict vignettes) featured more prosocial themes (social construction, cohesion, and accommodation) than that of aggressive boys.

DEVELOPMENTAL ASSOCIATIONS BETWEEN EMPATHY AND CALLOUS-UNEMOTIONAL TRAITS

The potential for the construct of callous-unemotional traits to inform models of the association between empathy and antisocial behavior should be evident from the findings reviewed herein. However, the construct of empathy also holds the potential to inform the conceptualization of callous-unemotional traits in ways that have rarely been explored. Low levels of empathy have been consistently emphasized as a core feature in definitions of childhood callous-unemotional traits. It is surprising then that no known studies of callous-unemotional traits have examined facets of empathy as distinct trait variables. Rather, this literature has focused on the broader profile of callous-unemotional traits, within which different deficits in empathy might be subsumed. As such, while empathy and callous-unemotional traits are generally conceptualized as closely (negatively) related constructs, the extent to which they can be considered distinct during childhood has remained largely unexamined, as has the precise relationship between these constructs.

A recent study by the authors aimed to disentangle the construct of empathy from the broader profile of callous-unemotional traits. In more detail, Dadds et al. (2009) examined the unique associations between callous-unemotional traits and the cognitive and affective components of empathy, as assessed using the GEM. This study also explored how these associations are transformed during development across childhood and adolescence and further investigated gender differences identified in previous research (e.g., Dadds, Hawes, et al., 2008). The study involved a community sample of children aged from 3 to 13 years (n = 2,760; 1,393 male, 1,367 female) who were divided into four age categories for analysis of developmental effects (3–4 years, 5–6 years, 7–9 years, 9–13 years). Based on support for operationalizing callous-unemotional traits as a categorical variable (see, e.g., Vasey, Kotov, Frick, & Loney, 2005), the sample was split further into four levels of callous-unemotional traits, with 40.7% categorized as showing zero levels of these traits, 30.9% showing low levels, 15.6% showing moderate levels, and 12.8% showing high levels. Those with the highest level represented children in the highest ranges on both callous-unemotional traits and antisocial behavior.

As predicted, high levels of callous-unemotional traits were found to be associated with low parent ratings of affective empathy; however, this association was unique to males. Across all age groups, boys with higher levels of callous-unemotional traits were rated as showing greater deficits in affective empathy, while, in girls, callous-unemotional traits were unrelated to parent ratings of affective empathy. Given the emphasis on reduced empathy in the most widely used definitions of callous-unemotional traits, this finding suggests that the conceptualization of callous-unemotional traits in females may warrant reformulation.

This finding is consistent with evidence from adult offender research that suggests the specific presentation of psychopathy differs between males and females (Cale & Lilienfeld, 2002; Salekin, Rogers, Ustad, & Sewell, 1998; Vitacco, Neumann, & Jackson, 2005; Vitale, Smith, Brinkley, & Newman, 2002). For example, research examining the factor structure of the Psychopathy Checklist-Revised has found that some of the features that characterize general antisocial behavior among nonpsychopathic male offenders (e.g., poor behavioral controls, impulsivity, irresponsibility) appear to be markers of psychopathy in female offenders (Salekin, Rogers, & Sewell, 1997). Likewise, it is consistent with the general thesis that the causal mechanisms that shape developmental trajectories of antisocial behavior are gender-specific (Silverthorn & Frick, 1999). While difficult to explain at present, the absence of a relationship between callous-unemotional traits and affective empathy in females, and the previous indications of some positive association between affective empathy and antisocial behavior in females (Dadds, Hawes, et al., 2008), may reflect a range of underlying gender differences. These potentially include greater comorbidity between antisocial behavior and anxiety or depression in females with callous-unemotional traits as well as increased susceptibility to adverse family or peer environments and greater impairments in emotion regulation.

The study by Dadds et al. (2009) also produced some unexpected findings related to parent ratings of cognitive empathy in children with callous-unemotional traits. As noted, research with adult offenders has found that those with psychopathic traits appear to be characterized by broad deficits in affective but not cognitive empathy. In contrast to this, Dadds et al. (2009) found a significant association between callous-unemotional traits and reduced cognitive empathy, as indexed by the GEM, in their child sample. Critically, however, this association was moderated by sex and age in such a way that points to potentially important gender specific developmental processes. Specifically, males and females with high levels of callous-unemotional traits showed deficits in cognitive empathy throughout childhood, but males with high levels of callous-unemotional traits showed a clear recovery to comparatively normal levels of cognitive empathy in the oldest 9- to 12-year-old age group, despite their affective empathy remaining compromised. Females with high levels of callous-unemotional traits, however, showed no such recovery in cognitive empathy.

There are various explanations as to why adolescent males with callous-unemotional traits may have appeared to overcome the deficits in cognitive empathy that they demonstrated at younger ages in this sample. It is possible that the formal verbal operations that develop with adolescence perform a compensatory function, eventually supporting the development of cognitive empathy—albeit through (abnormal) processes that are somewhat distinct from those involved at earlier developmental periods (when cognitive empathy appears to rely somewhat more directly on those processes associated with automatic affective empathy). Alternatively, this finding may reflect a developmental process more specific to the method by which empathy was measured in this study. As this study used parent reports of their child's demonstrations of empathy, it is possible that by the time males with callous-unemotional traits enter adolescence, they have become more skilled in masking their difficulties with cognitive empathy—only appearing to become increasingly competent in understanding the emotions and thoughts of others. Likewise, it is possible that the visibility of these deficits may be reduced across this period as children become more effective in manipulating or avoiding situations that directly confront their impairments in these skills.

While the use of a parent report measure allowed for the collection of a large enough sample to examine developmentally important age and sex interactions, experimental research involving the multimodal/multi-informant assessment of empathy and related domains will be necessary to confirm the reliability of these findings and determine the mechanisms underlying these specific effects. It is also important to recognize that, while research involving dimensional approaches to psychopathy in typically developing children has yielded considerable progress in the past decade (Frick & White, 2008), it is possible that research with more extreme groups such as clinic-referred conduct-problem children or forensic samples of juvenile offenders may yield quite different results from those discussed here.

CONCLUSIONS

Research examining empathy in children with antisocial behavior has been characterized historically by largely discrepant findings. Emerging developmental models of antisocial behavior suggest that inconsistencies in this evidence may have stemmed from a failure to characterize the heterogeneity of traits and behaviors within populations of these children as well as a failure to operationalize empathy in terms of its dissociable components. Current conceptualizations of empathy suggest distinct cognitive and emotional components, each associated with unique behavioral, psychophysiological, and neurocognitive correlates and neural architecture. There is growing evidence that these components relate differentially to distinct subtypes of childhood antisocial behavior marked by high versus low levels of callous-unemotional traits. Importantly, affective empathy (that facet of empathy most commonly emphasized in traditional unidimensional definitions of the construct) appears to be reduced only in the subgroup of antisocial children with high levels of callous-unemotional traits.

Experimental studies of the mechanisms underlying the unique patterns of empathic dysfunction associated with these subgroups have implicated amygdala-related dysfunction (Blair, 2008) and disruption to the allocation of attention to emotionally salient cues (Dadds, Hawes, et al., 2008). However, the demands associated with administering lab-based measures of empathy to large cohorts of children has meant that little is known about the normative trajectories of empathy-related domains, against which to differentiate the atypical trajectories of children with antisocial behavior. The recent validation of a parent report measure of empathy—the Griffith Empathy Measure—can be seen as an important step forward toward addressing this limitation of previous research (Dadds, El Masry, et al., 2008).

Preliminary findings using this measure have revealed that associations between callous-unemotional traits and different components of empathy vary across age as well as sex (Dadds et al., 2009). Males with high levels of callous-unemotional traits have shown evidence of consistent deficits in affective empathy across childhood and adolescence. Findings also suggest that cognitive empathy may be more impaired in these males than previously thought, albeit at younger ages only—by early adolescence their deficit appears to be overcome. It seems then that the characteristic disconnect between cognitive and affective empathy seen in adult males with psychopathy may crystallize during the pubertal years. Among females a somewhat different relationship between psychopathic traits and these components of empathy appears to unfold over time. Like younger males, younger females with callous-unemotional traits appear to exhibit a deficit in cognitive empathy; however, unlike males this deficit appears to persist—at least into puberty. Most surprisingly, it appears that dysfunction in affective empathy—a stable correlate of callous-unemotional traits in males—may in fact be unrelated to such traits in prepubescent and pubescent females (Dadds et al., 2009).

It should be emphasized that the parent report evidence reported by Dadds et al. (2009) pertains to the observable performance of empathy rather than the skills or capacities for empathy that underlie such performance. As such, it will be important to replicate these findings using experimental paradigms that assess such skills more directly. Furthermore, in the research reviewed here empathy was conceptualized as a persisting trait variable. Models relating empathy to antisocial behavior are likely to benefit also from applying the competence–performance distinction to investigate individuals who may have empathic skills but who choose not to use them or show difficulties in applying these skills only under specific environmental conditions.

REFERENCES

Adolphs, R. (2003). Cognitive neuroscience of human social behavior. *Nature Reviews Neuroscience, 4*, 165–178.

American Psychiatric Association (APA). (2000). *Diagnostic and statistical manual of mental disorders* (4th ed., text rev.). Washington, DC: Author.

Anastassiou-Hadjicharalambous, X., & Warden, D. (2008). Physiologically-indexed and self-perceived affective empathy in conduct-disordered children high and low on callous-unemotional traits. *Child Psychiatry and Human Development, 39*, 503–517.

Aniskiewicz, A. S. (1979). Autonomic components of vicarious conditioning and psychopathy. *Journal of Clinical Psychology, 35*, 60–67.

Barnett, M. A. (1987). Empathy and related responses in children. In N. Eisenberg & J. Strayer (Eds.), *Empathy and its development* (pp. 146–162). Cambridge, UK: Cambridge University Press.

Barnett, M. A., Howard, J. A., Melton, E. M., & Dino, G. A. (1982). Effect of inducing sadness about self or other on helping behavior in high- and low-empathic children. *Child Development, 53*, 920–923.

Barry, C. T., Frick, P. J., DeShazo, T. M., McCoy, M. G., Ellis, M. L., & Loney, B. R. (2000). The importance of callous–unemotional traits for extending the concept of psychopathy to children. *Journal of Abnormal Psychology, 109*, 335–340.

Birbaumer, N., Veit, R., Lotze, M., Erb, M., Hermann, C., Grodd, W., et al. (2005). Deficient fear conditioning in psychopathy: A functional magnetic resonance imaging study. *Archives of General Psychiatry, 62*, 799–805.

Blair, R. J. R. (1999). Responsiveness to distress cues in the child with psychopathic tendencies. *Personality and Individual Differences, 27*, 135–145.

Blair, R. J. R. (2005). Responding to the emotions of others: Dissociating forms of empathy through the study of typical and psychiatric populations. *Consciousness and Cognition, 14,* 698–718.

Blair, R. J. R. (2008). Fine cuts of empathy and the amygdala: Dissociable deficits in psychopathy and autism. *Quarterly Journal of Experimental Psychology, 61,* 157–70.

Blair, R. J. R., Budhani, S., Colledge, E., & Scott, S. (2005). Deafness to fear in boys with psychopathic tendencies. *Journal of Child Psychology and Psychiatry, 46,* 327–336.

Blair, R. J. R., & Coles, M. (2000). Expression recognition and behavioral problems in early adolescence. *Cognitive Development, 15,* 421–434.

Blair, R. J. R., Colledge, E., Murray, L., & Mitchell, D.V.G. (2001). A selective impairment in the processing of sad and fearful expressions in children with psychopathic tendencies. *Journal of Abnormal Child Psychology, 29,* 491–498.

Blair, R. J. R., Jones, L., Clark, F., & Smith, M. (1997). The psychopathic individual: A lack of responsiveness to distress cues? *Psychophysiology, 34,* 192–198.

Blair, R. J. R., Mitchell, D. G. V., Peschardt, K. S., Colledge, E., Leonard, R. A., Shine, J. H., et al. (2004). Reduced sensitivity to others' fearful expressions in psychopathic individuals. *Personality & Individual Differences, 37,* 1111–1122.

Blair, R. J. R., Sellars, C., Strickland, I., Clark, F., Williams, A., Smith, M., et al. (1996). Theory of mind in the psychopath. *Journal of Forensic Psychiatry, 7,* 15–25.

Bryant, B. K. (1982). An index of empathy for children and adolescents. *Child Development, 53,* 413–425.

Burke, D. M. (2001). Empathy in sexually offending and nonoffending adolescent males. *Journal of Interpersonal Violence, 16,* 222–233.

Cale, E. M., & Lilienfeld, S.O. (2002). Sex differences in psychopathy and antisocial personality disorder: A review and integration. *Clinical Psychology Review, 22,* 1179–1207.

Caspi, A. (2000). The child is father of the man: Personality continuities from childhood to adulthood. *Journal of Personality and Social Psychology, 78,* 158–172.

Christian, R. E., Frick, P. J., Hill, N. L., Tyler, L., & Frazer, D. R. (1997). Psychopathy and conduct problems in children: II. Implications for subtyping children with conduct problems. *Journal of the American Academy of Child and Adolescent Psychiatry, 36,* 233–241.

Cohen, D., & Strayer, J. (1996). Empathy in conduct-disordered and comparison youth. *Developmental Psychology, 32,* 988–998.

Crick, N. R., & Dodge, K. A. (1996). Social information-processing mechanisms in reactive and proactive aggression. *Child Development, 67,* 993–1002.

Dadds, M. R., El Masry, Y., Wimalaweera, S., & Guastella, A. J. (2008). Reduced eye gaze explains "fear blindness" in childhood ppsychopathic traits. *Journal of the American Academy of Child and Adolescent Psychiatry, 47,* 455–463.

Dadds, M. R., Fraser, J., Frost, A., & Hawes, D. (2005). Disentangling the underlying dimentions of psycopathy and conduct problems in childhood: A Longitudinal community study. *Journal of Consulting and Clinical Psychology, 73,* 400–410.

Dadds, M. R., & Hawes, D. (2004). *The Interpersonal Reward Task.* Author: The University of New South Wales, Sydney, Australia.

Dadds, M. R., Hawes, D. J., Frost, A. D., Vassallo, S., Bunn, P., Hunter, K., et al. (2008). A measure of cognitive and affective empathy in children using parent ratings. *Journal of Child Psychiatry and Human Development, 39,* 111–122.

Dadds, M. R., Hawes, D. J., Frost, A. D., Vassallo, S., Bunn, P., Hunter, K., et al. (2009). Learning to "talk the talk": The relationship of psychopathic traits to deficits in empathy across childhood. *Journal of Child Psychology and Psychiatry, 50,* 599–606.

Dadds, M. R., Perry, Y., Hawes, D. J., Merz, S., Riddell, A. C., Haines, D. J., et al. (2006). Attention to the eyes and fear-recognition deficits in child psychopathy. *British Journal of Psychiatry, 189,* 280–281.

Dadds M. R., Whiting, C., Bunn, P., Fraser, J., Charlson, J. H., & Pirola-Merlo, A. (2004). Measurement of cruelty in children: The Cruelty to Animals Inventory. *Journal of Abnormal Child Psychology, 32,* 321–334.

Dadds, M. R., Whiting, C., & Hawes, D. J. (2006). Associations among cruelty to animals, family conflict, and psychopathic traits in childhood. *Journal of Interpersonal Violence, 21,* 411–429.

Davis, M. H. (1983). Measuring individual differences in empathy: Evidence for a multidisciplinary approach. *Journal of Personality and Social Psychology, 44,* 113–126.

de Wied, M., Goudena, P. P., & Matthys, W. (2005). Empathy in boys with disruptive behavior disorders. *Journal of Child Psychology and Psychiatry, 46,* 867–880.

Decety, J., & Jackson, P. L. (2004). The functional architecture of human empathy. *Behavioral and Cognitive Neuroscience Reviews, 3,* 71–100.

Dodge, K. A., Lochman, J. E., Harnish, J. D., Bates, J. E., & Pettit, G. S. (1997). Reactive and proactive aggression in school children and psychiatrically impaired chronically assaultive youth. *Journal of Abnormal Psychology, 106,* 37–51.

Dodge, K. A., & Pettit, G. S. (2003). A biopsychosocial model of the development of chronic conduct problems in adolescence. *Developmental Psychology, 39,* 349–371.

Dodge, K. A., Pettit, G. S., McClaskey, C. L., & Brown, M. (1986). Social competence in children. *Monographs of the Society for Research in Child Development, 51,* 1–85.

Dolan, R. J. (2002). Emotion, cognition, and behavior. *Science, 298,* 1191–1194.

Eisenberg, N., Cumberland, A., Spinrad, T. L., Fabes, R. A., Shepard, S. A., Reiser, M., et al. (2001). The relations of regulation and emotionality to children's externalizing and internalizing problem behavior. *Child Development, 72,* 1112–1134.

Eisenberg, N., & Fabes, R. A. (1990). Empathy: Conceptualization, measurement, and relation to prosocial behavior. *Motivation and Emotion, 14,* 131–149.

Eisenberg, N., & Lennon, R. (1983). Sex differences in empathy and related capacities. *Psychological Bulletin, 94,* 100–131.

Eisenberg-Berg, N., & Hand, M. (1979). The relationship of preschoolers' reasoning about prosocial moral conflicts to prosocial behavior. *Child Development, 50,* 356–363.

Endresen, I. M., & Olweus, D. (2001). Self-reported empathy in Norwegian adolescents: Sex differences, age trends, and relationship to bullying. In A. C. Bohart & D. J. Stipek (Eds.), *Constructive and destructive behavior: Implications for family, school, and society* (pp. 147–165). Washington, DC: American Psychological Association.

Feshbach, N. D. (1978). Studies of empathic behavior in children. In B. Maher (Ed.), *Progress in experimental personality research,* (vol. 8, pp. 1–47). New York: Academic Press.

Feshbach, N. D., & Roe, K. (1968). Empathy in six- and seven-year olds. *Child Development, 39,* 133–145.

Fisher, L., & Blair, R. J. R. (1998). Cognitive impairment and its relationship to psychopathic tendencies in children with emotional and behavioral difficulties. *Journal of Abnormal Child Psychology, 26,* 511–519.

Frick, P. J., Cornell, A. H., Barry, C. T., Bodin, S. D., & Dane, H. E. (2003). Callous–unemotional traits and conduct problems in the prediction of conduct problem severity, aggression, and self-report of delinquency. *Journal of Abnormal Child Psychology, 31,* 457–470.

Frick, P. J., Cornell, A. H., Bodin, S. D., Dane, H. E., Barry, C. T., & Loney, B. R. (2003). Callous-unemotional traits and developmental pathways to severe conduct problems. *Developmental Psychology, 39,* 246–260.

Frick, P. J., & Hare, R. D. (2001). *The antisocial processes screening device.* Toronto: Multi-Health Systems.

Frick, P. J., Lilienfeld, S. O., Ellis, M. L., Loney, B. R., & Silverthorn, P. (1999). The association between anxiety and psychopathy dimensions in children. *Journal of Abnormal Child Psychology, 27,* 383–392.

Frick, P. J., & Morris, A. S. (2004). Temperament and developmental pathways to conduct problems. *Journal of Clinical Child and Adolescent Psychology, 33*, 54–68.

Frick, P. J., Stickle, T. R., Dandreaux, D. M., Farrell, J. M., & Kimonis, E. R. (2005). Callous-unemotional traits in predicting the severity and stability of conduct problems and delinquency. *Journal of Abnormal Child Psychology, 33*, 471–487.

Frick, P. J., & White, S. F. (2008). Research review: The importance of callous-unemotional traits for developmental models of aggressive and antisocial behavior. *Journal of Child Psychology and Psychiatry, 49*, 359–375.

Frith, U. (2001). Mind blindness and the brain in autism. *Neuron, 32*, 969–979.

Gill, K. L., & Calkins, S. D. (2003). Do aggressive/destructive toddlers lack concern for others? Behavioral and physiological indicators of empathic responding in 2-year-old children. *Development and Psychopathology, 15*, 55–71.

Gladstein, G. A. (1983). Understanding empathy: Integrating counseling, developmental, and social psychology perspectives. *Journal of Counseling Psychology, 30*, 467–482.

Gonzalez, K. P., Field, T. M., Lasko, D., LaGreca, A., & Lahey, B. (1996). Social anxiety and aggression in behaviorally disordered children. *Early Child Development and Care, 121*, 1–8.

Goodman, R. (1997). The Strengths and Difficulties Questionnaire: A research note. *Journal of Child Psychology and Psychiatry, 38*, 581–586.

Hare, R. D. (1991). *The Hare psychopathy checklist-revised*. Toronto: Multi-Health Systems.

Harris, P. (1989). *Children and emotion: The development of psychological understanding.* Oxford, UK: Basil Blackwell.

Hart, S. D., & Hare, R. D. (1996). Psychopathy and antisocial personality disorder. *Current Opinion in Psychiatry, 9*, 129–132.

Hart, S. D., & Hare, R. D. (1997). Psychopathy: Assesment and association with criminal conduct. In D. M. Stoff, J. Brieling, & J. Maser (Eds.), *Handbook of antisocial behavior* (pp. 22–35). New York: Wiley.

Hatfield, E., Cacioppo, J. T., & Rapson, R. (1994). *Emotional contagion*. New York: Cambridge University Press.

Hawes, D. J., & Dadds, M. R. (2005). The treatment of conduct problems in children with callous-unemotional traits. *Journal of Consulting and Clinical Psychology, 73*, 737–741.

Hemphill, J. F., Hare, R. D., & Wong, S. (1998). Psychopathy and recidivism: A review. *Legal and Criminological Psychology, 3*, 139–170.

Hoffman, M. L. (1984). Interaction of affect and cognition in empathy. In C. Izard, J. Kagan, & R. B. Zajonic (Eds.), *Emotions, cognitions and behavior* (pp. 103–131). Cambridge, UK: Cambridge University Press.

Hoffman, M. L. (2000). *Empathy and moral development: Implications for caring and justice*. New York: Cambridge University Press.

House, T. H., & Milligan, W. L. (1976). Autonomic responses to modeled distress in prison psychopaths. *Journal of Personality and Social Psychology, 34*, 556–560.

Hubbard, J. A., Smithmyer, C. M., Ramsden, S. R., Parker, E. H., Flanagan, K. D., Dearing, K. F., et al. (2002). Observational, physiological, and self-report measures of children's anger: Relations to reactive versus proactive aggression. *Child Development, 73*, 1101–1118.

Jones, A. P., Laurens, K., Herba, C., Barker, G.J., & Viding, E. (2009). Amygdala hypoactivity to fearful faces in boys with conduct problems and callous-unemotional traits. *American Journal of Psychiatry, 166*, 95–102.

Kiehl, K. A. (2006). A cognitive neuroscience perspective on psychopathy: Evidence for paralimbic system dysfunction. *Psychiatry Research, 142*, 107–128.

Kimonis, E. R., Frick, P. J., Fazekas, H., & Loney, B. R. (2006). Psychopathy, aggression, and the emotional processing of emotional stimuli in non-referred girls and boys. *Behavioral Sciences and the Law, 24*, 21–37.

Kruh, I. P., Frick, P. J., & Clements, C. B. (2005). Historical and personality correlates to the violence patterns of juveniles tried as adults. *Criminal Justice and Behavior, 32,* 69–96.

LeDoux, J. E. (1998). *The emotional brain.* London: Weidenfeld & Nicholson.

Lee, M., & Prentice, N. M. (1988). Interrelations of empathy, cognition, and moral reasoning with dimensions of juvenile delinquency. *Journal of Abnormal Child Psychology, 16,* 127–139.

LeSure-Lester, G. E. (2000). Relation between empathy and aggression and behavior compliance among abused group home youth. *Child Psychiatry and Human Development, 31,* 153–161.

Litvack-Miller, W., McDougall, D., & Romney, D. M. (1997). The structure of empathy during middle childhood and its relationship to prosocial behavior. *Genetic, Social, and Genetic Psychology Monographs, 123,* 303–324.

Loney, B. R., Frick, P. J., Clements, C. B., Ellis, M. L., & Kerlin, K. (2003). Callous-unemotional traits, impulsivity, and emotional processing in adolescents with antisocial behavior problems. *Journal of Clinical Child and Adolescent Psychology, 32,* 66–80.

Loney, B. R., Frick, P. J., Ellis, M. L., & McCoy, M. G. (1998). Intelligence, callous-unemotional traits, and antisocial behavior. *Journal of Psychopathology and Behavioral Assessment, 20,* 231–247.

Lovett, B. J., & Sheffield, R.A. (2007). Affective empathy deficits in aggressive children and adolescents: A critical review. *Clinical Psychology Review, 27,* 1–13.

MacQuiddy, S. L., Maise, S. J., & Hamilton, S. B. (1987). Empathy and affective perspective-taking skills in parent-identified conduct-disordered boys. *Journal of Clinical Child Psychology and Adolescent Psychology, 16,* 260–268.

Marcus, R. E., Roke, E. J., & Bruner, C. (1985). Verbal and nonverbal empathy and prediction of social behavior of young children. *Perceptual and Motor Skills, 60,* 299–309.

Marsh, A. A., & Blair, R. J. R. (2008). Deficits in facial affect recognition among antisocial populations: A meta-analysis. *Neuroscience & Biobehavioral Reviews, 32,* 454–65.

Marsh, A. A., Finger, E. C., Mitchell, D. G., Kosson, D. S., Reid, M. E., Sims, C., et al. (2007). Reduced amygdala response to fearful expressions in children and adolescents with callous-unemotional traits and disruptive behavior disorders. *American Journal of Psychiatry, 165,* 712–720.

Martin, G. B., & Clark, R. D. (1982). Distress crying in neonates: Species and peer specificity. *Developmental Psychology, 18,* 3–9.

Mehrabian, A., & Epstein, N. (1972). A measure of emotional empathy. *Journal of Personality, 40,* 525–543.

Miller, P. A., & Eisenberg, N. (1988). The relation of empathy to aggressive and externalizing/antisocial behavior. *Psychological Bulletin, 103,* 324–344.

O'Brien, B. S., & Frick, P. J. (1996). Reward dominance: Associations with anxiety, conduct problems, and psychopathy in children. *Journal of Abnormal Child Psychology, 24,* 223–240.

Pardini, D. A., Lochman, J. E., & Frick, P. J. (2003). Callous/unemotional traits and social-cognitive processes in adjudicated youths. *Journal of the American Academy of Child and Adolescent Psychiatry, 42,* 364–371.

Pardini, D., Lochman, J., & Wells, K. (2004). Negative emotions and alcohol use initiation in high-risk boys: The moderating effect of good inhibitory control. *Journal of Abnormal Child Psychology, 32,* 505–518.

Preston, S. D., & de Waal, F. B. M. (2002). Empathy: Its ultimate and proximate bases. *Behavioral and Brain Sciences, 25,* 1–72.

Pulkkinen, L., & Hamalainen, M. (1995). Low self-control as a precursor to crime and accidents in a Finnish longitudinal study. *Criminal Behavior and Mental Health, 5,* 424–438.

Redl, F., & Wineman, D. (1951). *Children who hate.* Glencoe, IL: Free Press.

Richell, R. A., Mitchell, D. G., Newman, C., Leonard, A., Baron-Cohen, S., & Blair, R. J. (2003). Theory of mind and psychopathy: Can psychopathic individuals read the "language of the eyes"? *Neuropsychologia, 41,* 523–526.

Roberts, W., & Strayer, J. (1996). Empathy, emotional expressiveness, and prosocial behavior. *Child Development, 67,* 449–470.

Salekin, R. T., Neumann, C. S., Leistico, A. R., & Zalot, A. A. (2004). Psychopathy in youth and intelligence: An investigation of Cleckley's hypothesis. *Journal of Clinical Child and Adolescent Psychology, 33,* 731–742.

Salekin, R. T., Rogers, R., & Sewell, K. W. (1997). Construct validity of psychopathy in a female offender sample: A multitrait–multimethod evaluation. *Journal of Abnormal Psychology, 106,* 576–585.

Salekin, R. T., Rogers, R., Ustad, K. L., & Sewell, K. W. (1998). Psychopathy and recidivism among female inmates. *Law and Human Behavior, 22,* 109–128.

Sharp, C., Van Goozen, S., & Goodyer, I. (2006). Children's subjective emotional reactivity to affective pictures: Gender differences and their antisocial correlates in an unselected sample of 7–11 year-olds. *Journal of Child Psychology and Psychiatry, 47,* 143–150.

Shields, A., & Cicchetti, D. (1998). Reactive aggression among maltreated children: The contributions of attention and emotion dysregulation. *Journal of Clinical Child Psychology, 27,* 381–395.

Silverthorn, P., & Frick, P. J. (1999). Developmental pathways to antisocial behavior: The delayed-onset pathway in girls. *Development and Psychopathology, 11,* 101–126.

Singer, T. (2006). The neuronal basis and ontogeny of empathy and mind reading: Review of literature and implications for future research. *Neuroscience and Biobehavioral Reviews, 30,* 855–863.

Singer, T., Seymour, B., O'Doherty, J., Kaube, H., Dolan, R. J., & Frith, C. D. (2004). Empathy for pain involves the affective but not sensory components of pain. *Science, 303,* 1157–1161.

Stevens, D., Charman, T., & Blair, R.J.R. (2001). Recognition of emotion in facial expressions and vocal tones in children with psychopathic tendencies. *Journal of Genetic Psychology, 162,* 201–211.

Strayer, J., & Roberts, W. (2004). Empathy and observed anger and aggression in five-year-olds. *Social Development, 13,* 1–13.

Vasey, M. W., Kotov, R., Frick, P. J., & Loney, B. (2005). The latent structure of psychopathy in youth: A taxometric investigation. *Journal of Abnormal Child Psychology, 33,* 411–429.

Vitacco, M. J., Neumann, C. S., & Jackson, R. L. (2005). Testing a four-factor model of psychopathy and its association with ethnicity, gender, intelligence, and violence. *Journal of Consulting and Clinical Psychology, 73,* 466–476.

Vitale, J. E., Smith, S. S., Brinkley, C. A., & Newman, J. P. (2002). The reliability and validity of the Psychopathy Checklist–Revised in a sample of female offenders. *Criminal Justice and Behavior, 29,* 202–231.

Vreeke, G. J., & van der Mark, I. L. (2003). Empathy, an integrative model. *New Ideas in Psychology, 21,* 177–207.

Waldman, I. D. (1996). Aggressive boys' hostile perceptual and response biases: The role of attention and impulsivity. *Child Development, 67,* 1015–1033.

Waschbusch, D. A., Carrey, N. J., Willoughby, M. T., King, S., & Andrade, B. F. (2007). Effects of methylphenidate and behavior modification on the social and academic behavior of children with disruptive behavior disorders: The moderating role of callous/unemotional traits. *Journal of Clinical Child and Adolescent Psychology, 36*, 629–644.

Wicker, B., Keysers, C., Plailly, J., Royet, J.-P., Gallese, V., & Rizzolatti, G. (2003). Both of us disgusted in my insula: The common neuron basis of seeing and feeling disgust. *Neuron, 40*, 655–664.

Widom, C. S. (1978). An empirical classification of female offenders. *Criminal Justice and Behavior, 5*, 35–52.

Woodworth, M., & Waschbusch, D. (2008). Emotional processing in children with conduct problems and callous/unemotional traits. *Child: Care, Health, and Development, 34*(2), 234–244.

Youngstrom, E., Loeber, R., & Stouthamer-Loeber, M. (2000). Patterns and correlates of agreement between parent, teacher, and male adolescent ratings of externalizing and internalizing problems. *Journal of Consulting and Clinical Psychology, 68*, 1038–1050.

Zahn-Waxler, C., Cole, P. M., Richardson, D. T., & Friedman, R. J. (1994). Social problem solving in disruptive preschool children: Reactions to hypothetical situations of conflict and distress. *Merrill-Palmer Quarterly, 40*, 98–119.

Zahn-Waxler, C., Robinson, J. L., & Emde, R. N. (1992). The development of empathy in twins. *Developmental Psychology, 28*, 1038–1047.

4

Fiction, Imagination, and Ethics

IAN RAVENSCROFT

Flinders University, Adelaide, Australia

A number of authors have argued that reading fiction can improve our moral capacities. Martha Nussbaum has claimed both that exposure to fiction can play a significant role in children's moral development and that consuming fiction can enhance adults' moral capacities. According to Nussbaum, both of these effects are mediated by fiction's positive impact on the capacity for empathy. In this chapter I assess the empirical support for both of these claims and draw connections between emotional responses to fiction and recent work on imagination and imitation. I argue that fiction provides opportunities to practice empathetic responses and thereby develop the capacity for empathy in adults. Following work by Prinz, I also argue that fiction may play a role in the child's moral development. However, it is apparent that the imitative mechanisms that plausibly underlie fiction's capacity to enhance empathetic responses may also be responsible for the impact of violent media on aggressive behavior. Identifying the properties of fictions that facilitate empathetic development and those that facilitate aggressive behavior are important issues for future research.

INTRODUCTION

*M*any have claimed that reading fiction can enhance one's moral capacities. Among philosophers we find Aristotle (1996), Rousseau (1762/2007), and Nussbaum (1995, 1997) proposing versions of this thesis. Among dramatists and novelists we find expression of this view in, for example, Sophocles (2003) and Dickens (1854/2003). And we find the view expressed by literary theorists such as Trilling (1950/2008) and Booth (1988). In addition, it seems likely that dramatists and writers, from Aeschylus to William Shakespeare to Salman

Rushdie, who explore morally serious themes in their work took it for granted that their work would enhance the moral capacities of their readers. Presumably they did not see themselves as mere purveyors of entertainments.

I begin this chapter by sketching Martha Nussbaum's views about the role of fiction in the development and exercise of moral capacities (see especially Nussbaum, 1995, 1997). Her thesis begins, in the spirit of Hume (1751/1998) and Smith (1759/1976), with the idea that sympathy or compassion plays a central role in moral life. She then proposes that exposure to the right sort of fiction can enhance the capacity for compassion and that, consequently, fiction can play a role in enhancing moral capacities. It is clear that, for Nussbaum, our emotional engagement with the lives of fictional characters is paramount. In her view, there exists an important connection among imagination, emotion, and ethics.

I set out Nussbaum's views in the next section and draw attention to two theses she advances: what I call the *nondevelopmental thesis,* which focuses on the ethical capacities of adults; and what I call the *developmental thesis,* which focuses on the child's acquisition of moral capacities. The claims Nussbaum makes about fiction and ethics are empirical ones; she does not, though, appeal to the growing empirical literature on fiction, ethics, and related themes. Following this, I discuss empirical evidence in support of the nondevelopmental thesis. In the *Poetics,* Aristotle (1996) defines poetry—which he took to include a wide range of fictional forms—as a "medium of imitation." This is a highly suggestive phrase. There is a large contemporary literature on the human capacity to imitate and on the neurobiological basis of imitation. This literature provides a way of modeling emotional engagement with both real and fictional others. I then examine the empirical evidence in support of the developmental thesis, drawing on the work of Prinz (2005). The empirical research vindicates Nussbaum to a considerable degree; however, once the central notion of imitation of fictional characters is connected to the growing empirical literature on imitation and its neurobiological basis, much darker elements must be considered. Following Susan Hurley (2004), I argue that portrayals of violence in fiction can lead to morally abhorrent, aggressive behavior. Finally, I conclude with some brief suggestions about the kinds of research my thesis makes imperative.

One final prefatory comment: I use the term *fiction* rather than Nussbaum's preferred term *literature.* This is in part because, while literature is typically used to pick out a certain class of written texts, my discussion includes film and television as well as stories that are related orally. In addition, the written texts the term "literature" is used to identify are usually thought of as in some way canonical or culturally significant, and I do not intend to restrict my discussion to such texts. Since some of the fictions I will consider are watched or heard rather than read, the term *reader* is not sufficiently general for my needs. Consequently, I will talk about the *consumers* of fiction; I apologize in advance for introducing this rather ugly term.

NUSSBAUM ON FICTION AND ETHICS

Nussbaum postulates a number of theses about fiction and moral capacities and also restricts the scope of her claims in various ways. In this section I sketch two theses she advances and outline two restrictions she makes. Before beginning, it should be noted that while both *Poetic Justice* (Nussbaum, 1995) and *Cultivating Humanity* (Nussbaum, 1997) make substantial claims about the relations between fiction and moral capacities, in these works her focus is on, broadly speaking, political issues. In *Poetic Justice* she advocates a role for what she calls the *literary imagination*—that is, an imaginative capacity nurtured by or expressed in works of fiction—in the social sciences, legal scholarship and practice, and social policy. And in *Cultivating Humanity* she advocates a role for the literary imagination in the education of what she terms the *world citizen*. But these are both strongly normative works. Her aim in *Poetic Justice* is to propose ways to improve people's lives via better social science, law, and policy. Her aim in *Cultivating Humanity* is to put forward an approach to liberal education that will make students more sensitive to the aspirations and needs of other human beings.

At the heart of Nussbaum's ideas about the relationship between consuming fiction and developing and exercising moral capacities is a claim about the relationship between compassion (or *sympathy*) and ethics.[1] I take compassion to involve a capacity to reenact another's emotional states and to respond in morally appropriate ways to their situation.[2] I use the term *empathy* to refer to the capacity to reenact another's emotional states.[3] It is important to stress that when X empathizes with Y who feels (say) sad, X does not merely attribute sadness to Y but experiences sadness herself. (Indeed, X may be capable of an empathetic response without being able to attribute mental states to others. Developmentally, some aspects of empathy are prior to theory of mind: see Prinz, 2005, p. 275.) It is also important to note that when Nussbaum draws a connection between compassionate responses and ethics, she is not making a definitional point—she is not defining ethical behavior as behavior that is motivated by compassion. Rather, she is identifying a capacity that, she claims, plays a crucial role in an ethical human life. Thus, she writes that "an ethics of impartial respect for human dignity will fail to engage real human beings unless they are made capable of entering imaginatively into the lives of distant others and to have emotions related to that participation" (Nussbaum, 1995, p. xvi). In a similar vein she remarks that "habits of empathy and conjecture conduce to a certain type of citizenship and a certain form of community: one that cultivates a sympathetic responsiveness to another's needs…" (Nussbaum, 1997, p. 90).

Having stressed the central role of compassion in ethical life, Nussbaum advances two theses linking fiction and compassion, thus drawing a connection between fiction and the ethical life:

1. A nondevelopmental thesis. Nussbaum believes that literature can promote, via an enhanced capacity for sympathy, the ethical capacities of the adult reader. Thus, she writes that "narrative art has the power to make us see the lives of the different with more than a casual tourist's interest—with involvement and sympathetic understanding…" (Nussbaum, 1997, p. 88). In a similar vein she remarks of classical Greek tragedy that "by inviting spectators to identify with the tragic hero … the drama makes compassion for suffering seize the imagination. This emotion is built into the dramatic form" (Nussbaum, 1997, p. 93).

2. A thesis about moral development in children. At some points, Nussbaum's focus is on the child's acquisition of moral capacities via exposure to fiction: "When a child and a parent begin to tell stories together, the child is acquiring essential moral capacities" (Nussbaum, 1997, p. 89). She goes on to makes it clear that stories facilitate the development of a capacity for compassion:

> As children grow older, the moral and social aspects of these literary scenarios become increasingly complex and full of distinctions, so that they gradually learn how to ascribe to others ... not only hope and fear, happiness and distress ... but also more complex traits such as courage, self-constraint, dignity, perseverance, and fairness.... As children grasp such complex facts in imagination, they become capable of compassion. (Nussbaum, 1997, p. 90)

Stories, compassion, and ethics are then brought together:

> As children explore stories, rhymes and songs—especially in the company of the adults they love—they are led to notice the sufferings of other living creatures with a new keenness. At this point, stories can then begin to confront children more plainly with the uneven fortunes of life, convincing them emotionally of their urgency and importance. (Nussbaum, 1997, p. 93)

At times Nussbaum seems to want to make the very strong claim that exposing children to fiction is essential to the development of compassion and thereby moral capacities. For example, she writes that "the child deprived of stories is deprived, as well, of certain ways of viewing other people" (Nussbaum, 1997, p. 89). Similarly, she remarks that "in these various ways, narrative imagination is an essential preparation for moral interaction" (p. 90). It may be, though, that she wants only to endorse the weaker claim that fiction very often plays a significant role in developing compassion and moral capabilities in children.

In this chapter I am principally concerned with connecting Nussbaum's theses with empirical work on imagination and imitation. With respect to Nussbaum's nondevelopmental claim, I provide empirical evidence that reading fiction provides opportunities to rehearse empathetic responses to real people and thereby strengthen our capacity to make moral responses. With respect to Nussbaum's developmental claim, I briefly sketch a model of moral development proposed by Prinz (2005; see also Huesmann, 2005a). Central to Prinz's model is the claim that children reenact or recreate the emotions of people around them and are aware of the resulting emotional congruence. I argue that children can also recreate the emotional states of fictional characters and thus that consuming fiction can play a role in moral development on Prinz's model.

I have mentioned that Nussbaum wants to restrict her theses in various ways. To begin with, she accepts that fiction may have only limited power to effect moral change (Nussbaum, 1995, pp. xvi–xviii). We shall see that the literary imagination may be a lot more powerful than many people believe. She is also aware that the question "Which fictions develop our moral capacities?" urgently needs to be addressed (Nussbaum, 1997, pp. 88–89). The discussion of fiction and violence later in the chapter will bring that question into very sharp focus.

THE NONDEVELOPMENTAL THESIS

In recent decades, a number of researchers have attempted to directly measure the ethical impact of consuming fiction. In a survey of the literature, Hakemulder (2000) found 54 studies demonstrating evidence that consuming fiction enhanced moral development and empathy or changed the consumer's norms, values, or self-concepts (Hakemulder was careful to reject studies that did not meet basic methodological standards). Hakemulder (2001) investigated the impact on moral attitudes of consuming fiction compared with nonfiction. One group of subjects read a chapter of a novel about the harsh life of an Algerian woman; a second group read a (nonfiction) essay on the lack of women's rights in Algeria. Subjects in the first group were later found to be more critical of the way women are treated in Algeria than those in the second group. Oatley, Mar, and colleagues have undertaken numerous studies of this type that demonstrate the impact of reading fiction on the consumer's theory of mind and empathetic capacities (for a useful summary see Mar, 2009; see also Oatley, 2008).

How might this effect come about? Oatley and colleagues appeal to the idea of simulation (Mar, Oatley, Hirsch, de la Paz, & Peterson, 2006; Mar, Djikic, & Oatley, 2008; Oatley, 1999; Oatley, 2008). In everyday life we use our theory of mind mechanisms to navigate around the social world. According to Oatley and Mar, when we read fiction we use the same mechanisms to understand the social aspects of the story. Reading fiction thus gives us the opportunity to practice our theory of mind mechanisms in much the same way that a pilot can improve her skills on a flight simulator (Oatley, 2008). As a consequence, reading fiction tends to improve theory of mind skills. Oatley and Mar put forward a similar hypothesis connecting the reading of fiction and empathy. Observing the plight of another person in real life sometimes brings about in us an empathetic emotional response. On the simulation model, the plight of a fictional character sometimes engages the cognitive mechanisms responsible for empathy. The extra practice that novel readers receive leads to an improved capacity to empathize outside the fictional context.

In this section I examine two ways of developing the Oatley–Mar simulation hypothesis, first by connecting it to work on imagination and then by developing links to work on imitation. As we have seen, Oatley and Mar offer simulationist theories of fiction's capacity to enhance both empathy and theory of mind. In what follows, the primary focus will be on empathy, although theory of mind is briefly discussed in the context of empathy.

The term *imagination* and its cognates are used in a wide range of ways. Currie and Ravenscroft (2002) proposed a general account of what we take to be a significant subset of mental activities commonly dubbed acts of imagination.[4] To a first approximation, we characterized the imagination as a general capacity to recreate or reenact mental states. Visual imagination provides a paradigm example of our approach. Phenomenologically, visual imagery is very much the re-creation of visual experience: When we close our eyes and imagine a favored scene it is as though we are actually seeing that scene. Moreover, a number of subtle features of vision are recreated in visual imagery. For example, the time it takes to scan between two points on a visual image of a map is directly proportional to the distance between the points, just as it is when scanning between points on a real map (Kosslyn, Ball, & Reiser, 1978). Similarly, the visual field has a boundary whose shape can be determined only experimentally; the imaged visual field has a boundary of the same shape (Finke & Kurtzman, 1981). In addition, many deficits of vision due to damage to the visual cortex are reproduced in visual imagery. For example, Bisiach and Luzzatti (1978) showed that patients suffering from hemispatial neglect exhibited a parallel neglect of one side of their imaged visual field. Finally, there is considerable overlap of the brain areas that subserve vision and those that subserve visual imagery (Farah, 1989; Goldenberg, Podreka, Steiner, Willmes, Suess, & Deecke, 1989; Goldenberg, Podreka, Uhl, Steiner, Willmes, & Deecke, 1989; Kosslyn et al., 1993; Roland & Friberg, 1985).[5]

Motor imagery is similarly recreative of motor performance (Currie & Ravenscroft, 1997; see also Currie, 1995; Morton, 1994). The temporal and kinematic properties of motor images match those of motor performance. In one experiment, subjects were shown a picture of a hand and asked whether it was a left or right hand. Subjects often reported experiencing motor imagery of moving their own hand when answering the question. Intriguingly, response times were a function of the factors that affect actual movements: handedness of subject, origin of movement, length of trajectory, and awkwardness of target position (Parsons, 1987a, 1987b). Similarly, there exists a strong correlation between the duration of an actual movement and that of the corresponding imagined movement (Parsons, 1994). Deficits in motor performance due to Parkinson's disease are reproduced in motor imagery (Dominey, Decety, Brousolle, Chazot, & Jeannerod, 1995), and (as we might expect) there are close correlations between the brain areas involved in motor performance and those involved in motor imagery (Parsons et al., 1995).

A very striking fact about motor imagery is that it can enhance motor performance (Currie & Ravenscroft, 1997). It has long been appreciated that forming and focusing on appropriate mental images can enhance athletic performance (Richardson, 1967). Yue and Cole (1992) compared the increase in strength of subjects who actually trained with that of subjects who merely generated the corresponding motor imagery. Actual training resulted in a 30% increase in mean maximal force; imagined training resulted in a 22% increase. Yue and Cole ensured that the subjects in the imagery group did not make covert muscle contractions during their imagined training, and Jeannerod (1994) demonstrated that improved athletic performance due to mental rehearsal cannot simply be attributed to improved motivation. The advantages of imagined motor rehearsal have also been demonstrated for musicians (Pascual-Leone, 2001). These findings strongly suggest that the training effect of motor imagery is due to improved motor control. Enhanced motor performance due to motor imagery is not surprising given the overlap of the neural substrates of motor imagery and motor performance. Motor imagery provides additional opportunities to exercise and strengthen the neural pathways used in motor performance. On this view, imagining provides opportunities to rehearse—and thereby improve—performance, and does so in a way that minimizes costs: It is generally cheaper to imagine performing than to actually perform. Indeed, this may be an important key to the evolutionary origin of imagination.

In the spirit of off-line simulation theory (see especially Goldman, 1989; Stich & Nichols, 1992), Currie and I suggested that propositional attitudes such as beliefs and desires can be imaginatively recreated, including other people's beliefs and desires (Currie & Ravenscroft, 2002, especially Ch. 3). In this view, theory of mind tasks such as predicting another's behavior involve recreating relevant parts of the target's set of propositional attitudes. Another extension of the theory describes empathetic states as imaginative states because they involve recreating the emotional states of another person (Ravenscroft, 1998).

Stories and other fictions are often described as "works of the imagination" because their creation requires extensive use of the author's imaginative capacities, and, in turn, they bring about acts of imagination in the consumer. Well-executed fictions induce in the attentive consumer a wide range of imaginative states including visual and aural images, propositional imaginings, and empathetic states. Fictions can be seen as scaffolding or supporting the imaginative processes of the consumer, assisting them to have a range of imaginings they otherwise may not have been capable of having. If, as the literature on motor imagery suggests, imagining can improve performance by providing opportunities for rehearsal or practice, fiction may provide opportunities for rehearsal that the consumer would not otherwise be able to have. I suggested earlier that one of the evolutionary advantages of imagination may be that imaginings can function as low-cost rehearsals prior to real performances. It may also be that one of the evolutionary advantages of storytelling is that it promotes and scaffolds such rehearsals.

I have described the imagination as a capacity to reenact or recreate the mental states of oneself and others, including fictional others. Imitation also involves reenactment or re-creation: The young child who imitates her mother's smile is reenacting or recreating the mother's smile. We can distinguish between the goal of an action and the bodily movements aimed at achieving that goal. A *full-fledged imitation* of an action reenacts both the goal and the behavior. In contrast, *goal emulation* reenacts only the goal, which might be achieved in ways other than the observed behavior (Tomasello, 1999). While goal emulation is not uncommon among nonhuman animals, full-fledged imitation is found only among humans and a small number of other highly intelligent animals (Byrne, 1995; Heyes & Galef, 1996; Tomasello & Call, 1997). Young children imitate, even reproducing behaviors that are awkward to carry out or inefficient at achieving the goal. For example, 14-month-old children, having observed an experimenter touch a panel with his forehead (rather than his hand), touched the panel with their forehead even after a week's delay (Meltzoff, 1988). Adults are also highly imitative. Chartrand and Bargh (1996, 1999, 2002) showed that subjects who observe another's behavior are more likely to engage in that behavior than subjects who have not witnessed the behavior. Subjects who interact with someone who rubs his or her foot will rub their own foot; if they then interact with someone who rubs his or her face, they will rub their own face. Strikingly, the effect occurs even if the subjects are unconscious of having observed the behavior and typically deny that their behavior is imitative.

The tendency of adults to imitate appears to be so strong as to constitute a kind of default mode of behavior in that imitation occurs unless social or other conditions lead to its inhibition (Kinsbourne, 2005). Thus, patients who have sustained damage to the frontal brain areas responsible for inhibiting socially undesirable behavior automatically imitate such behavior. For example, one patient, having observed the experimenter wearing two pairs of glasses at the same time, also put on two pairs of glasses (Lhermitte, 1986; Lhermitte, Pillon, & Serdaru, 1986).

Over the last 15 years neuroscience has discovered mirror neurons, which may contribute to the neurological basis of a wide range of imitative behaviors. Mirror neurons fire when either of two conditions is satisfied: (1) the agent observes an actor performing an action, or (2) the agent herself performs that same action. For example, firing might occur both when the agent observes an actor grasp an object and when the agent grasps an object herself. In monkeys the mirroring seems to represent only the actor's goal, whereas in humans the mirror system may represent both the actor's goal and the actor's movements directed toward that goal (Hurley, 2004, pp. 173–174). This distinction appears to echo the goal emulation–full-fledged imitation distinction noted earlier. Intriguingly, mirror neurons are concentrated around the Sylvian fissure, which is known to be involved in imitation (Iacoboni, 2005). As Hurley observes, the areas around the Sylvian fissure are markedly different in humans and monkeys (p. 174).

While the distinction between emulation and full-fledged imitation is interesting, it is excessively narrow for present purposes because it makes it definitional that only goals and the actions directed at them can be imitated. Like a number of other authors, I am interested not only in the reproduction of action–goal pairs but also the imitation of emotions. For present purposes I follow Prinz's (2005, pp. 275–276) broader definition of imitation:

> Imitation is a process by which one organism comes to exhibit a state or behavior exhibited by another organism through perceiving the other organism exhibit that state or behavior. Roughly speaking, imitation is mentally mediated replication.

Notice that, in Prinz's definition, the set of imitative states overlaps the set of imaginative states as Currie and I (2002) conceive them. While imitating another's bodily movements necessarily involves reproducing those movements, imagining another's bodily movements can occur without overtly reproducing them. Moreover, imitative states can recreate only other people's states, whereas in imagination we can recreate our own past states, or states that no identifiable person has had.

Prinz's (2005) definition allows that another's emotions can be imitated. Earlier I drew attention to the idea that empathetic acts are imaginative acts because they involve the reenactment of the target's emotions. Various authors have suggested the following mechanism by which empathetic imagination may occur (see, e.g., Prinz, 2005, p. 275). Even children only a few hours old exhibit a remarkable capacity to imitate the emotional expressions of those around them, although this may involve only behavioral imitation so soon after birth (Field, Woodson, Greenberg, & Cohen, 1982; Meltzoff & Moore, 1983). As we might expect, it has been suggested that these responses involve mirror neurons (Gallese, 2001). In addition, it has been widely noted that producing an emotional expression tends to bring about the corresponding emotional expression in an observer, sometimes in more attenuated form (see, e.g., Zajonc, Murphy, & Inglehart, 1989). So X observes Y's sad expression, imitates that sad expression, and consequently feels sad herself. I call this the *expression-first* empathy mechanism. While the expression-first mechanism is plausible for some kinds of empathetic response, it is unlikely to be the whole story. Notice that we can have an empathetic response to someone whose emotional expressions we cannot see or hear and therefore cannot behaviorally imitate. For example, I might empathetically experience terror when told that someone is trapped in a mine even though I cannot observe the trapped miner. In this case it is implausible that I behaviorally imitate the observed emotional expressions of the trapped miner and consequently experience their mental state of terror; it is far more likely that I mentally imitate their state of terror, and, as a consequence, my visage physically changes to match their look of terror. The processes whereby such empathetic responses arise are highly cognitive, taking as input a description of a person's situation (trapped in a mine) and yielding as output an attribution of an emotion (terror) to that person. The attribution then evokes a corresponding empathetic response by way of mental imitation of the other's terror, which, in turn, brings about the corresponding emotional expression. In other words, such empathetic responses would appear to require a prior exercise of mental attribution or theory of mind (Ravenscroft, 1998).[6] I refer to this as the *attribution-first* empathy mechanism.[7]

I suggested earlier that fictions can scaffold imaginative experiences. Of great significance to consumers of fiction are the empathetic experiences they have in response to fiction. In dramas and films, the consumer may be able to directly observe the character's emotional expressions and thus be able to behaviorally imitate them. As mentioned earlier, recreating emotional expressions can lead to experiencing the corresponding emotion. In other words, the expression-first model of empathetic responses may be plausible for some forms of fiction. However, it clearly is not plausible for many fictions. Consider the following passage that appears at the very end of Hemingway's *A Farewell to Arms* (1929/2005). Tenente's partner, Catherine, has been in labor with their child who has died. Tenente asks the medical staff about his wife's condition:

> "Is she dead?"
> "No, but she is unconscious."
> It seems she had one hemorrhage after another. They couldn't stop it. I went into the room and stayed with Catherine until she died. She was unconscious all the time and it did not take her very long to die....
> But after I had got them out and shut the door and turned out the light it wasn't any good. It was like saying good-by [sic] to a statue. After a while I went out and left the hospital and walked back to the hotel in the rain. (p. 293)

Hemingway makes no attempt to describe Tenente's emotional expressions and barely hints at his emotions: "it wasn't any good" and "It was like saying good-by to a statue" are the closest Hemingway comes to describing Tenente's interior life. Catherine is described only as "unconscious."[8] Many readers will, though, feel the emotional pull of the characters' plights. In cases like this, it is clear that the expression-first model of empathy isn't plausible. Empathy in such cases seems to be the outcome of highly cognitive processes that derive an emotional attribution from the description of the character's situation. The consumer then imaginatively enacts the attributed emotions. Many empathetic responses to fiction seem to be best captured by the attribution-first model.

I have stressed that imaginings may improve performance by a process of rehearsal (*off-line rehearsal,* as the simulation theorists would say). And I have suggested that, by scaffolding the imagination, fiction may provide additional opportunities for rehearsal. I have also stressed that empathetic states are imaginative/imitative states and that fiction can bring about empathetic states. Putting this together, fiction can scaffold empathetic experiences and thereby improve our ability to respond empathetically. Practice makes perfect. Nussbaum's nondevelopmental thesis is thus supported by our current understanding of imaginative and imitative processes.

I close this section by briefly mentioning one other line of support for Nussbaum's nondevelopmental thesis. Nussbaum's thesis assumes that there exists a crucial link between empathetic responses and ethical behavior. Psychopaths often engage in amoral behavior and purportedly fail to grasp the distinction between moral and merely conventional transgression (Blair, 1995; although see Langdon & Delmas, Chapter 5, this volume, for a critique of the commonly accepted interpretation of Blair's data). Strikingly, studies of psychopaths strongly indicate that they have emotional deficits. According to Hare (1991), psychopaths typically have flat affect and lack remorse, guilt, and empathy. They also have difficulty in recognizing other people's emotional states, in particular, other people's sad and fearful facial expressions (for further discussion see Hawes & Dadds, Chapter 3; Langdon & Delmas, Chapter 5; McIlwain et al., Chapter 6, this volume). We therefore have some grounds for hypothesizing a link between moral and emotional deficits in psychopathically inclined individuals (see Prinz, 2005, for discussion). This in turn provides some support for Nussbaum's views on the general relationship between emotions and ethics. Indeed, my account of the role of imagination in strengthening empathetic responses suggests that psychopathically inclined people may be particularly deficient in their imaginative imitation of others' mental lives.[9]

THE DEVELOPMENTAL THESIS

Prinz (2005) puts empathy at the heart of his model of the child's moral development and identifies three stages of early moral development (see de Rosnay & Fink, Chapter 2; Hawes & Dadds, Chapter 3, this volume, for further discussion of normal and abnormal moral development). The first stage involves empathetic responses to others based on what I call the expression-first mechanism (Prinz, 2005, pp. 274–276). Children only a few hours old behaviorally imitate the emotional expressions of caregivers and others (Meltzoff & Moore, 1983). On the expression-first model of empathy, this can lead to the child coming to experience the emotion of the caregiver. In particular, the child will tend to be happy when the caregiver is happy and sad when the caregiver is unhappy. At this point, children can exhibit what Prinz calls *first-order concern*: The child is distressed because the other is distressed.

The next stage occurs in the second year of life when toddlers begin to take active steps toward consoling others who are experiencing distress (Prinz, 2005, pp. 276–277). One possible explanation of their behavior is that, by reducing the other's distress, they reduce their own imitative distress. Imitation thus grounds early moral behavior. However, as it stands this account is less than satisfactory, for it leaves unexplained why the child reduces her own distress by consoling the other rather than by turning away. If the child were to distance herself from the person who is distressed, her imitative distress would be minimized (assuming, of course, that imitative distress is turned off by distance from the distressed person).[10] An alternate approach is found in Sugden's (2005) discussion of Prinz's theory. Sugden draws attention to Adam Smith's (1759/1976) observation that "[the] correspondence of the sentiments of others with our own appears to be a cause of pleasure, and the want of it a cause of pain" (p. 14). Say that child X is distressed and that child Y empathetically experiences X's distress. If Smith is right, both children's distress will at least to some extent be reduced by their mutual recognition of their mutual distress. On the other hand, if Y turns away from X and does not experience her distress, Y may be pained (as Smith would put it) by the discordance between her emotions and X's emotions. So empathy, coupled with the recognition of shared emotion, may lead children to attend closely to those in distress (see de Rosnay & Fink, Chapter 2, this volume).

The final stage occurs when the child begins to acquire an understanding of normative rules (Prinz, 2005, pp. 279–278). If a child causes distress in another, they are likely to empathetically experience the other person's distress and thereby become conditioned against causing the behavior that induced the other's distress (see Langdon and Delmas, Chapter 5, this volume, for discussion of Blair's violence inhibition model of the development of care-based morality). Caregivers may play a special role at this point: The caregiver's distress at the child's antisocial behavior can in turn lead to empathetic distress on the part of the child. Prinz elaborates this idea in terms of his theory that basic emotions such as sadness can be calibrated so that they are elicited by a new set of conditions (Prinz, 2004). In this view, guilt is a form of sadness elicited by harming another who is not deserving of that harm. Calibration leads to moral emotions such as guilt emerging from the basic biological emotional repertoire. By reflecting on the circumstances in which such emotions occur, the child can begin to identify simple normative rules of behavior.

We can see that all three stages of early moral development recognized by Prinz rest on imitative capacities. The child's capacity for expression-first empathetic responses grounds first-order concern. First-order concern, perhaps coupled with Smithian responses to concordant emotional states, grounds early prosocial behaviors like condolence. Finally, recognizing that they are distressed by another's distress—including a caregiver's distress at their inappropriate behavior—leads to the formation of simple normative rules. In Prinz's model, a lack of empathic capacities would lead to the failure of moral development, and, as he stresses, this is exactly what we find in the psychopath (Prinz, 2005).

I argued in the previous section that empathetic responses are imaginative or imitative states that can be scaffolded by fiction and that imaginative states can play an important role in rehearsing and thus improving performance. By enhancing empathetic responses, fiction may play a role in moral development. Picture books often display the facial expressions of the story's characters, usually in highly exaggerated ways. This may facilitate expression-first empathetic responses. In addition, picture books are almost always presented to the child by an adult, and the child may respond empathetically via the emotional expressions that the pictures and story elicit in the adult (recall Nussbaum's emphasis on adults and children reading or telling stories together; see Nussbaum, 1997, pp. 89, 93).

What of the attribution-first empathy mechanism? This mechanism will undergo a period of development that parallels the development of mental attribution or theory of mind. Children acquire an understanding of some mental states earlier than others; for example, they acquire an understanding of desire before they acquire an understanding of belief (see, e.g., Wellman, 1990). As is well known, children do not grasp that beliefs can be false until they are about 4 1/2 years old (Wimmer & Perner, 1983). The ability of children to empathize with fictional characters using the attribution-first mechanism will depend on how far they are along the theory of mind developmental pathway and what kinds of mental states are relevant to the accurate attribution of emotional states to the characters involved. To empathize with some fictional characters, a range of mental states must be attributed to them. For example, it is sometimes necessary to recognize that a character was deceived to appreciate her emotional states, and that in turn may require a grasp of false belief. Limitations on children's theory of mind capacities will therefore limit their attribution-first empathetic capacities and so limit their ability to gain much from certain fictions.

FICTION AND VIOLENCE

There is growing empirical evidence that exposure to violent media increases violent behavior (Hurley, 2004, p. 177). A meta-analysis of studies of exposure to media violence and aggressive behavior reported a strong positive correlation between the degree of exposure and aggressive behavior (Paik & Comstock, 1994). In a typical study of this type, Johnson, Cohen, Smailes, Kasen, and Brook (2002) tracked the amount of television watched by 707 individuals for 17 years and found a significant positive correlation between exposure to television in adolescence and early adulthood and subsequent aggressive behavior. Moreover, the impact of exposure to media violence on aggressive behavior is not inconsequential. Bushman and Anderson (2001) argue that this impact exceeds that of exposure to asbestos on the likelihood of developing cancer.

It is important to stress that there is considerable evidence that exposure to violent media not only is correlated with violent behavior but also causes violent behavior. For example, institutionalized boys were assessed for aggressiveness and then randomly assigned to one of two groups. The first group was shown nonviolent films, and the second group was shown violent films. The boys in the second group subsequently showed a marked increase in aggressiveness, whereas those in the first group did not. The impact of the violent films was most marked on boys who scored lower on the initial test of aggressiveness (see Berkowitz, 1993, pp. 207–208.) Longitudinal cross-lagged correlation studies have also been used to demonstrate a causal relationship between exposure to violent media and subsequent aggressive behavior. If it were simply the case that those inclined to violence were attracted to violent media, we would expect to find children's exposure to violent media correlated with their subsequent aggressive behavior and degree of aggression in children correlated with their subsequent consumption of violent media. But this is not the observed pattern. One relevant study showed that consumption of violent media by 8-year-old boys was strongly correlated with their aggressive behavior 10 years later; however, aggressive behavior by 8-year-old boys was not strongly correlated with the amount of violent media consumed 20 years later (see Huesmann, 2005b; Hurley, 2004).

A number of theorists have proposed that the impact of observing media violence on subsequent aggressive behavior should be understood in terms of imitation (see especially Huesmann, 2005b; Hurley, 2004). The human tendency toward action imitation has been demonstrated for a wide range of behaviors (Chartrand & Bargh, 1996, 1999, 2002). As Hurley (2004) remarks, "There is no apparent reason to exempt violent actions from these general tendencies" (p. 182). I noted earlier that there is considerable evidence that imitation occurs automatically in the absence of impulse control in neurological patients (Kinsbourne, 2005; Lhermitte, 1986; Lhermitte et al., 1986). Since impulse control tends to be relatively underdeveloped in children, the impact of exposure to violent media on aggressive behavior is likely to be strong among children (Hurley, 2004, p. 183). I also noted earlier that motor imagery improves motor behavior, and thus it can be seen as a kind of covert practice. Hurley (2004, p. 183) draws attention to this phenomenon, suggesting that media violence affords opportunities for covertly practicing violent behavior.

Notice that media violence is very often fictional. (There are exceptions, of course, such as news reports of violent behavior.) It follows that we have very considerable evidence of a direct causal link between a class of fictions and a class of unethical behaviors. Fictions are not magical texts that automatically guide us toward the ethical life. Human imitative mechanisms are exceedingly powerful, but they are, as it were, value neutral: We imitate the bad along with the good. So although recent work on imagination and imitation provides broad support for Nussbaum's views on fiction and the ethical life, they also underscore the fact that certain kinds of fictions are immensely destructive. The significance of the effect of exposure to violent media on aggressive behavior, plus the enormous prevalence of violent media, mean that the "dark side" of fiction is very dark indeed (Hurley, 2004, p. 178).

Violent fictions pose a conundrum. Since they represent people suffering, we would expect them to engage the empathetic mechanisms that generate sympathetic responses. This in turn should, by the arguments I advanced in the two previous sections, promote ethical behavior. But as we have seen, violent fictions do no such thing. I think that the key to this puzzle lies in the fact that, as we have seen, there exist (at least) two kinds of imitative responses to fictions. On one hand, fictions can engage imitative mechanisms that bring about the reenactment of the characters' emotions, and, on the other hand, fictions can engage imitative mechanisms that bring about the reenactment of the characters' actions. It is possible that a single work of fiction can engage both kinds of imitative mechanisms simultaneously. In the case of violent fictions, these imitative mechanisms may pull in opposite directions, with the mechanisms for emotional reenactment bringing about an empathetic response in the consumer and the mechanism for action reenactment bringing about violent behavior. The prevalence of aggressive responses to violent media suggests that, in many cases, the reenactment of action trumps the reenactment of emotion.

Support for the existence of parallel imitative systems is provided by Blair (2005), who argues for the dissociation of emotional, motor, and cognitive empathy. The first of these approximates to what I have called simply *empathy*, the second to what I have called *action imitation*, and the third to what is commonly called *theory of mind*. Blair reports that people with autism typically exhibit considerable deficits of motor and cognitive empathy but not emotional empathy. In contrast, individuals with psychopathy exhibit marked deficits of emotional empathy but not motor or cognitive empathy.

CONCLUSION

I have argued that consuming fiction can have important consequences for the consumer's ethical life. If I am right about this, two important questions immediately arise: Which fictions promote amoral violent behavior in consumers, and which promote ethical behavior? There is evidence that very realistic depictions of violence are more effective at promoting violence than less realistic depictions, and there is evidence that violence cast in an approving light, humorously presented, or perpetrated by attractive people is more likely to promote violence than other presentations of violence (Berkowitz, 1993, pp. 209–211; Smith & Donnerstein, 1998). Clearly, this is an important area for further research.

Nussbaum asked, "What sort of literary works ... should we promote in order to foster an informed and compassionate vision of the different?" (Nussbaum, 1997, pp. 88–89). Recall that I said compassion involves empathizing with another and ethically responding to their situation. So we can ask which aspects of fictions best enhance the consumer's capacity for empathy and which aspects enhance the consumer's ethical response. Very little is known about these issues. Extrapolating from the case of violent media just discussed, it may be that when a character's ethical responses are cast in a favorable light or when ethical responses are humorously presented or made by attractive people, they have maximum impact on the consumer's behavior. Nussbaum's own view is that our ethical responses will be nurtured by fictions that present lives very different from our own. Thus, she approvingly presents Marcus Aurelius's view:

> We must ... cultivate in ourselves a capacity for sympathetic imagination that
> will enable us to comprehend the motives and choices of people different from

ourselves, seeing them not as forbiddingly alien and other, but as sharing many problems and possibilities with us.... Here the arts play a vital role, cultivating powers of imagination that are essential for citizenship. (Nussbaum, 1997, p. 85)

It may be that the match between our empathetic response to those very different from ourselves and our emotional responses to our own situation promotes an ethical identification with the other. Intriguing though this idea is, it awaits empirical confirmation.

Establishing which circumstances enhance ethical behavior and which promote violence are vital tasks in the contemporary world. We urgently need to understand the basis of human normative behavior.[11]

REFERENCES

Aristotle. (1996). *Poetics* (M. Heath, Trans.). London: Penguin.

Berkowitz, L. (1993). *Aggression: Its causes, consequences, and control.* New York: McGraw-Hill.

Bisiach, E., & Luzzatti, C. (1978). Unilateral neglect of representational space. *Cortex, 14,* 129–33.

Blair, R. (1995). A cognitive developmental approach to morality: Investigating the psychopath. *Cognition, 57,* 1–29.

Blair, R. (2005). Responding to the emotions of others: Dissociating forms of empathy through the study of typical and psychiatric populations. *Consciousness and Cognition, 14,* 698–718.

Booth, W. (1988). *The company we keep: An ethics of fiction.* Berkeley: University of California Press.

Bushman, B., & Anderson, C. (2001). Media violence and the American public: Scientific facts vs. media misinformation. *American Psychologist, 56,* 477–489.

Byrne, R. (1995). *The thinking ape: Evolutionary origins of intelligence.* Oxford, UK: Oxford University Press.

Chartrand, T., & Bargh, J. (1996). Automatic activation of impression formation and memorization goals: Nonconscious goal priming reproduces effects of explicit task instructions. *Journal of Personality and Social Psychology, 71,* 464–478.

Chartrand, T., & Bargh, J. (1999). The chameleon effect: The perception–behavior link and social interaction. *Journal of Personality and Social Psychology, 76,* 893–910.

Chartrand, T., & Bargh, J. (2002). Nonconscious motivations: Their activation, operation, and consequences. In A. Tesser, D. A. Stapel, & J. V. Wood (Eds.), *Self and motivation: Emerging psychological perspectives* (pp. 13–41). Washington, DC: American Psychological Association.

Currie, G. (1995). Visual imagery as the simulation of vision. *Mind and Language, 10,* 25–44.

Currie, G., & Ravenscroft, I. (1997). Mental simulation and motor imagery. *Philosophy of Science, 64,* 161–180.

Currie, G., & Ravenscroft, I. (2002). *Recreative minds: Imagination in philosophy and psychology.* Oxford, UK: Oxford University Press.

Dickens, C. (1854/2003). *Hard times.* London: Penguin.

Dominey, P., Decety, J., Brousolle, E., Chazot, G., & Jeannerod, M. (1995). Motor imagery of a lateralized sequential task is asymmetrically slowed in hemi-Parkinson's patients. *Neuropsychologia, 33,* 727–741.

Farah, M. (1989). The neural basis of mental imagery. *Trends in Neurosciences, 12,* 395–399.

Field, T., Woodson, R., Greenberg, R., & Cohen, D. (1982). Discrimination and imitation of facial expression by neonates. *Science, 218,* 179–181.

Finke, R., & Kurtzman, H. (1981). Mapping the visual field in mental imagery. *Journal of Experimental Psychology: General, 110,* 501–517.

Gallese, V. (2001). The "Shared Manifold" hypothesis: From mirror neurons to empathy. *Journal of Consciousness Studies, 8,* 33–50.

Goldenberg, G., Podreka, I., Steiner, M., Willmes, K., Suess, E., & Deecke, L. (1989). Regional cerebral blood flow patterns in visual imagery. *Neuropsychologia, 27,* 641–664.

Goldenberg, G., Podreka, I., Uhl, F., Steiner, M., Willmes, K., & Deecke, L. (1989). Cerebral correlates of imagining colors, faces and a map. *Neuropsychologia, 27,* 1315–1328.

Goldman, A. (1989). Interpretation psychologized. *Mind and Language, 4,* 161–185.

Hakemulder, J. (2000). *The moral laboratory: Experiments examining the effects of reading literature on social perception and moral self-concept.* Amsterdam: Benjamins.

Hakemulder, J. (2001). How to make alle Menschen Bruder: Literature in a multicultural and multiform society. In D. Schram & G. Steen (Eds.), *The psychology and sociology of literature. In honor of Elrund Ibsch* (pp. 225–242). Amsterdam: Benjamins.

Hare, R. (1991). *The Hare psychopathy check list: Revised.* Toronto: Multi-Heath Systems.

Hemingway, E. (1929/2005). *A farewell to arms.* London: Vintage.

Heyes, C., & Galef, B. (1996). *Social learning in animals: The roots of culture.* San Diego: Academic Press.

Huesmann, L. (2005a). Acquiring morality by imitating emotions. In S. Hurley & N. Chater (Eds.), *Perspectives on imitation: From neuroscience to social science* (Vol. 2, pp. 386–388). Cambridge, MA: MIT Press.

Huesmann, L. (2005b). Imitation and the effects of observing media violence on behavior. In S. Hurley & N. Chater (Eds.), *Perspectives on imitation: From neuroscience to social science* (Vol. 2, pp. 257–266). Cambridge, MA: MIT Press.

Hume, D. (1751/1998). *An enquiry concerning the principles of morals* (T. L. Beauchamp, Ed.). Oxford, UK: Oxford University Press.

Hurley, S. (2004). Imitation, media violence, and freedom of speech. *Philosophical Studies, 117,* 165–218.

Hurley, S., & Chater, N. (2005). *Perspectives on imitation: From neuroscience to social science* (2 volumes). Cambridge, MA: MIT Press.

Iacoboni, M. (2005). Understanding others: Imitation, language and empathy. In S. Hurley & N. Chater (Eds.), *Perspectives on imitation: From neuroscience to social science* (Vol. 1, pp. 77–99). Cambridge, MA: MIT Press.

Jeannerod, M. (1994). The representing brain: Neural correlates of motor intention and imagery. *Behavioral and Brain Sciences, 17,* 187–202.

Johnson, J., Cohen, P., Smailes, E., Kasen, S., & Brook J. (2002). Television viewing and aggressive behavior during adolescence and adulthood. *Science, 295,* 2468–2471.

Kinsbourne, M. (2005). Imitation as entrainment: Brain mechanisms and social consequences. In S. Hurley & N. Chater (Eds.), *Perspectives on imitation: From neuroscience to social science* (Vol. 2, pp. 163–172). Cambridge, MA: MIT Press.

Kosslyn, S., Alpert, N., Thompson, W., Maljkovic, V., Weise, S., Chabris, C., et al. (1993). Visual mental imagery activates topographically organized visual cortex: PET investigations. *Journal of Cognitive Neuroscience, 5,* 263–287.

Kosslyn, S., Ball, T., & Reiser, B. (1978). Visual images preserve metric spatial information: Evidence from studies of image scanning. *Journal of Experimental Psychology: Human Perception and Performance, 4,* 47–60.

Lhermitte, F. (1986). Human autonomy and the frontal lobes, Part II. *Annals of Neurology, 19,* 335–343.

Lhermitte, F., Pillon, B., & Serdaru, M. (1986). Human autonomy and the frontal lobes, Part I. *Annals of Neurology, 19*, 326–334.

Mar, R. (2004). The neuropsychology of narrative: Story comprehension, story production and their interrelation. *Neuropsychologia, 42*, 1414–1434.

Mar, R. (2009). Empirical research on reading and watching narrative fiction. In D. Schram (Ed.), *Reading and watching: What does the written word have that images don't?* (pp. 53–61). Delft: Eburon Academic.

Mar, R., Djikic, M., & Oatley, K. (2008). Effects of reading on knowledge, social abilities, and selfhood: Theory and empirical studies. In S. Zyngier, M. Bortolussi, A. Chesnokova, & J. Auracher (Eds.), *Directions in empirical literary studies: In honor of Willie van Peer* (pp. 127–137). Amsterdam: Benjamins.

Mar, R., Oatley, K., Hirsh, J., de la Paz, J., & Peterson, J. (2006). Bookworms versus nerds: Exposure to fiction versus non-fiction, divergent associations with social ability, and the simulation of fictional social worlds. *Journal of Research in Personality, 40*, 694–712.

Meltzoff, A. N. (1988). Infant imitation after a 1-week delay: Long-term memory for novel acts and multiple stimuli. *Developmental Psychology, 24*, 470–476.

Meltzoff, A., & Moore, M. (1983). Newborn infants imitate adult facial gestures. *Child Development, 54*, 702–709.

Morton, A. (1994). Motor simulation. *Behavioral and Brain Sciences, 17*, 215.

Nussbaum, M. (1995). *Poetic justice: The literary imagination and public life.* Boston: Beacon Press.

Nussbaum, M. (1997). *Cultivating humanity: A classical defense of reform in liberal education.* Cambridge, MA: Harvard University Press.

Oatley, K. (1999). Why fiction may be twice as true as fact: Fiction as cognitive and emotional simulation. *Review of General Psychology, 3*, 101–117.

Oatley, K. (2008, June 28). The science of fiction. *New Scientist*, pp. 42–43.

Paik, H., & Comstock, G. (1994). The effects of television violence on anti-social behavior: A meta-analysis. *Communication Research, 21*, 516–546.

Parsons, L. (1987a). Imagined spatial transformations of one's body. *Journal of Experimental Psychology: General, 116*, 172–191.

Parsons, L. (1987b). Imagined spatial transformations of one's hands and feet. *Cognitive Psychology, 19*, 178–241.

Parsons, L. (1994). Temporal and kinematic properties of motor behavior reflected in mentally simulated action. *Journal of Experimental Psychology: Human Perception and Performance, 20*, 709–730.

Parsons, L., Fox, P., Downs, J., Glass, T., Hirsch, T., Martin, C., et al. (1995). Use of implicit motor imagery for visual shape discrimination as revealed by PET. *Nature, 375*, 54–58.

Pascual-Leone, A. (2001). The brain that plays music and is changed by it. *Annals of the New York Academy of Sciences, 930*, 315–329.

Prinz, J. (2004). *Gut reactions: A perceptual theory of emotion.* New York: Oxford University Press.

Prinz, J. (2005). Imitation and moral development. In S. Hurley & N. Chater (Eds.), *Perspectives on imitation: From neuroscience to social science* (Vol. 2, pp. 267–282). Cambridge, MA: MIT Press.

Ravenscroft, I. (1998). What is it like to be someone else? Simulation and empathy. *Ratio, 11*, 170–185.

Ravenscroft, I. (2010). Folk psychology as a theory. In E. Zalta (Ed.), *Stanford encyclopedia of philosophy*. Retrieved December 21, 2010 from http://plato.stanford.edu/entries/folkpsych-theory/

Richardson, A. (1967). Mental practice: A review and discussion (Parts 1 & 2). *Research Quarterly, 38*, 95–107, 262–273.

Roland, P., & Friberg, L. (1985). Localization of cortical areas activated by thinking. *Journal of Neurophysiology, 53*, 1219–1243.

Rousseau, J.-J. (1762/2007). *Emile: or, On education* (B. Foxley, Trans.). Sioux Falls, SD: NuVision Press.

Smith, A. (1759/1976). *The theory of moral sentiments* (D. D. Raphael & A. L. Macfie, Eds.). Oxford, UK: Oxford University Press.

Smith, S., & Donnerstein, E. (1998). Harmful effects of exposure to media violence. In R. Geen & E. Donnerstein (Eds.), *Human aggression: Theories, research, implications for social policy* (pp. 167–202). San Diego: Academic Press.

Sophocles. (2003). *Philoctetes* (C. Phillips, Trans.). New York: Oxford University Press.

Stich, S., & Nichols, S. (1992). Folk psychology: Simulation or tacit theory? *Mind and Language, 7*, 35–71.

Sugden, R. (2005). Mirror neurons and Adam Smith's theory of sympathy. In S. Hurley & N. Chater (Eds.), *Perspectives on imitation: From neuroscience to social science* (Vol. 2, pp. 388–391). Cambridge, MA: MIT Press.

Tomasello, M. (1999). *The cultural origins of human cognition*. Cambridge, MA: Harvard University Press.

Tomasello, M., & Call, J. (1997). *Primate cognition*. New York: Oxford University Press.

Trilling, L. (1950/2008). *The liberal imagination*. New York: New York Review of Books.

Wellman, H. (1990). *The child's theory of mind*. Cambridge, MA: MIT Press.

Wimmer, H., & Perner, J. (1983). Beliefs about beliefs: Representation and constraining function of wrong beliefs in young children's understanding of deception. *Cognition, 13*, 103–128.

Yue, G., & Cole, K. (1992). Strength increases from the motor program: Comparison of training with maximal voluntary and imagined muscle contractions. *Journal of Neurophysiology, 67*, 1114–1123.

Zajonc, R., Murphy, S., & Inglehart, M. (1989). Feeling and facial efference: Implications of the vascular theory of emotion. *Psychological Review, 96*, 395–416.

ENDNOTES

1. Some may want to draw a distinction between sympathy and compassion; however, Nussbaum uses these terms interchangeably, and so will I.

2. There is more to compassion than this. As Nussbaum reminds us, a compassionate response is directed at someone who "has suffered some significant pain or misfortune in a way for which that person is not, or not fully, to blame" (Nussbaum, 1997, pp. 90–91).

3. Empathy, as I have defined it, necessarily involves the re-creation or reenactment of another's emotional states. It is therefore closer to affective empathy than to cognitive empathy (for a review of the literature on the distinction between affective and cognitive empathy see Blair, 2005; see also Hawes & Dadds, Chapter 3, this volume).

4. We claimed only to have captured a significant subset of those mental activities commonly dubbed acts of imagination because some uses of the term imagined mean (roughly) "falsely believed." For example, it might be said that "Columbus imagined he had discovered a new route to India." In this case it is being claimed that Columbus believed that he had discovered a new route to India but was not entitled to his belief (see Currie & Ravenscroft, 2002, pp. 8–9).

5. For discussion of the parallels between vision and visual imagery, see Currie (1995) and Currie and Ravenscroft (1997).

6. I use the term "theory of mind" here very loosely to identify the cognitive processes, whatever they are, that underpin our capacity to predict and explain behavior. I don't intend, by using the term, to rule out the possibility that predicting and explaining behavior is underpinned by simulation. For a guide to some of the terminological confusions with which this field abounds, see Ravenscroft (2010).
7. Notice that the distinction between expression-first and attribution-first mechanisms is distinct from that between affective and cognitive empathy. Both the expression-first mechanism and the attribution-first mechanism bring about episodes of affective empathy.
8. Hemingway is well known for eschewing direct descriptions of his characters' interior lives, preferring to convey their emotions by describing their situations in surprisingly simple language. For Hemingway, less was more.
9. I owe this observation to Robyn Langdon.
10. As Prinz (2005) remarks, mere empathetic distress is compatible with a selfish response to another's distress (p. 276).
11. I would like to thank Robyn Langdon and Catriona Mackenzie for their patience, comments, and encouragement and Jason Tillett and Tamara Zutlevics for extensive discussion of the themes explored in this paper.

5

Moral Reasoning and Psychopathic Tendencies in the General Community

ROBYN LANGDON

Macquarie University

KRISTY DELMAS

University of New South Wales

Research investigating deficient moral agency in human adults has tended to focus on neurological patients with acquired moral deficits and incarcerated individuals with developmental psychopathy. We argue for the importance of also investigating such factors in nonclinical, nonincarcerated individuals with psychopathic tendencies. Studies of this type avoid confounds inherent in work with clinical or incarcerated populations and offer important advances in understanding the so-called successful psychopaths of today's world—psychopathically inclined individuals who avoid legal scrutiny yet appear capable of causing great social and economic harm. Toward this end, we review evidence that psychopathically inclined individuals in the general community self-report restricted empathic responsiveness toward others but not impoverished cognitive understanding of others' mental lives—a dissociation that likely facilitates their callous manipulative intent. We then report evidence that nonincarcerated individuals with varying levels of psychopathic attributes distinguish equally between moral and conventional transgressions, whereas those with higher levels of psychopathic attributes are significantly more likely to endorse emotionally aversive acts in moral dilemmas. We conclude by discussing the implications of our findings for three prominent approaches to moral judgment—the Humean, Humean–Kantian, and Rawlsian models.

INTRODUCTION

*I*ndividuals with psychopathic tendencies profess morally aversive attitudes and act in amoral ways. Research into the differences between individuals with and without psychopathic tendencies may advance understanding of the factors—developmental, neural, and cognitive—that sustain the acquisition and deployment of fully developed moral agency. In this chapter, we adopt a *continuity* approach to examine these differences in nonclinical, nonincarcerated adults with varying levels of psychopathic attributes. We focus primarily on two laboratory-based, behavioral tests of moral reasoning. One test requires participants to make the moral–conventional distinction when judging the seriousness of transgressions; the other test involves judging the "right" or "wrong" of acts in moral dilemma scenarios. In the latter test, participants must choose between endorsing and rejecting an emotionally aversive act of harming another person to benefit the majority. Laboratory-based tests of this type are less complex and less nuanced than are real-world demands on moral decision making and thus are ill-suited to inform understanding of the full spectrum of factors that impact healthy adults when they navigate today's social world (see Mackenzie, Chapter 11; Kennett, Chapter 12, this volume, for further discussion of the complexities of real-world moral challenges). Nevertheless, tests of this type allow for a greater degree of experimental control when specifying the differences between individuals with and without psychopathic tendencies that might explain the deficiencies of moral agency in the former group. We chose to focus on these two particular tests in our own work, since previous studies that have used these tests with clinical or incarcerated psychopathic individuals have been very influential in the philosophical literature. We have reservations, however, about some of the commonly accepted interpretations of the data from these previous studies, as discussed in more detail later.

In the following sections, we begin by describing the nature of psychopathy, before reviewing and critiquing previous studies of the moral–conventional distinction in clinical or incarcerated psychopathic individuals. Our reservations about some of the inevitable confounds that are inherent in conducting behavioral research with forensic populations, and our associated doubts about the commonly accepted interpretations of some of the forensic data, lead us to advocate for a continuity approach to also study psychopathic tendencies in nonclinical, nonincarcerated individuals. We review empirical findings that validate an assumption of continuity between clinical or forensic psychopathy and less extreme nonclinical and nonforensic manifestations of psychopathic attributes in the general community. The latter are commonly assessed using self-report inventories, which we describe and illustrate with some examples. We then review our own work on the moral–conventional distinction in nonincarcerated adults with varying levels of psychopathic attributes and report the performances of these same individuals when asked to judge the right or wrong of acts in moral dilemmas. We conclude by considering the implications of our findings for three prominent models of moral judgment, as summarized by Hauser (2006a) and illustrated in Figure 5.1:

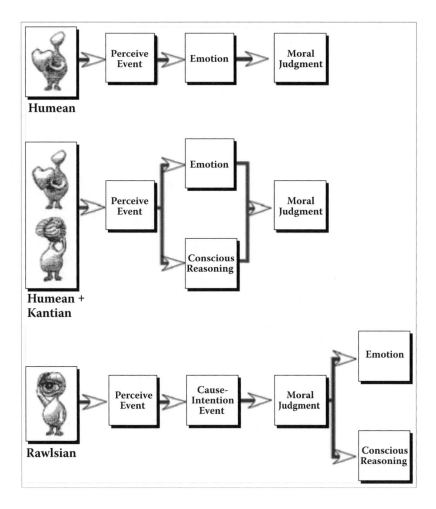

Figure 5.1   Three toy models of the sources of our moral judgments. (From Hauser, *Social Cognitive and Affective Neuroscience, 1,* pp. 214–220, 2006. With permission.)

1. *The Humean model,* according to which a perceived act triggers an automatic emotional response, which, in turn, unconsciously triggers an intuitive judgment as to whether the perceived act is morally right or wrong, perhaps best exemplified by the modern writings of Haidt (2001)
2. *The Humean–Kantian model,* according to which a perceived act triggers parallel emotional responses and conscious reflection, which may or may not be in conflict, perhaps best exemplified in the current work of Greene and colleagues (e.g., Greene, Nystrom, Engell, Darley, & Cohen, 2004; Greene, Sommerville, Nystrom, Darley, & Cohen, 2001)
3. *The Rawlsian model,* according to which a perceived act triggers an unconscious analysis of causal and intentional properties of the perceived act leading to a moral judgment, which, in turn, triggers emotional responses

and conscious reasoning, perhaps best exemplified today in Hauser and colleagues' (Hauser, 2006a, 2006b; Huebner, Dwyer, & Hauser, 2009) theory of a universal moral grammar

PSYCHOPATHY

Psychopathy is a developmental disorder characterized by enduring and maladaptive patterns of affective, interpersonal, and behavioral responses. It manifests early in life (see Hawes & Dadds, Chapter 3, this volume) and lasts a lifetime, proving difficult to treat. In his influential book, the *Mask of Sanity*, Cleckley (1976) outlined two sets of criteria for identifying the adult psychopath: (1) those related to the emotional nonresponsiveness and poor social relatedness of the psychopath (e.g., a lack of remorse or shame, absence of affective responsiveness, egocentricity and inability to love, manipulative deceitfulness and insincerity, absence of loyalty, and a lack of genuine insight into the condition); and (2) those related to the behavioral impulsivity and recklessness that is also associated with psychopathy (e.g., irresponsibility, sexual promiscuity, impulsive antisocial acts, failure to learn from experience, and absence of a clear life plan). Cleckley also noted that these deficiencies occur in the absence of intellectual disability, delusions, or irrationality and in the presence of a cunning social adroitness.

Drawing on Cleckley's (1976) classic description, Hare (1980) developed the Psychopathy Checklist (PCL) to assess psychopathy in adult criminal offenders. Later versions of this instrument, the PCL-R (Hare, 1991) and its second edition (Hare, 2003), are among the most widely used clinical tools today for assessing forensic psychopathy. In line with Cleckley's original description, factor-analytic studies of the PCL-R have reliably identified two relatively independent factors, one of which reflects the callous manipulative attributes of the psychopath and the other of which reflects the impulsive, bored, and antisocial attributes (e.g., Hart, Hare, & Harpur, 1992). While findings of this type suggest that psychopathy is related to antisocial personality disorder, antisocial behavior is not sufficient for a diagnosis of psychopathy. This is because psychopathy is conceived as characterized primarily by the emotional and moral deficits that manifest in a lack of empathy, callous manipulation of others, and failure to feel remorse (e.g., Blair, 2001; Cleckley, 1976; Hare, 1998; refer also to McIlwain et al., Chapter 6, this volume, for further discussion of possible relations between psychopathy and antisocial personality disorder).

While theoretical models of the underlying causes of psychopathy differ, many researchers have focused on the role of aberrant conditioning or biologically driven intuitive emotional responses. Some developmental psychopathologists have, for example, considered the impact of a lack of secure attachment early in life and the learning of a coercive manipulative style—that is, when a young child's noncompliance and temper cause a parent to give in, the child's coercive behavior is reinforced; likewise, when the parent gives in and the child terminates the coercion, the parent's permissive behavior is reciprocally reinforced (see, e.g., Patrick, Fowles, & Krueger, 2009, for discussion). There is also evidence that clinical or incarcerated psychopaths process fear-related stimuli abnormally, showing deficits, for example, in aversive conditioning (Flor, Birbaumer, Hermann, Ziegler, & Patrick, 2002) and a failure to generate autonomic responses to anticipated threat (Hare, 1982). This evidence has been taken to support the claim that psychopathy is a consequence of an impaired modulation of fear responses (e.g., Eysenck, 1964). According to Blair (1995), however, this claim assumes that normal moral development relies fundamentally on the use of fear and punishment, which is inconsistent with evidence that the use of reasoning, rather than punishment and authoritarian parenting, better achieves moral socialization in young children.

Blair (1995) took a developmental, cognitive-neuroscientific approach to psychopathy and proposed a model that features a violence inhibition mechanism (VIM). On his account, human beings typically develop a VIM, which is normally activated by others' distress cues (e.g., their sad and fearful facial expressions), and initiates a withdrawal response. Over time, the aversive arousal induced by the VIM comes to be paired with representations of others' distress. These representations are further fleshed out by imagining oneself in the "mental shoes" of another person. It is this pairing that purportedly underpins the physiological tendency to avoid others' suffering. The VIM-related aversive arousal also contributes to the experiencing of moral emotions, such as guilt and shame, which become increasingly more fine-grained and sophisticated as social concepts are acquired and refined during childhood and into adolescence (see, e.g., de Oliveira-Souza & Moll, Chapter 7, this volume, for discussion of the interplay of semantic and emotional facets of morality). In the case of individuals with psychopathy, however, the detection and processing of others' emotional signals, in particular their distress displays, are compromised, and a VIM fails to develop properly. These individuals thus fail to feel aversive arousal at the sight (or thought) of another's distress, fail to develop fully formed moral emotions, and lack a genuine appreciation of the heinousness of moral violations.

These developmental failures in psychopathically inclined individuals have been linked to compromise of the amygdala and ventromedial prefrontal cortex (VMPC; see, e.g., Glenn & Raine, 2009, for a recent review, and also de Oliveira-Souza & Moll, Chapter 7, this volume). Blair (2007) suggests that amygdala dysfunction in psychopathically inclined individuals impairs not only the detection and recognition of others' distress signals (e.g., their sad facial expressions) but also the pairing of perceived or imagined acts of harming others with aversive reinforcement. Information about this reinforced aversive expectancy would normally feed forward to the VMPC to inhibit morally aversive acts—an automatic curb on amoral behavior that is diminished in the psychopath. Within the VMPC, the orbitofrontal cortex (OFC) may be particularly important for integrating moral semantic knowledge with emotion cues (Moll, Oliveira-Souza, Bramati, & Grafman, 2002) and for inhibiting antisocial impulses (Brower & Price, 2001). Evidence that damage to the OFC can result in psychopathic attributes, such as callous affect and a lack of guilt or remorse, also supports the claim that the OFC plays a pivotal role in moral agency (Anderson, Bechara, Damasio, Tranel, & Damasio, 1999).

Behavioral findings of abnormal emotion and fear processing in psychopathically inclined individuals include that clinical or incarcerated psychopaths show (1) reduced *skin conductance responses* (SCRs: an indicator of autonomic arousal) to others' distress cues when compared with nonpsychopathic controls (Blair, Jones, Clark, & Smith, 1997), and (2) absence of startle reflex when presented with aversive images (e.g., a picture of a burn victim) and when compared with nonpsychopathic controls (Patrick, Bradley, & Lang, 1993). Facial expressions of negative affect, such as sadness and fear (and less commonly, disgust; Kosson, Suchy, Mayer, & Libby, 2002), are also poorly recognized by incarcerated psychopathic adults (Blair & Coles, 2000; Blair, Colledge, Murray, & Mitchell, 2001; Blair et al., 2004) as well as by children (Blair et al., 2001; Stevens, Charman, & Blair, 2001) and adolescents with psychopathic tendencies (Blair & Coles, 2000). One of the most influential set of findings to support a failure to develop empathetic care-based morality in psychopathically inclined individuals has come from studies of the moral–conventional distinction in clinical or incarcerated psychopaths. Some philosophers have taken these findings to provide strong support for a sentimentalist approach to moral reasoning. Prinz (2006), for example, describes psychopaths as the perfect test case for the claim that intact emotion processing is developmentally necessary to make moral judgments. He draws on the reported findings of emotion deficits in psychopaths, as well as Blair's (1995) finding of a failure to make the moral–conventional distinction in psychopathic prison inmates and other related findings, to argue that deficient emotion processing underpins the psychopath's failures to develop normal moral concepts and to act in moral ways. Because of these emotional deficits, he says, psychopaths "treat moral wrongs as if they were merely conventional … [and they treat] the word 'wrong' as if it simply meant 'prohibited by local authorities'" (p. 32). However, as we spell out in more detail herein, it is not quite correct to interpret Blair's findings as showing that psychopaths "treat moral wrongs as if they were conventional."

THE MORAL–CONVENTIONAL DISTINCTION

Moral transgressions involve violations of the rights and welfare of others, whereas conventional transgressions involve rule breaking (e.g., swearing, public nudity). The moral–conventional distinction refers to the differences in judgments and justifications generated by adults and children when they evaluate moral versus conventional transgressions. Moral transgressions are judged to be less permissible and more serious than conventional transgressions. They are also judged to be less authority dependent—in other words, moral transgressions, but not conventional transgressions, are still judged impermissible even when an authority figure says a transgression is okay. Justifications of the judgments of transgressions also differ. For example, both adults and children refer more to avoiding harm to a victim when justifying their judgments of moral transgressions, whereas they refer more to social norms and rule breaking (e.g., "It's just wrong") when the transgressions are conventional. The moral–conventional distinction is observed in children as young as 39 months (Smetana, 1981), even when children have suffered abuse (Smetana, Kelly, & Twentyman, 1984), and across cultures (e.g., Song, Smetana, & Kim, 1987).

That the moral–conventional distinction is such an early sign of moral social-ization in young children made it such a striking result when Blair (1995) reported evidence of a failure to make the moral–conventional distinction in 10 adult crimi-nal psychopaths (identified using the PCL) who he compared with 10 inmates with-out psychopathic tendencies. There were no other important differences between the two groups that might have accounted for Blair's findings—for example, all of the participants were male and incarcerated in a forensic psychiatric hospital for committing violent crimes, and the two groups were also well matched on age and IQ. Blair presented the adult criminal participants with very simple stories that were taken from the developmental literature: four moral stories (about, e.g., a child hitting another child) and four conventional stories (about, e.g., a boy wearing a skirt). After each story, the participants were then asked the following:

1. Was it OK for X to do Y?
2. On a scale of 1–10, how bad was it for X to do Y?
3. What if the teacher said … that anybody can do Y if they want to. Would it be OK for X to do Y if the teacher says X can?
4. Why was it bad for X to do Y?

(Question 4 actually came before Question 3; we have reordered to simplify the description of the plots in Figure 5.2). Figure 5.2 summarizes Blair's results.

While it is clear that the psychopathic inmates failed to distinguish between the moral and conventional transgressions, whether reporting their judgments of *impermissibility, seriousness,* or *authority modifiability,* it is also striking that the psychopaths treated the moral transgressions just as seriously as the nonpsycho-pathic inmates and across all criteria. Where they differed from the nonpsycho-pathic inmates was in treating the conventional transgressions as more serious, as

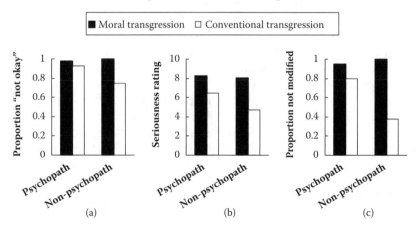

Figure 5.2   Illustration of Blair's (1995) data: (a) Proportion of transgressions judged impermissible (i.e., "not okay"). (b) Mean seriousness rating. (c) Proportion of "not okay" transgressions still "not okay" even if permitted by authority figure. (From Blair, R. J. R., *Consciousness and Cognition, 14,* 698–718, 2005. With permission.)

more like the moral transgressions. In other words, the psychopathic inmates produced higher than expected ratings for the conventional transgressions rather than lower than expected ratings for the moral transgressions. As Blair (1995) put it, "The psychopaths treated conventional transgressions as if they were moral" (p. 23), and not the other way around, as Prinz (2006) and others summarized his findings.

However, Prinz's (2006) description of Blair's (1995) findings is understandable, since Blair went on to interpret his data as entirely consistent with the claim that the psychopathic inmates genuinely responded to the moral transgressions as if they were less serious—as if they were merely conventional. The finding that the psychopathic inmates reported higher than expected ratings for conventional transgressions was put down to the inmates wanting to impress authority figures by inflating their ratings. We will flesh out Blair's argument in more detail next, but then we want to argue that Blair's data are just as consistent with the claim that the psychopathic inmates did genuinely distinguish between the moral and conventional transgressions—a moral–conventional distinction that was then obscured in their manipulated responses. Our take-home message is that the behavioral responses of incarcerated psychopathic individuals need to be treated with great caution—a point that Blair was also at pains to make in his 1995 paper.

So, let us focus on Blair's (1995) argument first. As he cautioned, working with incarcerated populations involves inevitable confounds; in particular, it is likely that all of the inmates were strongly motivated to impress authority figures (including the experimenter) to maximize their chances of early release. To summarize Blair's argument, the psychopathic inmates' genuine (or nonconfounded) ratings of transgressions, if these could have been directly assessed, would have been equally low for the moral and conventional transgressions and equal to the low ratings of the conventional transgressions reported by the nonpsychopathic inmates. But since the psychopathic inmates wanted to impress the authorities with their "respect for rules," they then inflated their reported ratings, and by an equivalent degree across the moral and conventional transgressions. Thus, their reported ratings ended up at equally high levels rather than equally low levels. The nonpsychopathic inmates, in contrast, were just as motivated to inflate their ratings, but they were starting from genuine unequal levels, so they ended up reporting unequal levels. To strengthen his interpretation, Blair noted that the two groups of inmates also differed in their justifications of transgression judgments; in particular, the psychopathic inmates generated fewer harm-based justifications (e.g., "He hurt him") than the nonpsychopathic inmates when justifying their judgments of moral transgressions. In contrast, the two groups were alike in generating rule-based justifications when the transgressions were conventional (e.g., "It's wrong" in answer to Question 4).

But these differences between psychopathic and nonpsychopathic inmates, when justifying their judgments of moral transgressions, need not indicate any differences in the processes that were invoked earlier when the two groups actually made their judgments. Hauser (2006a) makes a similar point (see also the Rawlsian model in Figure 5.1) when he comments that people sometimes have no idea about why they make the moral judgments they do, although one might respond by suggesting that people just cannot adequately articulate their genuine reasons. Setting aside the differences in justifications generated by the psychopathic and nonpsychopathic inmates, there is an alternate, equally plausible, interpretation of Blair's (1995) data. This is that the inmates' genuine (nonconfounded) ratings of moral transgressions were already close to ceiling for both groups; after all, these transgressions are far more heinous than conventional transgressions. If so, then any manipulative inflation on the part of the psychopathic inmates would have had very little effect on these already high ratings and would have affected only those ratings where there was more room to move—that is, when rating the conventional transgressions. In this case, the psychopathic inmates would have obscured their genuine capacity to make the moral–conventional distinction by manipulatively inflating their reported ratings. In contrast, the nonpsychopathic inmates might not have inflated their genuine ratings at all; after all, by definition, they would not be calculating and manipulative like the psychopaths. In this case, their genuine capacity to make the moral–conventional distinction was transparently evident in their reported ratings.

In sum, we think that Blair's (1995) data do not rule out that the psychopathic inmates knew the difference between moral and conventional transgressions, even though the two groups differed in their reported ratings of conventional transgressions and in their post hoc justifications of moral-transgression judgments. Adding to our doubts is that Blair et al. (1997) failed to replicate Blair's (1995) pattern of data. In this later study, Blair and colleagues reexamined the moral–conventional distinction in 18 adult psychopathic inmates and 18 nonpsychopathic controls. Now the researchers found that the psychopathic inmates did register a significant moral–conventional distinction with regard to their ratings of the seriousness of transgressions, although not with regard to either their judgments of impermissibility or authority modifiability. A similar group difference in the seriousness ratings for moral versus conventional transgressions, although not significant, can also be seen in Blair's earlier 1995 data (refer again to Figure 5.2b).

Doubts about how best to interpret Blair's (1995) data from manipulative incarcerated adults makes it all the more telling that later studies of the moral–conventional distinction in children with psychopathic tendencies, who were not incarcerated in prison hospitals at the time of testing, failed to replicate the 1995 pattern. In 1997, Blair tested 16 psychopathically inclined children (mean age of 13.2 years) and 16 children without psychopathic attributes (mean age of 12.8 years), identified thus using the Psychopathy Screening Device (PSD; Frick & Hare, 2000). The children were all aggressive or hyperactive and were considered too difficult to educate in mainstream schools, so they were resident in a special boarding school for children with "emotional and behavioral difficulties" at the time of testing. Counter to Blair and colleagues' earlier results, these difficult children with and without psychopathic tendencies made the moral–conventional distinction to the same degree in their reported judgments of impermissibility and seriousness. The children with psychopathic tendencies did, however, judge the moral transgressions to be more modifiable via authority than the children without psychopathic tendencies. Nevertheless, the psychopathically inclined children still registered the distinction between moral and conventional transgressions, even on the authority modifiability question, although not to the same degree. Of further note, the two groups did not differ in their justifications of moral-transgression judgments. A later study of similarly aged children with and without psychopathic tendencies, who were likewise resident in a special boarding school, revealed largely similar results (see Blair, Monson, & Frederickson, 2001).

We suggest that these inconsistencies between forensic and nonforensic studies cast serious doubt on the robustness of the claim that psychopaths fail to make the moral–conventional distinction. We also suggest that these inconsistencies highlight the importance of studying moral reasoning in nonincarcerated adults with psychopathic tendencies. So we turn now to consider the "continuity approach" and the use of the individual differences methodology to study psychopathy.

THE CONTINUITY APPROACH TO PSYCHOPATHY

The continuity, or dimensional, approach assumes that common factors, of perhaps varying severity, underpin both nonclinical (and nonforensic), and clinical (or forensic) manifestations of psychopathic attitudes and behaviors (Board & Fritzon, 2005). In keeping with this approach, Cleckley (1976) described successful people, who might be respected surgeons or business people in society but who nevertheless still showed similar impairments in emotion processing to the deficits seen in criminal psychopaths. In comparison to the 15–25% of incarcerated criminals who are estimated to be psychopathic, only 1% of the general nonincarcerated population is estimated to show a similar degree of pathological psychopathy to criminal psychopaths (Kirkman, 2002). Psychopathy may be more common in certain social groups within the general community however (e.g., the snakes in suits of today's corporate world) as suggested by Hare. More importantly, though, these estimated rates of psychopathic tendencies in noncriminal populations may actually be underestimating the true extent of nonincarcerated psychopathy. This is because previous studies that have assessed psychopathic tendencies in nonclinical nonincarcerated populations (e.g., Forth, Brown, Hart, & Hare, 1996) have tended to use screening versions of the forensic/clinical PCL-R (PCL:SV; Hart, Cox, & Hare, 1995), or similar clinical tools. Tools of this type emphasize criminal deviancy and so are unlikely to be sufficiently sensitive to detect psychopathic tendencies in nonincarcerated individuals, who have likely found other, strictly legal, yet still amoral, outlets for their callous, manipulative tendencies (see, e.g., Patrick et al., 2009, for discussion). These so-called successful psychopaths may also possess other qualities, such as higher levels of intelligence or executive control (when compared with incarcerated psychopaths), that would help them to elude detection by authorities and also by experimenters, who are relying on fairly transparent clinical tools.

To overcome these limitations, researchers have begun to use the individual differences methodology to assess varying levels of psychopathic attributes in nonincarcerated adults. This methodology relies upon anonymous self-report inventories such as the Psychopathic Personality Index (PPI; Lilienfield & Andrews, 1996), the Levenson Primary and Secondary Psychopathy Scales (LPSP; Levenson, Kiehl, & Fitzpatrick, 1995), and the Self-Report Psychopathy Scale II (SRP-II; Hare, Harpur, & Hemphill, 1989). In our own work, we have chosen to use later versions of the SRP (e.g., the SRP-III; Williams, Nathanson, & Paulhus, 2003; Paulhus,

Hemphill, & Hare, in press). This is because the SRP was developed originally to mirror the PCL-R and thus shares a close theoretical association with one of the gold-standard measures of forensic psychopathy (Williams & Paulhus, 2004). Self-report ratings on the SRP provide subscale scores for the following:

1. Callous affect (example items include "Most people are wimps" and "I never feel guilty over hurting others")
2. Interpersonal manipulation (example items include "I purposely flatter people to get them on my side" and "I get a kick out of 'scamming' someone")
3. Erratic impulse lifestyle (example items include "I enjoy doing wild things" and "I keep getting in trouble for the same things over and over")
4. Antisocial tendencies (example items include "Every now and then I carry a weapon, knife, or gun" and "I have threatened people into giving me money, clothes, or makeup")

The SRP-III is psychometrically sound with reported internal consistencies (measured using Cronbach's α) of .74, .76, .67, and .91 for the four subscales and an overall scale reliability of .88 (Williams, Nathanson, & Paulhus, 2003). Good validity has also been shown with strong positive correlations between the SRP-III total and subscale scores and other established psychopathy measures, including, for example, the Levenson Self-Report Psychopathy Scale (Williams et al., 2003). Further evidence of validity comes from factor-analytic studies that have shown that the SRP taps two personality-based factors (interpersonal manipulation and callous affect) and two behavioral factors (erratic lifestyle and antisocial tendencies) that largely mirror the factor structure of the PCL-R (Williams, Paulhus, & Hare, 2007).

Mahmut, Homewood, and Stevenson (2008) also provided behavioral evidence to validate the SRP-III. They showed that nonincarcerated adults with higher (compared with lower) SRP scores performed like incarcerated psychopaths in making significantly riskier decisions on the Iowa Gambling Task. Moreover, these researchers found that high SRP scorers also self-reported lower levels of empathetic responsiveness on the Emotional Empathy Questionnaire (EEQ; Mehrabian & Epstein, 1972). In other related experimental work, Aylett, Mahmut, Langdon, and Green (2005) also used the SRP to show that the identification of negative facial expressions (e.g., fear, disgust) is relatively impaired in university students with higher compared with lower levels of psychopathic attributes. This latter result is consistent with reports of similar emotion recognition deficits in clinical or incarcerated psychopaths. Aylett and colleagues also found that images of emotional facial expressions presented subliminally, just before an abstract drawing, failed to influence the psychopathically inclined participants' ratings of likeability of drawings; in contrast, the participants with lower SRP scores were unconsciously influenced by the emotional primes. An earlier forensic study of affective and semantic priming, which had used word rather than pictorial stimuli, reported largely similar results (Blair, Richell, Mitchell, Leonard, Morton, & Blair, 2006); the psychopathic inmates in that study were found to show less affective priming than the nonpsychopathic inmates but equivalent semantic priming.

In other related work in our lab, we have examined whether nonincarcerated individuals with higher levels of psychopathic attributes resemble clinical or incarcerated psychopaths in showing a dissociation between intact theory of mind (or understanding of other people's cognitive mental states, such as intentions and beliefs) and impaired empathic responsiveness (see Blair, 2005, for discussion of intact cognitive empathy and impaired affective empathy in psychopaths; and also Hawes & Dadds, Chapter 3, this volume). In one such study, 340 university students were screened using the SRP. Respondents with ratings in the upper and lower 20th percentile (according to gender, since females generally self-report lower SRP scores) were then asked to complete the Interpersonal Reactivity Index (IRI; Davis, 1980), which comprises four subscales, as follows:

1. Empathic concern (feeling compassion and concern for others)
2. Perspective-taking (an ability to adopt the mental viewpoints of others, or theory of mind)
3. Personal distress (feeling unease and discomfort in reaction to others' emotions)
4. Fantasy (an engagement with fictitious characters in books or movies)

In accord with Blair (2005), we expected the high SRP scorers (11 males, 12 females) to differ from the low SRP scorers (10 males, 11 females) only on the empathic concern and personal distress subscales. In other words, we expected the high SRP scorers to self-report lower levels of empathic concern and personal distress, alongside similar levels of perspective-taking and fantasy to the low SRP scorers. Counter to our expectations, however, the high SRP scorers also self-reported lower levels of perspective-taking, as well as lower levels of empathic concern and personal distress. Lower levels of perspective-taking would not be predicted if theory of mind abilities are unrelated to psychopathic attributes. Closer examination of the IRI items revealed, however, that the perspective-taking items on this scale tend to focus on imaginative projection to understand another person's inner world (e.g., "I sometimes try to understand my friends better by imagining how things look from their perspective"). Perhaps psychopaths do not use their imagination to understand what another person might want or believe; perhaps they rely instead on third-person theory of mind reasoning rather than first-person perspective taking. To explore this idea further, another one of our colleagues (Berry, 2007) went on to use a different empathy and mentalizing scale that comprises items worded more neutrally with regard to how a cognitive understanding of others' mental lives might be achieved. This scale is the abridged Empathy Quotient (EQ; Muncer & Ling, 2006), which comprises three subscales assessing the following:

1. Empathetic concern (an example item is "I really enjoy caring for other people")
2. Social skills (an example item is "I find it hard to know what to do in a social situation": reverse-scored)

3. Cognitive empathy (or theory of mind; example items include "I am good at predicting how someone will feel" and "I can easily work out what another person might want to talk about")

A total of 48 university students with SRP scores in the upper or lower quartiles (12 males and 12 females per low or high group), drawn from an initial sample of 222, were called back to complete the abridged EQ. Results once again revealed significant group differences, but now only for the empathetic concern scores (which were lower in the high SRP scorers) and not for the cognitive empathy and social skills scores, entirely consistent with the dissociation that has been found in clinical or incarcerated psychopaths between impaired affective empathy (reflected in the psychopath's callousness) and intact theory of mind (consistent with the psychopath's adroit social manipulation). Berry's finding of no association between self-reported measures of cognitive empathy and psychopathic attributes also accords with Aylett and colleagues' (2005) earlier behavioral data showing no differences in the theory of mind task performances of nonincarcerated adults with high versus low SRP scores. Having thus reassured ourselves of the validity of the SRP in our own lab, we went on to examine the moral–conventional distinction in groups of individuals with high and low SRP scores.

THE MORAL–CONVENTIONAL DISTINCTION IN NONCLINICAL NONINCARCERATED ADULTS WITH VARYING LEVELS OF PSYCHOPATHIC ATTRIBUTES

University students with high and low SRP scores in the upper and lower 20th percentile by gender as well as a medium group that fell within the 10th percentile above or below the median were called back from an initial sample of 340 to perform the moral–conventional distinction task. Full results are reported in Langdon and Delmas (in preparation). There were 21 participants in the Low-P group (11 females), 19 in the Mid-P group (10 females), and 23 in the High-P group (12 females). Our task was similar to that used by Blair (1995), although we also included some nontransgression stories to provide more of a contrast with the transgression stories (there were no differences among the three groups on these nontransgression stories). We also presented the stories on a computer monitor with the participants being asked to judge the impermissibility of the transgression (i.e., whether the behavior is okay or not okay). When an act was judged not okay, the participants were then asked the following:

1. On a scale of 1 (slightly) to 10 (extremely), how not okay was it for the child to do X? (to examine their seriousness ratings)
2. Why was it not okay for the child to do X? (to examine the content of justifications)
3. Would it be okay for the child to do X if the teacher says the child can? (to examine authority modifiability)

When scoring justifications, we focused on empathetic concern and assigned each justification to one of three categories based on the degree to which a participant made reference to others' welfare: (1) explicit mention of others' welfare, (2) implicit reference to others' welfare or multiple justifications containing at least one reference to others' welfare, and (3) no mention of others' welfare. We hypothesized that, if psychopathic tendencies affect the moral–conventional distinction in nonincarcerated adults, whose responses are unlikely to be confounded by a motivation to inflate responses, there will be a decreasing differential between moral and conventional transgressions as levels of psychopathic attributes increase. The results are illustrated in Figure 5.3.

Some effects were significant; for example, across groups, the proportion of not okay moral transgressions was significantly higher than the proportion of not okay conventional transgressions (all p's ≤ .001). The seriousness results also revealed significant main effects of (1) type of transgression ($p < .0005$), such that, across all participants, moral transgressions were judged more serious ($M = 8.44$) than conventional transgressions ($M = 6.72$); and (2) group ($p = .012$), such that, across transgressions, the Low-P group ($M = 8.14$) judged all transgressions as more serious than the Mid-P ($M = 7.39$) and High-P ($M = 7.20$) groups. The results for justifications also revealed a significant main effect of category ($p < .0005$) and a significant transgression by category interaction ($p < .0005$). The main effect occurred because justifications that made no mention of others' welfare were generally more common. The transgression by category interaction occurred because all participants were more likely to make explicit or implicit mention of others' welfare when justifying their judgments of moral compared with conventional transgressions.

But, as for our primary research question, we found no evidence that increasing levels of psychopathic attributes associated with a decreasing distinction between moral and conventional transgressions, whether we considered impermissibility, seriousness, authority modifiability, or the content of justifications. While our data were thus generally consistent with the pattern of data reported by Blair et al. (1997) when he and his colleagues examined children from special boarding schools with and without psychopathic tendencies, we were concerned that the

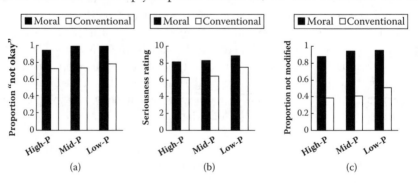

Figure 5.3   (a) Impermissibility: proportion of transgressions judged "not okay." (b) Mean seriousness rating of "not okay" transgressions. (c) Authority modifiability: proportion of "not okay" transgressions still "not okay" even if permitted by authority.

levels of psychopathic attributes in our nonincarcerated sample might not have varied sufficiently to produce any significant effects on moral reasoning tasks. So we went on to test these same individuals using moral dilemmas as the test stimuli.

HOW DO NONCLINICAL, NONINCARCERATED ADULTS WITH VARYING LEVELS OF PSYCHOPATHIC ATTRIBUTES JUDGE ACTS IN MORAL DILEMMAS?

Moral psychologists and social-cognitive neuroscientists have become increasingly interested in the utilitarian and nonutilitarian moral judgments that have long interested philosophers. This relatively new line of psychological research considers the role of intuitive emotional processes and emotion-related areas of the brain in moral judgments and was spearheaded by Greene and colleagues (Greene et al., 2001, 2004), who proposed a distinction between personal and impersonal moral dilemmas. An example of a personal moral dilemma is the classic footbridge scenario (Foot, 1967; Thomson, 1976):

> A runaway trolley is headed for five people who will be killed if it proceeds on its present course. You happen to be standing next to a large stranger on a footbridge that spans the tracks, in between the oncoming trolley and the five people. The only way to save the five people is to push this stranger off the bridge, onto the tracks below. He will die if you do this, but his body will stop the trolley from reaching the others. Should you save the five and push the stranger to his death? Should you maximize utilitarian outcomes or should you avoid a personal moral violation?

Most people judge the act to be inappropriate. An example of an impersonal moral dilemma is a variant of the trolley scenario in which the choice being presented is to pull a switch rather than push the man; the switch will turn the trolley onto an alternate set of tracks where it will kill one person rather than the five. Now more people judge the act to be appropriate.

Inspired, in part, by differences of this type, Greene and colleagues (2001) proposed a dual-process model of moral judgment in which automatic, intuitive emotional responses and effortful conscious reasoning are both engaged when people make moral judgments (see Mackenzie, Chapter 11, this volume, for critical discussion of Greene's philosophical claims). These intuitive and reflective processes are purportedly subserved by dissociable neural systems (Greene, 2003; Greene & Haidt, 2002; Greene et al., 2004). Support for Greene's model comes from evidence that participants take longer to accept, rather than reject, acts that maximize utilitarian outcomes in personal moral dilemmas, whereas they show no such difference when the acts are impersonal (although, see McGuire, Langdon, Coltheart, & Mackenzie, 2009, for a critique of this behavioral support for the personal–impersonal distinction and Greene's, 2009, response). Setting aside the putative personal–impersonal distinction, emotion-based accounts of moral judgment have drawn general support from (1) studies of neurological patients who show a relation between impoverished emotional responses and aberrant moral behavior; (2) neuroimaging studies that show moral judgments in healthy adults activate areas of the emotional brain; (3) clinical research on patients with VMPC brain damage, who show an abnormally utilitarian pattern of judgments when compared with controls; and (4) behavioral studies that purportedly manipulate affective state so as to alter moral judgments (see, e.g., Koenigs et al., 2007, for an overview of these findings; see also Case, Oaten, & Stevenson, Chapter 9, this volume, for a critique of studies that have purported to affect moral judgments by directly manipulating affective state).

Our own interest in these moral dilemmas stems from the claim that they trigger an interaction between automatic emotional aversion to the proposed act, which is putatively subserved by normal functioning of the VMPC (a brain region believed to be compromised in psychopathy), and utilitarian calculation of maximizing the greater good, which is purportedly underpinned by effortful reasoning and cognitive control. Given our interest in nonincarcerated individuals with psychopathic tendencies, Koenigs and colleagues' (2007) study was of most relevance to us. These researchers tested six patients with VMPC lesions who displayed emotional blunting and reduced SCRs to emotionally charged social stimuli (e.g., pictures of social disasters). Patients of this type have sometimes been referred to as *acquired sociopaths* since they show a callous disregard of others' feelings, although they do not show the same calculated manipulation that is seen in developmental psychopaths (see, e.g., Blair, 2007). Koenigs and colleagues also tested 12 brain-damaged control participants with lesions that did not involve the emotion structures of the brain (i.e., the VMPC, amygdala, insula) as well as 12 healthy controls. The groups were matched on age, gender, and ethnicity. Participants were asked to judge the appropriateness of acts in 50 dilemma scenarios, comprising nonmoral, personal-moral, and impersonal-moral scenarios, adapted from the stimuli used by Green et al. (2004). The results are illustrated in Figure 5.4.

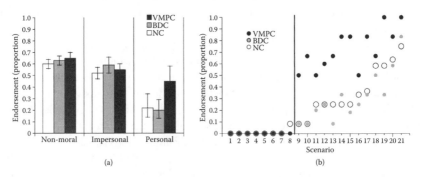

Figure 5.4 (a) Proportion of acts in nonmoral, impersonal, and personal (moral) dilemmas judged appropriate by VMPC patients, brain-damaged controls (BDC), and normal controls (NC). (b) Proportions of subjects per group for each of the 1–21 personal dilemmas (numbered along x-axis from those with the lowest overall endorsement rate to those with the highest overall endorsement rate). (From Koenigs, M., Young, L., Adolphs, R., Tranel, D., Cushman, F., Hauser, M., et al., *Nature*, 446, 908–911, 2007. With permission.)

In brief, the VMPC patients were significantly more likely to endorse acts in personal-moral dilemmas. This pattern was present for each personal-moral dilemma, with the exception of those that were rejected by 100% of the participants (see Figure 5.4b). These findings were taken to support the view that the VMPC, a brain region that is known to be normally activated by socially aversive stimuli (e.g., faux pas stories: Stone, Baron-Cohen, & Knight, 1998), plays a crucial role when healthy adults judge the right or wrong of acts in morally complex scenarios.

So we wanted to see whether the same nonincarcerated adults with psychopathic tendencies, who had distinguished between moral and conventional transgressions just like the individuals with lower levels of psychopathic attributes, would perform like the VMPC patients in the Koenigs et al. (2007) study or the controls when judging moral dilemmas. If the latter proved to be the case, this would suggest that levels of psychopathic attributes in our nonincarcerated sample did not vary sufficiently to affect any sort of moral judgment; if the former proved to be the case, this would suggest that the moral–conventional distinction task and moral dilemmas trigger different processes or the same processes to varying degrees.

Given the debate about the validity of the personal-impersonal distinction (see, e.g., McGuire et al., 2009), we focused on the high-conflict dilemmas that best discriminated between VMPC patients and controls. We also included five nonmoral dilemmas for baseline comparison purposes. In addition, we distinguished between five self-preservation moral dilemmas, where the central theme involved sacrificing another person for the benefit of not only other people but also oneself (e.g., to stay alive), and five altruistic dilemmas, where there was no direct benefit to self. An example of a self-preservation scenario is as follows:

> You and a group of ecologists are studying wildlife in a remote jungle when you are captured by terrorists and held hostage. One of the terrorists takes a liking to you. He tells you that his leader intends to kill you and the other hostages. He is willing to help you all escape, but he needs some assurance that you won't go to the police. So, he will videotape you while you kill one of your colleagues. The tape will ensure your silence and make it possible for the remainder of you to escape. Is it appropriate for you to kill one of your colleagues to save yourself and the others?

We also extended the paradigm to ask: "On a scale from 1 (not at all likely) to 10 (very likely), how likely is it that you would perform such an act yourself?" In accord with Koenigs and colleagues (2007), we predicted that, if psychopathic tendencies in the general community have similar effects to known VMPC brain damage, higher levels of psychopathic attributes will be associated with (1) higher endorsement rates of acts in moral dilemmas, and (2) higher ratings of the likelihood of performing such an act oneself. We also speculated that, given the characteristic egocentricity of psychopathic individuals, these patterns might be more pronounced for the self-preservation dilemmas.

Figure 5.5 summarizes our results (for full details see Langdon & Delmas, in preparation). Despite the null findings from our earlier study of the moral–conventional distinction, psychopathic tendencies in the general community were

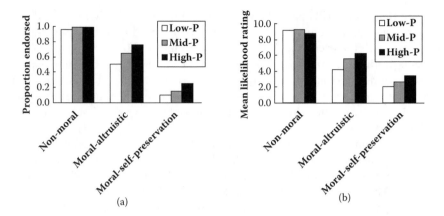

Figure 5.5 (a) Proportion of acts in nonmoral, "moral-altruistic," and "moral-self-preservation" dilemmas judged appropriate by groups of nonincarcerated adults with low, medium, and high levels of psychopathy (Low-P, Mid-P, and High-P, respectively). (b) Mean likelihood (1–10) of performing the act oneself in the three groups.

found to associate significantly with differential responses to the moral dilemmas in accord with the performances of VMPC patients. Across the two types of moral dilemmas (self-preservation and altruistic), there was a significant main effect of group, such that higher levels of psychopathic attributes were associated with a higher endorsement rate for emotionally aversive acts that maximized the greatest good ($p = .011$). Likewise, the more likely were the participants with higher levels of psychopathic attributes to rate themselves as being prepared to perform such acts ($p = .001$). Somewhat to our surprise we found that this pattern was no more marked for the self-preservation than altruistic scenarios. Participants, in general, were less prepared to endorse acts in self-preservation scenarios. Thus, it seems generally less okay to perform emotionally aversive acts, even if these are for the greater good, if there is also some benefit to the self. However, we urge caution here since the self-preservation and altruistic scenarios were not matched, so we cannot be sure that it was the presence versus absence of a self-preservation theme that was making for the critical difference here.

We conclude by summarizing our findings and considering whether they might offer some insights concerning the three prominent approaches to moral judgments illustrated previously in Figure 5.1.

SUMMARY AND POSSIBLE IMPLICATIONS FOR MODELS OF MORAL JUDGMENT

Studies of differences between individuals with and without psychopathic tendencies may inform understanding of the factors that sustain fully developed moral capacities. Previous findings that adult criminal psychopaths fail to make the moral–conventional distinction when judging simple transgressions, when even young children can appreciate this distinction, have been taken to provide strong support for a sentimentalist (or emotion-based) approach to moral reasoning. Our review of these findings highlighted confounds inherent in researching incarcerated populations. Blair (1995) interpreted his data from 10 psychopathic and 10 nonpsychopathic inmates of prison hospitals as consistent with the claim that the psychopathic inmates genuinely responded to the moral transgressions as if they were less serious, like conventional transgressions, and then inflated their genuinely lower ratings to impress authorities. We suggested, instead, that his data can just as plausibly be interpreted to suggest that the psychopathic inmates could genuinely distinguish between the moral and conventional transgressions. The psychopathic inmates (but not the nonpsychopathic inmates) then manipulatively inflated their reported ratings, which affected their ratings of conventional transgressions, but not their ratings of moral transgressions, which were already close to ceiling. We also cautioned that Blair's finding of fewer references to harming or hurting others in the psychopathic inmates' justifications of moral-transgression judgments, when compared with the nonpsychopathic inmates' justifications, need not imply any differences in the processes that were engaged when the two groups made their earlier judgments.

Our suspicions that the psychopathic inmates might, in fact, have known the difference between moral and conventional transgressions grew when we reviewed follow-up studies of the moral–conventional distinction in difficult children with and without psychopathic tendencies, who were resident in special boarding schools and not incarcerated in prison hospitals. The findings of these later studies are arguably more robust since it seems unlikely that the children were motivated to manipulate authority figures to gain their release. These studies of difficult children provided substantial evidence that pathologically clinical psychopathic individuals do know the difference between moral and conventional transgressions, at least as indexed by their ratings of impermissibility, seriousness, and authority modifiability. Although we acknowledge that the psychopathic groups generally made fewer references to harming or hurting others when justifying their judgments of moral transgressions, nevertheless, even with regard to the findings for justifications, there was still evidence that the psychopathic children made a moral–conventional distinction, just not as much of a distinction as the nonpsychopathic children.

In light of these inconsistencies between forensic and nonforensic studies and the difficulties with interpreting data from incarcerated populations, some of whom are known to be manipulative by virtue of the very nature of the psychopathy that one is trying to research, we advocated for a greater focus on psychopathic tendencies in nonincarcerated adults. Work of this type adopts a continuity approach and assumes that common factors, of perhaps varying severity, underpin both clinical (or forensic) and nonclinical (and nonforensic) manifestations of psychopathy. We argued that these successful psychopaths and snakes in suits warrant closer scientific attention in their own right, not only because of the great social and economic harm that they can cause but also because they may show a purer form of the emotional and moral dysfunctions that purportedly lie at the core of psychopathy. In other words, by investigating such individuals we avoid confounds of impulsive criminal deviancy that may be a feature of incarcerated psychopaths.

We then went on to review empirical support for the continuity approach and the use of individual differences methodology to study psychopathic tendencies. This support included that psychopathic tendencies in the general population, identified via self-report inventories, associate with some of the same factors (e.g., poor recognition of negative emotional facial expressions and an absence of affective priming) that distinguish between psychopathic and nonpsychopathic groups in clinical or incarcerated populations.

In our own lab, we also validated the continuity approach by demonstrating that psychopathically inclined individuals, identified via self-report, also self-report restricted empathic responsiveness toward others but not impoverished cognitive understanding of others' mental lives—a dissociation that is also seen in clinical or incarcerated psychopaths and accords with findings of intact theory of mind task performances in nonincarcerated individuals with psychopathic tendencies.

Our own work on the moral–conventional distinction in nonincarcerated adults with varying levels of psychopathic attributes then revealed a similar pattern of data reported in previous studies of psychopathically inclined children, who were resident in special boarding schools. That is, psychopathic attributes did not associate with differential responses to moral and conventional transgressions, whether we considered either the participants' ratings of impermissibility, seriousness, and authority modifiability or their justifications of judgments. It is acknowledged here, though, that previous studies of clinical or incarcerated psychopathic individuals generally report less of a tendency to generate harm-based justifications of moral-transgression judgments. In sum, when confounds inherent in work with incarcerated populations are avoided, findings suggest that psychopathically inclined individuals, who show relative deficiencies of moral agency, nevertheless do know the difference between moral and conventional transgressions, at least when that knowledge is indexed by explicit judgments and justifications. We then went on to consider their automatic proclivities to amoral behavior.

A potential criticism of the null findings from our first study is that levels of psychopathic attributes might not have varied sufficiently in our university student sample to reveal any significant association between psychopathic attributes and moral reasoning, even though similar previous studies of nonincarcerated psychopathy have revealed significant relations between levels of psychopathic attributes and recognition of others' facial affect as well as responses to subliminal emotional primes. Nevertheless, tasks inevitably differ in their sensitivity. This is why it was imperative that we use another moral-reasoning paradigm with the same participants. So, we followed Koenigs and colleagues' (2007) work. These researchers showed that patients with VMPC lesions, who are emotionally unresponsive to others in daily life, are also more prepared to endorse emotionally aversive acts that maximize the greater good in moral dilemmas. We used similar moral dilemmas with the same nonincarcerated adults who had shown an equivalent appreciation of the moral–conventional distinction across varying levels of psychopathic attributes. Now we found a pattern of data that closely mirrored the data reported by Koenigs and colleagues—that is, nonincarcerated adults with higher levels of psychopathic attributes were more prepared to endorse the emotionally aversive acts and also rated themselves as more likely to carry out such acts. We take the view that the relation between levels of psychopathic attributes and endorsement rates of acts in moral dilemmas is mediated by the degree of aversive arousal triggered automatically by the thought of personally harming another person. Remember that the moral dilemmas elicit a first-person perspective—what would you do?—while the moral–conventional distinction task asks participants to make an explicit third-person judgment about transgressions (see Kennett, Chapter 12, this volume, who also contrasts first-person and third-person moral judgments).

In sum, our studies of moral reasoning suggest no effects of psychopathic attributes on moral reasoning when the moral judgment involves third-person knowledge of the right or wrong and the seriousness of different kinds of transgressions. It was only when the judgment task tapped an automatic emotional curb on tendencies to personally harm another person that we saw a significant effect of psychopathic attributes on task results. Psychopathically inclined individuals may thus know, in a third-person way, that amoral acts are more serious than conventional transgressions; perhaps they have learned this distinction in childhood through observing the more serious consequences of the former even though they don't appear to react to those more serious consequences in the same way that nonpsychopathically inclined individuals do (e.g., showing deficits in aversive conditioning). In contrast, it appears that psychopathically inclined individuals do not respond intuitively to the thought of personally harming another person as aversively as do individuals with lower levels of psychopathic attributes. As Blair (1995, 2005) suggests, individuals who are not psychopathically inclined may have developed a care-based moral agency that derives, at least in part, from automatic aversive curbs on calculated acts of aggression toward others. Sometimes (but not always) this care-based morality manifests in a spontaneous tendency to generate more harm-based justifications of moral-transgression judgments.

We now consider the implications of our findings for the three models of moral judgment illustrated in Figure 5.1. Recall that we had hypothesized that if psychopathic attributes in a nonincarcerated sample affect responses to moral dilemmas but not performances on the moral–conventional distinction task, this would suggest that moral dilemmas and the moral–conventional distinction task tap different processes or the same processes to varying degrees. We have already speculated about some of the different processes that might be involved (e.g., explicit third-person judgments versus an automatic aversion to personally harming another). If so, it seems that our findings are most consistent with the Humean–Kantian model, since this model allows for an interaction between aversive emotional responses and conscious reasoning.

According to the Humean–Kantian model, one might argue, for example, that both the moral dilemmas and the transgression judgments were mediated primarily by the nonemotional conscious reasoning of the individuals with higher levels of psychopathic attributes. When they were presented with the moral dilemma scenarios, these more psychopathically inclined individuals thus reacted with less emotional aversion to the perceived acts of personally causing harm to another person, explaining their higher endorsement rates. And, in the case of the transgression scenarios, the psychopathically inclined individuals showed a moral–

conventional distinction solely because of their conscious reasoning and learned knowledge about relative right and wrong.

We digress slightly at this point to consider just what sort of learning or acquisition of moral knowledge might be involved here. Recall that individuals with higher levels of psychopathic attributes show no relative impairments on theory of mind tasks and self-report similar levels of cognitive perspective-taking as individuals with lower levels of psychopathic attributes, at least when questionnaire items are neutral with regard to how a cognitive understanding of others is achieved, although not when the items probe imagining what it would be like to be in the mental shoes of another person. Perhaps then, psychopathically inclined individuals develop, in childhood, an understanding of others' mental lives and a degree of moral knowledge by being observant little third-person scientists rather than imaginative empathizers.

Turning back now to consider a Humean–Kantian interpretation of the performances of adults with lower levels of psychopathic attributes on the two moral reasoning tasks, one would simply argue that these individuals were more influenced by their intuitive emotional responses than their conscious reasoning. This is why they were less likely to endorse the acts that involved causing personal harm to others on the moral dilemmas task. As for their performances on the moral–conventional distinction task, both their emotional responses and their conscious reasoning would have reinforced each other, resulting in their generating more severe judgments of moral versus conventional transgressions.

In contrast, we think that our results are more problematic for a purely Humean approach (see Kennett, Chapter 12, this volume, who also doubts a purely Humean, or simple sentimentalist, view). This is the view that a perceived (or imagined) act triggers an automatic emotional response, which, in turn, unconsciously triggers an intuitive judgment as to whether the perceived act is morally right or wrong. On this view, any conscious reasoning comes into play only after the moral judgment has been made, when making post hoc rationalizations. If so, and if conscious reasoning cannot mediate the influence of an automatic emotional response, why was there sufficient variation in the automatic emotional response of our sample to influence participants' moral dilemma judgments but not their transgression judgments? Certainly, the perceived acts in the moral dilemmas appear more emotionally aversive. But if the differences across tasks are due solely to a stronger emotional signal in the dilemma scenarios compared with transgression scenarios, there is a problem. This is because the psychopathically inclined individuals performed just like the individuals with lower levels of psychopathic attributes when judging the less emotionally evocative transgressions. So they must have had sufficient sensitivity to these less aversive stimuli to allow them to perform just like the individuals with lower levels of psychopathic attributes. Yet these same psychopathically inclined individuals must have had insufficient sensitivity when it came to processing the more evocative moral dilemmas to cause them to perform significantly different from the individuals with fewer psychopathic attributes. This does not follow; hence, we doubt that any differences in the emotional evocativeness of the dilemma versus transgression scenarios can adequately account for our findings on a purely Humean account.

However, some other differences between the two tasks might be confounding our results. First, not all moral transgressions involve personally harming another person (e.g., some involve damaging property). But, once again, that would seem to suggest that less rather than more of an emotional response is triggered by the transgression versus dilemma scenarios. Second, the implications of the acts in the two types of scenario differ. For example, there are immediate implications with regard to maximizing the greater good in the moral dilemma scenarios (i.e., saving more lives in the end) that do not feature in the simple moral transgression stories (e.g., in the latter case, a child is hit or a playground swing is broken). So, a pure Humean might want to argue that there are fundamentally different types of perceived acts and that moral dilemmas and the moral–conventional distinction task fall into fundamentally different categories of moral judgment. As noted already, the two tasks do differ with regard to eliciting a first-person versus third-person perspective. But, whether one argues for different categories of first-person versus third-person moral judgments or different contextual influences that shape the perception of acts and, in turn, modulate the emotional response, it is not obvious how one would augment a purely Humean model to incorporate such influences on moral judgments, not if one wants to retain a purely Humean focus on the emotional response doing all of the causal work.

As for a Rawlsian model, this can do a fairly good job of explaining our data from the moral–conventional distinction task since, on this account, emotion does not play a role when making moral judgments, and influences only post hoc reactions and justifications. Thus, this view is entirely consistent with the psychopathically inclined individuals, who show relative emotional deficiencies, judging the impermissibility, seriousness, and authority modifiability of moral transgressions just like individuals with lower levels of psychopathic attributes. It would only be when the individuals with and without psychopathic tendencies generate post hoc justifications of their judgments of transgressions that their differing emotional proclivities might sometimes show effects, although not in our own data. Explaining the data from the moral dilemmas task is more problematic, however. Perhaps a Rawlsian might respond to this data set by suggesting that the unconscious analysis of causal and intentional properties of perceived acts needs to be carved up in some principled way such that some subdomain that is critical for moral dilemmas (and not transgression scenarios) is relatively compromised in psychopathically inclined individuals. Perhaps differences between first-person versus third-person perspectives might come into play here, although it is not immediately obvious how.

Alternatively, one might augment the Rawlsian model to incorporate a two-stage process. There might, for example, be a first-stage, intuitive, and nonemotional judgment of right vs. wrong of the perceived act and a later second-stage explicit judgment that follows a more deliberative weighing-up of various, and sometimes conflicting, emotions, motivations, and evaluations of context, including the likely consequences of an act. On this augmented account—which may be closer to Rawls's (1971) own view since he focuses on potentially revisable intuitions and considered judgments—the judgments that are made on the very simple moral–conventional distinction task would be determined largely by the intuitive nonemotional first stage, since these stories are quite simple and straightforward.

And this would be why the psychopathically inclined individuals performed like the individuals with lower levels of psychopathic attributes on this task. In contrast, differences between individuals with low versus high levels of psychopathic attributes would show up when judging the moral dilemmas, since these scenarios are more complex, with more implications of the act to be taken into account, including how one would feel about personally harming another person, before explicitly reporting one's moral judgment—feelings that would seem to differ between individuals with and without psychopathic tendencies.

CONCLUSIONS

We did not set out to present data that would definitively adjudicate among the three models of moral judgments. Our aims were first to urge caution with regard to relying too heavily on the potentially confounded data from incarcerated psychopathic populations, which have been interpreted to show a failure to make the moral–conventional distinction in psychopathically inclined individuals. We also wanted to highlight that noncriminal samples of pathologically clinical children with and without psychopathic attributes have provided just as much evidence, if not more, that psychopathically inclined individuals do know the difference between moral and conventional transgressions, including when justifying the wrongness of transgressions. Next we sought to illustrate the potential of adopting a continuity approach to also study psychopathic attributes in the general community. Our own work adopting this approach suggests that nonincarcerated, psychopathically inclined individuals do know that moral transgressions are more blameworthy than conventional transgressions—a form of third-person moral knowledge that might have been acquired, in childhood, through scientific observation and rule acquisition rather than imaginative empathizing with others' mental lives. Where these psychopathically inclined individuals differ from individuals with lower levels of psychopathic attributes is in their reduced automatic aversion to acts of personally harming another person, a relative compromise that causes their greater preparedness to act in ways that conform to utilitarian judgments.

We leave others to debate whether that's the sort of morality that we ought to prefer since it's a sort of noncaring morality, at least at the level of an automatic emotional curb on harming others. While there is no doubt that utilitarian judgments sometimes require that we override our automatic emotional responses, we do not think that this should be taken to mean that our automatic emotional inclinations are morally misleading, not all of the time, and perhaps not even most of the time. Indeed, our own and others' data on moral judgments in psychopathically inclined individuals suggest that intuitive feelings of aversion at the thought of harming another person play a critical role in protecting against the development of amoral psychopathic tendencies.

With regard to the implications of our findings for current models of moral judgments, we take the view that our results count against either a purely Humean or purely Rawlsian approach and support a Humean–Kantian model.

REFERENCES

Anderson, S. W., Bechara, A., Damasio, H., Tranel, D., & Damasio, A. R. (1999). Impairment of social and moral behavior related to early damage in human prefrontal cortex. *Nature Neuroscience*, 2, 1032–1037.

Aylett, M., Mahmut, M., Langdon, R., & Green, M. (2005). Social cognition in non-forensic psychopathy. *Acta Neuropsychiatrica*, 18, 328.

Berry, S. (2007). *Psychopathy: An abnormality in the mirroring of others' emotions.* Unpublished thesis.

Blair, K. S., Richell, R. A., Mitchell, D. J. V., Leonard, A., Morton, J., & Blair, R. J. R. (2006). They know the words, but not the music: Affective and semantic priming in individuals with psychopathy. *Biological Psychology*, 73, 114–123.

Blair, R. J. R. (1995). A cognitive developmental approach to morality: Investigating the psychopath. *Cognition*, 57, 1–29.

Blair, R. J. R. (1997). Moral reasoning and the child with psychopathic tendencies. *Personality and Individual Differences*, 22, 731–739.

Blair, R. J. R. (2001). Neurocognitive models of aggression, the antisocial personality disorders, and psychopathy. *Journal of Neurology, Neurosurgery & Psychiatry*, 71, 727–731.

Blair, R. J. R. (2005). Responding to the emotions of others: Dissociating forms of empathy through the study of typical and psychiatric populations. *Consciousness and Cognition*, 14, 698–718.

Blair, R. J. R. (2007). The amygdala and ventromedial prefrontal cortex in morality and psychopathy. *Trends in Cognitive Sciences*, 9, 387–392.

Blair, R. J. R., & Coles, M. (2000). Expression recognition and behavioural problems in early adolescence. *Cognitive Development*, 15, 421–434.

Blair, R. J. R., Colledge, E., Murray, L., & Mitchell, D. G. V. (2001). A selective impairment in the processing of sad and fearful expressions in children with psychopathic tendencies. *Journal of Abnormal Child Psychology*, 29, 491–498.

Blair, R. J. R., Jones, L., Clark, F., & Smith, M. (1997). The psychopathic individual: A lack of responsiveness to distress cues? *Psychophysiology*, 34, 192–198.

Blair, R. J. R., Mitchell, D. G. V., Peschardt, K. S., Colledge, E., Leonard, R. A., Shine, J. H., et al. (2004). Reduced sensitivity to others' fearful expressions in psychopathic individuals. *Personality & Individual Differences*, 37, 1111–1122.

Blair, R. J. R., Monson, J., & Frederickson, N. (2001). Moral reasoning and conduct problems in children with emotional and behavioural difficulties. *Personality & Individual Differences*, 31, 799–811.

Board, B. J., & Fritzon, K. (2005). Disordered personalities at work. *Psychology, Crime and Law*, 11, 17–32.

Brower, M. C., & Price, B. H. (2001). Advances in neuropsychiatry: Neuropsychiatry of frontal lobe dysfunction in violent and criminal behaviour: a critical review. *Journal of Neurology, Neurosurgery and Psychiatry*, 71, 720–726.

Cleckley, H. (1976). *The mask of sanity* (5th ed.). St. Louis, MO: Mosby.

Davis, M. (1980). A multidimensional approach to individual differences in empathy. *JSAS Catalog of Selected Documents in Psychology*, 10, 85.

Delmas, K. (2006). *Psychopathy, empathy and moral reasoning.* Unpublished thesis.

Eysenck, H. J. (1964). *Crime and personality.* London: Routledge & Kegan Paul.

Flor, H., Birbaumer, N., Hermann, C., Ziegler, S., & Patrick, C. J. (2002). Aversive Pavlovian conditioning in psychopaths: Peripheral and central correlates. *Psychophysiology*, 39, 505–518.

Foot, P. (1967). The problem of abortion and the doctrine of double effect. *Oxford Review*, 5, 5–15.

Forth, A. E., Brown, S. L., Hart, S. D., & Hare, R. D. (1996). The assessment of psychopathy in male and female noncriminals: Reliability and validity. *Personality and Individual Differences, 20*, 531–545.

Frick, P. J., & Hare, R. D. (2000). *The psychopathy screening device.* Toronto: Multi-Health Systems.

Frick, P. J., & Hare, R. D. (2001). *Antisocial process screening device.* Toronto: Multi-Health Systems.

Glenn, A. L., & Raine, A. (2009). Psychopathy and instrumental aggression: Evolutionary, neurobiological, and legal perspectives. *International Journal of Law and Psychiatry, 32*, 253–258.

Greene, J. (2003). From neural "is" to moral "ought": What are the moral implications of neuroscientific moral psychology? *Nature Reviews: Neuroscience, 4*, 847–850.

Greene, J. D. (2009). Dual-process morality and the personal/impersonal distinction: A reply to McGuire, Langdon, Coltheart, and Mackenzie. *Journal of Experimental Social Psychology, 45*, 581–584.

Greene, J., & Haidt, J. (2002). How (and where) does moral judgment work? *Trends in Cognitive Sciences, 6*, 517–523.

Greene, J., Nystrom, L. E., Engell, A. D., Darley, J. M., & Cohen, J. D. (2004). The neural bases of cognitive conflict and control in moral judgment. *Neuron, 44*, 389–400.

Greene, J., Sommerville, B. R., Nystrom, L. E., Darley, J. M., & Cohen, J. D. (2001). An fMRI investigation of emotional engagement in moral judgment. *Science, 293*, 2105–2108.

Haidt, J. (2001). The emotional dog and its rational tail: A social intuitionist approach to moral judgment. *Psychological Review, 108*, 814–834.

Hare, R. D. (1980). A research scale for the assessment of psychopathy in criminal populations. *Personality and Individual Differences, 1*, 111–119.

Hare, R. D. (1982). Psychopathy and physiological activity during anticipation of an adversive stimulus in a distraction paradigm. *Psychophysiology, 19*, 266–271.

Hare, R. D. (1991). *The Hare psychopathy checklist—revised.* Toronto: Multi-Health Systems.

Hare, R. D. (1996). Psychopathy: A clinical construct whose time has come. *Criminal Justice and Behavior, 23*, 25–54.

Hare, R. D. (1998). Psychopaths and their nature: Implications for the mental health and criminal justice systems. In T. Millon, E. Simonsen, M. Birket-Smith, & R. D. Davis (Eds.), *Psychopathy: Antisocial, criminal, and violent behavior* (pp. 188–212). New York: Guilford Press.

Hare, R. D. (2003). *The Hare psychopathy checklist—revised (PCL-R),* 2nd ed. Toronto: Multi-Health Systems.

Hart, S., Cox, D., & Hare, R. D. (1995). *Manual for the psychopathy checklist: Screening version (PCL:SV).* Toronto: Multi-Health Systems.

Hart, S. D., Hare, R. D., & Harpur, T. J. (1992). The psychopathy checklist—revised (PCL-R): An overview for researchers and clinicians. In J. C. Rosen & P. McReynolds (Eds.), *Advances in psychological assessment* (vol. 8, pp. 103–130). New York: Plenum Press.

Hare, R. D., Harpur, T. J., & Hemphill, J. F. (1989). *Scoring pamphlet for the Self-Report Psychopathy Scale, SRP-II.* Unpublished document, Simon Fraser University, Vancouver, Canada.

Hauser, M. D. (2006a). The liver and the moral organ. *Social Cognitive and Affective Neuroscience, 1*, 214–220.

Hauser, M. D. (2006b). *Moral minds: How nature designed our universal sense of right and wrong.* New York: Ecco/Harper Collins.

Huebner, B., Dwyer, S., & Hauser, M. (2009). The role of emotion in moral psychology. *Trends in Cognitive Sciences, 13*, 1–6.

Kirkman, C. A. (2002). Non-incarcerated psychopaths: Why we need to know more about the psychopaths who live amongst us. *Journal of Psychiatric and Mental Health Nursing, 9*, 155–160.

Koenigs, M., Young, L., Adolphs, R., Tranel, D., Cushman, F., Hauser, M., et al. (2007). Damage to the prefrontal cortex increases utilitarian moral judgments. *Nature, 446*, 908–911.

Kosson, D. S., Suchy, Y., Mayer, A. R., & Libby, J. (2002). Facial affect recognition in criminal psychopaths. *Emotion, 2*, 398–411.

Langdon, R., & Delmas, K. (in preparation). Moral reasoning and non-criminal psychopathy. *Journal of Research in Personality.*

Levenson, M. R., Kiehl, K. A., & Fitzpatrick, C. M. (1995). Assessing psychopathic attributes in a noninstitutionalized population. *Journal of Personality and Social Psychology, 68*, 151–158.

Lilienfield, S. O., & Andrews, B. P. (1996). Development and preliminary validation of a self-report measure of psychopathic personality traits in noncriminal populations. *Journal of Personality Assessment, 66*, 488–524.

Mahmut, M. K., Homewood, J., & Stevenson, R. J. (2008). The characteristics of non-criminals with high psychopathy traits: Are they similar to criminal psychopaths? *Journal of Research in Personality, 42*, 679–692.

McGuire, J., Langdon, R., Coltheart, M., & Mackenzie, C. (2009). A reanalysis of the personal/impersonal distinction in moral psychology research. *Journal of Experimental Social Psychology, 45*, 577–580.

Mehrabian, A., & Epstein, N. (1972). A measure of emotional empathy. *Journal of Personality, 40*, 525–543.

Moll, J., Oliveira-Souza, R., Bramati, I. E., & Grafman, J. (2002). Functional networks in emotional moral and nonmoral social judgments. *NeuroImage, 16*, 696–703.

Muncer, S. J., & Ling, J. (2006). Psychometric analysis of the empathy quotient (EQ) scale. *Personality and Individual Differences, 40*, 1111–1119.

Patrick, C. J., Bradley, M. M., & Lang, P. J. (1993). Emotion in the criminal psychopath: Startle reflex modulation. *Journal of Abnormal Psychology, 102*, 82–92.

Patrick, C., Fowles, D. C., & Krueger, R. F. (2009). Triarchic conceptualization of psychopathy: Developmental origins of disinhibition, boldness, and meanness. *Development and Psychopathology, 21*, 913–938.

Paulhus, D. L., Hemphill, J. D., & Hare, R. D. (in press). *Manual for the Self-Report Psychopathy scale.* Toronto: Multi-Health Systems.

Prinz, J. (2006). The emotional basis of moral judgments. *Philosophical Explorations, 9*, 29–43.

Raine, A., & Yang, Y. (2006). Neural foundations to moral reasoning and antisocial behavior. *Social, Cognitive, and Affective Neuroscience, 1*, 203–213.

Rawls, J. (1971). *A theory of justice.* Cambridge, MA: Harvard University Press/Belknap Press.

Smetana, J. G. (1981). Preschool children's conceptions of moral and social rules. *Child Development, 52*, 1333–1336.

Smetana, J. G., Kelly, M., & Twentyman, C. T. (1984). Abused, neglected, and nonmaltreated children's conceptions of moral and social-conventional transgressions. *Child Development, 55*, 277–287.

Song, M., Smetana, J. G., & Kim, S. Y. (1987). Korean children's conceptions of moral and conventional transgressions. *Developmental Psychology, 23*, 577–582.

Stevens, D., Charman, T., & Blair, R. J. R. (2001). Recognition of emotion in facial expressions and vocal tones in children with psychopathic tendencies. *Journal of Genetic Psychology, 162*, 201–211.

Stone, V. E., Baron-Cohen, S., & Knight, R. T. (1998). Frontal lobe contributions to theory of mind. *Journal of Cognitive Neuroscience, 10*, 640–656.

Thomson, J. J. (1976). Killing, letting die, and the trolley problem. *Monist*, 59, 204–217.

Williams, K. M., Nathanson, C., & Paulhus, D.L. (2003). Structure and validity of the Self-Report Psychopathy Scale-III in normal populations. 111th Annual convention of the American Psychological Association, Toronto, Canada.

Williams, K. M., & Paulhus, D. L. (2004). Factor structure of the self-report psychopathy scale (SRP-II) in non-forensic samples. *Personality and Individual Differences*, 37, 765–778.

Williams, K. M., Paulhus, D. L., & Hare, R. D. (2007). Capturing the four-factor structure of psychopathy in college students via self-report. *Journal of Personality Assessment*, 88, 205–219.

6

Strange Moralities
Vicarious Emotion and Moral Emotions in Machiavellian and Psychopathic Personality Styles

DORIS MCILWAIN, JESS EVANS, ELENI CALDIS,
FRED CICCHINI, AVI ARONSTAN,
ADAM WRIGHT, and ALAN TAYLOR

Macquarie University

Not all manipulative characters of dubious morality are detected by the criminal justice system. Individuals with psychopathic and Machiavellian tendencies are well represented in the general population. Using McIlwain's cascading constraints model of personality styles we suggest that the different affective deficits of psychopathically inclined and Machiavellian individuals are precursors to deficient and strategic empathy and that empathy deficits in turn predispose these individuals to develop *strange moralities* with little concern for harming another, for which we offer detailed evidence, including a new scale. We asked these dark personalities to make decisions in moral dilemma scenarios (our variants of the Trolley Problem) and to give their rationales. We show the role played by callous unemotionality and blunted, strategic empathy in the display of strange moralities where others are viewed as objects in self-serving accounts cloaked in moral language.

INTRODUCTION

*P*sychopathically inclined and Machiavellian people are relatively amoral, charming manipulators. They have affective deficiencies in the scope and intensity of directly experienced emotion. Psychopathically inclined people have specific deficits in discerning emotions in others, whereas Machiavellians are seen as having a more across-the-board affective muting. Does this also extend to the emotion that they feel on behalf of others—termed *vicarious emotion*? How does empathic capacity relate to morality?

First, we offer a conceptual analysis and a psychometric picture of the overlap and distinctness of the two personality styles in previous research and offer new findings of our own. We then define personality style in terms of *cascading constraints* (McIlwain, 2007, 2008, 2010b). Our focus is on callous-unemotional traits as we see these as most relevant to morality, and we establish that these unemotional traits are shared by psychopathically inclined and Machiavellian individuals.

Our original studies illustrate the cascading constraints approach: Study 1 reveals that psychopathically inclined and Machiavellian people share callous unemotionality, in Study 2a we then link this to a lack of empathy, Study 2b reveals that these individuals also share a strategic use of empathy, and Study 3 links empathy deficiencies to the manifestation of *strange moralities*. We argue that strange moralities—moralities that are self-centered in focus and *harm-blind* in terms of outcome for the other—in psychopathically inclined and Machiavellian people arise as a result of affective deficits that impair the full development of empathy and impede the development of a sense of others as subjects who should not be harmed. We use our original variant of a moral dilemma scenario not only exploring the decisions made by psychopathically inclined and Machiavellian people but also considering in detail the rationales offered. Looking at the words as they are spoken enables us to reveal subtle differences in the moralities of psychopathic and Machiavellian personality styles.

DEFINING THE PERSONALITY STYLES: CONCEPTUALIZATION AND MEASUREMENT

Psychopathy

Early accounts of psychopathy outlined the moral deficiencies of psychopathic characters and the diverse views as to their origin, with references to "innate moral depravity" (Rush, 1812/1947, cited in Smith, 1984) and "acquired moral insanity" (Prichard, 1835, cited in Benn, 1999). By the turn of the nineteenth century, psychopathically inclined people were portrayed as immoral savages without insight into their condition and beyond remediation, requiring asylum for their own safety and that of others (Krafft-Ebing, 1905/2007). Contemporary accounts also suggest that psychopathic people lack moral responsibility, viewing them as unable to form other-regarding moral beliefs or to act for prudential reasons—unable to act in the present moment in ways to secure what they believe to be in their long-term best interest (Adshead, 1999; Fields, 1996). However, whether they lack moral responsibility, not all psychopathically inclined people are recidivist criminals or serial killers. Psychopathic inclinations are at similar levels in the incarcerated and nonincarcerated North American populations; around 1% of the general population show levels of these attributes similar to those seen in incarcerated psychopathic populations (Hare, 1996, 1999; Kirkman, 2002). Psychopathically inclined people are not inevitably detected by the criminal justice system. Hare (1998) suggests that those who escape formal detection can still be charming, if violent, manipulators. He describes them in the following way:

> [These] individuals [,] ... lacking in conscience and feeling for others, find it easy to use charm, manipulation, intimidation and violence to control others and to satisfy their own selfish needs. They ... form a significant proportion of persistent criminals, drug dealers, spouse and child abusers, swindlers and con men, mercenaries, corrupt politicians, unethical lawyers, terrorists, cult leaders, black marketeers, gang members, and radical political activists. (pp. 128–129)

Many psychopathically inclined people have no criminal records and are well represented in the business and corporate world (Kirkman, 2002), where a lack of morality may be of benefit when unaccompanied by vivid displays of antisocial, criminal, or self-defeating behavior. Many so-called successful psychopaths may thus evade detection and seem to function normally in society.

Until recently, research into psychopathy has focused primarily on incarcerated male offenders (although see Belmore & Quinsey, 1994; Ishikawa, Raine, Lencz, Bihrle, & Lacasse, 2001). We are interested in examining psychopathic tendencies in the general population and accordingly adopt a dimensional approach, seeing psychopathy as a matter of degree. We focus on personality traits rather than antisocial behaviors, following Cleckley's (1941/1964) work, which pioneered a personality-based conception of psychopathy. His empirical case studies and the personality profiles developed over years of clinical work drew attention to the following personality traits as well as rash and antisocial behavior: superficial charm in the presence of good *intelligence* and an absence of delusions and other signs of irrational thinking, absence of *nervousness* or psychoneurotic manifestations, unreliability, untruthfulness and insincerity, lack of remorse and shame, poor judgment and failure to learn by experience, pathologic egocentricity and incapacity for love, general poverty in major affective responses, specific loss of insight, and unresponsiveness in general interpersonal relations.

While the early *Diagnostic and Statistical Manual of Mental Disorders*, 1st ed. (*DSM-I*; APA, 1952) was consistent with Cleckley's conception and had emphasized personality features, the current *DSM-IV* (APA, 1994) focuses on defining antisocial personality disorder (ASPD) according to strictly observable behaviors to promote reliability (Lilienfeld, 1994; Lilienfeld & Andrews, 1996). However, we suggest that psychopathic tendencies characterize only a subset of people with ASPD and that, in turn, only a subset of those with psychopathic tendencies show callous unemotionality (as shown in Figure 6.1). Callous unemotionality refers to "characteristics of interpersonal callousness such as a lack of guilt or remorse,

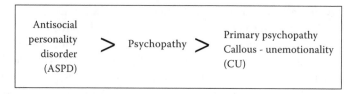

Figure 6.1 Clarifying the relations among ASPD, psychopathy, and callous unemotionality.

an absence of empathy and compassion for others, and shallow and constricted emotions that interfere with the formation of meaningful attachments" (Kerig & Stellwagen, 2009, p. 1). Since there will also be those with callous-unemotional traits who do not exhibit marked antisocial behaviors, we think it is important to distinguish between the personality traits associated with psychopathy as a personality style and the antisocial behaviors that associate with an array of personality disorders.

With regard to assessing psychopathic tendencies in the general community, Lilienfeld (1994) notes that the earlier measures based on observable behavior are likely to overlook successful psychopaths, while Hill (2003) suggests that more behavioral definitions are overinclusive and may include those with ASPD. A focus on observable behaviors also ignores culturally different motivations for antisocial behavior (Lilienfield, 1994, p. 23), potentially confounding personality predispositions with the effects of long-term institutionalization (Kirkman, 2002).

Hare has also contributed to the psychometric assessment of psychopathy. In 1980, he developed the Psychopathy Checklist (PCL) and later the revised version of the scale (PCL-R; Hare, 1991). The PCL-R was found to show two distinct factors. The first factor assessed callous unemotionality and predatory aggression (not necessarily physical), including items to tap pathological lying and emotional poverty. The second factor comprised items addressing antisocial, impulsive behaviors and is closer to the *DSM-IV* (APA, 1994) diagnostic criteria for ASPD. These two factors echo the distinction made by Karpman (1948), who first distinguished *primary* and *secondary* psychopathy. Recent research with the PCL-R shows some researchers arguing for a four-factor solution (Neumann, Hare, & Newman, 2007) and others suggesting the data support either a two-factor or a four-factor solution (Bishopp & Hare, 2008). The PCL-R, while a comprehensive tool involving an interview and a review of collaborative data, was not designed for use with nonincarcerated samples.

To assess larger general-community samples, researchers have developed a number of self-report measures of psychopathic tendencies, such as the Self-Report Psychopathy Scale (LSRP; Levenson, Kiehl, & Fitzpatrick, 1995). The LSRP was designed to measure primary and secondary psychopathy, mirroring the PCL-R factors 1 and 2, respectively. This divide between primary and secondary psychopathy appears to be stable across different measurement scales and across time (Mealey, 1995). For example, in a longitudinal study using a broadband measure of normal personality traits (Multidimensional Personality Questionnaire; Tellegen, 1982), Blonigen, Hicks, Krueger, Patrick, and Iacono (2006) found two broad factors, *fearless dominance* and *impulsive antisociality*, and suggested that these "may reflect separable trait dimensions of personality with distinct etiologic processes" (p. 92). Indeed, twin studies show evidence that two allied risk factors for psychopath—callousness and neuroticism—are both highly heritable and have a high degree of genetic independence (see Viding, 2004, for discussion). Viding suggests that those high in callousness show distinct neurocognitive profiles (e.g., showing emotion processing abnormalities) and distinct patterns of offending: Psychopathic people who are callous start acting against others earlier and are more versatile, showing an emphasis on predatory rather than reactive violence. Frick (1995) and Frick, Cornell, Bodin, Dane, Barry, and Loney (2003) also note that only a subset of children with conduct disorder exhibit the interpersonal characteristics of psychopathy, which are important indicators of future problem behavior.

Machiavellianism

Another personality style marked by a certain affective coolness is Machiavellianism. The concept of the Machiavellian arose from Christie and Geis's (1970) psychological interpretations of the writings of Florentine diplomat Niccolo Machiavelli (1469–1527). His political and social commentaries *The Prince* (Machiavelli, 1513/2003) and *The Discourses* (Machiavelli, 1513/1970) advocate expediency, duplicity, and opportunism while maintaining power and influence in society. The delicate balance required of an individual between the socially cooperative, "what you see is what you get" openness and a more power-oriented willingness to manipulate appearances and to strategically shift tactics can be directly observed in Machiavelli's *The Prince,* where he states of a leader, "It will be well for him to seem and, actually, to be merciful, faithful, humane, frank and religious. But he should preserve a disposition which will make a reversal of conduct possible in case the need arises" (p. 57). Christie and Geis (1970) were the first psychologists to study Machiavellianism as a personality variant. They identified four characteristics of a Machiavellian manipulator: (1) a relative lack of empathy in interpersonal relationships (it is easier to manipulate one viewed as an object than one with whom there is emotional attachment), (2) a lack of concern with conventional morality (a utilitarian view of interactions with others is optimal for manipulation), (3) a lack of gross psychopathology (objective reality testing is not muddied), and (4) low ideological commitments with an emphasis on getting things done.

Using excerpts from *The Prince* and *The Discourses*, Christie and Geis developed a number of self-report scales (Mach II, Mach IV, Mach V) to measure participants' agreement with Machiavelli's statements, such as, "Anyone who completely trusts anyone else is asking for trouble." The research reported in this chapter uses the earlier Mach II, which includes the original 71 items and permits detailed analysis of the subscales; in contrast, the later Mach IV includes only 20 of these items. Three subscales in the Mach II assess the following: (1) views, whether others are portrayed as vain, self-deluded, and out for themselves (e.g., "It is safer to assume most people have a vicious streak"); (2) tactics like flattery and deceit that expediently take advantage of those human weaknesses (e.g., "It is wise to flatter important people"); and (3) morality, which justifies actions with beliefs such as, "Others would do the same if given the chance" (e.g., "There is no point in keeping a promise if it is to your advantage to break it"). High and low scorers on these tests are often referred to in the literature as high and low Machs, respectively.

In line with the prevailing view of psychopathy, Machiavellianism has been found to be unrelated to intellectual ability, gross psychopathology, and (interestingly) economic status (Cherulnik, Way, Ames, & Hutto, 1981; Christie & Geis, 1970). "While not normally considered disordered, dangerous or even overtly antisocial, high Machs are characterized by manipulation, deceit and coercion and exhibit (a) a distinctly cynical view of others, and (b) an apparent lack of affect in interpersonal relations" (Kinner, 2004, p. 41). Findings to date have demonstrated that the Machiavellian is characterized by a preparedness to use manipulative and exploitative strategies and a cluster of attitudes toward the interpersonal world (McIlwain, 2003). For example, Machiavellians are prepared to use others against the interests of those others, armed with strategies like deceit and flattery to target human vanities (Kligman & Culver, 1992), a cynical worldview that suggests such preemptive action is warranted before others get in first and a relativistic morality. Hunter, Gerbing, and Boster (1982) established statistically that the development of cynicism arises before the exploitative, competitive behaviors. Overall, Machiavellian people, like psychopathically inclined people, are charming manipulators who do not think very highly of their fellow humans.

The Psychometric Overlap Between Psychopathically Inclined and Machiavellian People

Some suggest that it is among the subclinical, successful variants of psychopathic people that one finds Machiavellians. Thus, psychopathy is argued by some to be the broader construct, subsuming Machiavellianism. That these two constructs have been researched separately is attributed to professional boundaries by McHoskey, Worzel, and Szyarto (1998); while clinical psychiatrists, criminal psychologists, and more recently experimental cognitive scientists have explored the concept of a psychopathic person, it is largely personality and social psychologists who have investigated the concept of the Machiavellian.

The two personality styles certainly have many descriptive attributes in common (McIlwain, 2008). Early studies conducted by Smith and Griffith (1978) and Ray and Ray (1982) found weak-to-moderate correlations between the two constructs. McHoskey et al. (1998) found that Machiavellian scores were positively correlated with levels of both primary and secondary psychopathy and concluded that Machiavellianism was similar to global psychopathy. They asserted that high Machs represent the successful, white-collar psychopaths in society. However, other researchers have argued that the Machiavellian and psychopathic personalities are overlapping yet distinct constructs (Paulhus & Williams, 2002; Smith, 1999). One reason for these conflicting views is that people use different measures to assess the two constructs, but there may also be subcultural variation. There is overlap as shown by statistical correlation, but differences may emerge using different methodologies. We expect that there will be psychometric overlap between the two personality styles since at the very least we see them as each having a high degree of callous unemotionality.

STUDY 1: STATISTICAL RELATIONSHIPS BETWEEN PSYCHOPATHIC TENDENCIES AND MACHIAVELLIANISM

The following findings are the authors' own initial explorations of the relations between psychopathy and Machiavellianism.

Aims and Methods

To explore the overlap and distinctness of psychopathic and Machiavellian profiles, we assessed a sample of 107 (75 female) voluntary participants, 91.6% of whom were first-year psychology students and 8.4% of whom were recruited from elsewhere. We used the Mach II (Christie & Geis, 1970) and the LSRP (Levenson et al., 1995).

Results and Discussion

There is definite overlap between the two constructs. We found a strong positive correlation of .68 between the mean scores on the Mach II and the overall mean psychopathy score, as assessed using the LSRP (Table 6.1). In line with our expectations, Machiavellianism overlaps strongly (r = .66) with the primary psychopathy, which includes callous-unemotional traits. Primary psychopathy scores were moderately linked to all three Mach II subscales—morality, cynical views, and tactics—used to exploit and play on the vanity of victims. Links between Machiavellianism and primary psychopathy are considerable, while the links between Machiavellianism and secondary psychopathy are weaker but still significant.

Follow-up analyses were conducted to identify the best predictors of Mach II scores. Results confirmed our expectation that the primary psychopathy score is a better predictor, since secondary psychopathy scores did not add much value to predicting Mach II scores once the primary psychopathy scores had been taken into account.

Thus, while the Mach II and LSRP scales may be measuring similar constructs, it seems that factor 1 of the LSRP, which assesses callous unemotionality as a part of primary psychopathy, is more powerfully linked to Machiavellianism. To better understand these subtle differences and how they might relate to morality, we then sought to explore in more detail the theoretical profiling of the affective capacities of these two personality styles. Our general theoretical framework was to adopt a cascading constraints model.

TABLE 6.1　Correlations Among the Mach II and LSRP Psychopathy Subscales

Variable	Global Mach	Global Psychopath	Primary Psychopath	Secondary Psychopath	Mach View	Mach Morality	Mach Tactics
Global Mach scale							
LSRP Global Psychopathy scale	.68°°						
LSRP Primary Psychopathy subscale	.66°°						
LSRP Secondary Psychopath subscale	.43°°		.34°°				
Mach View subscale		.53°°	.50°°	.36°°			
Mach Morality subscale		.61°°	.59°°	.38°°	.45°°		
Mach Tactics subscale		.61°°	.59°°	.37°°	.64°°	.52°°	

Note: N = 107.
°° $p < .01$.

A Cascading Constraints Model of How Personality Styles Arise

Affective deficits are a central defining feature of psychopathically inclined and Machiavellian people. What does this imply for their morality? Psychopathically inclined people might know the language but do not "feel the music" of emotion. Machiavellian people can remain emotionally detached while manipulating and lying to others, seemingly bypassing empathy (McIlwain, 2003). Early studies (e.g., Christie & Geis, 1970; Geis & Levy, 1970) characterized Machiavellian people as having a *cool syndrome*; they are able to make realistic, cognitively based judgments of others without betraying any of their own affective experiences. McIlwain (2003) outlines how the cool syndrome is an advantage to a manipulator. A lack of affective expressivity is likely to make behavioral manipulation contingently successful, since the manipulator does not give themselves away with blushes or anxiety; a lack of affective resonance to the distress of another minimizes any possible internal sanction due to shame, guilt, and anxiety that might otherwise arise in the course of exploiting others.

On this account both (1) affective sensitivity (resonancing) and (2) expressivity have implications for morality. Affective insensitivity predisposes a person to deficient feeling on behalf of another (termed *vicarious feeling* or *affective resonancing*) and an inability to discern that another is being harmed from their distress cues. Thus, Machiavellians are likely to lack the hot, affective inputs to empathy that arise from within their own bodily economy as a result of perceiving others' distress. The inability to feel for another's distress may rob the viewer of informational and motivational input that might lead to correctly identifying emotion and promote morally responsible actions. This is of significance for later development from basic empathy to more nuanced morality. This lack of awareness of (or possibly an entire lack of) affective responses on witnessing another's suffering means they lack the inner signals that, on self-reflection, might be the basis of the formation of self-reflective moral emotions like guilt and shame. So this early affective deficit may in turn contribute to the development of strange moralities where the lack of vicarious emotion means decisions are justified with a focus on the outcome for oneself rather than any consideration of minimizing harm toward another. There may be the use of moral language, but closer analysis may reveal that there is a deep assumption of "the other as object" rather than the other as a knowing, feeling subject to whom respect and care are to be accorded. They use moral language but are harm-blind.

The second feature, a lack of affective expressivity, means that psychopathically inclined and Machiavellian people are likely to be highly successful manipulators, since emotional agitation is not going to alert victims to the fact that they are being exploited. It means that for the manipulator there is not the bodily clout of affect to overcome when strategically donning whatever emotional masks the situation requires.

Affective insensitivity is not portrayed as a single causal path to callous amorality since there may be other contributing factors, like a predatory fusion of sexuality and violent conquest in some psychopathically inclined people (McIlwain, 2007). We suggest that the flow on from affective deficit to empathic and moral deficiency is one possible broad tracing of influence. Overall, we view these psychopathically inclined and Machiavellian personality styles as arising contingently via a dynamic interplay of processes producing cascading constraints whereby early deficits have knock-on consequences for later development (McIlwain, 2007, 2008, 2010a). Constraint on parameters in early development restricts which other parameters are free to vary later in personality by a kind of *developmental shunting* (Alder & Scher, 1994). Formative early difficulties can close off certain developmental pathways while making others more likely. While traits vary along a continuum, being extremely low in a certain trait early in one's life may restrict variation on other traits later and make certain multidimensional constellations more likely than others. Psychopathy and Machiavellianism are multidimensional constructs, each dimension of which may have different developmental inputs and trajectories. Only people with the full constellation of dimensions have the full personality style, which may resemble a qualitatively different personality disorder (McIlwain, 2010a). This view suggests qualitatively different personality styles can arise from a cluster of extreme scores in a constellation of personality traits that are themselves dimensional parameters. Someone who is extreme on some but not all parameters may be socially gifted; for example, someone skilled at controlling facial expressivity may become a diplomat, psychotherapist, or a hostage negotiator—they have fully intact affective sensitivity under strategic expressive control, retaining at least one basis of inner moral sanction.

Traits exist to varying degrees in everyone, but innate predisposition or early experiences may influence whether one moves more toward the low or high end of any given parameter. A pertinent example for Machiavellianism is dispositional trust at first encounter with others (Gurtman, 1992). If early experience predisposes one to hostile distrust as the default option in first encounters, this radically shapes resultant social exchanges and the pattern of interpersonal difficulties faced. Cascading constraints may arise from either acquired traits, such as a lack of trust, or innate deficits, such as the fearlessness purportedly associated with psychopathy (see Kochanska, 1993; Lykken, 1957; Saltaris, 2002). Fearless children may lose the direct emotional experience that forms the basis of discerning such experiences in others. Indeed Blair and colleagues (Blair, Colledge, Murray, & Mitchell, 2001; Blair et al., 2002, 2004) present evidence that supports such a link. They found that some psychopathically inclined children are deficient in discerning experiences of fear and distress in the facial expressions and voices of others.

Unlike the specific deficits in regards to fear and distress that have been established for fledgling psychopathically inclined people, theory and research suggest that Machiavellian people have an across-the-board affective blunting. We suggest that Machiavellians bypass inconvenient emotions (McIlwain, 2003, 2010b); fleeting emotional signals are defensively dealt with so swiftly that these signals are insufficient to provide inner sanction to prevent exploitative behavior.

Psychopathically inclined people do not spontaneously discern the relevance of moral emotions like guilt. For example, Blair, Sellars, et al. (1995) found that although psychopathic and nonpsychopathic people performed similarly in attributing happiness, sadness, and embarrassment to characters in stories, the psychopathically inclined people attributed less guilt to story characters. Machiavellians seem to avoid inconvenient moral emotions by automatically attributing causality and blame to external sources (Mudrack, 1990). They are not entirely Teflon-coated when it comes to handling shame and blame, however. There is some evidence that Machiavellian people experience anxiety (Fehr, Samson, & Paulhus, 1992), encounter situations in which they feel unwilling to manipulate others (Barber, 1994), and experience narcissistic wounds and vulnerabilities (McIlwain, 2003; Sheppherd & Socherman, 1997). However, McIlwain (2003, 2010b) noted that an external attribution bias may diminish any adversely felt, shameful effects of exploiting others. There is evidence to support this view; for example, an external locus of control (i.e., a tendency to attribute the cause of events to powerful others, fate, or circumstances) is a robust indicator of Machiavellianism (Mudrack, 1990). Braginsky (1970) described Machiavellian young girls who spontaneously attributed to the experimenter responsibility for these young girls' imposition of an onerous task (of eating quinine-soaked biscuits) on another child whose exploitation was carried out by, and benefited, the young Machiavellian girls. In this way Machiavellian people avoid personal responsibility for their exploitative actions, and this may enable them to bypass shame (McIlwain, 2010b) and empathy (McIlwain, 2003). They also have a cynical worldview to further deal with any moral twinges, presuming everyone would manipulate if given the chance. Machiavelli stated that "a man would be a fool to throw away his sword when other men are only hiding theirs" (Machiavelli, 1513/1966, pp. 62–63; cited in Leary, Knight, & Barnes, 1986, p. 80). Our point is simple: If a cynical worldview and an external attribution bias prevent lingering experience of emotions indicating that another is suffering harm, then it is likely that the experience of empathy will be restricted or absent and other-oriented moral beliefs about preventing harm and suffering are unlikely to develop. We suggest that important (but possibly different) precursors to the development of empathy are lacking in both psychopathically inclined and Machiavellian people. So we expect that both personality styles will be deficient in their reporting of empathy.

Empathy in Psychopathically Inclined and Machiavellian People

Empathy hinges on vicarious experience in that the observed experiences of others come to affect our own bodily economy, feelings, and thoughts. It entails the ability to step outside of one's own frame of reference, a kind of decentering, and being able to suppress temporarily one's perspective on events to take on another's. Optimally, this perspective taking facilitates the anticipating of conflict, acknowledging the legitimate claims of others, and working toward compromise and accommodation. Historically, empathy has been divided into quick, hot, involuntary reactions and a more intellectualized ability to recognize the state of another independent of the vicarious experience of that person's state. Davis (1980), in his Interpersonal Reactivity Index (IRI) measure of empathy, distinguishes between *hot* spontaneous, emotional responses to another's emotional state such as empathic concern (EC) and personal distress (PD), and *cold* cognitive appreciation of another's emotional state such as perspective taking (PT) and fantasy (F). Cold empathy is more attitudinal and entails cognitive appraisal of the perspective of the other. It can include the fantasy projection of oneself into the position of the other as a more imaginative variant. Pellarini (2001, cited in McIlwain, 2003) found that Mach scores were significantly, negatively associated with empathic concern and positively correlated with levels of fantasy. However, research has failed to find a significant relationship between Mach scores and IRI personal distress scores (McIlwain, 2003).

A number of researchers (Baron-Cohen, 2004; Baron-Cohen & Wheelwright, 2004) have observed that the hot and cold aspects of empathy appear doubly dissociable. Individuals with autistic spectrum disorder purportedly lack the cold aspects of empathy while retaining some relatively normal reactions to emotional stimuli (Baron-Cohen & Wheelwright, 2004; Kinner, 2004). The opposite is the case for psychopathically inclined and Machiavellian people, who show intact cognitive ability to recognize the thought processes of another in *theory of mind* tests while lacking an ability to vicariously experience what another is experiencing. While (cognitive) theory of mind is intact, it is still in question whether psychopathically inclined and Machiavellian people report even cold, intellectually based empathy. Further, existing empathy scales were designed for use with prosocial populations. So we conducted two studies of empathy in these dark personalities. In Study 2a we sought to further explore the forms of empathy that psychopathically inclined and Machiavellian people self-report. Using our original scale of strategic empathic concern, we then explored in

Study 2b whether they acknowledge that they have the ability to discern what another is feeling but have control over whether this knowing influences them.

STUDY 2A: PSYCHOPATHY, MACHIAVELLIANISM, AND THE INTERPERSONAL REACTIVITY INDEX (IRI)

Aims and Method

To examine the relations among empathy, psychopathic tendencies, and Machiavellianism, we first asked the same 107 participants mentioned in Study 1 to also complete the IRI (Davis, 1980), which assesses separately the hot aspects of empathy via the empathetic concern (EC) and personal distress (PD) subscales, and the cold cognitive aspects, via the fantasy (F: placing oneself in the life situation of fictitious others) and perspective-taking (PT: the cognitive ability to understand another's affective state) subscales.

Results and Discussion

The full array of findings is reported in Table 6.2. There was no relationship between LSRP psychopathy or Mach scores and a tendency to experience personal distress at another's suffering or to be willing to project oneself into the situation of another by fantasy means. As expected, levels of psychopathy (primary and secondary) and Mach scores were significantly negatively associated with the IRI hot empathy subscale, empathic concern. Strikingly, there were also negative relations with IRI perspective-taking ability, a cold empathy subscale (see also Langdon & Delmas, Chapter 5, this volume).

STUDY 2B: STRATEGIC EMPATHY (MCILWAIN & WRIGHT)

Aims and Method

The finding that both Machiavellian and psychopathic tendencies related negatively to perspective taking, a form of cold empathy, puzzled us. Given that

TABLE 6.2   Empathy, as Assessed Using the IRI in Psychopathically Inclined and Machiavellian People

Variable	Global Mach Scale	Global Psychopathy	Primary Psychopathy	Secondary Psychopathy
IRI global empathy	−.35°°	−.39°°	−.47°°	−.11
IRI perspective taking	−.38°°	−.46°°	−.44°°	−.29°°
IRI empathetic concern	−.51°°	−.59°°	−.65°°	−.24°
IRI personal distress	.02	−.04	−.11	.10
IRI fantasy	.02	.11	.05	.16

Note: $N = 107$.
° $p < .05$.
°° $p < .01$.

psychopathically inclined and Machiavellian people are such good manipulators, which seems to entail their being able to discern the need the state of other to exploit that other, how do they do it if they are lacking in hot and cold empathy? One possibility is that our existing scales do not address the kinds of empathy they have. Like all empathy scales, the IRI was devised for prosocial populations and makes heavy use of feeling-saturated language. While entirely appropriate in the populations for which the scale was devised, psychopathically inclined and Machiavellian people may not reveal to a full extent the skills that they possess, because they may be unprepared to represent themselves on dimensions assessed by feeling-language items. Further, the IRI conflates a capacity to feel for another or take the perspective of the other, with the inevitable use of these abilities, since normatively if we have these skills we tend to use them. But in the personalities we have been discussing, capacity and use may be dissociable.

As part of a larger project with a sample of 62 first-year psychology students, we sought to address the dissociability of having an empathic capacity or skill and being able to turn that skill on or off depending on what would produce the best outcome for the protagonist. We used a new empathy scale we hope may complement Davis's (1980) IRI. We[1] devised new empathy items for the Strategic Emotional Control (SEC) scale that address the ability and tendency of participants to respond in an empathic way strategically, only when it suits their interests (e.g., "I can pick up on what others are feeling, but then it is my decision whether I let this influence me"). The scale is composed of seven items and shows reasonable internal reliability and no significant gender differences. We used it with the IRI and Mach IV.

Results and Discussion

In our sample of 62, the SEC scale significantly correlated moderately and positively with both primary psychopathy and Mach IV scores (see Table 6.3). Thus, psychopathically inclined and Machiavellian people are inclined to withhold their feelings of empathy toward others if necessary. McIlwain (2003) suggested that Machiavellians may initially experience the emotional responses of others, but they "may only experience them just long enough to get the information relevant to manipulation and then 'turn them off' or 'block them from awareness' in some way in order to better to exploit the person" (p. 51). The positive associations of SEC scores with both primary psychopathy and Mach IV scores suggest that both personalities characterized by affective coolness/deficits are inclined to self-report themselves as having this ability.

Both primary psychopathy and Mach IV scores correlated moderately negatively with empathic concern (EC; Table 6.3), confirming the idea that psychopathically inclined and Machiavellian people are less inclined to self-report feeling hot empathy for others. Neither primary nor secondary psychopath scores were associated with being affected by others' distress. This is consistent with the findings of different neurocognitive profiles and action dispositions in psychopathically inclined people when they respond to the distress cues of others. In one relevant study, Blair, Jones, Clark, and Smith (1995) presented a series of threatening,

TABLE 6.3   Correlations Among LSRP Psychopathy Scores, Mach IV Scores, IRI Measures of Empathy, and Scores for Strategic Emotional Control (SEC)

	IRI Fantasy Subscale	IRI EC Subscale	IRI PT Subscale	IRI PD Subscale	IRI Total	SEC
LSRP primary psychopathy	−.320*	−.510**	ns	ns	−.372**	.441**
LSRP secondary psychopathy	ns	ns	−.496**	ns	ns	ns
Mach IV	ns	−.391**	ns	ns	−.329*	.544**

Notes: EC, empathic concern. PT, perspective taking. PD, personal distress. SEC, strategic emotional control. ns, nonsignificant.
* $p < .05$.
** $p < .01$.

neutral and distressing visual stimuli to 18 psychopathic inmates and 18 non-psychopathic controls and compared their electrodermal responding. While the groups did not differ in their responses to the first two conditions (threatening and neutral), the psychopathic inmates showed little electrodermal response to the distress cues. Levenston, Patrick, Bradley, and Lang (2000), using skin conductance reactivity, heart rate, and facial expressions as indices, found that those high on primary psychopathy scores are slower to show the expected startle response when viewing stimuli most people consider aversive, such as images of starving children and mutilation. They conclude that "psychopathy involves a deviation in affective response at the most fundamental level—that of evoked action dispositions" (Levenston et al., 2000, p. 382). As suggested already, this affective coolness may protect the manipulator from vicariously experiencing the effects they have had on the other person in exploiting them and may make that exploitation less likely to be detected by the other in the first place.

In the next section, we consider what has variously been termed the *innate moral depravity, acquired moral insanity* of psychopaths, and ethical pathology that has been ascribed to psychopathically inclined and Machiavellian people alike. What forms of morality are acquired by individuals with these personality styles, so often portrayed as being without shame, guilt, and remorse?

Strange Moralities

Psychopathically inclined people understand morality enough to use it in exploiting others and to feign remorse at the right time. Having entertained claims that psychopathically inclined people ascribe to, in extreme forms, "the actual morality of society rather than the idealized morals that we would like to think pertain" (Fields, 1996, p. 267), Fields concludes that psychopaths differ more widely from the general population than this. He suggests they lack moral responsibility, that they are "incapable of acting for other-regarding moral reasons" (Fields, 1996, p. 267), adding that psychopaths do not act through rational calculation but "on a whim" and cannot act for prudential reasons in taking seriously their own best future interests.

How well do psychopathically inclined people understand morality when questioned? Evidence suggests that they fail to discriminate moral from conventional transgressions (Blair, 1995). However, the specific finding was that psychopathic men rated conventional transgressions as being as serious as moral transgressions, and this may have been a function of an incarcerated sample with parole on their minds (see also Langdon & Delmas, Chapter 5, this volume). They may have rated all transgressions highly for reasons of social desirability. Other researchers argue that this failure to distinguish moral from conventional transgressions is indicative of psychopaths' deficient empathy and failure to grasp the concept of harm to another. The focus is more on their own selfish gain and the whims of the moment. For example, Frick and Ellis (1999) noted that psychopaths' callous, unemotional superficial charm, coupled with impulsivity, a dysfunctional inhibition system, and a lack of guilt and shame, is a dangerous combination as these people also possess socially selfish tactics and a ready-made capacity for immoral behavior. The psychopaths' general poverty of affective reactions, especially those that would be triggered by the suffering of others (remorse, sympathy), condemnation by others (shame, embarrassment), or attachment to others (love, grief; Haidt, 2001, p. 822), renders feasible acts like murdering parents to collect the life insurance money or stealing from friends.

Machiavellians are associated with cunning guile but less with such overt and whimsically motivated violence. One of the underlying assumptions is that Machiavellians do not share conventional morality (Leary, Knight, & Barnes, 1986). For example, people with higher levels of Machiavellianism are *not* more likely to cheat than those with lower levels, but they are less likely to confess; they are only more likely to steal when being supervised if the supervisor clearly does not trust them, while people with low levels of Machiavellianism steal regardless of their supervisor's attitudes to them (Exline, Thibaut, Hickey, & Gumpert, 1970). Leary et al. (1986) found that Machiavellians think relativistic standards of behavior should apply in all situations and so are described (strangely enough) as *absolute relativists*: "Machiavellian individuals subscribe to a system of situationally-based ethics in which moral decisions are based upon a personal set of relativistic ethical guidelines rather than upon moral absolutes" (Leary et al., 1986, p. 76). Leary and colleagues examined two ethical dimensions: *relativism*, which rejects the notion that absolute moral principles exist that apply to all contexts; and *idealism*, the degree to which people believe that morally right behavior always leads to good consequences. They found a (weak) significant positive correlation between relativism and Mach scores, and that idealism was moderately and significantly negatively correlated with the Mach scores: Machiavellian people thus tended to hold the view that morally right behaviors will not always lead to the desired outcome.

Machiavellians do not see others as moved by ideals and so tend to be preemptively pragmatic (Pitkin, 1984). There needs to be something personally at stake for them for them to exploit or lie—such as stealing from under the nose of a distrustful supervisor.

Hot Inputs to Moral Reasoning and Feelings About Feelings

The suggestion that emotions and personal motivations are relevant to morality, the "sentimentalist" account of morality, is not a new stance. Hume proposed that "reason can let us infer that a particular action will lead to the death of many innocent people, but unless we care about those people, unless we have some sentiments that value human life, reason alone cannot advise against taking the action" (Haidt, 2001, p. 816).

The social intuition model of Haidt (2001) puts forward a delightfully Machiavellian theory of morality. Haidt claims that moral judgments are caused by quick moral intuitions and followed by post hoc moral reasoning. This model proposes that moral reasoning is therefore not a search for unbiased truth but "is likely to be hired out like a lawyer by various motives, employed only to seek confirmation of preordained conclusions" (Haidt, 2001, p. 824). Our own approach differs from Haidt's; we suggest there is not such a clean divide between fast intuitions and moral reasoning—the two become developmentally intertwined. We suggest that there are quick, almost involuntary inputs into moral judgments, namely, the hot components of empathy, and that, like developmentally primary emotions, these are quick, fast, and automatic. However, the specific form they take depends on a whole suite of available competencies and abilities, like the capacity for self-reflection, which changes as the person develops (with which they are "co-assembled"[2]) and characterizes a person at a given developmental moment. So, swift inputs can result in complex, nested, and self-reflective emotions. We suggest that in developing morality a vital preliminary stage is to develop reflective feelings about vicariously evoked feelings. Normally we experience feelings arising in response to another person being harmed as aversive. These "feelings about feelings" motivate us to stop the harm to the other. Feelings about feelings, or meta-emotions, include feeling shame for longing to depend on others or feeling anguish at perceiving another's distress (McIlwain, 2007).

However, hot, vicarious emotions elicited upon witnessing the experience of another are still vital inputs to morality, optimally providing instant bodily feedback that another is being harmed. We suggest normative morality will not be in evidence in those who lack it. Study 2a established that primary psychopathically inclined people and Machiavellians are particularly lacking in hot empathy in the form of empathic concern. We suggest these individuals will have strange moralities.

Cooler cognitive processes are also relevant to empathy or its bypassing. Literature on moral judgment and reasoning implicates the attitudes people hold about others as one of the central determining factors of personal morality. One form of attitude formation can be described as a set of automatic processes based on first impressions (Albright, Kenny, & Malloy, 1988). A pertinent example for Study 3 (in the next section) is the finding in Western society that overweight individuals are perceived as less active, less attractive, less intelligent, less popular, less hardworking, and less successful than individuals of an average weight (Hebl & Heatherton, 1998). Because our society views obesity as a controllable condition, larger individuals are also viewed as weak-willed, self-indulgent, and even immoral (Hebl & Mannix, 2003). If this kind of swift stereotyping response is commonplace in the general population and likely to be modulated in its verbal avowal by social desirability concerns and tempered by compassion, then, we reasoned, psychopathically inclined and Machiavellian people might represent an extreme of this kind of swift stereotyping stance, minus the compassion and minus the social desirability concerns.

Barber (1994) also proposes that morality is moderated by the extent of relatedness between the helper and recipient. Individuals frequently restrict prosocial behavior to members of their own family or social group (Hamilton, 1964, cited in Barber, 1994; Wilson, Near & Miller, 1996). However, Barber (1994) noted that Machiavellianism is one example of the biological concept of social selfishness, characterized by social detachment, competitiveness, and manipulation. This even extends to their kin, as Barber found that kinship had little influence on Machiavellians' ratings of their future behavior. They actually showed more favor toward close friends than toward family members.

Using this literature as background, we put to the test the moral decisions made by those high in psychopathy or Machiavellian scores to explore their moral judgments and the rationales they offer in hindsight. This approach allows us to consider whether these individuals might make similar judgments for different reasons. If so, such findings would suggest that different processes might underpin their exploitative capacities.

STUDY 3: PART ONE: ETHICAL DECISIONS AND THE TROLLEY PROBLEM

One way that philosophers and students of ethics and law have examined moral reasoning and its relation to moral action is the hypothetical Trolley Problem (Figure 6.2). This is a reasoning experiment in ethics that was introduced by Thomson (1976).

In what we call Dilemma 1 (Figure 6.3), the traditional problem is as follows:

> A train trolley is running out of control down a track. In its path are four people who have been tied to the track (Track A). You can flip the switch to divert the train onto a different track; however, there is one person tied to that track (Track B), a person who would survive if you did not act. The dilemma is this: Should you flick the switch or not?

Thomson (1976) also introduced a "large person variation" of the Trolley Problem (which we call Dilemma 2; see Figure 6.4) in which you are a bystander on a bridge, watching the whole event take place. Next to you stands a fat man. The decision you must make is whether you would push the large person onto the tracks to stop the train before it kills the people tied to the tracks?

In Dilemma 1 people generally think that it is their moral responsibility to flick the switch, whereby the decision to sacrifice one life for four is permissible. However, in Dilemma 2, individuals are less likely to judge it morally permissible to push the larger person, purportedly because direct harm to another is an integral part of the plan (Thomson, 1985).

Figure 6.2   The trolley problem—a runaway train. (Drawing by Jess Evans.)

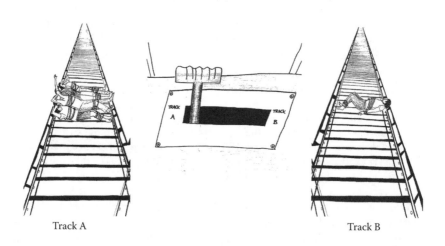

Track A   Track B

Figure 6.3   Dilemma 1: The runaway train will kill three people tied to Track A unless the switch is pulled, diverting the train to Track B—to which one person is tied. (Drawing by Jess Evans.)

Figure 6.4   Dilemma 2: The large person variation of the Trolley problem—would you throw him on the tracks to stop the train? (Drawing by Jess Evans.)

Aims and Method

In response to a workshop presentation by Greene in 2006, we planned research to extend his paradigm to consider how different personality styles would respond to a modified Trolley Problem (to which we also added some additional dimensions). As well as looking at the traditional yes or no decisions people make about flicking the switch or pushing the large person, we also included questions that tap into the moral–conventional distinction, questions that look at relatedness, such as, "What if the single person tied to the track was your family member or friend?" and questions that looked at responses to possible distress cues, such as, "What if the large person was unconscious or conscious at the time of being pushed?" To profile Machiavellianism and psychopathy in richer and more nuanced detail, we included open-ended questions to tap into post hoc moral reasoning. Open-ended questions permit us to discern whether moral language and other-oriented beliefs figure in the reasons given for judgments made as well as explore whether the decisions were made for primarily self-centered reasons. Our sample was the same 107 people mentioned in Study 1.

Results and Discussion

Dilemma 1: Flicking the Switch to Save Four   Overall, the majority of our participants indicated they would flick the switch ($n = 89/107$) to Track B, sacrificing

one to save four people, with only a minority leaving the train on Track A ($n = 18/107$). However, there were no significant differences for people higher and lower in psychopathy and Mach scores in their decision to flick or not flick the switch. Although, among the very highest scorers ($n = 8$) we did find a strong and significant association between higher psychopathy scores and the decision not to flick the switch.

Dilemma 1a: Sacrificing Four to Save a Family Member or a Friend
Given Barber's (1994) finding that kinship influenced less the altruistic decision making of Machiavellians, we also asked individuals what they would do if the single person on Track B were a family member over four strangers. Normatively, most participants avoid killing a family member than a friend on Track B. While 58 participants would change their initial decision to flick the switch and divert the train away from the more populated Track A for a family member or a friend, nine said they would change their initial decision only for a family member and not a friend. A total of 11 respondents wrote maybe for their response to the friend tied to the track option. One participant's open-ended response was of interest: Would s/he save a friend? "Possibly... I'd have to think about this one, unlike the immediate decision I made concerning the family member. In this case I would need to weigh up the friend's good and bad points...." However, there were no effects of psychopathy or Mach scores on decisions to save friends or family.

Dilemma 2: The Fat Man Variant
We also varied whether people were prepared to push a fat man on to a track as well as whether it would make a difference to decisions if he were conscious (Dilemma 2a) or unconscious (Dilemma 2b). We also varied the numbers of people on the tracks. Would people push him onto the tracks to save four people (Dilemma 2c)? Would they push him to save one person (Dilemma 2d)? We thought Dilemma 2d to be the strangest, since it entails killing one person to save one person. Discussion is restricted to Dilemma 2d since personality differences were in evidence.

Dilemma 2d: Pushing the Conscious Fat Man Onto a Track to Save One Person
In terms of killing one to save one, we found a significant (weak) correlation between the primary psychopathy score and the decision to push a large conscious person in front of Track B ($r = .21$, $p < .05$). An independent t-test showed that the group that would not push the large conscious person had a significantly lower psychopathy score ($M = 1.96$, $SD = .47$) than the group saying they would push him ($M = 2.41$, $SD = .64$). So those with higher levels of primary psychopathy were more likely to push the larger person, even when it was only to save one person tied to Track B.

STUDY 3: PART TWO: PERSONAL RATIONALES FOR DECISIONS ON THE TROLLEY PROBLEM

Aims and Method

We included open-ended questions with the Trolley Problem to understand how psychopathically inclined and Machiavellian people justify ethical decisions.

Based on the research by Braginsky (1970) and the robust meta-analytic findings of Mudrack (1990), we expected that there would be more blame shifting in the qualitative responses of those high on Machiavellian measures compared with those low on these measures. Specifically, we expected that high scorers' responses would show more evidence of an externalizing of control, rationalization, callousness, and a failure to become involved or take responsibility in the moral scenario. We expected that the large-person variant would produce the most unusual post hoc moral reasoning in those high on Machiavellian and psychopathy scores.

The participants were the same 107 participants. We asked participants to explain what went through their mind as they made their judgments. In response to the large-person variant, a person high on primary psychopathy said, "The person has the right to decide whether he/she wants to do it or not. If he/she is unconscious then his/her thoughts can't be heard." Moral terms are used, but the decision does not consider the unconscious fat man as a subject who should not have harm imposed on him. Another participant, high in primary psychopathy, viewed the fat man as somehow expendable: "To sacrifice someone who is 'okay to die' to save 4 lives or one life sounds reasonable." A person with a high Mach score said, "I assume (perhaps incorrectly) that the larger person does not appreciate their life as much as the person on the track does. They have let themselves go physically and do not appear to appreciate life to the fullest," so this participant would sacrifice the fat man to save one life or four.

We took all rationales and rated them on the basis of 14 theoretically and evidence-based categories that were scored on a three-point scale, where 1 = no evidence of this category, 2 = sometimes shows evidence of this category, and 3 = often or always shows evidence of this category. These categories were as follows:

1. Perspective taking (ability to see from another's perspective)
2. Fantasy (participants' ability to step into the scenario)
3. Empathy (use of hot emotional words like *pain* and *sad*)
4. Moral compliance (use of phrases such as "It's murder")
5. Direct distress (self-focused distress)
6. Vicarious distress (other-focused distress)
7. Fear (answers which include words like *scared, afraid, panic*)
8. Shame (the object of concern is the entire self, where the whole person is conceptualized as bad. Answers expressing a desire to escape the interpersonal situation, for example, "I couldn't bear to face the families of the victims.")
9. Guilt (object of concern is a particular bad action or a failure to act and answer which are characterized by feelings of remorse and regret)
10. Rationalization (assigning value to particular people on the track that made their death seem justified, for example, "They have probably done something bad if they are tied to the track," or "The large person will probably die of diabetes anyway")
11. External locus of control (answers that refer to fate or displace the blame)

12. Cold or callous (answers that go beyond just distancing themselves from the characters to answers that show sparks of cruelty and no hint of empathy)
13. Refusal to immerse (answers that say things like, "This is a rubbish scenario")
14. Refusal to involve (answers that included phrases like, "I would walk away")

Results and Discussion

Interater reliability for the 11 categories was acceptable. Correlations with single categories showed that those high on psychopathy gave rationales with a significant absence of perspective taking and significant evidence of refusal to involve. The justifications of people with high Mach scores were characterized by significant evidence of callousness.

Since it was unlikely that a single category would be a good predictor of psychopathy and Mach scores, we also examined what clusters of categories intercorrelated. A factor analysis extracted five independent factors of items (see Table 6.4).

Five numeric scores were then created for each of these factors. We then looked at how these factors were linked to the rationales offered by psychopathically inclined and Machiavellian people. People with higher Mach scores were most concerned with protecting their own egos—their rationales were largely self-centered: Factor 2, callous self-defense, showed a weak, positive association with Mach scores, indicating people with higher Machiavellian tendencies showed more evidence of fantasy, rationalization, and callousness in their qualitative rationales. An excerpt from a participant who gained among the highest Mach scores clearly demonstrates a propensity toward cool moral reasoning: "A lie is only a lie if other people find out. If I can save the lives of these people and the large person didn't know he was being murdered then it would be OK. The saved [sic] would probably be a greater asset to society anyway." Levels of psychopathy scores were not associated with factor 2 scores.

We were wise to pay attention to the subscales of the Mach as the morality subscale showed a significant positive correlation with factor 4, detachment, which is a combination of responses that evidence an external locus of control and a refusal to involve ($r = .22, p < .05$). Those with higher Mach morality scores would shift the blame—sometimes on to the people on the tracks themselves—and would say that they would walk away, which is even more detached than deciding not to flick the switch. For example, one such participant noted in response to the question as to whether they would flick the switch: "No. I have no intention of getting involved … best to walk away and let it run its course. Nobody innocent gets put in front of a train." These results partially confirmed our expectation that Machiavellians are characterized by detachment and blame shifting. Notably though, factor 4 did not show a significant relationship with either of the other Mach subscales or with psychopathy scores.

Factor 1 seems to be an empathy factor,[3] which also taps a willingness to immerse in the moral scenario and entertain it as real. This factor was negatively

TABLE 6.4   Factor Analysis Solution

	Factor 1 Empathy	Factor 2 Callous Self- Defense	Factor 3 Moral Emotions	Factor 4 Detachment	Factor 5 Too Fearful to Comply
[Q] Perspective Taking	**.79**	.30	.05	−.08	−.03
[Q] Fantasy	.31	**.57**	.28	−.05	.34
[Q] Empathy	**.78**	−.10	.16	−.02	−.04
[Q] Moral Compliance	.23	−.44	.18	.15	**−.56**
[Q] Direct Distress	−.03	.01	.47	−.17	**.51**
[Q] Vicarious Distress	**.53**	−.09	.39	.17	.14
[Q] Fear	.15	−.14	−.01	.19	**.75**
[Q] Shame	−.01	−.16	**.74**	−.18	−.16
[Q] Guilt	.35	−.03	**.73**	.02	.10
[Q] Rationalization	.14	**.77**	.09	.09	−.15
[Q] External Locus	−.01	.36	−.07	**.71**	.21
[Q] Callousness	−.23	**.81**	−0.4	.16	.00
[Q] Refusal to Immerse	**−.69**	−.19	.03	.33	−.10
[Q] Refusal to Involve	−.17	−.02	−.11	**.81**	−.11

Notes: [Q], Qualitative. Bold signifies component in which each category was included.

associated with levels of global psychopathy ($r = -.19, p < .05$) and more particularly with levels of primary psychopathy ($r = -.25, p < .05$). The justifications of more psychopathically inclined people showed: less empathy, less perspective-taking, less vicarious personal distress, and a higher likelihood of a refusal to immerse— a preemptive strike against having to make decisions where there was nothing to gain for them. One participant who scored high on psychopathy wrote, "Why should I put myself in personal jeopardy for a group of strangers in an unknown dilemma—not enough information for me to risk acting a hero and looking a fool."

To consider the profiles of those highest on the psychopathy and Mach measures, the data were filtered to include only participants whose mean scores fell above the 75th percentile. Eight participants fell into this category; note that the small numbers dictate caution here. More extreme Mach and secondary psychopathy scores within this extreme subgroup were linked with a refusal to be involved in the scenario by taking any action. But it was higher psychopathy scores in this extreme subgroup that associated most with post hoc rationales characterized by the constellation of a lack of hot and cold empathy and refusal to immerse in the scenario at all, or if they do, showing an unwillingness to flick the switch.

General Discussion of Study 3: Strange Moralities

There are indeed strange moralities: Rationales are cloaked in moral language, but even where moral terms are used there is a fundamental lack of concern for harm toward another—they have the words but not the music of morality. Both personality styles give rationales that conceive of others as objects, and their rationales are largely self-centered, such as electing to push the unconscious rather than the conscious person to avoid hearing screams. The qualitative profiling suggests that Machiavellians are prepared to immerse themselves in the fantasy scenario but are not prepared to be actively involved, electing to walk away, unlike psychopathically inclined people who were preemptively unlikely to immerse in the first place. This illustrates an interesting feature of the Trolley Problem. Immersing in the fantasy scenario at all means that any decision has personal costs. Once immersed someone will die if one acts, and walking away means one is still implicated in deaths. This has interesting connections with recent work by DeScioli, Bruening, and Kurzban (2009) that explores the moral implications of omissions (e.g., where not acting is viewed less severely than acting, even if the causal outcome is still the same).

We found that high Mach scorers gave more callous and cynical reasons for their decisions—attributing blame to the victims on the track. Psychopathy scores were instead negatively related to using empathic terms, while no such negative relationship pertained for Mach scores. There are thus complex differences in the moral rationales associated with the two personality styles.

We cannot do justice in this chapter to the richness of all the qualitative responses. Some detail is lost collapsing open-ended responses into categories for analysis. More detailed focus on the content of the qualitative responses of psychopathically inclined and Machiavellian people is required. Although we attempted to control for variability in scoring and had four separate coders, there was still room for interpretation bias. However, the interrater agreement was high for the majority of categories, and the qualitative results mirrored the quantitative results, which lends some support to the overall reliability of our qualitative approach. Finally, we note that hypothetical moral reasoning, as we have examined, may not translate into real-world action. Hence, ecological validity concerns remain.

CONCLUSIONS

Regarding construct overlap, we found that psychopathy and Machiavellianism are closely related psychometrically; however, primary psychopathy is more closely related to Machiavellian traits than secondary psychopathy. Our psychometric analyses therefore support previous research that has shown links between the constructs (McHoskey et al., 1998; Ray & Ray, 1982; Smith & Griffith, 1978). We found that those who share callous unemotionality are also found to lack empathy; Study 2a confirmed that those who score higher on measures of psychopathy and Machiavellianism show less empathy and, in particular, less vicarious hot empathy, as argued elsewhere (Lauria, 2002; Pellarini, 2001, cited in McIlwain, 2003). However, across two studies, using the IRI (Davis, 1980) our findings did not support the view that psychopathically inclined and Machiavellian people possess intact, even enhanced, cold empathy or the ability cognitively to recognize the emotional responses and thought processes of others without vicariously experiencing them.

Different processes may well underlie empathic deficiencies; this requires further research. For those high on psychopathy, poor self-reported perspective taking, as assessed using the IRI, may reflect deficiencies in vicarious emotional experience of fear and distress. For those who score high on Machiavellianism, their poor perspective taking may result from flattened affect in general, arising from a cynical worldview and blame-shifting external attribution bias that function to detach them emotionally from the situation and presume the worst in others.

The mystery of how Machiavellian and psychopathically inclined people can be such good manipulators if they lack all capacity to discern the need states of others may be clarified by our Study 2b showing that these individuals share a strategic capacity to use empathy when it suits their purposes. They are prepared to report empathic ability when questions retain a distinction between a capacity to discern another's feelings and control over how that understanding is implemented in action. Our new empathy scale has promise.

Different moral profiles emerge in the themes prominent in rationales offered for decisions made in our variations of the Trolley Problem. These personality constructs are overlapping, but distinct, in accord with Paulhus and Williams (2002) and Smith (1999). Machiavellians' moral reasoning has a self-defensive quality, characterized by callousness and rationalization— as if emotions impact them and are swiftly dealt with. For psychopathically inclined people it is as if vicarious emotions do not impact in the first place and immersion in the scenario just does not happen. The moral justifications of psychopathically inclined people are primarily characterized by a lack of empathetic resonance, an absence of vicarious distress, and an inability to see from another's perspective. This same pattern of underlying differences has been suggested in the literature where it is argued that, while psychopathically inclined people lack the actual ability to fully experience empathy (Cleckley, 1941/1964; Hare, 1998; Johns & Quay, 1962) or to recognize distress (Blair, Jones, et al., 1995), Machiavellians may bypass vicarious emotion (McIlwain, 2003) or use it strategically. This ability to detach or gain reflective distance from the experience of empathy may be facilitated by the Machiavellian's deeply ingrained cynical worldview and the propensity to rationalize and place the blame elsewhere.

In conclusion, our study highlights the promise of qualitative techniques to explore differences in reflection on moral reasoning. As our cascading constraints model suggested, we found that those with affective deficits and high on callous unemotionality were also those lacking in empathy and those with the most deviant moral reasoning. We also found a link between unusual reasoning and a callous capacity to detach from responsibility by refusing to become involved in the scenarios (as shown by the high Mach scorers) and from preemptive refusal to immerse in fantasy scenarios in the first place (as shown by the high psychopathy scorers). While only a small number of individuals overall in our studies would be classified as high in psychopathic and Machiavellian tendencies relative to the levels seen in incarcerated populations, the very fact that we found such results within a population largely composed of undergraduate students lends further support to the view that such traits exist to a varying degree in the noninstitutionalized population.

Perhaps future research will reveal that many of those higher on psychopathic and Machiavellian tendencies in our society are not the "monsters" traditionally portrayed as vicious, antisocial criminals but are wolves in sheep's clothing—students who walk among us, future business women and men, journalists, politicians.

REFERENCES

Adshead, G. (1999). Commentary: Psychopaths and other-regarding beliefs. *Philosophy, Psychiatry, and Psychology, 6*, 41–44.

Albright, L., Kenny, D. A., & Malloy, T. E. (1988). Consensus in personality judgments at zero acquaintance. *Journal of Personality and Social Psychology, 55*, 387–395.

Alder, A. G., & Scher, S. J. (1994). Using growth curve analyses to assess personality change and stability in adulthood. In T. F. Heatherton & J. L. Weinberger (Eds.), *Can personality change* (pp. 149–173). Washington, DC: American Psychological Association.

American Psychiatric Association. (APA). (1952). *Diagnostic and Statistical Manual of Mental Disorders,* 1st ed. Washington, DC: Author.

American Psychiatric Association. (APA). (1994). *Diagnostic and Statistical Manual of Mental Disorders,* 4th ed. Washington, DC: Author.

Barber, N. (1994). Machiavellianism and altruism: Effect of relatedness of target person on Machiavellian and helping attitudes. *Psychological Reports, 75*, 403–422.

Baron-Cohen, S. (2004). Autism: Research into causes and intervention. *Journal of Paediatric Rehabilitation, 7*, 73–78.

Baron-Cohen, S., & Wheelwright, S. (2004). The Empathy Quotient (EQ): An investigation of adults with Asperger's syndrome or high functioning autism, and normal sex differences. *Journal of Autism and Developmental Disorders, 34*, 163–175.

Belmore, M. F., & Quinsey, V. L. (1994). Correlates of psychopathy in a non-institutional sample. *Journal of Interpersonal Violence, 9*, 339–349.

Benn, P. (1999). Freedom, resentment, and the psychopath. *Philosophy, Psychiatry and Psychology* 6, 29–39.

Bishopp, D., & Hare, R. D. (2008). A multidimensional scaling analysis of the Hare PCL-R: Unfolding the structure of psychopathy. *Psychology, Crime & Law, 14*, 117–132.

Blair, R. J. R. (1995). A cognitive developmental approach to morality: Investigating the psychopath. *Cognition,* 57, 1–29.

Blair, R. J. R. (1997). Moral reasoning and the child with psychopathic tendencies. *Personality and Individual Differences, 22*, 731–739.

Blair, R. J. R. (1999). Responsiveness to distress cues in the child with psychopathic tendencies. *Personality and Individual Differences, 27*, 135–145.

Blair, R. J. R. (2003). Neurobiological basis of psychopathy. *British Journal of Psychiatry, 182*, 5–7.

Blair, R. J. R., & Coles, M. (2000). Expression recognition and behavioural problems in early adolescence. *Cognitive Development, 15*, 421–434.

Blair, R. J. R., Colledge, E., Murray, L., & Mitchell, D. G. V. (2001). A selective impairment in the processing of sad and fearful expressions in children with psychopathic tendencies. *Journal of Abnormal Child Psychology, 29*, 491–498.

Blair, R. J. R., Jones, L., Clark, F., & Smith, M. (1995). Is the psychopath "morally insane"? *Personality and Individual Differences, 19*, 741–752.

Blair, R. J. R., Jones, L., Clark, F., & Smith, M. (1997a). The psychopathic individual: A lack of responsiveness to distress cues? *Psychophysiology, 34*, 192–198.

Blair, R. J. R., Jones, L., Clark, F., & Smith, M. (1997b). The psychopathic individual: a lack of response to distress cues? *Psychophysiology, 34*, 192–198.

Blair, R. J. R., Sellars, C., Strickland, I., Clark, F., Williams, A. O., Smith, M. et al. (1995). Emotion attributions in the psychopath. *Personality and Individual Differences, 19,* 431–437.

Blair, R. J. R., Mitchell, D. G., Peschardt, K. S., Colledge, E., Leonard, R. A., Shine, J. H., et al. (2004). Reduced sensitivity to others' fearful expressions in psychopathic individuals. *Personality & Individual Differences, 37,* 1111–1122.

Blair, R. J. R., Mitchell, D. G., Richell, R. A., Kelly, S., Leonard, A., Newman, C., et al. (2002). Turning a deaf ear to fear: Impaired recognition of vocal affect in psychopathic individuals. *Journal of Abnormal Psychology, 111,* 682–686.

Blonigen, D. M., Hicks, B. M., Krueger, R. F., Patrick, C. J., & Iacono, W. G. (2006). Continuity and change in psychopathic traits measured via normal-range personality: A longitudinal-biometric study. *Journal of Abnormal Psychology, 115,* 85–95.

Braginsky, D. D. (1970). Machiavellianism and manipulative interpersonal behavior in children. *Journal of Experimental Social Psychology, 6,* 77–99.

Cherulnik, P. D., Way, J. H., Ames, S., & Hutto, D. B. (1981). Impressions of high and low Machiavellian men. *Journal of Personality, 49,* 388–400.

Christie, R., & Geis, F. (1970). *Studies in Machiavellianism.* New York: Academic Press.

Cleckley, H. M. (1941/1964). *The mask of sanity: An attempt to clarify some issues about the so-called psychopathic personality* (4th ed.). St. Louis: Mosby Company.

Cooke, D. J. (1998). Psychopathy across cultures. In D. J. Cooke, A. E. Forth, & R. D. Hare (Eds.), *Psychopathy: Theory, research and implications for society* (pp. 13–45). Dordrecht: Kluwer Academic Publishers.

Davis, M. H. (1980). A multidimensional approach to individual differences in empathy. *JSAS the Netherlands: Catalogue of Selected Documents in Psychology, 10,* 85.

DeScioli, P., Bruening, R., & Kurzban, R. (2009). *The omission effect and the design of moral psychology.* Manuscript submitted for publication.

Exline, R. V., Thibaut, J., Hickey, C. B., & Gumpert, P. (1970) Visual interaction in relation to Machiavellianism and an unethical act. In R. Christie & F. Geis (Eds.), *Studies in Machiavellianism* (pp. 53–75). New York: Academic Press.

Fehr, B., Samson, D., & Paulhus, D. M. (1992). The construct of Machiavellianism: Twenty years later. In C. D. Spielberger & K. M. Butcher (Eds.), *Advances in Personality Assessment* (pp. 77–116). Hillsdale, NJ: Erlbaum.

Fields, L. (1996). Psychopathy, other-regarding moral beliefs and responsibility. *Philosophy, Psychiatry & Psychology, 3,* 261–277.

Frick, P. J. (1995). Callous-unemotional traits and conduct problems: A two-factor model of psychopathy in children. *Issues in Criminological and Legal Psychology, 1,* 47–51.

Frick, P. J., Cornell, A. H., Bodin, S. D., Dane, H. E., Barry, C. T., & Loney, B. R. (2003). Callous-unemotional traits and developmental pathways to severe conduct problems. *Developmental Psychology, 39,* 246–260.

Frick, P. J., & Ellis, M. (1999). Callous-Unemotional traits and subtypes of conduct disorder. *Clinical Child and Family Psychology Review, 2,* 149–168.

Frick, P. J., & Hare, R. D. (2002). *The psychopathic screening device.* Toronto, Ontario, Canada: Multi-health Systems.

Geis, F., & Levy, M. (1970). The eye of the beholder. In L. Festinger & S. Schachter (Eds.), *Social psychology: A series of monographs, treatises, and texts.* New York: Academic Press.

Green, J. D. (2006). Morality and agency workshop. Hosted jointly by the Macquarie Centre for Cognitive Science and the Department of Philosophy, Macquarie University.

Greene, J., & Haidt, J. (2002). How (and where) does moral judgment work? *Trends in Cognitive Sciences, 6,* 517–523.

Gurtman, M. B. (1992). Trust, distrust and interpersonal problems: A circumplex analysis. *Journal of Personality and Social Psychology, 62,* 989–1002.

Haidt, J. (2001). The emotional dog and its rational tail: A social intuitionist approach to moral judgment. *Psychological Review, 108,* 814–834.

Hare, R. D. (1991). *The Hare psychopathy checklist—revised.* Toronto: Multi-Health Systems.

Hare, R. D. (1996). Psychopaths and antisocial personality disorder: A case of diagnostic confusion. *Psychiatric Times, 13,* 39–40.

Hare, R. D. (1998). Psychopathy, affect and behavior. In D. J. Cooke, A. E. Forth, & R. D. Hare (Eds.), *Psychopathy: Theory, research and implications for society* (pp. 105–137). Dordrecht, the Netherlands: Kluwer Academic Publishers.

Hare, R. D. (1999). *Without conscience: The disturbing world of the psychopaths among us.* New York: Guilford Press.

Hare, R. D., McPherson L. M., & Forth, A.E. (1988). Factor structure of the psychopathy checklist. *Journal of Consulting Psychology, 56,* 741–747.

Harpur, T. J., & Hare, R. D. (1994). Assessment of psychopathy as a function of age. *Journal of Abnormal Psychology, 103,* 604–609.

Hebl, M. R., & Heatherton, T. F. (1998). The stigma of obesity in women: The differences are black and white. *Personality and Social Psychology Bulletin, 24,* 417–426.

Hebl, M. R., & Mannix, L. M. (2003). The weight of obesity in evaluating others: A mere proximity effect. *Journal of Personality and Social Psychology Bulletin, 29,* 28–38.

Hill, J. (2003). Early identification of individuals at risk for antisocial personality disorder. *British Journal of Psychiatry, 182,* 11–14.

Hunter, J. E., Gerbing, D. W., & Boster, F. J. (1982). Machiavellian beliefs and personality: Construct validity of the Machiavellianism dimension. *Journal of Personality and Social Psychology, 43,* 1293–1305.

Ishikawa, S. S., Raine, A., Lencz, T., Bihrle, S., & Lacasse, L. (2001). Autonomic stress reactivity and executive functions in successful and unsuccessful criminal psychopaths from the community. *Journal of Abnormal Psychology, 110,* 423–432.

Johns, J. H., & Quay, H. C. (1962). The effect of social reward on verbal conditioning in psychopathic and neurotic military offenders. *Journal of Consulting Psychology, 26,* 217–220.

Karpman, B. (1948). The myth of the psychopathic personality. *American Journal of Psychiatry, 104,* 523–534.

Kerig, P. K., & Stellwagen, K. K. (2009). Roles of callous-unemotional traits, narcissism, and Machiavellianism in childhood aggression. *Journal of Psychopathology and Behavioral Assessment, 32,* 343–352.

Kinner, S. A. (2004). *Psychopathy, Machiavellianism, empathy and theory of mind: An integrative approach.* Unpublished doctor of philosophy dissertation, University of Queensland, Australia.

Kirkman, C. A. (2002). Non-incarcerated psychopaths: Why we need to know more about the psychopaths who live amongst us. *Journal of Psychiatric and Mental Health Nursing, 9,* 155–160.

Kligman, M., & Culver, C. M. (1992). An analysis of interpersonal manipulation. *Journal of Medicine and Philosophy, 17,* 173–197.

Kochanska, G. (1993). Toward a synthesis of parental socialization and child temperament in early development of conscience. *Child Development, 64,* 325–347.

Krafft-Ebing, R. (1905/2007). *Textbook of insanity* (C. G. Chaddock, Trans.). Kessinger Publishing Company.

Leary, M. R., Knight, P. D., & Barnes, B. D. (1986). Ethical ideologies of the Machiavellian. *Personality and Social Psychology Bulletin, 12,* 75–80.

Levenson, M. R., Kiehl, K. A., & Fitzpatrick, C. M. (1995). Assessing psychopathic attributes in a non-institutionalised population. *Journal of Personality and Social Psychology, 68,* 151–158.

Levenston, G. K., Patrick, C. J., Bradley, M. M., & Lang, P. J. (2000). The psychopath as observer: Emotion and attention in picture processing. *Journal of Abnormal Psychology, 109*, 373–385.

Lilienfeld, S. O. (1994). Conceptual problems in the assessment of psychopathy. *Clinical Psychology Review, 14*, 17–38.

Lilienfeld, S. O., & Andrews, B. P. (1996). Development and preliminary validation of a self-report measure of psychopathic personality traits in noncriminal populations. *Journal of Personality Assessment, 66*, 488–524.

Lykken, D. T. (1957). A study of anxiety in the sociopathic personality. *Journal of Abnormal and Social Psychology, 55*, 6–10.

Machiavelli, N. (1513/1966). *The prince*, D. Donno (Trans.). New York: Bantam Books.

Machiavelli, N. (1513/1970). *The discourses*. (L. J. Walker & B. Richardson, Trans.). Harmondsworth, UK: Penguin Books.

Machiavelli, N. (1513/2003). *The prince*. (G. Bull, Trans.). London: Penguin Books.

McHoskey, J. W., Worzel, W., & Szyarto, C. (1998). Machiavellianism and psychopathy. *Journal of Personality and Social Psychology, 74*, 192–210.

McIlwain, D. (2003). Bypassing empathy: A Machiavellian theory of mind and sneaky power. In B. Repacholi & V. Slaughter (Eds.), *Individual differences in theory of mind: Implications for typical and atypical development* (pp. 39–66). New York: Psychology Press.

McIlwain, D. (2007). Rezoning pleasure: Drives and affects in personality theory. *Theory and Psychology, 17*, 529–561.

McIlwain, D. (2008). Cascading constraints: The development of Machiavellianism and psychopathy. In S. Boag (Ed.), *Personality down under: Perspectives from Australia*. New York: Nova Science publishers.

McIlwain, D. (2010a). Living strangely in time: Emotions, masks and morals in psychopathically-inclined people. *European Journal of Analytic Philosophy, 6*, 75–94.

McIlwain, D. (2010b). Young Machiavellians and the traces of shame: Coping with vulnerability to a toxic affect. In C. Barry, P. Kerig, K. Stellwagen, & T. Barry (Eds.), *Narcissism and Machiavellianism in youth: Implications for the development of adaptive and maladaptive behavior*. Washington, DC: American Psychological Association.

McIlwain, D., & Warburton, W. (2005). The role of early maladaptive schemas in adult aggression. *Psychology, Psychiatry, and Mental Health Monographs, 2*, 17–34.

Mealey, L. (1995). Primary sociopathy (psychopathy) is a type, secondary is not. *Behavioral and Brain Sciences, 18*, 579–599.

Moore, D., & McDonald, J. (2000). *Transforming conflict*. Sydney: Transformative Justice Australia.

Mudrack, P. E. (1990). Machiavellianism and locus of control: A meta-analytic review. *Journal of Social Psychology, 130*, 125–126.

Naylor, M. B. (1988). The moral of the trolley problem. *Philosophy and Phenomenological Research, 48*, 711–722.

Neumann, C. S., Hare, R. D., & Newman, J. P. (2007). The super-ordinate nature of the psychopathy checklist—revised. *Journal of Personality Disorders, 21*, 102–117.

Paulhus, D. L., & Williams, K.M. (2002). The dark triad of personality: Narcissism, Machiavellianism and psychopathy. *Journal of Research in Personality, 36*, 556–563.

Pitkin, H. (1984). *Fortune is a woman: Gender and politics in the thought of Niccolo Machiavelli*. Berkeley: University of California Press.

Prichard, J. C. (1835). *A treatise on insanity and other disorders affecting the mind*. London: Sherwood, Gilbert, and Piper.

Ray, J. J., & Ray, J. A. B. (1982). Some apparent advantages of subclinical psychopathy. *Journal of Social Psychology, 117*, 135–142.

Rush, B. (1812/1947). *Medical inquiries and observation upon the diseases of the mind*. Philadelphia: Kimber and Richardson.

Saltaris, C. (2002). Psychopathy in juvenile offenders: Can temperament and attachment be considered as robust developmental precursors? *Clinical Psychology Review, 22,* 729–752.

Sheppherd, J. A., & Socherman, R. E. (1997). On the manipulative behavior of low Machiavellians: Feigning incompetence to "sandbag" an opponent. *Journal of Personality and Social Psychology, 72,* 1448–1459.

Smith, R. J. (1984). The psychopath as moral agent. *Philosophy and Phenomenological Research, 45,* 177–193.

Smith, R. J. (1999). Psychopathic behavior and issues of treatment. *New Ideas in Psychology, 17,* 165–176.

Smith, R. J., & Griffith, J. E. (1978). Psychopathy, the Machiavellian and anomie. *Psychological Reports, 42,* 258.

Tellegen, A. (1982). Manual for the multidimensional personality questionnaire. Unpublished manuscript.

Thomson, J. J. (1976). Killing, letting die, and the trolley problem. *Monist, 59,* 204–217.

Thomson, J. J. (1985). The trolley problem. *Yale Law Journal, 94,* 1395–1415.

Viding, E. (2004). Annotation: Understanding the development of psychopathy. *Journal of Child Psychology and Psychiatry, 45,* 1329–1337.

Widom, C. S. (1977). A methodology for studying noninstitutionalized psychopaths. *Journal of Consulting and Clinical Psychology, 45,* 674–683.

Wilson, D. S., Near, D., & Miller, R. R. (1996). Machiavellianism: A synthesis of the evolutionary and psychological literatures. *Psychological Bulletin, 119,* 285–299.

ENDNOTES

1. Barbara Nevicka helped to devise some of the items of this scale.
2. Co-assembly was a term coined by Tomkins in his affect theory to refer to a process which creates a unitary experience when an affect amplifies the signal from another psychological system (Moore & McDonald, 2000, p. 155).
3. Global IRI Empathy shows a significant, positive moderate correlation with Component One ($r = .34, p < 0.01$) and a significant, negative moderate correlation with Component Four ($r = -.25, p < 0.01$). This result indicated that those who scored higher on the IRI global empathy wrote qualitative responses that showed more evidence of perspective taking, empathetic concern, and less evidence of an external locus of control and failure to be involved in the scenario. This also gave support to the validity of our qualitative measures.

7

The Neurology of Morality

RICARDO DE OLIVEIRA-SOUZA and JORGE MOLL

D'Or Institute for Research and Education and the
Federal University of the State of Rio de Janeiro

The capacity for moral agency is one outstanding attribute of human beings and, as such, may be grounded on a dedicated neural organization that has been shaped by phylogenesis over the past 7 million years. Clues on the neurological organization of human morality are provided by neuroimaging studies of healthy volunteers and patients with brain damage. Data obtained from these neurologically oriented sources have informed, and in turn have been informed by, fields of knowledge such as economics and the social sciences, which were alien to neuroscientific enterprise until recently. This cross-fertilization is already breeding a composite scenario with the human brain as the main character, allowing the charting of unexplored territories of the human mind. The purpose of this communication is to discuss current knowledge of the neural underpinnings of human morality as an instance of a typical form of human cognition and behavior.

INTRODUCTION

*I*n this chapter, we examine the neurobehavioral processes that underlie emotion and reasoning about moral predicaments and the moral norms that are held by individuals pertaining to social groups like family, job, and church (Han & Northoff, 2008). We will not address the issue of how morality emerged in our species or how it relates to cognitive and motivational mechanisms observed in other social species.

Although moral beliefs and reasoning may be highly structured, deliberative, and complex and can be articulated explicitly, at least to some degree much of the mental processing that relates to human morality generally operates at the fringe of awareness in implicit and automatic ways (Bargh & Ferguson, 2000). Moral beliefs and reasoning emerge from a complex interaction of biological proclivities with cultural learning, a lengthy process that is not completed before adulthood (Vygotsky, 1934/1962). After important stages of development that begin in early infancy, morality is established by early adulthood as strongly held structures of belief, reasoning, and judgment systems, which have both sanctioning and forbidding aspects.

THE PSYCHOLOGICAL STRUCTURE OF MORALITY

Fully developed morality results from the concerted operation of three psychological domains: semantic, emotional, and motivational. The semantic domain is embodied in language (spoken and written) and in the visual arts, which are among the most efficient vehicles for the transmission of moral norms, attitudes, and beliefs. Language and art play a crucial role in providing concrete representations of moral beliefs through iconic symbols and figurative language, which enforce the intersubjective conformity to group norms and the social sharing of meanings. Fables, such as Aesop's, provide apt instances of a universal means of transmission of moral norms and beliefs in our culture.

Much of the complexity of moral reasoning and judgment systems lies in the semantic domain, which is represented by rich associations of conceptual knowledge. Although semantic aspects can be communicated through nonverbal channels (e.g., imitation and action knowledge), verbal language (written or spoken) provides the most powerful means of transmitting moral knowledge. The logico-verbal organization of the semantic system allows the encoding of morality into rules of conduct that categorize values into hierarchies and minimize logical incongruence. For example, the biblical commandment "Thou shalt not kill" conveys a clear message but may be suspended in certain circumstances, such as in legitimate self-defense.

The emotional domain of morality encompasses a family of subjective experiences known as *moral emotions* (Moll & Schulkin, 2009). In contrast to the *basic emotions* (e.g., happiness, fear), which are primarily related to the self-centered interests of the individual, the moral emotions are linked to "the interests or welfare either of society as a whole or at least of persons other than the judge or agent" (Haidt, 2003, p. 853). Moral emotions were already of interest to eminent researchers of the nineteenth century, as shown by their mention of "the muscles of joy and benevolence" (Duchenne, 1862/1990, pp. 69–73) and the "special expressions of man," which included joy, love, meditation, and determination (Darwin, 1872/1988). However, these early writings on the moral emotions were eclipsed by the far more intensive attention devoted to the basic emotions during the twentieth century (Ekman, 1992).

Notwithstanding their differences in psychological and neural architecture, both basic and moral emotions are conceived as discrete subjective experiences elicited by ideas[1] and perceptions endowed with personal relevance (Heilman, 1997). Emotional experiences are accompanied by changes in phasic autonomic activity that can be gauged even when they take place at the brink of conscious awareness or as purely introspective phenomena (Bauer, 1998). In this sense, emotions can imbue ideas and perceptions with subjective values that continuously affect the ways that individuals relate to the world (de Oliveira-Souza & Figueiredo, 1996). Emotional experience, in this sense, comprises a special kind of projective experience that "tags" ideas and perceptions with subjective qualities that do not exist as such in the physical world. It is within this conceptual framework that emotional experience, and the moral sense in particular, partakes in the *fundamental projective property*, in which the individual projects subjective qualities upon ideas, objects, and facts (Köhler, 1938). This emotional tagging must be distinguished from the attribution of emotions to perceived faces, intonations, and gestures, a cognitive process that draws on the physical characteristics of the stimulus and does not need the elicitation of emotional experiences in the observer to take place flawlessly (Adolphs, 2002; Heilman, Scholes, & Watson, 1975), although *emotional mimicking* of others' perceived emotions can occur and may facilitate emotion recognition. This contrast between emotion cue recognition and emotional tagging is exemplified by patients with acquired brain damage who lose the ability to experience emotions but not to infer them in others (de Oliveira-Souza & Figueiredo, 1996). Depending on lesion localization, this emotional tagging response can be damaged in modality-specific ways. For example, Bauer (1982) reported on the case of a 39-year-old patient with bilateral occipito-temporal hematomas who lost the ability to recognize familiar faces and places, and to experience emotions aroused by visual cues. For example, his galvanic skin responses to auditory narratives with a sexual content were twice as great as those elicited by the visual presentation of nudes or landscapes. A similar case, a 71-year-old man with a right posterior hemisphere lesion, was reported by Habib (1986).

The third domain of morality involves motivation. We have argued elsewhere that what distinguishes one's moral conduct from one's social behavior in general are the moral motivations (e.g., respect for moral rules and the inclination to behave altruistically) rather than just the effects of one's actions on others or outcomes (Moll, de Oliveira-Souza, & Zahn, 2008). The key for defining these motivations as *moral* is their ability to overcome the (proximate) interests of the self or agent. Although the description of the neural correlates of moral motivations is now within the reach of empirical science, the neural correlates of moral motivations in real life are much more difficult to establish.

In adults with normal moral agency,[2] the implementation of morally guided behavior, we assume, requires the engagement of an event-structured complex—a type of abstract procedural memory for the efficient execution of actions (overt physical acts and mental acts), such as habits, attitudes, routines, and skills, which is called into action by specific contexts (Wood, Knutson, & Grafman, 2005). Like any event-structured complex, the sensing of moral cues in certain stimulus configurations immediately retrieves the appropriate moral evaluation from memory (Moll, Zahn, de Oliveira-Souza, Krueger, & Grafman, 2005). The combined engagement of social knowledge, emotions, and motivations enables the emergence of well-defined psychological states—which we have called *event-feature-emotion complexes*—such as moral sentiments and activated moral values. Moral beliefs impose contextual structure upon the aforementioned semantic, emotional, and motivational domains and can be retrieved and enacted in an effortless, fluent, and intuitive manner to guide behavior. Moral belief and reasoning processes, by way of the emotional responses and motivations associated with these processes in specific situations, continuously tag the objects and events of the semantic domain as right or wrong (Shermer, 2006), fueled by patterned sets of culturally acquired values (Schwartz & Bilsky, 1987). This tagging process relies on the automatic recruitment of a host of basic and moral emotions tailored for specific circumstances (i.e., contexts) as well as momentary dispositions, which are conditioned by bodily homeostasis (e.g., fatigue, hunger), and enduring personality traits, such as openness to new experiences and the capacity to experience empathic concern (Mychack, Rosen, & Miller, 2001).

Established moral beliefs represent the main guides of ordinary social behavior because most daily situations faced by adults are variations around common themes on which crystallized opinions have long been formed (Bargh & Ferguson, 2000). There are other circumstances, however, in which established moral dispositions fall short of being efficient in regulating behavior. These circumstances invariably involve some kind of moral stalemate for which there are no legally sanctioned or generally agreed-upon courses of action. In such circumstances, previously appropriate ways of feeling and acting are no longer suitable and a process of moral calculus must be called upon, involving effortful, conscious deliberation (Moll & de Oliveira-Souza, 2008).

A few words can be said here about the uniqueness of the interplay between emotional tagging and semantic processing through the use of figurative language in ordinary communication and its importance for the organization of one's own moral ideas (Kövecses, 2000). In English (but probably in most other languages as well), the most conspicuous feature of emotionally imbued language is its metaphoric and metonymic nature. When semantic associations and emotional response concur to compound a metaphor, new meanings are attained that are not contained in the literal constituent parts of the metaphoric vehicle. The cultural universality of figurative language is a consequence of its relatedness to physiologic body states and semantic associations with events of the physical world. Figurative language is thus a major vehicle for the transmission of moral values and beliefs within and among cultural groups.

The tagging of ideas and external events with moral quality imparts morality to behavior, which is expressed as private thoughts and reasoning as well as through expressed opinions, arguments, and actions. Moral behavior is thus the product of a delicate balance between emotional experience, intuition, and calculus, in which the consequences of one's own actions on self and others are pondered against their possible outcomes, depending on the scenarios that present to the moral agent in different time frames (Moll & de Oliveira-Souza, 2008).

NEURAL UNDERPINNINGS OF MORALITY

The Supraordinate Nature of the Moral Sense

Lesion and neuroimaging studies indicate that the three domains—semantic, emotional, and motivational—are organized in neural assemblies that represent the material substrate of the innate moral sense shared by most human beings (Haidt, 2007). The moral quality of ideas and world events that we experience as a moral sense represents a supraordinate neurocognitive structure that integrates a set of more elementary cognitive-affective abilities for feeling empathy, figuring out the intentions and feelings of others, and attributing agency even to inanimate or ethereal beings (Bering, 2006). The supraordinate hypothesis implies that small neuronal assemblies subserving particular configurations of moral events mediate the experience of morality (Tonkonogy & Puente, 2009). For example, the formation of social bonds, which is a fundamental ingredient of the moral sense, depends on oxytocinergic and vasopressinergic neuronal systems localized in a limited number of subcortical nuclei, predominantly in the hypothalamus (Young, Young, & Hammock, 2005). In brief, the neuropeptides oxytocin and vasopressin are necessary for the establishment of social bonds, including parental care, pair bonding, and social memory (Baumgartner, Heinrichs, Volanthen, Fischbacher, & Fehr, 2008). Evidence that social bonding, underpinned by oxytocinergic and vasopressinergic neuronal systems, contributes to the development of morality comes from studies of previously institutionalized children. These children, who are often neglected by caregivers, frequently manifest a lack of wariness of strangers, atypical and disinhibited patterns of attachment, and difficulties in developing close friendships. Adopted children who were previously reared in institutions also show reduced levels of oxytocin and vasopressin after physical contact with their foster mothers, even after dwelling in stable, enriched, and nurturing family environments for an average of 3 years (Fries, Ziegler, Kurian, Jacoris, & Pollak, 2005).

The findings concerning neglected children concur with the proposal that the elementary neuronal systems that contribute to a fully developed moral sense—in this case, the attachment system—are anatomically discrete, chemically specified, and dependent on specific influences from the social environment over a critical period of individual development for their normal maturation (Moll & de Oliveira-Souza, 2009).

Neural Building Blocks of the Moral Sense

Visual perception is the product of distributed neural systems each contributing specific sensory elements (e.g., color, movement, shapes) to compound the gestaltic experience of the visual world. There is evidence that morality follows similar rules of organization in the neural space, as has also been argued with regard to religious and spiritual experience (Saver & Rabin, 1997). This organizational similitude was keenly intuited long ago by Maudsley (1876):

> It may be witnessed, even in young children, who, long before they have known what vice meant, have evinced an entire absence of moral feeling with the active display of all sorts of immoral tendencies—a genuine moral imbecility or insanity. As there are persons who cannot distinguish certain colors, having what is called colorblindness, and others who, having no ear for music, cannot distinguish one tune from another, so there are some few who are congenitally deprived of moral sense. Associated with this defect there is

frequently more or less intellectual deficiency, but not always; it sometimes happens there is a remarkably acute intellect with no trace of moral feeling. (Maudsley, 1876, p. 58)

In the following sections, we focus on work with patients showing impairments of moral behavior following brain lesions, along with related work using functional neuroimaging with healthy adults. In the following subsections, we will present a short review of the main cerebral systems that have been shown to underpin morality (schematically represented in Figures 7.1, 7.2, 7.3, and 7.4).

Isocortical Regions of the Hemispheric Convexity:[3] Anterior Temporal Lobes, Temporoparietal Junction, and Frontopolar Cortex

Gross disruptions of social and moral behavior are seen in cases of damage to the anterior temporal lobes (dorsolateral anterior and temporopolar). The syndrome caused by damage to the anterior temporal lobes was experimentally produced by Klüver and Bucy in chimpanzees (1939/1997). Its recognition in humans—the Klüver-Bucy syndrome—soon followed (Lilly, Cummings, Benson, & Frankel, 1983). The social abnormalities associated with the Klüver-Bucy syndrome include a hypersexuality that is often accompanied by changes in sexual orientation, loss of the ability to experience emotions, apathy, and disregard for social norms and adequacy (e.g., masturbation in public, acquired pedophilia).

Evidence for a critical role of the anterior temporal cortex in social conduct is also provided by patients with the temporal variant of frontotemporal dementia. These individuals present with aphasia when the degeneration is predominantly left-sided. When the degeneration is more severe in the right temporal lobe, they develop odd changes of personality characterized by irritability and impulsiveness, bizarre dressing styles, and fixed ideas and ritualized behaviors reminiscent of those seen in cases of obsessive-compulsive disorder (Edwards-Lee et al., 1997; Rankin et al., 2006).

That the anterior temporal lobes harbor the neural substrates of the semantic component of morality was also shown in a study in which normal adult volunteers of both sexes had to decide whether written word pairs depicting animal function concepts (e.g., nutritious–useful) and social concepts, both positive (e.g., honor–brave) and negative (e.g., tactless–impolite), were related in meaning (Zahn, Moll, et al., 2007). The word pairs varied with regard to their descriptiveness and meaning relatedness. The level of conceptual detail of the social concepts selectively correlated with the level of activation in the superior anterior temporal cortex, more on the right side, whereas both social and animal word pairs were associated with activation in the anterior middle temporal gyrus. The temporal lobe activations in this study were not due to either theory of mind mechanisms (also known to involve the temporal lobe) or emotional valence. With regard to the former, there was a lack of correlation of level of descriptiveness and meaning relatedness with activation in other cortical areas usually implicated in theory of mind (e.g., frontal regions); with regard to the latter, there was a lack of correlation between the levels of temporal activations and stimulus valence. In a follow-up study, Zahn, Moll, et al. (2009) confirmed that the anterior temporal cortices sustain stable

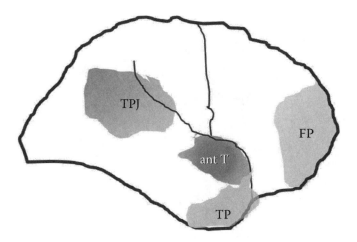

Figure 7.1   Schematic view of right cerebral hemisphere (dorsolateral surface) depicting the cortical areas discussed in the text: anterior temporal cortex (ant T), frontal pole (FP), temporal pole (TP), temporoparietal junction (TPJ).

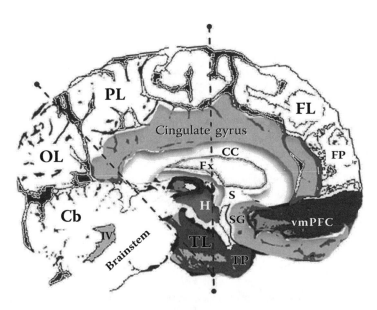

Figure 7.2   Schematic view of left cerebral hemisphere (medial surface) depicting some of the cortical and subcortical structures discussed in the text: cerebellum (Cb), corpus callosum (CC), frontal lobe (FL), frontal pole (FP), fornix (Fx), hypothalamus (H), fourth ventricle (IV), occipital lobe (OL), parietal lobe (PL), subgenual area (S), ventromedial prefrontal cortex (vmPFC), temporal lobe (TL), temporal pole (TP).

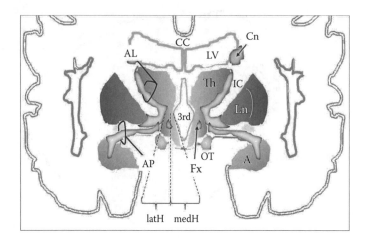

Figure 7.3   Frontal section of the cerebral hemispheres showing the rostral structures of Nauta's mesolimbic system: amygdale (A), ansa peduncularis (AP, ventral amygdalofugal pathway, which connects the amygdala and ventromedial hypothalamus), ansa lenticularis (AL, which connects the internal pallidal segment with the motor thalamic nuclei), caudate nucleus (Cn), fornix (Fx), internal capsule (IC), lateral hypothalamus (latH, medial forebrain bundle), medial hypothalamus (medH), lenticular nucleus (Ln), lateral ventricle (LV), optic tract (OT), thalamus (Th), third ventricle (3rd).

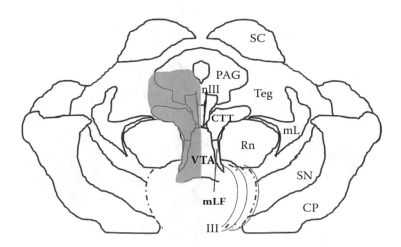

Figure 7.4   Transversal section of upper brainstem showing the caudal structures of Nauta's mesolimbic system (light gray, on left side of viewer): cerebral peduncle (CP), central tegmental tract (CTT), third cranial nerve (III), medial lemniscus (mL), medial longitudinal fasciculus (mLF), third nerve nucleus (nIII), periacqueductal gray substance (PAG), red nucleus (Rn), superior colliculus (SC), substantia nigra (SN), tegmentum of brainstem (Teg), ventral tegmental area (VTA).

representations of abstract social concepts, whereas activity in subcortical-limbic and prefrontal regions was modulated by emotional valence and agency respectively. These findings suggest that the anterior temporal lobes may represent some of the neural substrates of the semantic (conceptual) dimension of our tripartite model. They also concur with Eslinger et al.'s (2009) finding that the anterior temporal cortex becomes more active in moral judgment during development, reflecting the increasing acquisition of social concepts during childhood and adolescence.

The cortex at the temporoparietal junction is also known to underpin the construction of inferences concerning the mental state of others (Decety & Lamm, 2007; Saxe, 2006), which is a critical input with regard to our moral judgments of others' behavior. Other relevant findings concerning the frontopolar and posterior temporal cortices demonstrate that these regions are automatically engaged by stimuli endowed with moral content, as shown by a study in which healthy adult volunteers were exposed to scenarios portraying interpersonal transactions (Moll et al., 2002). In an example scenario of this type, subjects are passively exposed to emotional pictures with or without explicit moral content (e.g., war scenes in contrast to scenes of body mutilations). The former, and not the latter, stimuli were found to automatically activate the frontopolar and posterior temporal cortices.

Taken together, these findings speak for an important role of anterior temporal, temporoparietal, and frontopolar networks in moral sensitivity, irrespective of executive function requirements.

Nauta's Mesolimbic Circuit   Another important neural system for morality involves the limbic midbrain circuit. This circuit comprises a bidirectional collection of fibers that link the ventral tegmental area with rostral basal forebrain structures after establishing synaptic contacts with the intervening lateral hypothalamic nuclei and ventral striatum. The fiber systems that make up the mesolimbic circuit are highly heterogeneous regarding their neurotransmitter content, axon diameter, and degree of myelination.

A significant part of the rewarding effects of self-stimulation is mediated by neuronal systems that run in the medial forebrain bundle. For example, there is evidence that this system is engaged by the rewarding effects of basic stimuli, such as eating chocolate (Small, Zatorre, Dagher, Evans, & Jones-Gotman, 2001), as well as by altruistic behaviors such as those involved in charitable donations (Moll, Krueger, Zahn, Pardini, de Oliveira-Souza, & Grafman, 2006) and maternal love (Bartels & Zeki, 2004). The intimate association of the mesolimbic circuit with the hypothalamus and the ascending projections from brainstem nuclei conveying viscero-endocrine information suggests that this is a critical region for the modulation of social behavior by ongoing bodily states.

From an anatomical perspective, Nauta's mesolimbic circuit constitutes a bidirectional pathway for several fiber systems shared by subgenual-septal and basolateral circuit projections, as discussed in more detail in the next section.

Subgenual Area and Septal Nuclei   Direct stimulation of the septal area in humans evokes feelings of pleasure (Bishop, Elder, & Heath, 1963). Neuroimaging studies also indicate that the subgenual area acts in concert with the mesolimbic circuit to process reward from acts of benevolence toward others (Moll & de Oliveira-Souza, 2009). Subgenual activity is likewise associated with experiences of guilt; for example, subgenual activity in response to guilt-evoking scenarios is related to levels of self-reported emotional empathy as measured by the empathic concern subscale of the Interpersonal Reactivity Index (Zahn, de Oliveira-Souza, et al., 2009).

Selective damage to the rostromedial basal forebrain, involving the subgenual area and neighboring septal nuclei and preoptic area, is rare. When it happens though, it is associated with profound alterations in personality (Freeman & Watts, 1948), sexual disinhibition (Gorman & Cummings, 1992; Miller, Cummings, McIntyre, Ebers, & Grode, 1986), and outbursts of rage (Poeck & Pilleri, 1965).

Ventromedial Prefrontal Cortex, Temporal Pole, and Amygdala   The ventromedial prefrontal cortex (vmPFC), temporal pole (TP), and basolateral amygdala are closely interconnected by the uncinate fasciculus (Klinger & Gloor, 1960). The network thus constituted by these connections was called the *basolateral limbic circuit* by Livingston and Escobar (1971) to emphasize its privileged access to both interoceptive information (i.e., through the basal forebrain) and information from the external environment through the major sensory systems (Barbas, 2000; Nauta, 1986). The basolateral limbic circuit (or vmPFC-TP-amygdala circuit) rests in a strategic position to influence the activity of the whole forebrain. This influence is expressed through its effects on the organization of thought and behavior (Duncan, Emslie, Williams, Johnson, & Freer, 1996) and on the concomitant activation of the autonomic nervous system in response to personally relevant stimuli (Tranel, 2000).

The vmPFC encompasses a set of architectonically distinct regions on the medial third of the orbitofrontal (OF) cortex and lower medial frontal lobe. The work of Damasio and colleagues has fundamentally contributed to our understanding of the role of the vmPFC in social conduct (Damasio, 1995). This understanding has increased enormously during the past decade. Damage to the vmPFC gives rise to severe changes in moral character (Tranel, 1994), especially when the damage is bilateral and extends into the TP cortex and amygdala (Jurado & Junqué, 2000). Some examples of the consequences of such damage include (1) a previously gifted student who lost his talent and began to spend his days on simple manual tasks that had to be constantly organized and overseen by others (Mataró, Jurado, García-Sánchez, Barraquer, Costa-Jussà, & Junqué, 2001); and (2) a prosperous manager in a home-building firm, who was married with two children and active in church affairs before his brain damage and who became unable to stay on the job and incapable of maintaining short-term partnerships and relationships. This patient eventually lost his wife and children and moved in with his parents, unable to hold down any productive occupation (Eslinger & Damasio, 1985).

The mechanisms by which vmPFC damage leads to changes in personality of this type are still obscure, but they probably involve a loss of the capacity to anticipate action outcomes, a decrease of insight into one's own condition, and a loss of the regulatory role of moral emotions and moral reasoning on behavior (Moll &

Schulkin, 2009). This conclusion is based on the observation that vmPFC patients are impulsive and incapable of planning, a deficit that explains much of their failure in real life (Starkstein & Robinson, 1997).

Given the coincidence of so many different fiber systems in the small volume of tissue that delimits the basal forebrain (Heimer, van Hoesen, Trimble, & Zahm, 2008), lesions of the vmPFC region typically engender heterogeneous syndromes of which changes in personality and moral behavior are only a part (Alpers, 1940; Flynn, Cummings, & Tomiyasu, 1988; Poeck & Pilleri, 1965; Tonkonogy & Geller, 1992). Nevertheless, the changes in personality previously described are not always followed by a decrease in premorbid intelligence or gross impairments in social knowledge, language, memory, perception, and praxic skills (Saver & Damasio, 1991). Moreover, lesser degrees and variations of this acquired *dysmoral* syndrome are observed when the damage is unilateral (Mataró et al., 2001; Tranel, Bechara, & Denburg, 2002) and when the lesions are restricted to only parts of the vmPFC-TP-amygdala circuit (Cohen, Angladette, Benoit, & Pierrot-Deseilligny, 1999; Hayman, Rexer, Pavol, Strite, & Meyers, 1998; Mendez, Chow, Ringman, Twitchell, & Hinkin, 2000; Tonkonogy, 1991). Focal deficits in judgment have also been described and further exploration of these *moral scotomata* is a fruitful avenue for research. One example of such a restricted deficit is shown by a patient with acquired pedophilia due to a frontotemporal traumatic lesion who did not exhibit any other kinds of antisocial behavior. Another example of *moral selectivity* is the observation, in controlled settings, that vmPFC patients are far more indulgent about their own moral transgressions than the transgressions of others (Ciaramelli, Muccioli, Làdavas, & di Pellegrino, 2007). At the same time, they are deficient at judging the harmful intent of one agent against another agent in trivial life contexts (Young, Bechara, Tranel, Damasio, Hauser, & Damasio, 2010), yet their comprehension of moral situations may still be generally intact (Moll & de Oliveira-Souza, 2007).

Patients with epilepsy, who present with the syndrome of sensory-limbic hyperconnectivity, provide further evidence that moral ideation is dependent on dedicated neural circuits involving temporal regions (Bear, 1979). These patients display a heightened state of moral, religious, and philosophical convictions (Trimble & Freeman, 2006) with a proclivity to attach emotional significance to ordinary neutral stimuli (Bear, Schenk, & Benson, 1981). A few patients with bilateral anterior temporal epileptic foci experience the phenomenon of sudden religious conversion and enduring personality change (Dewhurst & Beard, 1970). In contrast, epileptic patients with *moral auras*, such as sensations of embarrassment (Devinsky, Hafler, & Victor, 1982) or unresolved moral issues (Cohen, River, & Abramsky, 1999), usually exhibit a right anterior temporal epileptic focus (Devinsky & Lai, 2008).

Interhemispheric Asymmetry   Finally, right hemisphere dominance for the neural underpinning of morality is indicated by the abnormally heightened sense of personal destiny that can be seen in the interictal personality disorder of temporal lobe epilepsy (Devinsky, 2000). The disintegration of the sense of self in cases of frontotemporal dementia that involve damage to the right frontal lobe also adds to the evidence concerning right hemisphere dominance for the organization of morality (Miller, Seeley, Mychack, Rosen, Mena, & Boone, 2001).

The preceding considerations indicate that the moral brain comprises an array of related cortical and subcortical structures. The specificity of this network to moral ideation is relative only insofar as the same structures may be engaged by distinct cognitive mechanisms. The neural subsystems that are specific to moral ideation remain to be elucidated. That they do exist is suggested by individuals with developmental psychopathy, who show a primary impairment of moral behavior with relative sparing of esthetical and religious sentiments (de Oliveira-Souza, Moll, Ignácio, & Hare, 2008). In these individuals, volumetric reductions have been found in regions previously shown to be part of the social brain (Moll et al., 2005), namely, in the frontopolar, OF, and TP cortices, superior temporal sulcus, and insula (de Oliveira-Souza, Hare, et al., 2008).

Other Neuroimaging Findings and the Interplay of Factors in Morality

In the past few years the neural organization of morality has been investigated with unprecedented depth. While there is general consensus with regard to the various neural networks that underpin morality, interpretation of the functional significance of the interplay of these various networks is debated.

For the most part, researchers have paid especial attention to the influence of emotional experience on morality by studying the performance and brain activity of normal individuals and patients with brain damage on a variety of moral dilemmas and economic games (Krajbich, Adolphs, Tranel, Denburg, & Camerer, 2009). Moral dilemma paradigms use scenarios that pit emotionally aversive acts (e.g., killing one person) against outcomes that maximize the greater good (e.g., saving the lives of another group of people; for an example of this paradigm see McIlwain et al., Chapter 6, this volume), while participants in economic games paradigms engage in competitive bargaining with other players. Thus, in paradigms of this type, there is a focus on conflict and competition.

The investigations carried out by Greene and coworkers have been particularly influential in this regard. Notwithstanding their importance, we believe that the interpretation of these studies have suffered from their being too strongly influenced by a long-held tradition that advocates an irreconcilable antagonism, or conflict, between cognition and emotion (Beach, 1955). One example of this way of thinking is exemplified by Cohen's (2005) assertion that "people do have the capacity to override emotional responses. This capacity relies in large measure on the most recently evolved parts of our brains that support forms of behavior that are more recognizably rational" (p. 3). In a somewhat similar vein, Greene et al. (2004) hypothesize a dual-process model of moral judgment, in which cognitive control mechanisms are recruited to resolve conflicts between fast, unconscious, and effortless emotional processing and conscious, effortful, cognitive processing that focuses on consequences.

Although a formal discussion of this work is outside the scope of this chapter, we would like to raise two points in support of our main argument, which may be summarized in the proposal that most prevailing models of emotional experience are heavily biased by concepts derived from work on nonhuman animals. These models have consequently overlooked or downplayed the most interesting aspects of human emotions, that is, their essential sociocultural nature. Although recent investigations apparently acknowledge this fact, as shown by the diversity of social paradigms employed as test stimuli, the influence of animal research still pervades the design and interpretation of the results in many instances, which is shown by the appeal to two prevalent paradigms, one anatomical and the other psychological. From an anatomical point of view, much of the interpretation of findings from neuroimaging studies that have used conflict paradigms of the type previously described attribute emotion processes to the limbic system. To do so has proven just as misleading as attributing cognitive processes to the neocortex. These conflict resolution interpretations stem from a varied mix of the Cartesian opposition between the passions of the soul and reason (Descartes, 1649), with fanciful evolutionary concepts that portray the human brain as the product of phylogenetic change by the addition of layers, the topmost and more recent being represented by the so-called neocortex (Kukuev, 1980). As aptly put by Striedter (2006), "many 'classic' notions about how vertebrate brains evolved (e.g., by adding neocortex to an ancestral 'smell-brain') continue to hold sway among many non-specialists … even though they have long been disproved" (p. 2). Indeed, recent anatomical findings show that the entire isocortex receives direct projections from principal mediobasal prosencephalic (limbic) structures, such as the hypothalamus, hippocampus, and amygdala (Saper, 1987), thus definitely refuting the idea that a limbic system can be defined by the subcortical and cortical structures that, in contrast to a neocortex, receive direct hypothalamic projections (Stephan & Andy, 1982). In short, the more we drift away from Broca's strict anatomical definition of *the great limbic lobe* (Broca, 1877), the more futile the very concept of a limbic system with specific extracognitive attributions becomes (Lautin, 2001).

From a psychological point of view, and with notable exceptions (Haidt, 2003), current neuroscientific studies on human emotions still tend to see them as basic Cartesian passions, leaving aside what is most human about them. This is that human emotions can be especially refined and versatile, enabling the subtlest forms of inner experiences, like those evoked by music (Koelsch, 2010) and the pursuit of transcendence (Schnall, Roper, & Fessler, 2010). In such cases, emotions instantiate novel experiences and attitudes toward life and the world that extend far beyond the ordinary realms to which basic sensory systems are biologically tuned (von Uexküll, 1934/1957).

CONCLUSIONS AND PROSPECTS

The neural underpinnings of morality have only begun to be experimentally explored. No matter how preliminary and tentative, data from studies on morality, religiousness, political inclinations, interpersonal attachment and bonding have begun to exert influence, for example, on practical aspects of the law such as lie detection and expert testimony (Markowitsch, 2008). Challenges for future research include a precise determination of the neurochemical systems and their specific roles in the various components of morality and how these can be pharmacologically modified. The identification of critical developmental periods, when these systems are open to environmental influences, and the nature of these influences may allow the establishment of large-scale programs for early interventions to mitigate disorders that become overtly severe much later, usually in early adulthood, such as antisocial personality and psychopathy. The theoretical importance of such studies is also obvious, as the neurology of morality may reveal an essential piece of the puzzle of our own humanness (Mendez & Lim, 2004).

ACKNOWLEDGMENTS

The authors are indebted to Professor Omar da Rosa Santos (Federal University of the State of Rio de Janeiro) for wise comments on an early version of the manuscript, and to Ms. Mônica Garcia and Mr. José Ricardo Pinheiro (Library of Instituto Oswaldo Cruz, Rio de Janeiro) for the diligent retrieval of classic texts.

REFERENCES

Adolphs, R. (2002). Recognizing emotion from facial expressions: Psychological and neurological mechanisms. *Behavioral and Cognitive Neuroscience Reviews*, *1*, 21–62.

Alpers, B. J. (1940). Personality and emotional disorders associated with hypothalamic lesions. *Psychosomatic Medicine*, *2*, 286–303.

Barbas, H. (2000). Connections underlying the synthesis of cognition, memory, and emotion in primate prefrontal cortices. *Brain Research Bulletin*, *52*, 319–330.

Bargh, J. A., & Ferguson, M. J. (2000). Beyond behaviorism: On the automaticity of higher mental processes. *Psychological Bulletin*, *126*, 925–945.

Bartels, A., & Zeki, S. (2004). The neural correlates of maternal and romantic love. *Neuroimage*, *21*, 1155–1166.

Bauer, R. M. (1982). Visual hypoemotionality as a symptom of visual-limbic disconnection in man. *Archives of Neurology*, *39*, 702–708.

Bauer, R. M. (1998). Physiologic measures of emotion. *Journal of Clinical Neurophysiology*, *15*, 388–396.

Baumgartner, T., Heinrichs, M., Vonlanthen, A., Fischbacher, U., & Fehr, E. (2008). Oxytocin shapes the neural circuitry of trust and trust adaptation in humans. *Neuron*, *58*, 639–650.

Beach, F. A. (1955). The descent of instinct. *Psychological Review*, *62*, 401–410.

Bear, D. M. (1979). Temporal lobe epilepsy: A syndrome of sensory-limbic hyperconnection. *Cortex*, *15*, 357–384.

Bear, D. M., Schenk, L., & Benson, H. (1981). Increased autonomic responses to neutral and emotional stimuli in patients with temporal lobe epilepsy. *American Journal of Psychiatry*, *138*, 843–845.

Bering, J. M. (2006). The cognitive psychology of belief in the supernatural. *American Scientist*, *94*, 142–149.

Bishop, M. P., Elder, S. T., & Heath, R. G. (1963). Intracranial self-stimulation in man. *Science*, *140*, 394–396.

Broca, P. (1877). Sur la circonvolution limbique et la scissure limbique. *Bulletins de la Société d'Anthropologie de Paris, 12,* 646–657.

Ciaramelli, E., Muccioli, M., Làdavas, E., & di Pellegrino, G. (2007). Selective deficit in personal moral judgment following damage to ventromedial prefrontal cortex. *Social Cognitive and Affective Neuroscience, 2,* 84–92.

Cohen, J. D. (2005). The vulcanization of the human brain. A neural perspective on interactions between cognition and emotion. *Journal of Economic Perspectives, 19,* 3–24.

Cohen, L., Angladette, L., Benoit, N., & Pierrot-Deseilligny, C. (1999). A man who borrowed cars. *Lancet, 353,* 34.

Cohen, O., River, Y., & Abramsky, O. (1999). Seizures induced by frustration and despair due to unresolved moral and political issues: A rare case of reflex epilepsy. *Journal of the Neurological Sciences, 162,* 94–96.

Damasio, A. R. (1995). *Descartes' error: Emotion, reason, and the human brain.* New York: Avon Books.

Darwin, C. (1872/1988). *The expression of the emotions in man and animals.* New York: Oxford.

Decety, J., & Lamm, C. (2007). The role of the right temporoparietal junction in social interaction: How low-level computational processes contribute to metacognition. *Neuroscientist, 13,* 580–593.

Descartes, R. (1649). *Les passions de l'âme.* Retrieved March 31, 2010 from http://www.hs-augsburg.de/~harsch/gallica/Chronologie/17siecle/ Descartes/des_pas0.html

de Oliveira-Souza, R., & Figueiredo, W. M. (1996). Iatrogenic multimodal apathy. *Arquivos de Neuropsiquiatria, 54,* 216–221.

de Oliveira-Souza, R., Hare, R. D., Bramati, I. E., Garrido, G. J., Ignácio, F. A., Tovar-Moll, F., et al. (2008). Psychopathy as a disorder of the moral brain: Fronto-temporo-limbic grey matter reductions demonstrated by voxel-based morphometry. *Neuroimage, 40,* 1202–1213.

de Oliveira-Souza, R., Moll, J., Ignácio, F. A., & Hare, R. D. (2008). Psychopathy in a civil psychiatric outpatient sample. *Criminal Justice and Behavior, 35,* 427–437.

Devinsky, O. (2000). Right cerebral hemisphere dominance for a sense of corporeal and emotional self. *Epilepsy and Behavior, 1,* 60–73.

Devinsky, O., Hafler, D. A., & Victor, J. (1982). Embarrassment as the aura of a complex partial seizure. *Neurology, 32,* 1284.

Devinsky, O., & Lai, G. (2008). Spirituality and religion in epilepsy. *Epilepsy and Behavior, 12,* 636–643.

Dewhurst, K., & Beard, A. W. (1970). Sudden religious conversions in temporal lobe epilepsy. *British Journal of Psychiatry, 117,* 497–507.

Duchenne, G. B. A. (1862/1990). *The mechanism of human facial expression* (R. A. Cuthbertson, Trans.). New York: Cambridge University Press.

Duncan, J., Emslie, H., Williams, P., Johnson, R., & Freer, C. (1996). Intelligence and the frontal lobe: The organization of goal-directed behavior. *Cognitive Psychology, 30,* 257–303.

Edwards-Lee, T., Miller, B. L., Benson, D. F., Cummings, J. L., Russell, G. L., Boone, K., et al. (1997). The temporal variant of frontotemporal dementia. *Brain, 120,* 1027–1040.

Ekman, P. (1992). An argument for basic emotions. *Cognition and Emotion, 6,* 169–200.

Eslinger, P. J., & Damasio, A. R. (1985). Severe disturbance of higher cognition after bilateral frontal lobe ablation: Patient EVR. *Neurology, 35,* 1731–1741.

Eslinger, P. J., Robinson-Long, M., Realmuto, J., Moll, J., de Oliveira-Souza, R., Tovar-Moll, F., et al. (2009). Developmental frontal lobe imaging in moral judgment: Arthur Benton's enduring influence 60 years later. *Journal of Clinical and Experimental Neuropsychology, 31,* 158–169.

Fisher, C. M. (1983). Abulia minor vs. agitated behavior. *Clinical Neurosurgery, 31,* 9–31.

Fisher, C. M. (1993). Concerning mind. *Canadian Journal of the Neurological Sciences*, *20*, 247–253.

Flynn, F., Cummings, J. L., & Tomiyasu, U. (1988). Altered behavior associated with damage to the ventromedial hypothalamus: A distinctive syndrome. *Behavioural Neurology*, *1*, 49–58.

Freeman, W., & Watts, J. W. (1948). Frontal lobe functions as revealed by psychosurgery. *Digest of Neurology and Psychiatry*, *16*, 62–68.

Fries, A. B. W., Ziegler, T. E., Kurian, J. R., Jacoris, S., & Pollak, S. D. (2005). Early experience in humans is associated with changes in neuropeptides critical for regulating social behavior. *Proceedings of the National Academy of Sciences USA*, *102*, 17237–17240.

Gorman, D. G., & Cummings, J. L. (1992). Hypersexuality following septal injury. *Archives of Neurology*, *49*, 308–310.

Greene, J. D., Nystrom, L. E., Engell, A. D., Darley, J. M., & Cohen, J. D. (2004). The neural bases of cognitive conflict and control in moral judgment. *Neuron*, *44*, 389–400.

Habib, M. (1986). Visual hypoemotionality and prosopagnosia associated with right temporal lobe isolation. *Neuropsychologia*, *24*, 577–582.

Haidt, J. (2003). The moral emotions. In R. J. Davidson, K. Scherer, & H. H. Goldsmith (Eds.), *Handbook of affective sciences* (pp. 852–870). New York: Oxford University Press.

Haidt, J. (2007). The new synthesis in moral psychology. *Science*, *316*, 998–1002.

Han, S., & Northoff, G. (2008). Culture-sensitive neural substrates of human cognition: A transcultural neuroimaging approach. *Nature Reviews of Neuroscience*, *9*, 646–654.

Hayman, L. A., Rexer, J. L., Pavol, M. A., Strite, D., & Meyers, C. A. (1998). Klüver-Bucy syndrome after bilateral selective damage of amygdala and its cortical connections. *Journal of Neuropsychiatry and Clinical Neurosciences*, *10*, 354–358.

Heilman, K. H. (1997). The neurobiology of emotional experience. In S. Salloway, P. Malloy, & J. L. Cummings (Eds.), *The neuropsychiatry of limbic and subcortical disorders* (pp. 133–142). Washington, DC: American Psychiatric Press.

Heilman, K. M., Scholes, R., & Watson, R. T. (1975). Auditory affective agnosia. Disturbed comprehension of affective speech. *Journal of Neurology, Neurosurgery and Psychiatry*, *38*, 69–72.

Heimer, L., van Hoesen, G. W., Trimble, M., & Zahm, D. S. (Eds.). (2008). *Anatomy of neuropsychiatry: The new anatomy of the basal forebrain and its implications for neuropsychiatric illness*. Amsterdam: Elsevier.

Jurado, M. A., & Junqué, C. (2000). Conducta delictiva tras lesiones prefrontales orbitales. Estudio de dos casos. *Actas Españolas de Psiquiatria*, *28*, 337–341.

Klinger, J., & Gloor, P. (1960). The connections of the amygdala and of the anterior temporal cortex in the human brain. *Journal of Comparative Neurology*, *115*, 333–369.

Klüver, H., & Bucy, P. C. (1939/1997). Preliminary analysis of functions of the temporal lobes in monkeys. *Journal of Neuropsychiatry and Clinical Neurosciences*, *9*, 606–620.

Koch, C., & Crick, F. (2001). The zombie within. *Nature*, *411*, 893.

Koelsch, S. (2010). Towards a neural basis of music-evoked emotions. *Trends in the Cognitive Sciences*, *14*, 131–137.

Köhler, W. (1938). *The place of values in a world of facts*. New York: Liveright.

Kövecses, Z. (2000). *Metaphor and emotion: Language, culture, and body in human feeling*. New York: Cambridge University Press.

Krajbich, I., Adolphs, R., Tranel, D., Denburg, N. L., & Camerer, C. F. (2009). Economic games quantify diminished sense of guilt in patients with damage to the prefrontal cortex. *Journal of Neuroscience*, *29*, 2188–2192.

Kukuev, L. A. (1980). The concept of nervous system levels. *Neuroscience and Behavioral Physiology*, *10*, 1–5.

Lautin, A. (2001). *The limbic brain*. New York: Plenum.

Lilly, R., Cummings, J. L., Benson, D. F., & Frankel, M. (1983). The human Klüver-Bucy syndrome. *Neurology, 33,* 1141–1145.

Livingston, K. E., & Escobar, A. (1971). Anatomical bias of the limbic system concept. A proposed reorientation. *Archives of Neurology, 24,* 17–21.

Markowitsch, H. J. (2008). Neuroscience and crime. *Neurocase, 14,* 1–6.

Mataró, M., Jurado, A., García-Sánchez, C., Barraquer, L., Costa-Jussà, F. R., & Junqué, C. (2001). Long-term effects of bilateral frontal lobe lesion: 60 years after injury with an iron bar. *Archives of Neurology, 58,* 1139–1142.

Maudsley, H. (1876). *Responsibility in mental disease, third edition.* London: Henry S. King & Co.

Mendez, M. F., Chow, T., Ringman, J., Twitchell, G., & Hinkin, C. H. (2000). Pedophilia and temporal lobe disturbances. *Journal of Neuropsychiatry and Clinical Neurosciences, 12,* 71–76.

Mendez, M. F., & Lim, G. T. H. (2004). Alterations of the sense of "humanness" in right hemisphere predominant frontotemporal dementia patients. *Cognitive and Behavioral Neurology, 17,* 133–138.

Miller, B. L., Cummings, J. L., McIntyre, H., Ebers, G., & Grode, M. (1986). Hypersexuality or altered sexual preference following brain injury. *Journal of Neurology, Neurosurgery and Psychiatry, 49,* 867–873.

Miller, B. L., Seeley, W. W., Mychack, P., Rosen, H. J., Mena, I., & Boone, K. (2001). Neuroanatomy of the self: Evidence from patients with frontotemporal dementia. *Neurology, 57,* 817–821.

Moll, J., & de Oliveira-Souza, R. (2007). Moral judgments, emotions and the utilitarian brain. *Trends in Cognitive Sciences, 11,* 319–321.

Moll, J., & de Oliveira-Souza, R. (2008, February–March). When morality is hard to like. *Scientific American Mind,* 30–35.

Moll, J., & de Oliveira-Souza, R. (2009). "Extended attachment" and the human brain: Internalized cultural values and evolutionary implications. In J. Verplaetse, J. De Schrijver, S. Vanneste, & J. Braeckman (Eds.), *The moral brain: Essays on the evolutionary and neuroscientific aspects of morality* (pp. 69–85). New York: Springer.

Moll, J., de Oliveira-Souza, R., Eslinger, P. J., Bramati, I. E., Mourão-Miranda, J., Andreiuolo, P. A., et al. (2002). The neural correlates of moral sensitivity: A functional magnetic resonance imaging investigation of basic and moral emotions. *Journal of Neuroscience, 22,* 2730–2736.

Moll, J., de Oliveira-Souza, R., & Zahn, R. (2008). The neural basis of moral cognition: Sentiments, concepts, and values. *Annals of the New York Academy of Sciences, 1124,* 161–180.

Moll, J., Krueger, F., Zahn, R., Pardini, M., de Oliveira-Souza, R., & Grafman, J. (2006). Human fronto-mesolimbic networks guide decisions about charitable donation. *Proceedings of the National Academy of Sciences USA, 103,* 15623–15628.

Moll, J., & Schulkin, J. (2009). Social attachment and aversion in human moral cognition. *Neuroscience and Biobehavioral Reviews, 33,* 456–465.

Moll, J., Zahn, R., de Oliveira-Souza, R., Krueger, F., & Grafman, J. (2005). The neural basis of human moral cognition. *Nature Reviews Neuroscience, 6,* 799–809.

Mychack, P., Rosen, H., & Miller, B. L. (2001). Novel applications of social-personality measures to the study of dementia. *Neurocase, 7,* 131–143.

Nauta, W. J. H. (1986). Circuitous connections linking cerebral cortex, limbic system, and corpus striatum. In B. K. Doane & K. E. Livingston (Eds.), *The limbic system: Functional organization and clinical disorders* (pp. 43–54). New York: Raven Press.

Poeck, K., & Pilleri, G. (1965). Release of hypersexual behavior due to lesion in the limbic system. *Acta Neurologica Scandinavica, 41,* 233–244.

Posner, J. B., Saper, C. B., Schiff, N. D., & Plum, F. (Eds.). (2007). *Plum and Posner's diagnosis of stupor and coma,* 4th ed. New York: Oxford University Press.

Rankin, K. P., Gorno-Tempini, M. L., Allison, S. C., Stanley, C. M., Glenn, S., Weiner, M. W., et al. (2006). Structural anatomy of empathy in neurodegenerative disease. *Brain, 129,* 2945–2956.

Saper, C. B. (1987). Diffuse cortical projection systems: anatomical organization and role in cortical function. In F. Plum (Ed.), *Handbook of physiology I: The nervous system V: Higher functions of the brain* (pp. 169–210). Bethesda, MD: American Physiological Society.

Saver, J. L., & Damasio, A. R. (1991). Preserved access and processing of social knowledge in a patient with acquired sociopathy due to ventromedial frontal damage. *Neuropsychologia, 29,* 1241–1249.

Saver, J. L., & Rabin, J. (1997). The neural substrates of religious experience. *Journal of Neuropsychiatry and Clinical Neurosciences, 9,* 498–510.

Saxe, R. (2006). Uniquely human social cognition. *Current Opinion in Neurobiology, 16,* 235–239.

Schnall, S., Roper, J., & Fessler, D. M. T. (2010). Elevation leads to altruistic behavior. *Psychological Science, 21,* 315–320.

Schwartz, S. H., & Bilsky, W. (1987). Towards a universal psychological structure of human values. *Journal of Personality and Social Psychology, 53,* 550–562.

Shermer, M. (2006). *The science of good and evil.* New York: Times Books.

Small, D. M., Zatorre, R. J., Dagher, A., Evans, A. C., & Jones-Gotman, M. (2001). Changes in brain activity related to eating chocolate: From pleasure to aversion. *Brain, 124,* 1720–1733.

Starkstein, S. E., & Robinson, R. G. (1997). Mechanism of disinhibition after brain lesions. *Journal of Nervous and Mental Diseases, 185,* 108–114.

Stephan, H., & Andy, O. J. (1982). Anatomy of the limbic system. In G. Schaltenbrand & A. E. Walker (Eds.), *Stereotaxy of the human brain* (2d ed., pp. 269–292). New York: Georg Thieme Verlag.

Striedter, G. F. (2006). Précis of *Principles of brain evolution. Behavioral and Brain Sciences, 29,* 1–36.

Tonkonogy, J. M. (1991). Violence and temporal lobe lesion: Head CT and MRI data. *Journal of Neuropsychiatry and Clinical Neurosciences, 3,* 189–196.

Tonkonogy, J. M., & Geller, J. L. (1992). Hypothalamic lesions and intermittent explosive disorder. *Journal of Neuropsychiatry and Clinical Neurosciences, 4,* 45–50.

Tonkonogy, J. M., & Puente, A. E. (2009). *Localization of clinical syndromes in neuropsychology and neuroscience.* New York: Springer.

Tranel, D. (1994). "Acquired sociopathy": The development of sociopathic behavior following focal brain damage. *Progress in Experimental Personality and Psychopathology Research, 17,* 285–311.

Tranel, D. (2000). Non-conscious brain processes indexed by psychophysiologic measures. *Progress in Brain Research, 122,* 317–332.

Tranel, D., Bechara, A., & Denburg, N. L. (2002). Asymmetric functional roles of right and left ventromedial prefrontal cortices in social conduct, decision-making, and emotional processing. *Cortex, 38,* 589–612.

Trimble, M., & Freeman, A. (2006). An investigation of religiosity and the Gastaut–Geschwind syndrome in patients with temporal lobe epilepsy. *Epilepsy Behavior, 9,* 407–414.

von Uexküll, J. (1934/1957). A stroll through the worlds of animals and men: A picture book of invisible worlds. In C. H. Schiller (Ed., Trans.), *Instinctive behavior. The development of a modern concept* (pp. 5–80). New York: International University Press.

Vygotsky, L. S. (1934/1962). *Thought and language*. (E. Hanfmann & G. Vakar, Trans). New York: MIT Press.

Wood, J. N., Knutson, K. M., & Grafman, J. (2005). Psychological structure and neural correlates of event knowledge. *Cerebral Cortex, 15*, 1155–1161.

Young, L., Bechara, A., Tranel, D., Damasio, H., Hauser, M., & Damasio, A. (2010). Damage to ventromedial prefrontal cortex impairs judgment of harmful intent. *Neuron, 65*, 845–851.

Young, L. J., Young, A. Z. M., & Hammock, E. A. D. (2005). Anatomy and neurochemistry of the pair bond. *Journal of Comparative Neurology, 493*, 51–57.

Zahn, R., de Oliveira-Souza, R., Moll, J., Bramati, I. E., & Garrido, G. (2009). Subgenual cingulate activity reflects individual differences in empathic concern. *Neuroscience Letters, 457*, 107–110.

Zahn, R., Moll, J., Garrido, G., Krueger, F., Huey, E. D., & Grafman, J. (2007). Social concepts are represented in the superior anterior temporal cortex. *Proceedings of the National Academy of Sciences USA, 104*, 6430–6435.

Zahn, R., Moll, J., Paiva, M., Garrido, G., Krueger, F., Huey, E. D., et al. (2009). The neural basis of human social values: Evidence from functional MRI. *Cerebral Cortex, 19*, 276–283.

ENDNOTES

1. We use *ideation, idea*, and *ideational* as shortcuts for all kinds of mental events that make up the fleeting contents of conscious awareness at any given instant in the waking state (Fisher, 1993). The term was coined to designate the normal counterpart of *anideation*, a syndrome closely related to *abulia minor*, in which introspective awareness is lost as a result of brain damage (Fisher, 1984). Conceptually, ideation differs from *mind* (Posner, Saper, Schiff, & Plum, 2007) because it excludes the unconscious, which may play a significant part in the workings of the mind (Koch & Crick, 2001).

2. We use the word *normal* in a socio-occupational sense to refer to individuals who are autonomous and socially productive. Even if they fulfill diagnostic criteria for a physical or psychiatric disorder, by definition, these disorders are not of sufficient magnitude to compromise socio-occupational functioning and autonomy.

3. For reasons presented later on, we use the term *isocortex* instead of *neocortex* to refer to the six layered cortical tissue that makes up most of the human cerebral cortex.

Section *II*

Methodological and Philosophical Reflections on Experimental Moral Psychology

8

Cognitive Enhancement and Intuitive Dualism
Testing a Possible Link

NEIL LEVY

Florey Neuroscience Institutes

JONATHAN MCGUIRE

Macquarie University

Jonathan Haidt has argued that moral judgments might sometimes be caused by feelings generated by morally irrelevant aspects of the cases presented to subjects or of the context in which they are presented. We hypothesized that opposition to cognitive enhancements—pharmaceutical or neurological means of raising the cognitive capacities of normal individuals—might be due in part to a mechanism of this kind. Specifically, we hypothesized that the fact that cognitive enhancement violates dualistic intuitions, which appear to be nearly universal, might cause a feeling of unease that would then cause or constitute a negative moral appraisal of these enhancements. We used a cognitive load manipulation to test the hypothesis. Unfortunately, our data did not support our hypothesis. Nevertheless, we suggest that the methodology employed opens up further avenues for research on the relationship between emotions and moral judgments.

INTRODUCTION

*P*hilosophy has recently undergone an experimental turn. This turn might be regarded as the culmination of the discipline's earlier naturalistic turn. For more than 2 decades, much of the most exciting work in philosophy has been driven by, or at least responsive to, contemporary scientific advances. But the concerns of scientists and those of philosophers are not always identical, and the data that the first provide may not always address the questions of the second. Hence, the experimental turn: To answer their questions, philosophers have designed experiments to gather the specific data they need.

We applaud this development. Although we believe that there remains plenty of important work for more traditional philosophers to do, hands-on experience with experimental methods can only enrich naturalistic philosophy, and the data the experimental philosophers gather are invaluable, even if the results are null, as was the fate of the experiment we report in this chapter. Nevertheless, we believe that our chapter is not without interest. In particular, it illustrates how philosophers can expand their experimental methods beyond the intuition-gathering methods pioneered by Knobe (2010). The experiment reported here combined naturalistic philosophy with experimental philosophy and psychology: We empirically tested a philosophical hypothesis partially inspired by current theory in cognitive science. Even though our data failed to support our primary hypothesis, we think the results are informative, and we hope to inspire other philosophers to expand the range of experimental methods they employ as well as to inspire researchers in the cognitive sciences to collaborate with philosophers. Our null results ought not to obscure the potential power of methods beyond the survey-style methodologies that have been the main tool of experimental philosophers so far.

We used a different approach to the standard methodology of experimental philosophers because our question was different. Experimental philosophers have had two primary interests: (1) testing the features of cases (or scenarios) to which participants' intuitive responses are sensitive; and (2) assessing which philosophical views are intuitive to the folk. Knobe's (2010) work focused largely on hypotheses falling into the first category; in particular, he is concerned with whether ostensibly nonmoral causal judgments are sensitive to the normative features of cases, such as whether the effect is a harm or a benefit. In the second category belongs the extensive literature on whether the folk are compatibilists or incompatibilists about free will (i.e., whether they believe that agents are morally responsible for actions performed in causally deterministic universes; see, e.g., Nahmias, Morris, Nadelhoffer, & Turner, 2005, 2008; Nichols, 2006) and the work on cultural variation in responses to Gettier problems (Weinberg, Nichols, & Stich, 2001).[1] We were interested neither in what the folk generally thought nor in manipulating features of cases to see whether intuitive responses alter as a consequence. Rather, we had a specific hypothesis about how certain intuitions are generated that we aimed to test directly by manipulating the conditions under which participants responded. We hypothesized that opposition to cognitive enhancement was driven, in part, by participants' intuitive dualism. Before we sketch the hypothesis, some background is helpful.

COGNITIVE ENHANCEMENTS: THE CURRENT DEBATE

It is commonplace in bioethics (and now neuroethics) to distinguish two ways the mental and physical traits of persons can be improved. *Treatments* improve traits to compensate for or to cure a disease or dysfunction; *enhancements* improve traits that are not the product of disease or dysfunction. Typically (though not invariably) treatments aim at raising some trait (e.g., intelligence, strength, immune system efficiency) from below the normal range, whereas enhancements aim at raising traits above the normal range. The distinction is, at first sight, commonsensical: There is a clear difference, it seems, for example, between strengthening the muscles of someone who has suffered from a wasting disease and giving someone steroids so that they can become even stronger than they already are. Enhancements that target the elements of cognition (i.e., working memory, general intelligence, attention) are termed *cognitive enhancements*.

Some examples of possible cognitive enhancements might be helpful. Many actual or potential cognitive enhancements involve the off-label use of pharmaceuticals developed as treatments for mental dysfunctions. For instance, there is now allegedly a large market for methylphenidate (marketed as Ritalin) among American college students. Drugs of this type, developed for the treatment of attention deficit/hyperactivity disorder (ADHD), have been found to enhance concentration among normal subjects and thereby supposedly to improve examination marks (Forlini & Racine, 2009). In a large survey of the readers of *Nature*, one of the world's premier science journals, 44% of respondents reported using modafinil, a drug developed for the treatment of sleep disorders, again for the enhancement of concentration (Maher, 2008). Off-label use of antidepressants, such as the selective serotonin reuptake inhibitors of the Prozac family, to boost a feeling of well-being and confidence in normal individuals has been reported for nearly 20 years (Kramer, 1993). Drugs used to treat dementia are now being explored for possible use in enhancing normal memory (Farah, 2005). In addition, cognitive enhancements for any number of distinguishable mental functions either already exist or are the target of novel research efforts.

The distinction between treatments and enhancements is commonly regarded as morally significant. There are, it is commonly believed, very different statuses attaching to the two classes of intervention. Different thinkers place different weights upon the treatment and enhancement distinction. For some, it marks the distinction between the obligatory and the (merely) permissible. For thinkers in this camp, diseases place us under an obligation to provide the means of treatment, whereas enhancements do not obligate us. If this were right, we would be obligated, perhaps, to provide for treatment of disease through a subsidized public system, which is accessible to all regardless of their ability to pay while leaving the provision of enhancements in the hands of the market. We might use the distinction to argue that health insurance *must* provide for treatment, while it *may* provide for enhancement. On the other hand, some thinkers believe that the treatment and enhancement distinction marks the distinction between the obligatory and the impermissible. We might think that the state must provide for the treatment of disease, but it would be unethical to provide enhancements. Some go further, holding that enhancements ought to be banned.

The thinkers who hold that treatments have a different moral status to enhancements—probably a clear majority of those who have reflected on the issue—offer a broad range of reasons for this judgment. They have argued that enhancements constitute a way of cheating in the social competition; that enhancements are inauthentic; that they place undue pressure on others to follow suite; that they tend to promote inequality. In this chapter, we will not attempt directly to assess these arguments (one of us has done so in detail elsewhere; see Levy, 2007). Rather, we propose and report the results of an experiment designed to test a deflationary hypothesis concerning the intuition that there is something especially troubling about cognitive enhancements (indeed, about interventions aimed at the mind more generally). The hypothesis is that these intuitions are the product of an implicit commitment to substance dualism. If this explanation is correct, we have a strong reason to discount these intuitions.

MORALITY AND THE PLACE OF INTUITIONS

Haidt and colleagues (Haidt, 2001; Haidt, Koller, & Dias, 1993) argue that moral reasoning does not, usually at any rate, produce moral judgments; instead, its job is to defend such judgments. In Haidt's model, automatic systems operating without conscious input or rational guidance generate our moral intuitions. These systems encode information from two sources: innate dispositions and acculturated responses. These sources explain, respectively, the cross-cultural commonality with regard to basic moral responses and the cross-cultural diversity coupled with within-culture homogeneity of moral responses with regard to less fundamental questions. No matter what the source of our intuitions, though, Haidt argues that reason typically plays no direct role in generating them and that they are resistant to rational argument. Rational argument generally plays the role of seeking plausible explanations of our intuitions rather than generating or modifying them. We take ourselves to have good reasons for our responses, but these reasons are nothing more than post facto rationalizations of our responses. Haidt suggests that we are more like lawyers defending a client than judges searching for the truth in our use of reason.

Elsewhere, one of us has argued that Haidt underestimates the degree to which reason plays a role in moral thought (Levy, 2006, 2007). Levy argued that Haidt underplays the extent to which our acculturated moral responses are indirectly responsive to reason: not the reason of the person whose response it is but the reason-giving activity of the person's community. We should no more expect people to be able to justify their moral responses on the spot—or, indeed, ever—than we should expect them to be able to justify their scientific views. Justification is a distributed property, and individuals can be warranted in asserting claims when their community can justify them, even when they themselves cannot. Thus, the fact that people respond in ways they cannot justify should not lead us to think that their responses are unwarranted or irrational. Moreover, Levy argued that moral argument does play a role in altering agents' moral views. This process might be slow and uneven; nevertheless, it appears false to claim that our moral judgments are impervious to argument. However, while we think that Haidt underplays the role of reason in revising moral judgment, we want to apply his model of the processes whereby moral judgments are normally generated. In his view, intuitions, produced by mechanisms that encode innate and acculturated information, are at the heart of moral judgment.

Intuitions come in a variety of forms. For the purposes of this paper, we define *intuitions* as spontaneous "intellectual seemings" (Bealer, 1998, p. 208). To have the intuition that p is for it to seem that p is the case. It is not, by itself, to judge that p (though agents commonly regard their intuitions as good evidence and go on to form the correlative judgment). It can seem to someone that p even though they judge that p is not the case. For instance, when someone is confronted with what they know to be an instance of the Müller-Lyer illusion, it seems to them that the lines are of different lengths, but they do not judge that they are different lengths. In our terminology, these agents have the intuition that the lines are of different lengths. Normally, seeming to one that something is the case causes a person to form the correlative judgment; it is only in special circumstances that we do not automatically endorse the content of our intuitions. So understood, intuitions can be produced by different mechanisms and different causal routes. The intuitions on which Haidt focuses are produced by affective responses and are experienced as intuitive feelings; the intuition that the lines in the Müller-Lyer illusion are different lengths is produced by cold cognitive systems and is experienced as perceptions. On the functional account of intuitions presupposed here, this difference in causal routes is irrelevant: What matters is whether the process culminates in an intellectual seeming.

Intellectual seemings, as we just noted, can sometimes be overridden or trumped by other kinds of evidence. Nevertheless, they are almost always regarded as reason giving. In moral thought they have an especially prominent place. Plausibly, intuitions are our primary mode of generating moral claims: We are moral animals at all only because we have certain—to a large extent species-wide—intuitive responses to acts we conceptualize as unjust, vicious, unfair, or what have you (plausibly we can so conceptualize these actions only because we have these intuitive responses to these actions). Moral philosophers have long recognized the primacy of intuitions as a source of evidence for moral claims; it is this primacy that underlies the adoption of the methodology of reflective equilibrium (Rawls, 1971) as a principal means of testing moral claims and theories. This method of reflective equilibrium involves testing a moral claim by assessing its consistency with other moral claims and with moral theories. Using this method requires us to ask whether a particular principle, say, is consistent with the intuitions provoked by considering other possible cases, actual or hypothetical (Rawls, 1971).

We can, by way of argument and the consideration of possible cases, be led to reject some of our intuitions; since intuitions are sometimes inconsistent, such revision is required by the method of reflective equilibrium. But we never escape from intuitions. It is only when arguments are themselves backed up by powerful intuitions that they can hope to convince us to reject the way things seem.

Haidt's emphasis on their centrality to moral thought seems well placed. Moreover, it is also plausible that the causal route he emphasizes—an affect-based automatic route to their production—is likewise central to moral thought: Though we may sometimes generate moral intuitions by cold cognitive processes (say by induction or deduction from prior principles or by reference to paradigm cases), it seems likely that, especially when confronted by novel cases, our first-pass judgments will be driven by our intuitive affective responses.

Thus, it is likely that some of our intuitions, especially those that have not been widely discussed and challenged, are (as yet) little affected by conscious reason. Intuitions with regard to cognitive enhancement might well figure among those upon which, because they are relatively novel, we have not yet come to anything like a cultural consensus and regarding which we are especially likely to be driven by intuitive feeling. Cognitive enhancements represent (apparently) unprecedented means of altering the lives of people. They provide us with means of altering nothing less than the self, or at least constituent parts thereof: Our memories (both their capacities and their contents), our personalities, our desires, and our beliefs. Since these powers are new and unprecedented, we have devoted little thought to their application previously. Hence, we have not had the opportunity to think through our intuitions, to gauge their rationality and their consistency with our other beliefs, moral and nonmoral. Consequently, the chances that our responses to cognitive enhancements reflect gut feelings, and that the reasons we give for our responses are nothing more than post facto rationalizations, are very great. It is this hypothesis that we aimed to test.

In particular, we hypothesized that common responses to cognitive enhancement are the product of our intuitive dualism. No matter agents' explicit beliefs on the topic, it is hard for them to shake off the intuition that the thinking and feeling self is immaterial—embodied, perhaps, but only contingently linked to its fleshy envelope. If this is right, then intervening in the brain to affect that self is something that feels wrong—not perhaps morally wrong, at least not directly, but wrong inasmuch as it ought not to be (we cannot help feeling) possible. Intuitively, cognitive enhancement is a category violation—a violent yoking together of two incompatible kinds of things; changing minds using matter, whether chemicals or electrical pulses, mixes together two categories that are intuitively distinct. Hence, it is likely to spontaneously provoke anxiety; emotional responses like anxiety are easily mistaken for, or causally generate, aversive gut feelings of wrongness. When what is in question is a cognitive enhancement, rather than a treatment, this aversive feeling is not offset by the sense that such interventions are also treatments that are owed to sufferers; since it is unopposed, the intuitive aversive feeling is sufficient to generate the judgment that the cognitive enhancement is impermissible or at any rate morally suspect. That, at any rate, was our hypothesis. If it is correct, opposition to cognitive enhancement might often rest on the automatic anxiety such enhancements provoke and the reasons given for such opposition will represent rationalizations of our intuitions (which is not, of course, to say that these reasons are necessarily bad ones).

We believed that our hypothesis was plausible because there is independent evidence for two claims that support it: (1) that dualism is intuitive for most of us, and (2) that violations of intuitive categories can give rise to negative moral evaluations. We will review this evidence before presenting our experimental methodology and data.

EVIDENCE FOR INTUITIVE DUALISM

Dualism (more technically, *substance dualism*, to distinguish it from its more respectable cousin, *property dualism*) is the view that there are two fundamental kinds of matter.[2] This view is sometimes described as Cartesian dualism, after its best-known proponent René Descartes. Descartes thought that we were not essentially extended because we can coherently doubt the reality of any of our physical properties but not of our minds. *Pace* Descartes, it is controversial whether inconceivability is a good guide to impossibility (Gendler & Hawthorne, 2002). However, we can set Descartes' reasons for dualism aside: Descartes is by no mean responsible for the prevalence of the view. Rather, substance dualism is apparently a cultural universal, found in all places and periods in human history.

Part of the evidence for this claim is that religion is a cultural universal, and almost all religions postulate the existence of immaterial beings. Such beings—gods, spirits, ghosts—are thinking entities that are not (or that are only contingently) embodied. They are pure minds without substance. Afterlife beliefs are also near universal (Kluckhohn, 1962), and belief in the afterlife usually, and perhaps always, brings with it the belief that something—some essence of the person—can survive the death and decay of the body (some cultures seem to have held that survival after death requires the resurrection of the body, but it is unclear that they are counterexamples to the universality of dualism, since they seem to believe in the restoration of the body and therefore that the essence of the body survives its decay). Belief in an afterlife remains very common, even among educated people, and those of us who reject the claim intellectually, along with any other kind of substance dualism, nevertheless find it very easy to go along with such claims in imagination. Think of the attraction of narratives turning on the existence of immaterial beings or otherwise presupposing some kind of dualism: ghost story, tales of possession by spirits, or people swapping bodies.

There is also experimental evidence supporting the view that substance dualism comes naturally to people, though interpreting that evidence is somewhat difficult. Bering (2002) presented adult subjects with vignettes about a person's activities, at the end of which the person is killed. The participants were then asked about their views regarding the existence of an afterlife and were given a series of questions about the mental states of the dead person. As expected, participants who professed disbelief in any afterlife at all—*extinctivists*, in Bering's terminology—were significantly more likely to deny that the dead had any mental states at all than were participants who believed that death was not the end of existence. But extinctivists were significantly more likely to deny that the dead had mental states intuitively tied to the existence of the body, like being hungry, than they were to deny that they had mental states with no obvious ties to the body, like emotions. Thus, a fairly large minority of extinctivists maintained that the dead person in the vignette continued in the emotional or epistemic states they were in prior to their death, such as being angry, having desires, and having beliefs. Interestingly, the same pattern of responses—a greater propensity to deny that the dead have mental states intuitively linked to the body than mental states with no such intuitive link—was also exhibited by participants who professed a belief in the afterlife, regardless of the form such a belief took. Thus, whether these participants believed in reincarnation or in heaven or had a kind of mixed belief, they exhibited the same pattern (as did agnostic participants). In general, it seems it is harder to imagine the cessation of certain kinds of mental states than others.

Some of Bering's (2002) evidence also bears on the process leading to this pattern. Bering measured the time it took participants to make their responses and found that among those extinctivists who denied that the dead had any mental states at all, reaction times were slower when the question concerned the possible continuation of mental states with no intuitive link to the body—the same mental states that extinctivists and nonextinctivists were more likely to assert continued after death. Reaction time data of this type can be interpreted as reflecting the effortful overriding of a cognitive default; that is, the use of slow, usually conscious, processes to override the output of a fast, automatic process (the kind of process that generates an intuition). This suggests that, even for participants who explicitly denied that the dead had any mental states at all, it is intuitive that some mental states survive death, which suggests in turn an implicit dualism. This hypothesis is testable: If the response that mental states end with death is the product of the effortful overriding of an automatic intuition by conscious processes, it should be possible to bias against this response by using a *cognitive load* manipulation. When conscious processes are otherwise engaged, subjects should have fewer resources for overriding automatic intuitive output and therefore should be more likely to assert the continuity of mental states.

Why did participants have the intuition that mental states with no intuitive link to the body survive their agent's death? There are several possibilities. Bering (2002) suggests that the results are a product of our mind-reading machinery. We attribute mental states to others, he suggests, by running offline simulations of their mental states. This is known, in the theory of mind literature, as the *simulation* approach to mind reading; we attribute mental states to others by simulating their minds (the rival hypothesis is the *theory* theory, according to which mental state attributions are made by reference to an implicit theory; see Davies & Stone, 1995, for representatives of both sides of the debate). The important point, for our purposes, is that if we attribute mental states by simulation—even after the others' death—we should expect results like those in Bering's study.

The reason for this is that discontinuity is far easier to simulate for some mental states than others. If we use our own minds as a template to imagine others, we will be able to attribute to them only mental states that we can imagine ourselves having. It is easy to imagine ourselves having mental states that we actually have had, but it is much harder to imagine having mental states that we have never had. Hence, if we answer questions about the mental states of others after death by simulation, we are more likely to agree that they are no longer hungry than that they no longer have beliefs. Not being hungry is a common experience for us, whereas we have never experienced ourselves not having beliefs (nor do we know what it would be like not to have beliefs). This difficulty in imagining the cessation of mental states in creatures that have once had them might be the causal route to an intuitive dualism. People die, but we find it hard to accept that their mental states cease. Hence, we are disposed to conclude that thoughts and emotions can float free of bodies.

But there are other possible routes to intuitive dualism. Another possibility is hinted at by Bering (2002) and developed more fully in later work. It might simply be the apparent conceptual link between some mental states and the body that drives the responses. Bering and Bjorklund (2004) found that younger children are more likely to attribute continuity of body-linked mental states like hunger to dead beings than are older participants, suggesting that the growth in biological knowledge plays a role in intuitions of discontinuity. It may even be that explaining intuitive dualism by reference to some disposition or heuristic that has as its proper domain some other subject matter is a mistake: Perhaps intuitive dualism is more basic than that. Perhaps the pattern of responses might be explained by reference to the difference between (what folk psychology regards as) the *essential* properties of persons—mental states that make them the persons they are—and *inessential* states like hunger and thirst.[3]

In addition to the experimental and anthropological evidence for intuitive dualism, there is plenty of material suggestive of a commitment to intuitive dualism in popular discourse about the mind. As Bloom and Weisberg (2007) pointed out, popular presentations of neuroscientific findings often seem to draw a distinction between brains and persons, such that if a behavior is caused by the brain it is not caused by the person.

IMPLICIT DUALISM AND INTUITIONS ABOUT ENHANCEMENT

None of the evidence we have discussed shows that all of us accept dualism. It shows (at most) that dualism is a cognitive default position, toward which people are disposed. Further, it suggests that even those of us who reject every element of the dualist package (immaterial beings, ghosts, gods, reincarnation) will nevertheless find ourselves disposed to dualist intuitions. It will seem to us as if dualism is true, especially in novel circumstances where there are few conflicting automated or reflective processes to keep these intellectual seemings in check. If this is so, then we might find that all of us—especially those who accept one or more elements of the dualist package but also those who reject it all—also generate gut feelings of unease in response to interventions into the mind where mental states are mechanically altered.

In Haidt's (2001) model of moral judgments, intuitive feelings of unease provoked by contemplating an action or scenario are the basis of moral judgments. When such feelings are provoked by acts falling within the scope of an implicit theory of morality, they are automatically interpreted as intuitions of moral wrongness, but even when they do not automatically fall within this scope, say when the observed acts are novel, the feelings of unease may still be taken as evidence of wrongfulness. We believe we reason from our theories to our judgments, Haidt maintains, but we are wrong: Our rationales for our moral judgments are post hoc rationalizations of these judgments, not their causes. Haidt has two sets of evidence for these claims. First, he cites evidence from *moral dumbfounding* (Haidt, 2001; Haidt et al., 1993). Haidt and colleagues generated this phenomenon in studies in which participants were given scenarios describing taboo but victimless actions (e.g., cleaning a toilet with the national flag, having sex with a dead chicken before cleaning and cooking it) and then asked about the moral status of these actions. Many participants, especially lower socioeconomic status (SES) participants, held that these actions are wrong. When they were asked to justify this conviction, these participants turned to their folk moral theory, which is harm based. They cited possible harms the actions might cause, but the scenarios were carefully designed to rule out any such harm. When they were pressed, the participants were morally dumbfounded: They laughed, shook their heads, and confessed an inability to justify their responses but continued to insist that the action was wrong.

Moral dumbfounding is controversial: Its occurrence may show nothing more than that participants have a limited vocabulary with which to express their moral responses. More impressive, because more clearly demonstrating the generation of (what are taken to be) moral judgments by irrelevant factors is a second set of evidence for the claim that moral judgments are caused by gut feelings rather than reasoning. This set of evidence consists in studies showing that judgments of moral wrongness are intensified and even caused by irrelevant disgust responses. Wheatley and Haidt (2005) used posthypnotic suggestion to induce a disgust response to arbitrary words. They then presented the participants with vignettes describing morally wrong behavior and asked them to rate the degree of wrongness. If the case was described using the word that invoked a disgust response, participants rated it much more seriously wrong than the same case described using a synonym instead. That is, the feeling of disgust was interpreted as causing people to judge the action as more seriously wrong. Indeed, participants even thought that entirely innocent actions were slightly morally questionable if they were described using the target word. Once again, this evidence supports the view that moral judgment is the product of nonrational processes that produce an emotional output. Schnall, Haidt, Clore, and Jordan (2008) used a similar paradigm to intensify judgments of moral wrongness. They found that for participants who score in the upper half of a scale measuring consciousness of one's own body, being seated at a dirty desk led to stronger moral judgments. While one of us (McGuire) has reservations about the methodological rigor of these two studies, particularly in regard to the specificity and strength of the association between *core disgust* experiences and moral judgments (for similar reservations see Case, Oaten, & Stevenson, Chapter 9, this volume), these reported findings seem to support the claim that emotional responses can and do effect moral judgments.

If disgust responses can intensify or even cause judgments of moral wrongness, then it is plausible to think that the feeling of unease generated by violations of implicit dualism will have a similar effect. This was the hypothesis we aimed to test.

MOTIVATIONS FOR THE HYPOTHESIS

We hypothesized that participants would judge novel cognitive enhancements that violate substance dualism to be more wrong than those that do not violate substance dualism or do but seem more natural (e.g., exercising to improve mood). This hypothesis was motivated by two observations: (1) opposition to cognitive enhancement is often explicitly rooted in a feeling of unease; and (2) opponents of enhancement often resort to the language of dualism—though often in a self-consciously metaphorical way—when they attempt to articulate the content of that feeling.

Consider, as evidence of the first observation, Sandel's (2004) well-known expression of the antienhancement position. In his book *The Case Against Perfection*, Sandel claims that the moral concepts in terms of which we usually assess the permissibility of options are inadequate when it comes to cognitive enhancement, because they do not enable us to make sense of the sense of unease that we feel when we confront such interventions:

> When science moves faster than moral understanding, as it does today, men and women struggle to articulate their unease. In liberal societies they reach first for the language of autonomy, fairness, and individual rights. But this part of our moral vocabulary is ill equipped to address the hardest questions posed by genetic engineering. The genomic revolution has induced a kind of moral vertigo. (p. 9)

Sandel (2004) proceeds to discuss various possible objections to enhancement framed in terms of the "language of autonomy, fairness, and individual rights" (p. 9), arguing, reasonably persuasively, that these objections fail. An appeal to these concepts cannot, he claims, make sense of why we feel that cognitive enhancements are so disturbing. He concludes that we must leave behind such concepts to understand the wrongness of the enhancement project, and turns to elaborating the concept of giftedness as a way of giving expression to the unease enhancement provokes. We must come to understand our traits as gifts from nature, he claims, to which the right response is gratitude. Enhancement is wrong because it is incompatible with the kind of gratitude we ought to feel for our many gifts.

Sandel (2004) claims that *thick* concepts like giftedness (see FitzGerald & Goldie, Chapter 10, this volume, for further discussion of thick concepts and their role in moral psychology) help us to understand the unease the enhancement project generates in us; they also help us to see significant and substantial moral worries that outrun the framework of our *thin* concepts like rights and autonomy. In the light of Haidt's (2001) theory, however, a different way of understanding Sandel's views comes into light. Rather than the mismatch between our moral vocabulary and the feeling of unease generated by enhancement scenarios indicating the inadequacy of the former to capture the full range of moral problems, we might understand the mismatch as reflecting the extent to which our intuitions can respond to triggers beyond the domain of morality. It might suggest only that irrelevant factors can cause intuitions of the same kind that typically generate our moral responses. Intuitions might be no more than heuristics, prompting us to consider whether a certain kind of case is morally problematic: If we fail to explicitly identify a moral problem (one that can be expressed using our existing moral vocabulary), that might be a good reason to look for a different explanation of the intuition's cause—one that explains it as generated by morally irrelevant mechanisms—rather than looking to expand our moral vocabulary with new thick concepts.

The second observation motivating our hypothesis is that opponents of cognitive enhancement frequently use dualistic language in expressing their unease. One commonly expressed worry about enhancements, or indeed any technological means to altering personality traits or emotional states, is that such means risk inauthenticity. As Elliott (1998, p. 182) forcefully expressed the worry:

> It would be worrying if Prozac altered my personality, even if it gave me a bet-ter personality, simply because it isn't *my* personality. This kind of personality change seems to defy an ethics of authenticity.

The worry here seems to be of a mismatch between what *I* am and what the drug makes of me. But why does Elliott think that there is room for a gap between what I am and remain, even after taking the drug, and what the drug makes of me? To be sure, if the transformation is shallow—short-lived or only partial—we can easily answer this question. But Elliott's claim is not that Prozac cannot change me thoroughly and deeply; it is that it would be a bad thing if it did change me thoroughly and deeply because in changing me it would introduce a rift between my traits and who I deeply am and remain. This view supposes that I have a contentful essence, an essence that has a natural or typical behav-ioral expression, such that departure from this essence—at least departures that utilize the wrong means—is a departure from who I am. Elliott's acknowledged source here is Taylor (1992), for whom each of us has an original way of being human, "his or her own 'measure'" (p. 28), in accordance with which each of us is called to live. This measure is a value we are called upon to live up to; by living in accordance with it, we live by our own lights, and by failing to live up to it we live a lie. It is only by being true to what is within that we live fully meaningful lives: If I do not live authentically, "I miss the point of my life, I miss what being human is for *me*" (Taylor 1992, p. 29). As Elliott understands Taylor's claim, we each have an essential way of being to which we can conform or fail to conform and that remains untouched by the kinds of changes that can be wrought by psychopharmaceuticals.

That is, Elliott (1998) takes us to have an essence that is in principle beyond the reach of cognitive enhancements. Clearly this view does not commit Elliott to dualism by itself. An essence could be material (perhaps it's the genome, for instance). Nevertheless, since there are no good grounds to postulate any such material essence, it is permissible to suspect that Elliott's view is motivated by dualistic intuitions. Having sketched the motivation for our hypothesis, we now turn to the methods and data.

METHODOLOGY

Questionnaire Construction

Participants completed three novel self-report inventories designed to assess the constructs of interest.

Implicit Dualism Questionnaire

The Implicit Dualism Questionnaire (IDQ) was adapted from Bering's (2002) interview procedure and consists of two separate single-page vignettes. Each details a series of events in the morning of a fictional character, ending with the character's sudden death. In the course of the vignette, various physical, sensory, and mental states the character experiences are explicitly reported—for example, "He was extremely hungry," "Richard suspected that Martha was having an affair," and "The taste of the aspirin was very strong and chalky and almost made her gag." These states were all current at the point of the character's death.

Each vignette was followed by a 20-item questionnaire probing participants' attributions of mental states to the character once they were dead. Five subscales of four questions each probed different kinds of mental states: (1) psychobiological (e.g., "Do you think that Richard is still hungry?"), (2) perceptual (e.g., "Do you think Richard can hear the paramedics talking?"), (3) emotional (e.g., "Do you think Richard is now happy?"), (4) desire (e.g., "Do you think that Richard longs to see his wife?"), and (5) epistemic (e.g., "Do you think Richard knows he's dead?"). Full text of the vignettes and probes is included in Bering (2002).

Participants were asked to provide a yes or no answer and to give a brief reason for their answer if they chose no. This method was used because while a positive answer directly indicates that the participant considers that the state in question persists after death, a negative answer may not indicate that the participant believes that the state could not continue. For example, a negative answer to the probe "Do you think that Richard still loves his wife?" could indicate either a rejection of the possibility of a dead agent experiencing love or that the participant thinks that Richard no longer loves his wife because he believes she was unfaithful. Responses were classified as continuity responses (yes or no, accompanied by a reason referencing continuation of states) or discontinuity responses (no, accompanied by reasoning denying the possibility of continuation of the state post-death). Scores were obtained by calculating the proportion of continuity responses to questions in each category so that higher scores indicated a more dualist outlook.

Attitude to Enhancement Questionnaire

The Attitude to Enhancement Questionnaire (AEQ) is a vignette-based 18-item questionnaire assessing attitudes to three different types of enhancements of mental functioning. Four items assess attitudes to *mental interventions* (e.g., trying a special memory technique to boost memory), four items assess attitudes to *physical interventions* (e.g., using a sun lamp to treat seasonal affective disorder), and ten items assess attitudes to *pharmacological interventions* (e.g., taking a drug that boosts memory). For each item, participants were asked to rate how okay it would be for the agent to engage in the intervention on a five-point Likert scale (with anchors 1 = not at all okay, 3 = somewhat okay, 5 = totally okay). Scores were obtained by averaging the item scores in each category so that higher scores indicated a more permissive attitude to the intervention type. Full text of all vignettes is included in Appendix 8.1.

We included these three categories due to their different relations to dualism. Mental interventions do not violate dualist assumptions, as the mechanism of action is via mental states. However, both physical and pharmacological interventions violate simple dualist notions in that they use a physical mechanism to target mental states. Physical interventions of the type used here, however, are widely considered acceptable, whereas pharmacological interventions are controversial.

Appeal to Nature Questionnaire

Audience members at a previous presentation of the implicit dualism hypothesis raised concerns that participants may respond negatively to the perceived unnaturalness of cognitive enhancements. To control for this, we devised the Appeal to Nature Inventory (ANI), a 20-point self-report inventory designed to assess the extent to which participants equated what is *natural* with what is *good*. A total of 10 items expressed endorsements of the sentiment that what is natural is good—for example, "It is important to keep the natural order of things in mind when deciding what to do," and "Unnatural behaviors are morally unacceptable." Another 10 items expressed the sentiment that nature has no special moral status—for example, "Just because something is natural doesn't mean it is good," and "I don't worry about what's natural when deciding what to do." Participants rated their agreement with each item on a 5-point Likert scale ranging from 1 = strongly disagree to 5 = strongly agree. Negatively phrased items were reverse scored, and item scores were averaged to yield a total score for which a higher score indicated greater agreement that the natural is inherently good. The full text of all items is included in Appendix 8.2.

Experimental Design

Participants were 57 individuals (34 female, age range 17–35) who responded to an advertisement placed on a university subject website. Participants received $7.50 reimbursement for their participation and were randomized into either the *cognitive-load* or *no-load* condition and completed the three questionnaires in counterbalanced order.

Cognitive load was induced by playing a series of spoken words through headphones at a rate of one per second. A total of 20% of words were animal names, while the remainder were two- or three-syllable nouns unrelated to animals. Participants in the cognitive-load condition were instructed to tally the number of animal names they heard while they completed all the questionnaires. Participants in the no-load condition were instructed to ignore the words. This ensured that all participants experienced the same level of sensory input and distraction, with the only difference between conditions being the cognitive load imposed by the requirement to attend to and tally the animal names.

Hypotheses

We predicted that among implicit dualists, unease generated by enhancements produced by either pharmacological or physical means would cause participants to intuitively respond to such enhancements negatively, via the causal route suggested by Haidt and colleagues. We therefore expected degree of opposition to such enhancements to correlate with implicit dualism. It is likely, however, that some participants do not endorse the content of their intuitions and instead effortfully override them. The cognitive-load manipulation was designed to selectively interfere with this effortful override, thereby increasing the proportion of negative judgments.

Accordingly, we had four specific hypotheses:

H1. Attitudes to pharmacological interventions will be less permissive than for mental or physical interventions.

H2. Attitudes to pharmacological interventions will independently correlate with both appeal to nature and implicit dualism.

H3. The correlation between implicit dualism and attitudes to pharmacological interventions will remain significant when appeal to nature is controlled for.

H4. Participants undergoing cognitive load will be less permissive of pharmacological interventions, appeal to nature to a greater extent, and report higher levels of dualism.

RESULTS

Questionnaire Reliability

Reliability analyses yielded Chronbach's α's in the acceptable to excellent range for all scales bar physical interventions, which were excluded from further analyses.[4] Values are given in Table 8.1. With the exception of the ANI, data did not conform to assumptions of normality, requiring the use of nonparametric analyses. Three participants did not provide valid responses to the AEQ.

Hypothesis 1: Attitudes to pharmacological interventions will be less permissive than for mental interventions.

Participants were significantly more permissive of mental interventions ($M = 4.57$) than of pharmacological interventions ($M = 2.25$, $p < .001$) on the

Table 8.1   Questionnaire Reliability

Scale	Alpha
Appeal to Nature	.718
Mental Interventions	.777
Physical Interventions	.462
Pharmacological Interventions	.835
Psychobiological Dualism	.937
Perceptual Dualism	.872
Emotional Dualism	.946
Desire Dualism	.976
Epistemic Dualism	.941
Overall Dualism	.979

Attitude to Enhancement Questionnaire (AEQ). Of the 57 participants, only two rated pharmacological interventions more permissible than mental interventions. Interestingly, a near significant gender effect also obtained in that males ($M = 2.45$) were more permissive of pharmacological interventions than females ($M = 2.12$, $p = .053$).

> Hypothesis 2: Attitudes to pharmacological interventions will independently correlate with appeal to nature.
> Hypothesis 3: Attitudes to pharmacological interventions will independently correlate with implicit dualism.

Contrary to our second prediction, attitude to pharmacological enhancements did not correlate with any measure of either implicit dualism or appeal to nature, whether we considered the whole sample or participants in either the cognitive-load or no-load condition. The only correlations that were significant were strong positive correlations among all five subscales (i.e., psychobiological, perceptual, emotional, desire, and epistemic dualism) of our dualism questionnaire (Spearman's rho (r) between .59 and .86, all $p < .001$). Thus, it seems that dualists are consistently so across all mental states. In line with Bering's (2002) findings, scores for desire dualism were higher than for emotional or epistemic dualism, which in turn were higher than for psychobiological and perceptual dualism (all $p < .001$). Means are given in Table 8.2.

TABLE 8.2   Subscale Means

Scale	Mean	Std. Dev.
Psychobiological Dualism	.26	.37
Perceptual Dualism	.21	.30
Emotional Dualism	.58	.42
Desire Dualism	.70	.42
Epistemic Dualism	.57	.40
Overall Dualism	.48	.34

TABLE 8.3   Effect of Cognitive-Load and No-Load Conditions

	All participants		No Load		Load	
	Mean	Std. Dev.	Mean	Std. Dev.	Mean	Std. Dev.
Appeal to Nature	3.34	0.362	3.28	0.245	3.40	0.450
Mental Interventions	4.57	0.625	4.54	0.691	4.61	0.559
Physical Interventions	4.42	0.554	4.32	0.586	4.52	0.509
Pharmacological Interventions	2.25	0.691	2.22	0.652	2.29	0.739
Psychobiological Dualism	0.26	0.366	0.31	0.385	0.21	0.342
Perceptual Dualism	0.21	0.300	0.26	0.336	0.16	0.249
Emotional Dualism	0.58	0.421	0.59	0.444	0.57	0.400
Desire Dualism	0.70	0.423	0.67	0.439	0.74	0.411
Epistemic Dualism	0.57	0.397	0.57	0.421	0.58	0.375
Total Dualism	0.48	0.336	0.49	0.362	0.46	0.309

There were also some weak to moderate negative correlations between attitude to mental interventions (although not attitude to pharmacological intervention) and both psychobiological dualism ($r(52) = -.34$, $p = .013$) and overall dualism ($r(52) = -.28$, $p = .039$), with trends for similar negative correlations with epistemic dualism ($r(52) = -.27$, $p = .051$) and perceptual dualism ($r(52) = -.243$, $p = .076$). Thus, participants who are less inclined to dualism are more permissive of mental interventions.

> Hypothesis 4: Participants undergoing cognitive load will be less permissive of pharmacological interventions, appeal to nature to a greater extent, and report higher levels of dualism.

Again contrary to prediction, cognitive load did not have a main effect on attitudes to pharmacological enhancement on the AEQ. Similar null effects of cognitive load were found for the implicit dualism and appeal to nature scores (see Table 8.3 for means). In addition, no interactions of presence–absence of cognitive load by subscale were found.

Extinctivists Versus Immortalists

A significant minority of participants ($n = 11$) scored at floor on the IDQ, indicating a complete rejection of the possibility of any mental state continuing after death. Indeed, most explicitly wrote on their questionnaires that they did not think it was possible for a dead agent to experience a mental state. Borrowing a term from Bering (2002), we term these participants extinctivists, while those who allowed for some continuation of mental state after death ($n = 46$) we termed immortalists.[5]

Given that the aforementioned analyses failed to show an effect of implicit dualism on attitudes to cognitive enhancements, we analyzed the responses of these two groups to assess if explicit dualism bore on the attitudes. Unfortunately, again all analyses failed to show any differences between the ratings on the AEQ or the ANI given by extinctivists and immortalists.

DISCUSSION

Only one of our four hypotheses was supported by the data; moreover, the hypothesis supported—that participants would have less permissive attitudes toward pharmacological enhancements than other kinds—is unsurprising and therefore not especially interesting. Our main hypotheses about the role of implicit dualism in intuitive attitudes to cognitive enhancement (in particular, pharmacological interventions) therefore seem decisively disconfirmed; although we note some relation between implicit dualism and rejection of mental interventions such as memory techniques and counseling.

It may nevertheless be true that something like our hypothesis is still correct. Opposition to cognitive enhancement via pharmacological intervention might be generated by an intuitive feeling of unease caused by other morally irrelevant features of these cases. It may be, for instance, that it is the sheer novelty of pharmacological enhancements that explains opposition to them. However, the failure of the cognitive-load manipulation to increase the degree of opposition to cognitive enhancements is data that any such account must explain, and it is difficult to see how this is to be done. Cognitive load is not selective: It should interfere with the effortful overriding of any intuitive response. Given that scores for permissibility of cognitive enhancement via pharmacological intervention were not at ceiling or at floor, it seems reasonable to expect that the cognitive-load condition should increase effects of intuitive feelings on permissibility scores by reducing subjects' capacities to effortfully override such feelings. This very plausible hypothesis is not supported by our data.

Therefore, Haidt's (2001) model of moral judgment generation can be applied to the explanation of opposition to cognitive enhancement only if very little effortful overriding of initial intuitions is required or if our manipulation of cognitive load was not strong enough to sufficiently reduce access to effort. For example, our permissibility scores might have been relatively insensitive to a cognitive-load manipulation; in contrast, Bering's (2002) study used reaction time data to show effortful overriding of intuitive dualism. Another possibility is that subjects who oppose cognitive enhancements via pharmacological intervention have different intuitions from those who do not oppose them. We find this latter suggestion surprising but by no means inconceivable. At any rate, it suggests a further line for future research.

We welcome such future research. More generally, we hope to inspire experimental philosophers to broaden their range of experimental tools to include not only questionnaires but also the entire range of experimental paradigms that have been developed by psychologists and other cognitive scientists.

REFERENCES

Bealer, G. (1998). Intuition and the autonomy of philosophy. In M. R. DePaul & W. Ramsey (Eds.), *Rethinking intuition: The psychology of intuition and its role in philosophical inquiry* (pp. 201–239). Lanham, MD: Rowman & Littlefield Publishers.

Bering, J. M. (2002). Intuitive conceptions of dead agents' minds: The natural foundations of afterlife beliefs as phenomenological boundary. *Journal of Cognition and Culture, 2,* 263–308.

Bering, J. M., & Bjorklund, D.F. (2004). The natural emergence of reasoning about the afterlife as a developmental regularity. *Developmental Psychology, 40,* 217–233.

Bloom, P., & Weisberg, D.S. (2007). Childhood origins of adult resistance to science. *Science, 316,* 996–997.

Davies, M., & Stone, T. (Eds.). (1995). *Folk psychology: The theory of mind debate.* Oxford, UK: Basil Blackwell.

Elliott, C. (1998). The tyranny of happiness: Ethics and cosmetic psychopharmacology. In E. Parens (Ed.), *Enhancing human traits: Ethical and social implications* (pp. 177–188). Washington, DC: Georgetown University Press.

Farah, M. J. (2005). Neuroethics: The practical and the philosophical. *Trends in Cognitive Sciences, 9,* 34–40.

Forlini, C., & Racine, E. (2009). Autonomy and coercion in academic "cognitive enhancement" using methylphenidate: Perspectives of key stakeholders. *Neuroethics, 2,* 163–177.

Gendler, T., & Hawthorne, J. (Eds.). (2002). *Conceivability and possibility.* Oxford, UK: Oxford University Press.

Haidt, J. (2001). The emotional dog and its rational tail: A social intuitionist approach to moral judgment. *Psychological Review, 108,* 814–834.

Haidt, J., Koller, S. H., & Dias, M. G. (1993). Affect, culture, and morality, or is it wrong to eat your dog? *Journal of Personality and Social Psychology, 65,* 613–628.

Kluckhohn, C. (1962). *Culture and behavior.* New York: Free Press.

Knobe, J. (2010). Person as scientist, person as moralist. *Behavioral and Brain Sciences, 33,* 315–329.

Kramer, P. D. (1993). *Listening to Prozac.* London: Fourth Estate.

Levy, N. (2006). The wisdom of the pack. *Philosophical Explorations, 9,* 99–103.

Levy, N. (2007). *Neuroethics: Challenges for the twenty-first century.* Cambridge, UK: Cambridge University Press.

Maher, B. (2008). Poll results: Look who's doping. *Nature, 452,* 674–675.

Nahmias, E., Morris, S., Nadelhoffer, T., & Turner, J. (2005). Surveying freedom: Folk intuitions about free will and moral responsibility. *Philosophical Psychology, 18,* 561–584.

Nahmias, E., Morris, S., Nadelhoffer, T., & Turner, J. (2008). Is incompatibilism intuitive? In J. Knobe & S. Nichols (Eds.), *Experimental philosophy* (pp. 81–104). Oxford, UK: Oxford University Press.

Nichols, S. (2006). Folk intuitions on free will. *Journal of Cognition and Culture, 6,* 57–86.

Rawls, J. (1971). *A theory of justice.* Cambridge, MA: Harvard University Press.

Sandel, M. (2004, April). The case against perfection. *The Atlantic.*

Schnall, S., Haidt, J., Clore, G., & Jordan, A. (2008). Disgust as embodied moral judgment. *Personality and Social Psychology Bulletin, 34,* 1096–1109.

Taylor, C. (1992). *The ethics of authenticity.* Cambridge, MA: Harvard University Press.

Weinberg, J., Nichols, S., & Stich, S. (2001). Normativity and epistemic intuitions. *Philosophical Topics, 29,* 429–460.

Wheatley, T., & Haidt, J. (2005). Hypnotic disgust makes moral judgments more severe. *Psychological Science, 16,* 780–784.

APPENDIX 8.1: ATTITUDE TO ENHANCEMENT QUESTIONNAIRE ITEMS

MENTAL INTERVENTIONS

Ernesto really wants to do well in his exams, but he is finding the sheer amount of information he has to remember overwhelming. Then he reads an article in a magazine, outlining a special memory technique used by card players. The article says that this simple technique can dramatically improve recall.

Would it be okay for Ernesto to use the special technique?

Francine has self-esteem problems that prevent her from doing as well at university as her teachers think she can. A friend suggests that she tries counseling with a psychotherapist. A therapist in the area has a reputation for helping people with just the problem Francine has.

Would it be okay for Francine to see the therapist?

Bert is a writer. He has been disappointed with his writing over the past few weeks: It has seemed flat and uninspired. He resolves to do something about this. He decides that the best thing to do is to go back and immerse himself in the literature he loves and that inspired him to take up writing in the first place. He therefore resolves to take time out, relax, and just read for a few days.

Would it be okay for Bert to immerse himself in literature to try to recapture his inspiration?

Robin plays clarinet in a symphony orchestra. Recently, she feels that she has not been performing as well as she can. Her old mentor tells her that there is nothing really wrong, but a few technical faults have slipped in. She recommends that Robin put in an extra hour of practice a day for 2 weeks and thinks that this will solve the problem.

Would it be okay for Robin to practice extra to try to perform better?

PHYSICAL INTERVENTIONS

Jackie suffers from sleeplessness whenever the pressure at work gets to her. Her doctor tells her there is nothing physically wrong with her. A friend suggests that she do yoga: He had had similar problems, but after several months of yoga he started to feel much more relaxed.

Would it be okay for Jackie to do yoga to help her relax?

Mike has trouble concentrating at school. His parents think that he needs to be more self-disciplined. At the suggestion of his aunt, they consider enrolling him in karate classes, in the belief that a rigorous workout will help him burn off excessive energy and teach him the self-discipline he needs.

Would it be okay for Mike's parents to enroll him in karate classes to help him concentrate at school?

Ron suffers from seasonal affective disorder (SAD). That is, every winter he gets mildly depressed. His doctor says that there is nothing really wrong with him, but it might help if he gets a sun lamp and lies under it for 10 minutes a day.
Would it be okay for Ron to use the sun lamp to treat his mild sadness?

Danielle's performance at work is suffering. She is finding it difficult to concentrate on the demanding tasks she faces daily as a lawyer; just the other day she made a mistake that almost cost a client a great deal of money. A friend suggests that she might be deficient in vitamins: He urges her to try iron and vitamin C tablets to see if that helps her regain her concentration.
Would it be okay for Danielle to try vitamin tablets to help her performance at work?

PHARMACOLOGICAL INTERVENTIONS

John is worried about his upcoming law exams. It is important to him that he gets good marks, but he is finding the amount of information he needs to memorize intimidating. A friend advises him to take Refulen, a drug that has been shown to enhance memory. At first John is worried that the drug might not be safe, but his friend reassures him that many people have taken Refulen without ill effects.
Would it be okay for John to take Refulen?

Jan is a mathematician working on a new proof. She can make progress on her difficult work only if she can concentrate for many hours at a time. She is finding this very difficult. A colleague tells her about Modadin, a drug that can enhance the ability to concentrate without side effects.
Would it be okay for Jan to take Modadin?

Fred wishes he were more outgoing and better at making friends. In the waiting room at his doctor, he reads about a new drug that has been shown to make people more relaxed and more social, without any negative side effects. Fred wonders whether he should take the new drug.
Would it be okay for him to take the drug?

Rita loves to travel. She believes that her experience would be even more enjoyable if she were able to speak the language of the countries to which she is traveling. She has taken lessons but finds progress slow and frustrating. A friend tells her about Gabbatron, a drug that enables much more rapid than usual learning without negative side effects. This would help Rita easily absorb new languages.
Would it be okay for Rita to take Gabbatron?

Frank is a trumpet player. Before he performs, he gets very nervous. So far his nerves haven't prevented him playing his best, but he worries that his playing might suffer. A friend tells him about beta-blockers, a class of drugs that has been shown to calm nerves without drowsiness. Frank decides he will take some beta-blockers before his next performance.

Would it be okay for Frank to take the beta-blockers?

Jackie winces every time she remembers how embarrassed she was at her high school formal. She got drunk and ended up falling into the swimming pool—completely out-of-character behavior for her. Now she has moved on to university and no longer has much contact with anyone who knew her then. She would love just to forget about the incident. Someone tells her about Propozalm, a drug that enables the targeted deletion of memories. All Jackie has to do is take the drug while recalling (one last time) the incident; a few days later, the memory will be gone.

Would it be okay for Jackie to take the drug?

Geoff wants his daughter to do well at school. He has heard of a drug that will allow her to learn more easily and retain more information. At first he is worried that it might be bad for her, but a consultation with his general practitioner puts that worry to rest. He is able to obtain the drug.

Would it be okay for Geoff to give the drug to his daughter?

Madja is tone deaf: She can't tell Mozart from Mahler or Bach from the Beatles. Other people seem to get great enjoyment from music, and she wants to discover what she is missing out on. Testing shows that there is nothing wrong with her ears or auditory system. A musician tells her that he can teach her to appreciate music, but only if she takes a special drug; the drug will help develop the part of the brain involved in processing music. The drug is safe, but Madja isn't certain she should take it.

Would it be okay for Madja to take the drug?

Betsy is a teenager who has been in trouble with the police for shoplifting. Sometimes she is strongly tempted to steal, and sometimes she gives in to the temptation. She has been assessed by a psychiatrist, who concluded that there was nothing wrong with her: She just needs to exercise more self-control. But Betsy finds that difficult and wonders if there is some way to avoid having the temptations at all. She discovers that a drug developed for the treatment of obsessive-compulsive disorder greatly reduces the force of temptations. She therefore considers taking the drug.

Would it be okay for Betsy to take the drug?

Brett has been on Prozac for the treatment of depression. His psychiatrist tells him that he doesn't need it anymore; still, when he goes off the drug he feels less happy than when he is on it. His feelings are entirely normal, his psychiatrist says. But Brett thinks it is better to be happier and therefore is considering remaining on the drug.

Would it be okay for Brett to remain on Prozac?

APPENDIX 8.2: APPEAL TO NATURE INVENTORY ITEMS

Items with an asterisk are reverse scored.

1. Natural products are healthier for you.
2. *As Thomas Hobbes said, life in nature is "nasty, brutish, and short."
3. *Nature is just a resource for people to use.
4. I try to avoid purchasing processed items.
5. Nature gives us a good guide as to what is right and wrong.
6. *Ignoring the natural order has allowed humans to prosper.
7. *Just because something is natural doesn't mean it is good.
8. Unnatural behaviors are morally unacceptable.
9. *People should try to overcome nature when necessary.
10. *There is nothing morally special about nature.
11. People would be happier if they were closer to nature.
12. People shouldn't interfere with nature.
13. It is important to keep the natural order of things in mind when deciding what to do.
14. *There are plenty of natural things that are bad.
15. People should try to live in harmony with nature.
16. Maintaining the natural order is an end in its own right.
17. *Whether someone's behavior is natural has no bearing on whether it is right or wrong.
18. *Natural products are no better than processed ones.
19. Interfering with nature only causes problems.
20. *I don't worry about what's natural when deciding what to do.

ENDNOTES

1. The Gettier problem—so called due to its initial formulation by Edmund Gettier—is a problem in the analysis of knowledge. Prior to Gettier, most philosophers thought that the correct analysis of "knowledge" was simple: Knowledge is justified true belief. Gettier described cases in which agents have justified true beliefs that seemed not to be knowledge because the facts that justified the belief were not the facts that made the belief true.
2. Property dualism is the view that though there is just one kind of ontological substance, this substance has two essentially different properties. Proponents typically hold that one of these properties is not captured by standard physics.
3. We owe this suggestion to Catriona Mackenzie.
4. Upon further investigation, there appeared to be two groupings within the physical interventions category. Ratings of the two vignettes in which the intervention was a form of exercise intercorrelated, $r(55) = .398, p = .002$, as did the remaining vignettes, which involved use of a sunlamp and vitamins, $r(55) = .388, p = .003$. This is indicative that participants were sensitive to a distinction between these types of physical interventions. We therefore excluded physical interventions from analysis.

5. Although we borrowed Bering's terminology, we defined extinctivists and immortalists in a different manner. Bering relied on self-report, whereas we have extrapolated from questionnaire responses. Given that Bering found self-identified extinctivists who nonetheless allowed for continuation of some mental states after death, our criterion is stricter in identifying extinctivists.

9

Disgust and Moral Judgment

TREVOR I. CASE, MEGAN J. OATEN,
and RICHARD J. STEVENSON
Macquarie University

Intuitive emotions may be one means by which we make moral judgments, and disgust might be involved in this process. We explore this suggestion by examining data from three empirical approaches. The first approach involves inducing disgust and then examining its impact on moral and other judgments; this approach ensures that any observed effects must result from the induction of disgust. Unfortunately, few studies have adopted this method, and those that have often omit appropriate controls. The second approach examines trait differences in disgust sensitivity and moral judgments. The third approach focuses on the simultaneous experience of disgust while making moral judgments. While these approaches are of high ecological validity, they do not permit an examination of competing explanations of effects on moral judgments. We consider three contender accounts: (1) there is a causal link between judgments of moral violations and disgust, (2) moral violations are disgusting to the extent that they bring to mind core elicitors of disgust feelings, and (3) disgust is used metaphorically to describe complex reactions to moral violations. We conclude that moral violations might recruit disgust only to the extent that they also involve core disgust elicitors (e.g., contamination cues).

INTRODUCTION

*C*an emotions influence moral judgments? One tradition of thought suggests that moral judgments—judgments of what is right and wrong—are the domain of higher, deliberative (affect-free) processes. In contrast, another tradition holds that intuitive emotional responses have a substantial impact on our moral judgments (see, e.g., Haidt, 2001). The focus of this chapter is on this second approach. Whereas recent empirical evidence suggests a link between disgust and moral judgments, some researchers argue that emotions are only peripheral to moral judgment, confined to motivating morally relevant behavior, but not directly influencing moral judgment (e.g., Huebner, Dwyer, & Hauser, 2009).

In this chapter, we review and evaluate the empirical literature on the three approaches used to investigate the putative link between disgust and moral (as well as other) judgments. The first approach, for which we devote the most attention, involves studies of judgments (including moral judgments) influenced by incidentally induced disgust. We also describe three of our own experiments of induced disgust. The second approach involves studies whereby individual differences in trait disgust sensitivity are associated with differential moral judgments. The third approach involves studies of *integral* disgust evoked by the moral transgression itself (see later for further clarification). We evaluate the weight of the evidence from each of these approaches and discuss the methodological limitations of key studies. Finally, we consider the implications of the research findings from these three approaches.

THE EFFECTS OF INDUCED EMOTION ON MORAL (AND OTHER) JUDGMENTS

One of the main approaches used to investigate the link between emotions and people's thoughts, judgments, and behaviors has been to experimentally induce mood states. This line of research has shown that incidental affect can influence unrelated judgments (Lerner & Keltner, 2000; see Valdesolo & DeSteno, 2006, for a study on the influence of positive affect on moral judgments). In the typical mood-induction study, participants watch films or write about personal experiences intended to evoke positive or negative mood and then any effects of the mood inductions on subsequent judgments are compared (see Forgas, 1995, for a review). The methodology used in mood research provides a valuable paradigm for inferring the causal direction of the link between affect and judgments. Conversely, in studies of integral affect, it is impossible to impute causality because the emotion is purportedly evoked by the judgmental stimulus itself.

In one early study of incidental affect, Schwarz and Clore (1983) induced mood by asking participants to write about recent positive or negative life events. Those participants directed to write about negative events subsequently reported being sadder and less satisfied with their lives than those in the positive mood condition. Furthermore, in a naturalistic follow-up study, these investigators conducted a brief telephone survey of life satisfaction. Those responding to the survey on a warm, sunny day (the positive mood induction) reported greater life satisfaction than those responding on a rainy day (the negative mood induction). Overall, these and many other studies demonstrate that incidental mood can influence judgments in two general ways. First, affect can be recruited to directly inform unrelated judgments (i.e., Schwartz & Clore, 1983). Second, affective differences in information processing can influence judgments indirectly. Such indirect affective influence includes enhanced recall for mood-congruent memories. In addition, negative mood typically results in careful, detail-oriented processing, whereas positive mood promotes heuristic, shallow processing (Lerner & Keltner, 2000).

Although the types of judgment affected and the particular conditions under which mood states have their greatest influence have been extensively documented over the past several decades (Keltner, Anderson, & Gonzaga, 2002), the vast majority of research in this area has focused on the general valence of the induced mood to the exclusion of the effects of distinct emotions (Lerner & Keltner, 2000). Moods are conceived as diffuse, enduring, and of low intensity (Forgas, 2002). As such, they are less likely to be correctly attributed to their genuine cause and therefore might be well suited to subtly influencing judgments. On the contrary, emotions are typically short-lived, are of high intensity, and can often be attributed to a clear cause. Emotions might therefore be less likely to influence judgments than subtle mood states.

Nevertheless, although much of the wisdom gained from the literature on mood inductions does not apply to discrete emotions, there is evidence that specific emotional states can incidentally influence judgments. For example, emotions such as fear and disgust have been reported to affect judgments of risk (e.g., Lerner & Keltner, 2000) and judgments of moral transgressions (e.g., Schnall, Haidt, Clore, & Jordan, 2008). In general, however, negative mood effects do not hold for discrete negative emotions such as fear or anger. For instance, although anger has a negative valence, participants specifically induced to feel angry behave more like those induced to feel happy (i.e., relying more on heuristic cues such as stereotypes in both cases) rather than like those in a negative mood (Bodenhausen, Sheppard, & Kramer, 1994). Taking into account that emotions vary on (1) related appraisal dimensions (e.g., sense of control, certainty, pleasantness, attentional activity, anticipated effort, and responsibility; Smith & Ellsworth, 1985) and (2) the set of behavioral, physiological, communicative, and experiential responses they evoke, Lerner and Keltner (2000) argued that specific emotions should have unique effects on judgments.

In terms of the emotion of disgust, the evolutionary account holds that it serves as a disease avoidance function (Oaten, Stevenson, & Case, 2009). As such, the consequences for judgments and decisions might be a general tendency to expel or avoid stimuli that serve as disease reminders. Further, the grip of the disgust experience is so strong that it might be expected to produce rejection of stimuli in subsequent situations, unrelated to the initial disgust-eliciting event. On one hand, any carryover effects of incidental disgust might be limited to disease-relevant stimuli only. If the effects of incidental disgust are confined to disgust-relevant stimuli, it is unclear whether the effects are similar for directly disease-related stimuli (e.g., feces, vomit) and more complex stimuli such as moral disgust elicitors.

On the other hand, it is possible that the rejection tendency is general, with disgust also leading to rejection of stimuli that have no disease relevance.

Research on the Effects of Incidental Disgust on Various Judgments

In the tradition of the extensive research on mood and judgment, a small literature has emerged focusing specifically on the effects of incidental disgust on moral and other judgments. To investigate the specific effects of incidental disgust, the induction must be compared with appropriate control conditions. For example, comparing the effects on judgments of a disgust induction and a neutral affect induction does not preclude a general negative valence account of the disgust induction. That is, induced disgust might simply involve effects of nonspecific negative affect. Thus, inducing other negative emotions such as sadness, fear, or anger is important to determine whether any effects on judgments are specific to disgust.

Using an autobiographical writing task, Tiedens and Linton (2001) successfully induced happiness, disgust, fear, and hopefulness and then examined the effects of these inductions on a separate and unrelated judgment task: The participants were asked to rate their certainty of the occurrence of future events. The rationale for this study was that emotions such as disgust, anger, and happiness are associated with a feeling of certainty, a sense of understanding the current situation and what will happen next; in contrast, emotions such as fear, hope, and worry are associated with feeling uncertain. Despite being of opposing valence, induced happiness and disgust were expected to be associated with certainty appraisals and induced fear and hopefulness with uncertainty. Accordingly, happy and disgust inductions resulted in much more certain predictions of future events than did fear and hopeful inductions. This study provided some of the first evidence that incidental disgust can have subsequent carryover effects on emotion-irrelevant judgments. Moreover, the effects of these discrete emotions were independent of the general valence of the emotion.

In another experiment from the same series, *certainty emotions* were hypothesized to be characterized by an overreliance on heuristic cues such as stereotype information. Disgust (a certainty emotion) and fear (an uncertainty emotion) were induced by showing participants short extracts from films. Participants then made judgments about a hypothetical scenario in which a student was suspected of cheating. As expected, the disgust induction resulted in a greater reliance on stereotype (heuristic) information about the accused student (the student was described as an athlete; the stereotype athlete is a mediocre student and therefore more likely to cheat) than the fear induction. Thus, by virtue of its association with certainty appraisals, disgust appeared to produce shallow information processing, much like the mood induction literature has found for general positive mood.

Several other studies using a variety of methods (e.g., film, sounds, and vignettes or some combination of these) to successfully induce incidental disgust and fear were not as successful in demonstrating any unique effects for incidental disgust on attentional bias or memory. For example, Charash and McKay (2002) found that a disgust induction produced greater attentional bias to disgust words (assessed using a Stroop task) and increased recall of disgust words only for those individuals who reported high trait levels of disgust sensitivity. In a later study, Charash, McKay, and Dipaolo (2006) used the same induction with a more implicit measure of attentional bias (a masked Stroop task) and found that only the fear induction produced a bias for disgust words. As the authors acknowledged, one main limitation of these studies is that intensity of the fear and disgust induction stories were likely to be different.

In a study of blood-injection-injury phobics, a disgust film had no effect on a disgust-word Stroop task or a word-stem completion task (where participants are asked for the first word that comes to mind to complete a word stem) compared with a neutral condition, even though the disgust film successfully induced disgust (Sawchuk, Lohr, Lee, & Tolin, 1999). Finally, participants in a disgust induction condition did not differ from those in a fear induction condition in negative interpretational bias of threat–neutral homophones such as die–dye and flu–flew (Davey, Bickerstaffe, & MacDonald, 2006). Together, these several studies suggest that incidental disgust can be reliably induced but that its effects on attentional bias and recall is minimal or, at best, similar to the effects of fear.

Conversely, an interesting finding to emerge from the disgust induction literature is that incidental disgust can influence economic decision making. Using film clips to induce disgust, sadness, and neutral affect, Lerner, Small, and Loewenstein (2004) found that disgust, compared with a neutral condition, led to a reduction in the price for which participants would sell a set of highlighter pens that they had been given at the beginning of the experiment. Disgust also reduced the amount participants offered to purchase the pens, compared with a neutral condition. The behavior of the participants in the disgust induction condition was consistent with the appraisal tendencies related to disgust (associated, e.g., with expelling and avoiding): Selling for less ensures that the object is expelled and offering to buy for a low price reduces the likelihood that the other will sell (Lerner et al., 2004). As in Tiedens and Linton (2001), appraisal tendencies associated with the emotion of disgust (involving, e.g., certainty, expelling, avoiding) appear to carry over and show congruent effects on subsequent judgments.

Finally, a recent study induced disgust using a combination of slides (from the International Affective Picture System, or IAPS; Lang, Bradley, & Cuthbert, 2001), sounds (e.g., burp & vomit sounds), and vignettes and compared this with a neutral control condition of pictures, sounds (i.e., classical music), and vignettes (Olatunji & Armstrong, 2009). Participants completed several measures of individual trait differences, including a measure of contamination fear before the emotion induction. They were then taken to a public rest room and asked if they would touch five restroom objects representing increasing contagion risk (sink, trash can, toilet handle, toilet seat, and inside of the toilet). There was no main effect of the disgust induction on the propensity to touch the various restroom objects. Yet, within the disgust condition, those individuals high in contamination fear found the milder contagion risk restroom tasks (sink and toilet handle) more aversive that those low in contamination fear. Further, within the neutral condition, those individuals high in contamination fear found the more extreme contagion risk restroom tasks (touching toilet seat and inside of toilet) more aversive than those low in contamination fear.

The sparse research examining the effects of induced disgust on various judgments has produced several findings suggesting that feelings of disgust can carry over to subsequent judgments. Moreover, where effects have been detected, they tend to be consistent with an appraisal style that is characteristic of disgust (i.e., involving certainty, reliance on heuristic information, rejection, and disease avoidance). It also appears that incidental disgust influences judgments even when the target of judgment does not involve any disease-relevant or disgust-relevant features (e.g., rating certainty of the occurrence of future events; buying and selling highlighter pens). Nevertheless, several of these studies failed either to obtain disgust induction effects or to find any unique effects for disgust when compared with other negative emotion inductions. Whereas these differences likely reflect differences in the judgmental task under investigation, it is still too early to know which types of judgments are most prone to the influence of incidental disgust. One type of judgment that is thought to be specifically prone to the influence of disgust and that has received recent empirical attention is moral judgment.

Research on the Effects of Incidental Disgust on Moral Judgments

Whereas disgust is proposed to influence attentional and memory biases or judgments via associated appraisal tendencies in the previously reviewed studies, the link between disgust and moral judgment is thought to be more direct. For example, the amount of disgust one feels in response to reading a news story about a corrupt politician purportedly invokes harsher moral judgments of the protagonist. Experimental investigations of incidental disgust are therefore used to investigate whether disgust produced in one irrelevant situation can carry over and make subsequent moral judgments harsher. For example, in a study of incidental disgust, Wheatley and Haidt (2005) gave participants the posthypnotic suggestion to feel a "flash" of disgust when they read certain words (e.g., *often*). They then had participants rate a series of vignettes describing moral transgressions (e.g., theft, incest, bribery) and containing the hypnotic cue words. Overall, they found that the hypnotic suggestion increased both reported feelings of disgust and moral disapproval of the transgressions. Importantly, the authors acknowledged that this effect could not be isolated to disgust because the studies did not include any other comparison emotion hypnotic suggestions. As such, it is possible that similar levels of moral disapproval might have occurred if a negative mood induction were used. Furthermore, the hypnotic disgust induction even increased disgust and moral disapproval for the following control vignette that did not involve any sort of moral violation (Wheatley & Haidt, 2005, Study 2): "Dan is a student council representative at his school. This semester he is in charge of scheduling discussions about academic issues. He [tries to take/often picks] topics that appeal to both professors and students in order to stimulate discussion." This finding suggests that the incidental emotion (disgust) might have led to negative judgments in general rather than having a specific effect on judgments of moral transgressions.

In another investigation of incidental disgust, Schnall et al. (2008, Study 1) used an offensive odor to induce mild and strong disgust compared with a neutral condition. Although the mild odor did not differ from the neutral condition in self-report disgust, both disgusting and nondisgusting moral violations were met with moral disapproval from those who had smelled the mild and strong odors. Again, however, it is impossible to know whether the emotion of disgust is being recruited in the moral decision-making process or whether some other factor is responsible (e.g., irritation, distraction, general negative mood). Moreover, the finding that the strong odor did not lead to any appreciable differences in the moral ratings compared with the mild odor is inconsistent with the idea of a direct relationship between the dose intensity of felt disgust and moral disapproval; a direct causal relationship would be implied if a higher dose of incidental disgust produced greater moral disapproval.

One way to explain this dose insensitivity in Schnall et al.'s (2008) Study 1 draws upon the work by Schwarz and Clore (1983). Specifically, affect is less likely to be recruited to inform the judgment at hand when the source of the affect is obvious (e.g., when there is a strong offensive odor emanating from a nearby trash can). When respondents in Schwarz and Clore's (1983) telephone survey had their attention directed to the weather prior to making their ratings of life satisfaction, the ratings were no longer affected by the warm or rainy conditions. In Schnall et al.'s Study 1, it is therefore possible that participants could more clearly ascertain the source of their disgust when the odor was strong and easily noticed (indeed, participants in the strong odor condition reported greater awareness of the odor than those in the mild odor condition) and were therefore less likely to use how they currently felt to inform their moral judgments. Yet, when the offensive odor was only mild, the source of participants' disgust would have been less obvious and so more likely to influence moral judgments. Nonetheless, it is difficult to draw conclusions from this study because there was no evidence that the mild odor produced any disgust.

In subsequent studies in the same series, Schnall et al. (2008) used several different methods to induce disgust (i.e., dirty lab room, autobiographical writing task, and films), yet each of these experiments failed to replicate the direct influence of the disgust induction on moral condemnation of vignettes obtained in Study 1. Only when individual differences in attention to internal physical states assessed using the private body consciousness subscale (PBC; Miller, Murphy, & Buss, 1981) were taken into account did any effects emerge. Specifically, the disgust inductions led to greater moral condemnation (compared with control conditions) only for those scoring high on the PBC. Furthermore, this occurred whether the moral violation vignettes involved core[1] elicitors of disgust (e.g., a man who eats his dog) or did not (e.g., providing false information on a resume). Thus, the compelling suggestion is that the effect of incidental disgust does not appear to be confined to only moral vignettes that involve core disgust elicitors. Accordingly, incidental disgust might be expected to amplify moral condemnation of any moral judgment in accord with Haidt's (2001) views; however, several concerns with these studies cast doubt on this interpretation.

Of the four studies described in Schnall et al. (2008), only one included a negative mood induction (sadness; Study 4) as a comparison with the disgust induction. Therefore, it is unclear whether the effects obtained in the first three experiments were specific to disgust or were caused more generally by negative affect (or arousal). The inclusion of a sad mood induction in Study 4 resulted in amplified moral condemnation from those who undertook the disgust induction compared with the sad participants. But again, this effect was confined to only those individuals high in attention to internal physical states. It is also notable that the disgust condition did not differ from the neutral condition in moral condemnation. Thus, the finding has as much to do with the sadness induction decreasing moral condemnation as the disgust induction increasing it.

Another potential concern with Study 4 was that the film clip used to induce disgust might have inadvertently presented and primed morally relevant content, in addition to presenting the core disgust elicitor. The clip was taken from the popular film *Trainspotting* (Boyle, 1996) in which a drug addict desperately scrabbles through a heavily feces-soiled toilet (the core disgust elicitor) for his drugs. Even if a participant had not previously seen the movie, drugs would seem an obvious explanation to come to mind to account for the desperate protagonist frantically searching in the putrid toilet (other explanations might be money, jewelry). To the extent that participants could link the clip to drug dealing or addiction, the disgust induction is confounded with the depiction of an immoral behavior (drug dealer or addict). That is, it is possible that the depiction of this immoral protagonist (rather than the induction of core disgust) might have resulted in the amplified moral condemnation of the subsequent vignettes.

Another concern with the series of studies described in Schnall et al. (2008) involves the curious finding that moral condemnation after smelling an offensive odor (Study 1) was dose insensitive. We have already suggested that this pattern of results might have occurred because the source of the odor was more noticeable when it was strong and hence weakened its influence on subsequent moral judgments. This account, however, does not sit well with the findings from the remaining three studies, which all found that the effects of incidental disgust were confined to those individuals scoring high on the PBC. These individuals might be expected to notice their bodily changes at the onset of the disgust elicitor and correctly identify the source, reducing the likelihood of subsequent effects on their moral judgments. Thus, the different sets of results across the Schnall et al.'s (2008) studies are puzzling and difficult to reconcile. Based on the findings of Wheatley and Haidt (2005), it is surprising that Schnall et al. (2008) found no main effects of the disgust induction on moral condemnation in any of their studies. What is more, such an effect should have been amplified for those low (not high) in attention to internal physical states in the studies that used the PBC. As argued already, it is those with low levels of such traits who would be expected to be less likely to correctly identify the cause of their disgust feelings. These limitations and puzzling results from Wheatley and Haidt (2005) and Schnall et al. (2008) prevent any firm conclusions about the effects of incidental disgust on moral judgments.

A recent study of incidental disgust by Horberg, Oveis, Keltner, and Cohen (2009, Study 2) included a negative emotion (sadness) control condition and used moral scenarios representing two different moral domains:[2] (1) *purity* (e.g., "Purposely wearing unmatched clothing," "Buying music with sexually explicit lyrics"), and (2) *harm* (e.g., "Refusing to lend lecture notes to a classmate," "Ridiculing a stranger's clothing as she walks by"). Disgust (compared with sadness) increased moral condemnation of the moral scenarios from the purity domain but not from the harm domain. This was the first controlled study on incidental disgust to obtain a main effect for disgust on moral judgment. However, disgust was induced using the *Trainspotting* film clip (Boyle, 1996), which we already suggested might prime morally relevant content (drug dealing and addiction) in addition to including a core disgust elicitor. Indeed, one of the moral behaviors included in the Horberg et al. (2009) study concerned refraining from consuming drugs. In addition, many of the moral violations used in the study do not seem to represent what might conventionally be considered a moral violation. For example, it is difficult to see how "Purposefully wearing unmatched clothing" could be considered a moral violation: Can this action be considered morally right or wrong, and how does such an action bear on the wearer's character? Finally, the absence of a neutral control condition prevented a determination of the extent to which induced sadness decreased moral condemnation. Thus, the findings of this recent study are also limited in the light they shed on the effects of incidental disgust on moral judgment.

Based on the research reviewed thus far, the conclusion that can be drawn on the link that exists between incidental disgust and moral judgment is that this link is at best weak and might even depend on moderating variables before any effects emerge. One of the concerns with many of these studies is the omission of a suitable negative emotion control condition. Another more general limitation is that it is difficult to include more than one or two short judgment tasks after inducing the emotion because the induced emotion is likely to be short-lived. In the next section we describe some of our own research on incidental disgust, in which we have attempted to address some of the shortcomings of the previous research.

The Authors' Studies of Incidental Disgust

Here we briefly describe three studies that we conducted on incidental disgust and judgments. These studies used carefully balanced control conditions and presented participants with a wide variety of judgment tasks, ranging from judgments involving rudimentary perceptual processes (e.g., odor perception) to abstract judgments (e.g., moral judgments).

Study 1: The Effects of Induced Disgust on Judgments

In the first study, we explored the effects of incidental disgust (vs. negative vs. neutral conditions) on a wide range of tasks expected to be related to disgust. These tasks were (1) identification of emotion faces, (2) odor perception, (3) depictions of potential contamination risk, (4) individual differences in disgust sensitivity, (5) preference for cleansing products, and (6) ratings of unethical behaviors described in vignettes.

Participants were 64 introductory psychology students. The induction task comprised presenting participants with slides selected from the IAPS (Lang et al., 2001). A total of 20 slides were selected on the basis of their disgust content (e.g., rotting animal corpse, internal organs, cockroaches on food). The negative control condition comprised 20 slides depicting negative, but not disgusting, images (e.g., people huddled together crying, a distressed child, injured people leaving plane wreck). Most important, the overall valence and arousal of the negative images were equivalent to the disgust set. A further pool of slides contained neutral images (e.g., a chair, a fire hydrant, an electrical outlet).

As described already, an absence of appropriate controls has been a limitation of many incidental disgust inductions described in previous research. The advantage of including the arousal and valence matched negative condition and also including a neutral control condition was that any differences between the conditions could be firmly linked to the unique effect of incidental disgust. Another unique feature of this study was that we repeated the induction five times throughout the experimental session, each time followed by a different dependent measure and a manipulation check. This enabled us to prolong the induced emotion to obtain judgments of a series of different stimuli in just one experimental session.

At each of the five induction phases, participants viewed four slides for 10 seconds each, randomly selected from the appropriate pool of slides. They also completed one of the five randomized judgment tasks and gave ratings of their emotions (disgust, happy, sad, tense). Using a task adapted from Wheatley and Haidt (2005), participants were offered cookies from a plate at the end of the experiment, ostensibly to thank them for participating in the study. The number of cookies consumed actually served as a final behavioral manipulation check, and consistent with Wheatley and Haidt (2005) disgust was expected to result in reduced consumption.

The emotion ratings, made after each of the five induction phases, confirmed that the disgust induction reliably produced disgust compared with the negative or neutral inductions. Moreover, those in the disgust condition consumed significantly fewer cookies at the end of the experimental session than those in the negative or neutral conditions. Thus, the manipulation checks suggested that we had managed to successfully induce disgust, uniquely from the valence and arousal matched control condition. Any effects on the five judgment tasks could then be attributed to the unique effects of incidental disgust.

In terms of accuracy at identifying emotion faces, we adapted a task used by Sprengelmeyer et al. (1996) in which faces were displayed rapidly at differing saturations of disgust and fear (25%, 50%, and 100%). Using a specially labeled keypad, participants were required to identify which of six emotions was presented. Compared with the neutral induction, disgust improved identification accuracy when disgust faces were presented at the 100% saturation and impaired identification accuracy when the faces were presented at 25% saturation. However, the disgust induction and the negative induction did not reliably differ from each other, suggesting that any effects were not unique to incidental disgust.

To investigate the effects of incidental disgust on odor perception, we presented each participant with three odors to smell and evaluate for strength and liking: *pleasant* (mint), *neutral* (iso-borneal), and *negative* (parmesan cheese) odors. There were no differences between the disgust, negative, and neutral induction conditions and the evaluations of any of the odors. To the extent that the odor perception task and the emotion identification task involved low-level processes, induced disgust might have limited effects. Our remaining tasks used more constructive or elaborative processes and were therefore expected to be more likely to be influenced by induced emotion.

Another task required participants to rate slides depicting varying levels of contamination risk. One pair of slides depicted an unclean restaurant (a dirty wharf-side kiosk) and a clean restaurant (a set table with a white table cloth); another pair depicted a contagious person (a woman sneezing) and clean person (a well-presented woman). Participants rated how much they would like to eat at the restaurants and how they would feel about standing next to the person on a train. Predictably, ratings of the unclean restaurant and the contagious person were associated; however, there were no differences among the disgust, negative, and neutral induction conditions in ratings. Moreover, the induction had no effect on the ratings of disgust using a measure of sensitivity scale developed by Haidt, McCauley, and Rozin (1994) (participants are asked to rate how disgusted or bothered they would feel in a number of scenarios, e.g., "You see a bowel movement left unflushed in a public toilet").

Since it is possible that a less explicit judgment task than that required when rating the contamination slides or completing the disgust sensitivity scale might have been more sensitive to the effects of the induction, we also had participants rate their preference for supermarket products under the guise of a marketing task, based on Zhong and Liljenquist (2006). Most importantly, some of the products listed were cleansing products (e.g., Windex cleaner, Sunlight soap, Colgate toothpaste), and other products were not associated with cleansing (e.g., Energizer batteries, Post-it notes, Mars bars). It was expected that preference for the cleansing products over the other products would be driven by feelings of disgust. Indeed, Zhong and Liljenquist (2006) observed a preference for the cleaning products after participants had read a vignette describing an unethical event (vs. participants who read about an ethical event). Nevertheless, in our study, the only reliable difference to emerge was that the disgust induction led to a lower preference for Mars bars than the neutral condition (suggesting that the disgust induction might have suppressed appetite). Again, we failed to find any evidence that incidental disgust could carry over and influence subsequent judgments.

A final task required participants to make moral judgments about three vignettes describing unethical behavior: In the first vignette, an employee sabotages his colleague's chances at promotion; in the second, a man steals an iPod from a parked car; and in the third a politician, with a reputation for trustworthiness, is taking a bribe. We were careful to select unethical vignettes that did not involve any elements that might serve as confounds of disgust such as sex, death, and body envelope violations. Thus any effects of the disgust induction could be isolated to the unethical vignette and not to an amplification of disgust elements integral to the vignette. Consistent with the lack of effects obtained for the other tasks in this study, there were no differences between the emotion induction conditions in judgments of how morally wrong the acts in vignettes were. The only reliable difference to emerge was that those who received the disgust induction rated the vignettes as less disgusting than those in the negative and neutral conditions. We suspect that the graphic pictures used in the disgust induction made the unethical behaviors described in the vignettes seem weak by comparison.

Given the past findings for the effects of incidental disgust on various judgments and the fact that the self-reported and behavioral manipulation checks in our study suggest the slides did successfully induce the intended emotional states, we were surprised to find no significant effects of the disgust induction. Although we had included more rigorous controls than previous studies—the disgust induction and the negative induction were equivalent in valence and arousal—there was still a complete failure to detect any differences when the disgust condition was compared with the neutral condition. One plausible reason we failed to obtain any effects might have been that the induction phase was too close to the judgment tasks, rendering the induction slides too obvious a cause of the emotion. This might have prevented the participants' induced feelings of disgust from influencing their subsequent judgments. We attempted to explore this possibility in a second induction study.

Study 2: Induced Disgust With Delay and Distraction   Study 2 used the same method to repeatedly induce disgust, negative, and neutral states as Study 1. Furthermore, we retained two of the judgment tasks used in Study 1: (1) the depictions of potential contamination risk, and (2) the vignettes depicting unethical behaviors. We also included the self-reported and behavioral manipulation checks used in Study 1. However, Study 2 differed from Study 1 in that we manipulated the interval between the induction phase and the onset of the judgment task. Moreover, participants were given tasks designed to distract their focus away from the induction task. We introduced a new task to investigate the effects of the disgust induction on activation of disgust concepts (i.e., a word fragment completion task), and in keeping with the findings of Schnall et al. (2008) we included the same measure of attention to internal physical states—the PBC (Miller et al., 1981) as used in Schnall et al. (2008).

A total of 82 introductory psychology students completed a series of questionnaires, including the PBC. Participants were then exposed to four induction phases. To distract participants and obscure the link between the induction and the subsequent judgment task, participants were presented with a list of words or a seven-digit number to remember prior to each presentation of the induction slides. After each exposure to the induction slides they were asked to recall the word list or digits, and they then completed a judgment task and a manipulation check. An additional phase of the experiment, in which no induction slides were presented, was added at the end. In this last phase, participants completed manipulation checks, had a 5-minute rest during which they were offered cookies, and then completed (1) the depictions of potential contamination risk, (2) the vignettes depicting unethical behaviors, and (3) the word fragment completion task. This final phase of the experiment was included to investigate whether the disgust induction would have a greater effect on the dependent measures after a delay. In sum, we attempted to obscure the link between the induction and the subsequent judgment tasks by both incorporating a distraction (recalling word lists and seven-digit numbers) between the induction slides and the judgment task and by including a 5-minute delay condition. This enabled a comparison of judgments made immediately after the recall task with those made after the delay.

As in Study 1, the emotion ratings manipulation checks confirmed that the disgust induction reliably produced disgust compared to the negative or neutral inductions. Again, those in the disgust condition consumed significantly fewer cookies at the end of the experimental session than those in the negative or neutral conditions. It is noteworthy that despite incorporating distraction and delay to obscure the link between the induction and subsequent judgments, the self-reported and behavioral manipulation checks confirmed that the intended emotional states were successfully induced.

The slides depicting potential contamination risk (clean and unclean restaurant; contagious and well-presented woman) used in Study 1 were separated, so that one pair always randomly appeared after the 5-minute delay at the end of the experiment. As in Study 1, ratings of the unclean restaurant and the contagious person were associated; however, there were no differences among disgust, negative, and neutral induction conditions in judgments, whether the judgments were made immediately after the recall task or in the delay condition. Moreover, PBC and other individual differences did not reveal any moderating effects on the results.

In the next task, the two vignettes used in Study 1 depicting unethical behaviors (theft and corrupt politician) were separated so that one always randomly appeared after the delay. Again, there were no differences between the ratings of these vignettes between the emotion inductions in either the immediate or delay conditions, regardless of ratings of the PBC and other individual differences.

To establish that our disgust induction could produce some significant effects, we devised four lists of word fragments to represent the categories of disgust (e.g., V _ _ I T could be completed as either vomit or visit), clean (e.g., S O _ P could be completed as either soap or soup), disease (e.g., I N F _ _ T I O N could be completed as either infection or inflation), and negative (e.g., G _ _ O _ Y could be completed as either gloomy or groovy). There were eight words from each category plus eight neutral words, which were subdivided into two different versions that could be randomly positioned in either the immediate condition or the delayed condition. It was expected that the disgust induction would increase the mental accessibility of disgust and disease concepts more than the negative and neutral inductions. We included the clean category to explore whether feeling disgust might also activate cleansing concepts (see Zhong & Liljenquist, 2006). As such, we expected participants who received the disgust induction to convert more word fragments to disgust-, disease-, and clean-related words than participants who received the negative or neutral inductions. Furthermore, the negative induction was expected to increase the mental accessibility of negative concepts more than the disgust and neutral inductions. As expected, participants who undertook the disgust induction completed significantly more disgust-related words than those in the negative or neutral conditions, suggesting that induced disgust increases the mental accessibility of disgust-related concepts. In addition, the disgust induction significantly increased the tendency for participants to complete disease-related and clean-related words compared with the negative and neutral induction conditions. All of the effects obtained for the word fragment completion task occurred whether the word fragments were completed immediately after the induction or after a delay. Furthermore, self-ratings of attention to internal physical states and other individual differences had no effects on the results.

Unexpectedly, those who undertook the disgust induction also generated the most negative words. This suggests that induced disgust increased the accessibility of negative concepts (e.g., depressed, gloomy, alone, despair, sad) more than the negative induction. It is difficult to account for this outcome, given that the inducing slides used in the disgust and negative inductions were equated for valence (and arousal). Nevertheless, the significant effects of the disgust induction on the word fragment completions suggest that disgust increases the mental accessibility of disgust-related concepts, and showed that the method we have used to induce disgust can have measurable effects on tasks other than the manipulation checks.

Thus, although Study 2 produced evidence that disgust increases the mental accessibility of disgust-related concepts, this mental accessibility does not seem to translate into any other effects on behavior. Indeed, over the course of both studies, we explored a wide range of judgments, ranging from those involving rudimentary processes (identification of emotion faces and odor perception) through to more abstract moral judgments, yet none of these judgment tasks were influenced by the inductions. As reviewed already, the effects of disgust inductions have generally been underwhelming, and this may be particularly so when participants are explicitly aware of the cause of their disgust (e.g., the inducing pictures) and so do not misattribute greater disgust to the various disgust-relevant dependent measures (see Schwarz & Clore, 1983). However, our Study 2 addressed this possibility by including a distraction task and a delay manipulation to increase the likelihood that participants would misattribute their disgust to the stimuli.

Another possibility that might explain our null results is that the assorted disgust images we used to induce disgust were too general. That is, the effects of induced disgust might be greatest when the specific domain of disgust induced (e.g., pictures of cockroaches) is matched (e.g., rating disgust toward cockroaches) as opposed to mismatched (e.g., rating disgust toward body envelope violations) to the judgment task. At least one recent study has shown that prolonged exposure to a specific elicitor (cadavers) results in reliable domain-specific (e.g., death and body envelope violation disgusts) reductions in disgust sensitivity but not a reduction in other disgust domains (e.g., foods, animals, body products; Rozin, 2008). In an attempt to address this possibility, one of our colleagues, Amy-Rose McHolme (unpublished thesis, 2009), conducted a study to investigate if any carryover effects of a disgust induction are domain specific or domain general.

Study 3: Domain-General or Domain-Specific Effects?   In this study, 67 female introductory psychology students were randomly allocated to one of three induction conditions. In a *matched* condition, disgust-inducing slides representing several specific domains of disgust (animals, envelope violation, body products, and hygiene) preceded several matching domain-specific judgment tasks. In a *mismatched* control condition the same set of disgust-inducing slides were used, but they were always mismatched to the domain of the subsequent judgment tasks. Finally, in a neutral control condition neutral slides preceded each judgment task. This design afforded tight experimental control, since the slides used in the matched

and mismatched conditions were identical. Thus, the only difference between these conditions was the domain specificity of the subsequent judgment task.

Guided by Haidt et al.'s (1994) description of disgust domains, we selected five exemplar slides each of (1) cockroaches (animals domain), (2) body organs (envelope violation domain), (3) urine (body products domain), and (4) dandruff (hygiene domain). A neutral condition comprised the same neutral slides that were used in our previous studies. The set of 20 disgust slides were independently rated as more disgusting than the neutral set. Furthermore, a manipulation check at the end of the experiment showed that participants who saw the disgust slides (in the matched and mismatched conditions) rated higher levels of disgust than those in the neutral condition.

After exposure to a subset of five slides (e.g., five slides of cockroaches), participants rated scenarios that varied in their level of relevance to the domain of the inducing slides. For example, in the matched condition, the series of five slides of cockroaches were shown, and then participants rated how disgusting they found a specific domain-relevant scenario (i.e., "You see a cockroach scuttle across your kitchen bench and into your pantry"), a general domain-relevant scenario (i.e., "You see some maggots on the lid of your garbage bin"), and a domain-irrelevant scenario (i.e., "You see human organs as part of a biology class"). In the mismatched condition, the domain represented by the five slides (e.g., cockroaches) was never matched with domain-relevant scenarios (e.g., scenarios concerning cockroaches or animals). In a manipulation check toward the end of the experiment, participants were able to reliably discriminate scenarios that were domain relevant from those that were domain irrelevant.

The other main dependent measure comprised four behavioral avoidance tasks adapted from a method used in Rozin, Haidt, and Fincher (1999) and consisted of participant determined exposure to four stimuli chosen to represent each of the four domains: (1) cockroach (animals domain), (2) bedpan (body products domain), (3) sheep's kidney (envelope violations domain), and (4) used hair comb (hygiene domain). Each behavioral avoidance task comprised a series of steps designed to be increasingly disgusting (e.g., looking at the cockroach, touching it, holding it, holding the cockroach up to their nose and smelling it). Participants were scored on how far they would progress with the steps. Again, in the matched condition, the domain-relevant behavioral avoidance task followed the appropriate set of five induction slides (e.g., cockroach slides were followed by the cockroach behavioral avoidance task).

After completing a battery of measures of individual differences, including the measure of attention to internal physical states (PBC; Miller et al., 1981) used in Schnall et al. (2008), participants were presented with five induction slides and then rated three scenarios and completed the behavioral avoidance task. This procedure was repeated four times during the experiment, and at the end of the study participants completed the manipulation check items. The order of the scenarios and the behavior avoidance task was randomized, as was the position of the groups of five slides representing each domain.

The results indicated that those in the matched condition rated the scenarios equivalently to those in the mismatched and neutral conditions. Furthermore, whether participants undertook the matched, mismatched, or neutral condition had no effect on their behavioral avoidance scores. Thus, it is clear that there was no distinguishable carryover effect of the disgust-inducing slides to the subsequent judgments and behaviors whether these were specifically matched. There were also no moderating effects of individual differences in attention to internal physical states.

DISCUSSION OF INCIDENTAL DISGUST STUDIES

The three studies from our lab paint a bleak picture for the prospect of incidental disgust influencing subsequent judgments. Incorporating tight experimental control into each study to ensure that any effects could be attributed to the disgust induction (and not general negative mood or arousal), only the word fragment completion task produced results that differed significantly among conditions. For all other judgments, the neutral induction did not differ from the two emotion inductions across the three studies. It did not matter whether the judgments concerned rudimentary perceptual processes (e.g., odor perception) or abstract judgments (e.g., moral judgments). Nor did it matter if the judgments were relevant or irrelevant to the specific domain of the disgust-inducing slides.

A major difference between the designs we used and those used in other induction studies is that we incorporated multiple induction phases within a single experiment. It is possible that this might have made the slides an obvious cause of the participants' emotional states and hence reduced the carryover effects on subsequent judgments. However, other induction studies have used powerful and obvious disgust inductions such as film clips, slides, sounds, and smells, administered immediately prior to the judgment task (e.g., Lerner et al., 2004; Tiedens & Linton, 2001; Schnall et al., 2008) and have obtained significant effects. Furthermore, we attempted to address the possibility that our induction was too obviously the cause of the emotion by including a distraction and delay between the induction phase and the judgment task in Study 2, which had no effect. Finally, we attempted to disguise the purpose of the induction phase by informing participants that the slides were part of a memory task, for which they would be examined at the end of the experiment. None of these participants were able to identify the true purpose of the induction slides during debriefing. For these reasons, we think it unlikely that the inductions used in our studies interfered with carryover effects any more than those used in other induction studies.

Based on the previous research on the effects of induced disgust on judgments and our own experiments, it seems that induced disgust might increase mental accessibility of disgust-related concepts and that this might carry over to influence some subsequent judgments in a manner consistent with the appraisal-style characteristic of disgust (i.e., involving certainty, reliance on heuristic information, rejection, and disease avoidance). Nevertheless, this is by no means a robust effect, with many studies failing to obtain any effects of the induction on judgments, despite reliably inducing feelings of disgust. In terms of any influence that incidental disgust might have on moral judgments, the existing studies showing significant results used designs and methods that leave open the possibility that any effects are not uniquely due to disgust. Furthermore, our own studies failed to find any support for a relationship between incidental disgust and moral judgments. Thus we conclude that there is no firm replicable evidence for this relationship.

The Effects of Disgust Sensitivity on Moral Judgments

Based on the same rationale as the induction studies, another source of evidence that disgust is associated with moral judgments comes from correlational studies that measure individual differences in the propensity to experience disgust—*disgust sensitivity* (Haidt et al., 1994). Disgust sensitivity describes an individual's proneness to experiencing disgust easily and intensely. Just as disgust inductions elevate feeling of disgust, so too the person high in disgust sensitivity feels elevated disgust, and this elevated disgust is thought to increase disgust in response to entities from various classes of disgust elicitors (e.g., human and animal products such as feces, blood, gore; Haidt et al., 1994). In general, disgust sensitivity has been reported to predict a range of attitudes, biases, and behaviors that reflect concerns over moral violations. In one such study, individuals high in trait disgust reported a stronger inclination to punish impure behaviors (e.g., being sexually promiscuous; Hoberg, Oveis, Keltner, & Cohen, 2009). Trait disgust sensitivity has also predicted greater condemnation of criminal activity (Jones & Fitness, 2008). When presented with a vignette of a person accused of a heinous crime (e.g., ambiguous evidence about a man charged with murdering a young woman by strangulation), participants high (vs. low) in disgust sensitivity were more likely to find the suspect guilty, impose harsher penalties, and consider the suspect evil. High disgust-sensitive participants also demonstrated more pronounced moral biases insofar as they reported greater estimates of the extent of crime within the community and reported a preference for setting reasonable doubt thresholds for crime convictions at relatively low levels.

Individuals with high disgust sensitivity have also been found to show greater self-reported political conservatism (Haidt & Hersh, 2001; Inbar, Pizarro, & Bloom, 2009). This relationship was reported as being strongest for the sociomoral political issues of homosexuality (Haidt & Hersh, 2001), gay marriage, and abortion (Inbar, Pizarro, & Bloom, 2009). Specifically, high disgust sensitivity was related to a greater disapproval of homosexuality, gay marriage, and abortion. In addition, even when participants explicitly report that they are not morally opposed to homosexuality, those participants higher in disgust sensitivity are more likely to display antigay attitudes when using implicit measures of attitudes, such as the Implicit Association Test[3] (Inbar, Pizarro, Knobe, & Bloom, 2009). Relatedly, Olatunji (2008) found that high disgust sensitivity for core elicitors predicted homophobic attitudes (i.e., sex should be between a man and a woman), conservative attitudes toward sex (i.e., sex education should be restricted to the home), and religious principles (i.e., "I must try hard to avoid certain immoral thoughts").

Along these same lines, disgust sensitivity has also been related to intolerance toward nonconformists. Specifically, people high in disgust-sensitivity have a stronger attraction to the dominant ingroup and are more likely to adhere to their principles, values, and norms. In addition, high disgust sensitive people are more likely to be less tolerant of nonconformists because they view such individuals as potential threats (Brooks, 2008). This assertion is consistent with the finding that high disgust sensitivity predicts negative attitudes toward outgroups (e.g., immigrants and foreign ethnic groups; Hodson & Costello, 2007; Navarrete & Fessler, 2006). Finally, disgust sensitivity has also been associated with moral objections to cigarette smoking (Rozin & Singh, 1999). In this study, disgust reactions to cigarette smoking were associated with stronger beliefs that smoking is immoral and should be illegal. Furthermore, disgust measures correlated more strongly and positively with moral judgments of smoking than did smoking-related health concerns.

The rationale for examining differences in chronic disgust sensitivity in relation to moral judgments might appear parallel to the rationale for examining the effects of induced disgust on judgments. Nevertheless, the main limitation of the disgust sensitivity studies is that it is unclear whether disgust sensitivity or, alternatively, some other correlate of disgust sensitivity (e.g., neuroticism, perceived vulnerability to disease, sensation seeking) is directly responsible for the relationship. Furthermore, the reactions might depend on the presence of other disgust domains in the moral vignettes (e.g., sex, death, body envelope violations to evoke the amplified disgust reactions). For this reason the findings of the disgust sensitivity studies must be treated with caution because causality cannot be imputed from them.

The Effects of Integral Emotion on Judgment

Another experimental approach that has been used to explore the link between emotions and how people think and behave incorporates the manipulation of integral emotion (Schwarz, 1990; Schwarz & Clore, 1996). Integral emotion is the emotion that is directly elicited by a particular event and influences judgments made about that event (Lerner & Keltner, 2000). For example, a field study of public reactions to O. J. Simpson following his arrest for the alleged murder of his ex-wife found that participants who reported anger toward the crime endorsed more severe sentencing for that crime, whereas sympathy toward the crime predicted more lenient sentencing (Graham, Weiner, & Zucker, 1997).

The Effects of Integral Disgust on Moral Judgments

In terms of moral judgments, several findings suggest that disgust is elicited by moral infractions (e.g., feeling disgust toward a corrupt politician) that have little to do with the elicitors of core disgust. An obvious question then is whether this purported disgust response resembles the disgust triggered by exposure to disgusting physical contaminants. While there is growing empirical support for the view that these disgust responses are all similar, we argue that the support is problematic.

In two studies of integral disgust, Moll and de Oliveira-Souza (2007) and Moll et al. (2005) explored contrasting neural signatures of core disgust stimuli versus what they described as indignation stimuli (i.e., involving moral disgust) and argued that brain activity in individuals who contemplate morally disgusting acts compared with those contemplating elicitors of core disgust demonstrates substantial overlap in the brain regions activated for both. Nevertheless, as the authors noted, their indignation stimuli also relied on core disgust cues (e.g., "You took your mother out to dinner. At the restaurant, she saw a dead cockroach floating on the soup pan"), which confounds the resultant data.

Another functional magnetic resonance imaging (fMRI) study presented men with short statements describing various acts involving their sister (Borg, Lieberman, & Kiehl, 2008). Although overlap was observed in the brain regions activated for pathogen disgust and sociomoral disgust, the items used to instill pathogen disgust (e.g., sipping your sister's urine) were rated as more morally wrong than those in a neutral control condition. Moreover, (nonsexual) moral statements were rated as more disgusting than neutral items, and these moral statements contained some vivid disgust content (e.g., killing your sister's child) in addition to pure moral content (e.g., burglarizing your sister's home). Thus again, brain activation overlap might have been enhanced by overlap in the content of the statements across conditions.

This problem arises in yet another fMRI study. Harris and Fiske (2006) found that images of outgroups, images that included homeless people and drug addicts, were associated with activation in the amygdala and insula. This pattern of activation is reported as consistent with patterns triggered by core disgust but is also consistent with fear (Schäfer, Schienle, & Vaitl, 2005). Moreover, these images were embedded with core disgust cues (e.g., depictions of individuals injecting themselves with syringes), which suggests that the neural response was more likely produced by core disgust and had little to do with social categorization of outgroups. Similarly, a recent study by Horberg et al. (2009, Study 1) investigated disgust in relation to moral-purity violations, yet core disgust cues were embedded in the moral transgression (e.g., "A man goes to the supermarket once a week and buys a dead chicken. But before cooking the chicken, he has sexual intercourse with it. Then he cooks it and eats it"). To test whether moral disgust really is the same as core disgust, one needs to construct immoral events that do not contain features of core disgust. We know of only one such study: Chapman, Kim, Susskind, and Anderson (2009) found that the specific facial muscles activated in response to ingesting unpleasant substances and in response to core disgust elicitors are also activated when participants feel morally slighted. In their study, participants were morally slighted by receiving unfair monetary offers in an economic game designed to have clear fair and unfair options. However, as the authors note, emotional responses to unfairness were not characterized by disgust alone: Anger and sadness were also endorsed, suggesting that unfairness is associated with a blend of negative emotions. Moreover, the main facial marker of disgust used by Chapman et al.—the raised upper lip—is also activated by anger (Rozin et al., 2009). Until more research using different behavior and self-report measures emerges, the evidence implicating integral disgust in moral judgment is, at best, mixed.

Limitations of the Integral Disgust Studies

Although there is now one study of integral disgust to suggest that being morally slighted results in the same disgust experience as is provoked by core disgust elicitors (Chapman et al., 2009), there are good reasons to think that the emotional response to moral transgressions and the emotional response to core disgust elicitors (e.g., body envelope violations) are different. In their initial development of the disgust sensitivity scale, Haidt et al. (1994) reported that items assessing moral disgust did not correlate with the overall disgust scale score. They therefore removed the moral domain from the final version of their disgust scale. Other evidence that moral disgust and core disgust are separate constructs comes from a study comparing reactions with core and moral disgust pictures (e.g., a picture of vomit and urine compared with a depiction of racism; Simpson, Carter, Anthony, & Overton, 2006; see also Marzillier & Davey, 2004). Whereas both types of pictures resulted in similar levels of self-rated disgust, moral disgust pictures also evoked higher levels of self-rated anger and sadness. Moreover, ratings of disgust for the core pictures diminished over time, but ratings of disgust for the moral disgust pictures increased. There were no sex differences in the ratings of disgust for the moral disgust pictures, whereas women reacted with more intense disgust than men to the core disgust pictures. Finally, a neuropsychological study of impaired disgust recognition in patients with Huntington's disease (HD) found that HD patients recalled proportionally fewer examples of core disgust but more examples of moral disgust compared with controls (Hayes, Stevenson, & Coltheart, 2007). Overall, these divergent reactions to core and moral disgust suggest that the type of emotion produced by moral transgressions might be very different from the disgust experienced in reaction to core elicitors.

INTERPRETING THE FINDINGS OF THE THREE APPROACHES

In this chapter we reviewed the recent literature on the link between the emotion of disgust and judgments, with a particular focus on moral judgments. In light of the findings, we consider three possible ways that disgust might be linked to moral judgment: (1) there is a causal link between judgments of moral violations and the emotion of disgust, (2) moral violations are disgusting to the extent that they bring to mind elicitors of core disgust, and (3) disgust is used metaphorically to describe complex emotional and cognitive reactions to moral violations. We now examine each of these in turn.

If there is a causal link between judgments of moral violations and the emotion of disgust, there are two ways the causal arrow can point. First, disgust could amplify the harshness of moral violations. Second, moral violations could increase feelings of disgust. The findings from the research on incidental disgust suggest that rather than informing judgments directly, the influence of incidental disgust might be confined to indirect cognitive mediation on subsequent judgments. That is, disgust might prompt mental accessibility of disgust-related concepts and produce subsequent judgments consistent with the disgust appraisal style (involving, e.g., certainty, avoidance). Overall, however, there is no compelling evidence that induced disgust influences moral judgments. With regard to the research on disgust sensitivity, there is evidence to suggest an effect of trait disgust on moral judgments. However, this approach is not well equipped to rule out other correlates of disgust sensitivity as the cause of any obtained differences. Thus, it seems unlikely that disgust could directly amplify the harshness of moral violations.

Can moral violations cause feelings of disgust? The research on integral disgust might suggest that moral transgressions can produce disgust, yet only one study from this approach has used a moral task that is clean of core disgust elicitors (Chapman et al., 2009). Furthermore, there is evidence that moral disgust might not be the same as the disgust experienced in response to core disgust elicitors. Rather, moral disgust might be a mixture of anger, sadness, and disgust, with differing temporal properties and gender effects to core disgust (Marzillier & Davey, 2004; Simpson et al., 2006). More evidence will be required before it can be concluded that moral violations increase feelings of the core emotion of disgust. Thus, we conclude that the evidence that there is a causal link between judgments of moral violations and the emotion of disgust is, at best, weak.

As described earlier, one of the main problems with the studies of moral disgust is that the moral violations often include core disgust cues. Although we have criticized this as a potential confound, another implication is that moral violations might be disgusting to the extent that they bring to mind core disgust elicitors. This was a necessary feature of Horberg et al.'s (2009) Study 1 where only violations of moral purity (e.g., sex with a dead chicken) led to harsher moral judgments and higher disgust ratings. In the absence of other controlled studies that manipulate the presence and absence of core disgust cues in the moral scenarios used, it is difficult to gauge just how important the role of core disgust elicitors is; however, we suspect that this might point to an important prerequisite of moral disgust. This would also be consistent with a disease-avoidance account of disgust (Oaten et al., 2009), where abstract moral violations are not directly implicated in disease transmission and might therefore be less likely to recruit what is essentially a protective behavioral adaptation—that is, core disgust.

Finally, the tendency for the term *disgust* to commonly be associated with moral violations (see Haidt, Rozin, McCauley, & Imada, 1997) might reflect its metaphorical use (Royzman & Sabini, 2001). As a universal, basic emotion that represents extreme aversion, rejection, and dislike, proclaiming that one is disgusted by a corrupt politician provides a brief but emphatic and visceral way of communicating extreme disapproval. It might even be the case that the mere semantic activation of the emotion label *disgust* in response to moral violations produces a modified experience of disgust (Rozin et al., 2009). Nevertheless, based on existing evidence, it seems unlikely that moral violations have the power to increase felt disgust unless core disgust cues are incorporated into the moral violation.

CONCLUSION

Research on the relationships between moral judgments and incidental disgust, disgust sensitivity, and integral disgust have been interpreted to support important links. After reviewing this literature and the findings from our own studies, we suggest that a direct link between core disgust and moral judgment is likely to be spurious. Consistent with an evolutionary disease-avoidance perspective on disgust (Oaten et al., 2009), we suspect that moral violations might only be disgusting to the extent that they contain core disgust cues.

REFERENCES

Bodenhausen, G. V., Sheppard, L. A., & Kramer, G. P. (1994). Negative affect and social judgment: The differential impact of anger and sadness. *European Journal of Social Psychology, 24,* 45–62.

Borg, J. S., Lieberman, D., & Kiehl, K. A. (2008). Infection, incest, and iniquity: Investigating the neural correlates of disgust and morality. *Journal of Cognitive Neuroscience, 20,* 1529–1546.

Boyle, D. (Director). (1996). *Trainspotting* [Film]. Miramax Films.

Brooks, J. (2008). *The social function of disgust: A correlational study of disgust sensitivity, social desirability and conformity.* Unpublished thesis, Indiana University of South Bend.

Chapman, H. A., Kim, D. A., Susskind, J. M., & Anderson, A. K. (2009). In bad taste: Evidence for the oral origins of moral disgust. *Science, 323,* 1222–1226.

Charash, M., & McKay, D. (2002). Attention bias for disgust. *Journal of Anxiety Disorders, 16,* 529–541.

Charash, M., McKay, D., & Dipaolo, N. (2006). Implicit attention bias for disgust. *Anxiety, Stress, & Coping, 19,* 353–364.

Davey, G. C. L., Bickerstaffe, S., & MacDonald, B. (2006). Experienced disgust causes a negative interpretation bias: A causal role for disgust in anxious psychopathology. *Behaviour Research and Therapy, 44,* 1375–1384.

Forgas, J. P. (1995). Mood and judgment: The affect infusion model (AIM). *Psychological Bulletin, 117,* 39–66.

Forgas, J. P. (2002). Feeling and doing: Affective influences on interpersonal behavior. *Psychological Inquiry, 13,* 1–28.

Graham, J., Haidt, J., & Nosek, B. A. (2009). Liberals and conservatives rely on different sets of moral foundations. *Journal of Personality and Social Psychology, 96,* 1029–1046.

Graham, S., Weiner, B., & Zucker, G. S. (1997). An attributional analysis of punishment goals and public reactions to O. J. Simpson. *Personality and Social Psychology Bulletin, 23,* 331–346.

Haidt, J. (2001). The emotional dog and its rational tail: A social intuitionist approach to moral judgment. *Psychological Review, 108,* 814–834.

Haidt, J., & Hersh, M. (2001). Sexual morality: The cultures and emotions of conservatives and liberals. *Journal of Applied Social Psychology, 31,* 191–221.

Haidt, J., McCauley, C., & Rozin, P. (1994). Individual differences in sensitivity to disgust: A scale sampling seven domains of disgust elicitors. *Personality and Individual Differences, 16,* 701–713.

Haidt, J., Rozin, P., McCauley, C. R., & Imada, S. (1997). Body, psyche and culture: The relationship between disgust and morality. *Psychology and Developing Societies, 9,* 107–131.

Harris, L. T., & Fiske, S. T. (2006). Dehumanizing the lowest of the low: Neuro-imaging responses to extreme outgroups. *Psychological Science, 17,* 847–853.

Hayes, C. J., Stevenson, R. J., & Coltheart, M. (2007). Disgust and Huntington's disease. *Neuropsychologia, 45,* 1135–1151.

Hodson, G., & Costello, K. (2007). Interpersonal disgust, ideological orientations, and dehumanization as predictors of intergroup attitudes. *Psychological Science, 18,* 691–698.

Horberg, E. J., Oveis, C., Keltner, D., & Cohen, A. B. (2009). Disgust and the moralization of purity. *Journal of Personality and Social Psychology, 97,* 963–976.

Huebner, B., Dwyer, S., & Hauser, M. (2009). The role of emotion in moral psychology. *Trends in Cognitive Sciences, 13,* 1–6.

Inbar, Y., Pizarro, D. A., & Bloom, P. (2009). Conservatives are more easily disgusted than liberals. *Cognition and Emotion, 23,* 714–725.

Inbar, Y., Pizarro, D. A., Knobe, J., & Bloom, P. (2009). Disgust sensitivity predicts intuitive disapproval of gays. *Emotion, 9,* 435–439.

Jones, A., & Fitness, J. (2008). Moral hypervigilance: The influence of disgust sensitivity in the moral domain. *Emotion, 8,* 613–627.

Keltner, D., Anderson, C., & Gonzaga, G. C. (2002). Culture, emotion, and the good life in the study of affect and judgment. *Psychological Inquiry, 13,* 65–67.

Lang, P. J., Bradley, M. M., & Cuthbert, B. N. (2001). *International affective picture system (IAPS): Instruction manual and affective ratings.* Technical report A-5, The Center for Research in Psychophysiology, University of Florida.

Lerner, J. S., Small, D. A., & Loewenstein, G. F. (2004). Heart strings and purse strings: Carryover effects of emotions on economic decisions. *Psychological Science, 15,* 337–341.

Lerner, J. S., & Keltner, D. (2000). Beyond valence: Toward a model of emotion specific influences on judgment and choice. *Cognition and Emotion, 14,* 473–493.

Marzillier, S. L., & Davey, G. L. (2004). The emotional profiling of disgust-eliciting stimuli: Evidence for primary and complex. *Cognition & Emotion, 18,* 313–336.

McHolme, A. (2009). *The effect of inducing disgust on judgments and behaviour.* Unpublished honours thesis, Macquarie University.

Miller, L. C., Murphy, R., & Buss, A. (1981). Consciousness of body: Private and public. *Journal of Personality and Social Psychology, 41,* 397–406.

Moll, J., & de Oliveira-Souza, R. (2007). Moral judgments, emotions and the utilitarian brain. *Trends in Cognitive Sciences,* 11, 319–321.

Moll, J., de Oliveira-Souza, R., Moll, F. T., Ignácio, F. A., Bramati, I. E., Caparelli-Dáquer, E. M., et al. (2005). The moral affiliations of disgust: A functional MRI study. *Cognitive and Behavioral Neurology, 18,* 68–78.

Navarrete, C. D., & Fessler, D. M. T. (2006). Disease avoidance and ethnocentrism: The effects of disease vulnerability and disgust sensitivity on intergroup attitudes. *Evolution and Human Behavior, 27,* 270–282.

Oaten, M. J., Stevenson, R. J., & Case, T. I. (2009). Disgust as a disease-avoidance mechanism. *Psychological Bulletin, 135,* 303–321.

Olatunji, B. O. (2008). Disgust, scrupulosity and conservative attitudes about sex: Evidence for a mediational model of homophobia. *Journal of Research in Personality, 42,* 1364–1369.

Olatunji, B. O., & Armstrong, T. (2009). Contamination fear and effects of disgust on distress in a public restroom. *Emotion, 9,* 592–597.

Royzman, E. B., & Sabini, J. (2001). Something it takes to be an emotion: The interesting case of disgust. *Journal for the Theory of Social Behavior, 31,* 29–59.

Rozin, P. (2008). Hedonic "adaptation": Specific adaptation to disgust/death elicitors as a result of dissecting a cadaver. *Judgment and Decision Making, 3,* 191–194.

Rozin, P., Haidt, J., & Fincher, K. (2009). From oral to moral. *Science, 323,* 1179–1180.

Rozin, R., Haidt, J., McCauley, C. R. (2000). Disgust. In M. Lewis & J. M. Haviland-Jones (Eds.), *Handbook of emotions* (2nd ed., pp. 637–653). New York: Guilford Press.

Rozin, P., Haidt, J., McCauley, C., Dunlop, L., & Ashmore, M. (1999). Individual differences in disgust sensitivity: Comparisons and evaluations of paper-and-pencil versus behavioral measures. *Journal of Research in Personality, 33,* 330–351.

Rozin, P., & Singh, L. (1999). The moralization of cigarette smoking in the United States. *Journal of Consumer Psychology, 8,* 321–337.

Sawchuk, C. N., Lohr, J. M., Lee, T. C., & Tolin, D. F. (1999). Exposure to disgust-evoking imagery and information-processing biases in blood-injection-injury phobia. *Behaviour Research and Therapy, 37,* 249–257.

Schäfer, A., Schienle, A., & Vaitl, D. (2005). Stimulus type and design influence hemodynamic responses toward visual disgust and fear elicitors. *International Journal of Psychophysiology, 57,* 53–59.

Schnall, S., Haidt, J., Clore, G. L., & Jordan, A. H. (2008). Disgust as embodied moral judgment. Personality *and Social Psychology Bulletin, 34,* 1096–1109.

Schwarz, N. (1990). Feelings as information: Informational and motivational functions of affective states. In E. T. Higgins & R. Sorrentino (Eds.), *Handbook of motivation and cognition: Foundations of social behavior* (Vol. 2, pp. 527–561). New York: Guilford Press.

Schwarz, N., & Clore, G. L. (1983). Mood, misattribution and judgments of well-being: Informative and directive functions of affective states. *Journal of Personality and Social Psychology, 45,* 513–523.

Schwarz, N., & Clore, G. L. (1996). Feelings and phenomenal experiences. In E. T. Higgins & A. Kruglanski (Eds.), *Social psychology: Handbook of basic principles* (pp. 433–465). New York: Guilford.

Simpson, J., Carter, S., Anthony, S. H., & Overton, P. G. (2006). Is disgust a homogeneous emotion? *Motivation and Emotion, 30,* 31–41.

Smith, C. A., & Ellsworth, P. C. (1985). Patterns of cognitive appraisal in emotion. *Journal of Personality and Social Psychology, 48,* 813–838.

Sprengelmeyer, R., Young, A. W., Calder, A. J., Karnat, A., Lange, H., Homberg, V., et al. (1996). Loss of disgust: Perception of faces and emotions in Huntington's disease. *Brain, 119,* 1647–1665.

Tiedens, L. Z., & Linton, S. (2001). Judgments under emotional certainty and uncertainty: The effects of specific emotions on information processing. *Journal of Personality and Social Psychology, 81,* 973–988.

Valdesolo, P., & DeSteno, D. (2006). Manipulations of emotional context shape moral judgment. *Psychological Science, 17,* 476–477.

Wheatley, T., & Haidt, J. (2005). Hypnotic disgust makes moral judgments more severe. *Psychological Science, 16,* 780–784.

Zhong, C., & Liljenquist, K. (2006). Washing away your sins: Threatened morality and physical cleansing. *Science, 313,* 1451–1452.

ENDNOTES

1. Rozin, Haidt, and McCauley (2000) proposed that body products (e.g., feces), certain animals (e.g., maggots), and decayed or contaminated foods (e.g., spoiled milk) represent core elicitors of disgust. This is the most fundamental form of disgust, represented by aversive sensory experiences. Moral disgust (e.g., disgust at hearing about a theft) is proposed to have expanded from core disgust, thus sharing little in common with core elicitors.

2. Five moral domains have been identified: (1) harm–care, (2) fairness–reciprocity, (3) ingroup–loyalty, (4) authority–respect; and (5) purity–sanctity (e.g., Graham, Haidt, & Nosek, 2009).

3. The Implicit Association Test (IAT) measures the strength of association between concepts. It is a computerized test that requires rapid categorization of various exemplars (e.g., gay–straight, good–bad). Faster categorization responses represent stronger memory associations.

10

Thick Concepts and Their Role in Moral Psychology

CHLOË FITZGERALD

Centre de Recherche en Éthique de l'Université de Montréal

PETER GOLDIE

University of Manchester

Prurient, tedious, glamorous, stubborn, idle, screwy: These are a few of the terms that appear in an article in the *BBC News Magazine* online discussing a political scandal in the United Kingdom (Brooke, 2009). They are all examples of *thick evaluative concepts*. These are to be contrasted with *thin evaluative concepts*, such as *good, bad, right, wrong, beautiful, ugly, irrational*, and *imprudent*, only one of which appears in the article—imprudent. The content of the article is highly evaluative; it is a personal opinion on the moral and political significance of political representatives fiddling their expenses. Thick concepts are what we use most frequently to think about and discuss important moral issues, and thin concepts are less often used.

The title of this paper is deliberately ambiguous. The term "moral psychology" can be taken to mean the ways in which we think, feel, and reflect morally in our everyday lives (let this be *moral psychology*). Or it can refer to the practice of theorizing about our moral thoughts, feelings, and reflections (let this be *Moral Psychology*). The former is simply what takes place in our everyday moral lives, whereas the latter is an interdisciplinary field of research into what takes place in our moral lives, comprising philosophy, empirical psychology, social psychology, neuroscience, and anthropology, among other disciplines.

Our central claim is that thick concepts are predominant in moral psychology, yet they are scarcely to be found in Moral Psychology. In contrast, thin concepts are much less prevalent in moral psychology, yet they are predominant in Moral Psychology. We think it is time for this asymmetry to be put right, not by trying to change moral psychology but by trying to change Moral Psychology.[1]

In the first half of this chapter we will begin with a descriptive task, looking at the use of thick concepts in our moral psychology: explaining in more detail what they are, examining their pervasiveness in our moral (and other) thoughts and feelings, and exploring the varieties of psychological connection between judgments involving thick concepts and emotion, showing that emotions are by no means mere irrational gut feelings. In the second half of this chapter, we will take a prescriptive turn and suggest some ways thick concepts should be used in Moral Psychology—not unanalyzed or to the exclusion of thin concepts but as a starting point for the understanding and theoretical analysis of the richness and diversity of our moral psychology. It will turn out that our recommendations about thick concepts in Moral Psychology support, and gain support from, certain concerns about Moral Psychology that have recently been expressed by other people working in this area.

THICK CONCEPTS IN OUR EVERYDAY LIVES

What Thick Concepts Are

Thick concepts are not a philosopher's construct but rather something pervasive in our everyday lives—in our moral psychology. It was, however, a philosopher who first coined the term: Bernard Williams introduced *thick concepts* to moral philosophy, focusing particularly on thick ethical concepts.[2] He gives *treachery, promise, brutality, courage, lie,* and *gratitude* as examples of thick concepts and contrasts these with thin concepts such as *right* and *good* (Williams, 1985/2007, pp. 128–30, 140–146; see also Williams, 1965/1973).

As seen in the citations from the previously mentioned BBC article, thick concepts are very much part of the way we think and talk evaluatively in our judgments about the world around us. Think of the description one would give if a friend asked one to describe one's mother's character; the description would typically be full of thick concepts. For example, one might say that she was *kind* and *loving* but *unreliable*. It is less likely that one would say simply that she was *good* or that she always did the *right* thing.

We would like to draw attention to five characteristics of thick concepts.[3] We use the thick concept *shameful* to illustrate these in an example we call *American Beauty*, after the film in which something similar occurs (Mendes, 2000). Mary, a 16-year-old girl, is at a family party, and her father starts to flirt outrageously with her best friend, despite her mother's presence at the party. She thinks her father's conduct is shameful, and she feels ashamed.

The first characteristic is that thick concepts have more descriptive content than thin. This is why we tend to use them more in our daily interactions. If Mary describes her father's action as shameful, she tells you a lot more about his action than if she simply said that what he did was bad or wrong. This difference between thick and thin concepts is one of degree rather than a sharp distinction, as Samuel Scheffler (1987) argued; for instance, *good* is a thinner concept than *praiseworthy*, but *praiseworthy* is a thinner concept than *courageous*.

Second, thick concepts, like thin concepts in this respect, are evaluative. In *American Beauty*, when Mary judges that her father behaved shamefully she is evaluating his behavior, and she is evaluating it negatively, in an ethical and possibly also in a prudential way (as we shall soon see, these can overlap). Mary's judgment that her father behaved shamefully thus goes beyond a value-free way of describing his conduct, such as that he had an animated and flirtatious discussion with her friend.

The third characteristic of thick concepts is that the psychological force of judgments containing them cannot be adequately captured by replacing them with judgments containing a purely nonevaluative, descriptive element plus a thin negative evaluative element.[4] Mary is doing more than judging that her father had an animated and flirtatious discussion with her friend and that this behavior was wrong. Williams (1965/1973) has a nice example of the attempt to find a replacement to this judgment: "Of course, he went back on his agreement when he got to the meeting, the little coward." Williams asks if it possible to rephrase the sentence without the emotional element, without the "expletive addition" of "the little coward." This is how he suggests it might go: "As might have been predicted, he went back on his agreement at the meeting through fear; which he ought not to have done (or this was a bad thing)." This may be the same moral judgment as in the original, Williams says, in the simple sense that both original and replacement reveal that the speaker is against, or "con," what was done. But this is not enough if we are to take the notion of a moral judgment seriously. What matters, in addition to mere pro and con, are the "moral overtones," as Williams puts it (Williams 1965/1973, p. 213).[5]

One way the moral overtones of someone's response to a moral situation are revealed can be found in the fourth characteristic of thick concepts: There are *emotional* responses that are intimately connected to the use of thick concepts in judgment.[6] In some cases, there may be a relatively direct connection between the thick concept judgment and a cognate emotion, as Mary's judging her father's behavior to be shameful is connected with her feeling of shame. Similarly, the judgment that the pudding is disgusting will be relatively directly connected with the emotional response of disgust, and so on for dangerous–fear, embarrassing–embarrassment, and infuriating–fury. But this relatively direct connection between the thick concept judgment and the emotional response does not hold for all cases (for discussion, see Mulligan, 1998). For example, *disloyal, stubborn, promise, glamorous*, and *unjust* do not have a single emotion, cognate with the concept, that will typically arise with the judgment. However, it does not follow that emotions of various kinds will not typically be connected to the judgment, albeit not in such a direct way. For example, the judgment that something is unjust is typically connected to anger and resentment (and not typically connected to other emotions, such as surprise, fear, and jealousy).

The fifth characteristic of thick concepts is that their application in judgment is both "world-guided" and "action-guiding," as Williams puts it (Williams, 1985/2007, pp. 140–141). Thick concept judgments are world-guided because there are situations to which the concept can be correctly applied and situations to which it would be incorrect to apply it. In *American Beauty*, it is appropriate and correct for Mary to judge her father's conduct to be shameful. The world-guidedness of thick concepts is, in just this sense, normative, or subject to correctness conditions in its application. This normative aspect of thick concepts is captured by recent sentimentalist theories of value, such as Justin D'Arms's and Daniel Jacobson's version of *rational sentimentalism*: Their theory "explains the shameful in terms of fitting shame, the funny in terms of fitting amusement, and so forth" (D'Arms & Jacobson, 2010, p. 587). Thus, instead of arguing that the shameful is simply what causes shame in the average person, they claim that the shameful is that to which it is fitting or appropriate to respond with shame.

Of course, there remains the difficult task of determining on any particular occasion whether a thick concept judgment is fitting or appropriate. As Williams (1985/2007) notes, there may be disagreement even within a culture—for example, two people might reasonably disagree in their judgment about whether nude sunbathing on public beaches is shameful. But disagreement on its own is not sufficient to show that there is no correct application of the concept (pp. 140–141). Furthermore, within a culture, the evaluative import of thick concepts can change over time, sometimes because they are recruited by different social groups to advance their interests. Simon Blackburn (2009) gives the example of how in England in the seventeenth century the new commercial class succeeded in changing the previously negative import of *ambitious* to a positive evaluation and the previously positive *condescending* to a negative one (pp. 19–21). Evidence of this remains today when one notes that *ambitious* is still a predominantly negative term in many Catholic European cultures, except among business people who aspire to engage commercially with Anglo-Saxon markets. And today many investment bankers would consider *aggressive* to be a term of approbation (e.g., "an aggressive bond trader"), whereas most of us would still consider it a term of disapproval (e.g., "an aggressive attitude toward one's fellow passengers").

Thick concept judgments are action-guiding because they dispose us to act in ways appropriate to the situation. In *American Beauty*, when Mary judges her father's action to be shameful, she is disposed to act in particular ways, such as fleeing from the situation to avoid further exposure to this shameful act, trying to get her father to stop his outrageous behavior, or something else that might express her shame in some way. Of course, Mary might not act in any of these ways. For example, she might have an overriding reason not to, such as a desire to maintain family dignity and prevent a scene. In this particular case, it might not be possible to predict in which way Mary will act. Nevertheless, her action, whether running away or trying to get her father to stop what he is doing, will be intelligible in the light of the shame she is feeling, and her action will be justifiable by her through appeal to those aspects of her father's behavior in virtue of which it is shameful.[7]

To sum up the five characteristics of thick concepts: (1) they have more descriptive content that thin concepts, (2) they are evaluative, (3) a judgment containing a thick concept cannot be replaced by a judgment containing merely descriptive content plus a thin evaluative concept, (4) thick judgments are connected to emotion, and (5) thick judgments are world-guided and action-guiding. But thick judgments are, as we will see in more detail shortly, diverse, and they cannot be readily regimented; as Scheffler (1987) argued, "Our ethical vocabulary is very rich and diverse, and the ethical concepts we use vary along a number of dimensions, of which the dimensions of specificity or generality and agreement or disagreement in application are two" (p. 418).

The Pervasiveness and Interconnectedness of Thick Concepts Across Spheres of Discourse

Thick concepts are everywhere in moral psychology. Pick up a newspaper, read a novel, glance at an art review, watch a reality television program, engage in a gossipy conversation, discuss the manners or morals of people you know, engage in countless other activities, and you will be struck by how pervasive they are. Not only are thick concepts found in moral discourse, but there are thick prudential, aesthetic, and other kinds of evaluative concepts, too: *dangerous, rash, crude, embarrassing, tarnished,* and *elegant.*[8] In Figure 10.1, we give some examples of thick concepts, divided into three rough spheres of discourse: (1) the moral or *ethical*, (2) the *prudential*, and (3) the *aesthetic*. As the diagram shows, the three spheres overlap, with some thick concepts used in two or even all three of the

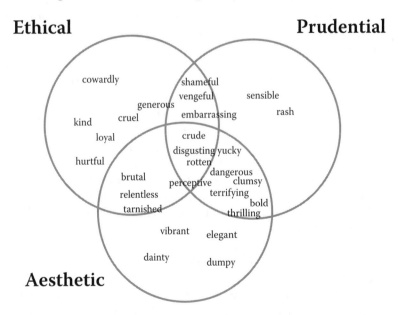

Figure 10.1   The pervasiveness and interconnectedness of thick concepts across different spheres of discourse.

different evaluative spheres. For example, *crude* can be applied aesthetically to an artwork, as in "the crude brushstrokes"; a description of someone's way of trying to amuse as "crude humor" could be either an ethical or an aesthetic indictment of their behavior; and one can talk of a "crude raft" or a "crude weapon," which is prudentially problematic because it serves only its basic purpose and cannot be relied on to last.

Thick Concept Judgments and Emotion: Varieties of Psychological Connections

It is helpful to think in terms of a paradigm case, such as *American Beauty*. In *American Beauty*, the paradigmatic process would be thus: Mary judges that her father's behavior is shameful and, as she is "fully emotionally engaged" with the concept, she feels shame and expresses her shame in action by abandoning the party or in some other way. [9]

The purpose of this section is briefly to explore some examples of common, everyday variation from the paradigm. We do not present them as counterexamples to our claims about thick concepts; on the contrary, they are, rather, variations on a theme—variations away from the paradigm, but in such a way that the variations could not exist as they do without the existence of the paradigm.

1. *The dispute arbitrator.* The dispute arbitrator is asked to arbitrate the dispute between A and B over whether the behavior of A was offensive to B. She judges that A's behavior was offensive to B's religion, but, because she is aiming at *cool* impartiality, she does not actually feel offense or resentment. Nevertheless, her use of the thick concept of *offense* is both sincere and engaged.

2. *The selfish toddler.* The toddler learns the thick concept *selfish* from his mother, as what she calls him when she's annoyed with his behavior toward his baby sister. He grasps some of the sense of the concept, feeling upset and being inclined to stop whatever he is doing when she calls him selfish. He also applies the concept to other children when he does not like their behavior toward him and feels anger at what they do. But he is not yet mature enough to feel the complex emotions of guilt and resentment. He is on the way to gaining a full grasp of the concept *selfish* and exhibits some of the corresponding emotional responses but does not yet fully grasp its meaning, its context of application, or its full range of emotional resonance.[10]

3. *The anthropologist.* In rural Catalonia (this is a real-life example), there is a thick concept expressed in Catalan as *pixapins* (literally "urinates on pine trees"). The concept is applied to Catalans from Barcelona who come to the countryside on the weekends and fail to show proper respect for the land. Among Catalan country people, the thick judgment that a Barcelona weekender is a *pixapins* is paradigmatically accompanied by feelings of contempt and resentment. Nevertheless, the anthropologist can learn to

correctly apply *pixapins* to Barcelona weekenders without her experiencing any of these associated feelings when she does so.[11]

4. *The theater-goer.* The theater-goer was raised in a strict religious sect where it was drilled into him that theater-going is *sinful*. As an adult, he now completely rejects this judgment. However, he cannot help feeling sinful when he goes to the theater (Rawls, 1972, p. 482), although he wants to rid himself of these feelings—the emotion is *recalcitrant* (Brady, 2007).

5. *The television viewer.* The television viewer watching the news of a genocide in a remote country exclaims, "How horrific! How cruel!" The viewer correctly applies these terms, as the situation fittingly provokes horror at what happened and sympathy for the victims, but the television viewer is not really emotionally engaged; he has become accustomed to this kind of news—he is suffering from what is often called *compassion fatigue.*

6. *The rude schoolboy.* An example from the developmental psychologist Lawrence Kohlberg, of what happened in a class when the teacher was not looking, was used by the philosopher R. M. Hare:

> In the front row, a boy said something to his neighbor, who retaliated by quietly spitting in his face. The first boy equally quietly slugged the other without leaving his seat, by which time the teacher noted the disturbance. She said calmly, "Stop that and get back to your workbooks." The boy who had done the slugging said, "Teacher, I hit him because he spit in my face." The teacher replied, "That wasn't polite; it was rude. Now get back to work, you're supposed to be doing your workbooks." As they went back to work, the boy who had done the spitting said to his opponent with a grin, "I will grant you that; it was rude." (Hare, cited in Goldie, 2009, p. 101)

The spitting boy's evaluative use of *rude* is reversed from the usual negative evaluative use. It is not that the rude schoolboy has failed to grasp the meaning of rude; it is rather that he chooses to reverse its evaluative import.

7. *The politician.* The politician avows loyalty to a colleague: "I will always remain loyal to you," he says, feeling the appropriate emotions and believing that he really means it—that he is sincere. However, when his colleague gets into trouble, he quickly disassociates himself from him and publicly disavows him, feeling no contrition. We can see from his hypocritical behavior that, even if he did not realize it, he was not really sincere in his earlier avowal of loyalty, even though, when he made the avowal, he had all the appropriate feelings.

8. *The Moral Psychology participant.* The participant is asked what she would think of someone cutting up her old national flag and using it to clean the bathroom (cf. Haidt, Koller, & Dias, 1993). The participant makes the thick judgment that it would be disgusting and that she would feel disgust if she witnessed such an action. However, as she is imagining the scenario only hypothetically, she cannot be sure how her actual

response would compare with how she imagines she would respond. The Moral Psychology participant imagines she would feel disgusted, but in fact, when she is actually confronted with the situation, she does not. In effect, somewhat like the politician, she misjudges what her emotional responses will be.

These few examples are intended to give a flavor of the variety of nonparadigmatic ways in which thick concepts are used in judgments and connected to the user's emotional responses. What matters here is that these variations do not undermine the importance of the psychological connection between thick concept judgments and emotional responses. These variations are variations from a paradigm; recognizing the wealth of variations from the paradigm is central to our understanding of moral psychology.

THICK CONCEPTS IN OUR THEORIZING ABOUT MORALITY

If we accept that thick concepts are everywhere in our moral psychology, then Moral Psychology ought to heed this fact. Without acknowledging the role of thick concepts in what Scheffler (1987) rightly calls our "very rich and diverse" moral discourse (p. 418), Moral Psychology will fail adequately to capture moral psychology as an object of understanding and theoretical analysis.

This failure is a real and present danger in Moral Psychology today, with its almost exclusive reliance on thin concepts such as *right, wrong, good, bad,* and on other concepts at the thinner end of the spectrum such as *harm* and *evil.* Our claim is not that researchers should abandon these thinner concepts but rather than they should widen their repertoire to allow thicker moral concepts and the related emotions a substantial role in the design of their empirical investigations and in the analysis of the data they obtain.

Aside from the fact that we see no obvious justification for restricting Moral Psychology to thin concepts, given that thick concepts are so prevalent in moral psychology, there are at least three positive reasons for recommending the use of thick concepts when researching moral psychology, which we will examine in the following sections. First, thick concepts help to open up the moral–nonmoral distinction in a way that complements recent proposals from others along these same lines. Second, thick concepts are at the intersection of emotional response and moral judgment and thus help us better to appreciate the complex connections between the two and to appreciate that emotion in our moral thought and talk is far from being mere gut feelings—at best, a source of ungrounded intuition. And third, thick concepts help to shed new light on the theory of dual-process thinking in psychology. Finally, having considered these three reasons, we will then consider possible objections to our claims.

Opening Up the Moral–Nonmoral Distinction

In the first half of this chapter, we aimed to show how thick concepts are interconnected across different spheres of discourse, using ethical, prudential, and aesthetic thick concepts as examples. Sometimes we make a thick concept judgment without committing ourselves to that judgment being in any particular sphere of discourse: Examples might include *crude, rotten, tarnished, embarrassing*, and *disgusting*. If I see someone feeding a child with human remains, I immediately judge that to be disgusting, and have an instant emotional reaction of disgust. This use of disgusting could be partly ethical (cannibalism is unnatural), partly prudential (this practice is not hygienic), and partly aesthetic (the child chomping on human fingers is not picturesque, to say the least!), but when I make the judgment I am not committed to which kind of evaluation I am giving: I feel disgust, I think that it was disgusting; and that is all. Once we see how people use thick concepts across different spheres of discourse, it becomes more difficult to pin down a particularly moral area of thinking to investigate in Moral Psychology.

Of course, researchers in Moral Psychology need somehow to delineate the area of human thought and action with which they are concerned, but this does not justify making a sharp moral–nonmoral distinction when such a sharp distinction is not to be found in moral psychology, in the domain of inquiry. When researchers theorize exclusively with thin ethical concepts, such as *good* and *bad*, *right* and *wrong*, they do often find themselves implicitly adopting a tight definition of the sphere of moral discourse; anything that seems to fall outside this tight definition is ignored, and interconnections between spheres remain disguised. For example, we have this claim: "morality refers to prescriptions of conduct based on concepts of fairness, justice, and welfare," where any norms encountered that do not fit this definition are labeled *conventional* (Nucci, Turiel, & Encarnacion-Gawrych, 1983, p. 470). Elsewhere: "moral transgressions have been defined by their consequences for the rights and welfare of others, and social conventional transgressions have been defined as violations of the behavioral uniformities that structure social interactions within social systems" (Blair, 1995, p. 5).

This kind of moral–conventional distinction identifies moral transgressions with seriousness, harmful effects on a victim and independence from authority; conventional transgressions are less serious, do not involve a victim, and are dependent on an authority for their validity. It is maintained that people from all cultures and from a young age can distinguish moral transgressions from conventional along these parameters (Nucci, 2001; Turiel, 2002). The kind of cases that have been used in experiments are hitting another child (moral transgression) and talking in class (conventional transgression). In a typical experiment, when interviewing children to see whether they distinguished between moral and conventional norms, the key question was along these lines: "What if there weren't a rule in the school against (some observed action), would it still be wrong to do it?" If the child said that it would still be wrong to do the action, the norm was considered moral. If they said it would no longer be wrong, it was conventional (Nucci et al., 1983, p. 475).

However, it is not obvious that moral or ethical discourse is so clearly marked off in the way suggested by this use of a moral–conventional distinction. The children being interviewed in the previous experiment are asked explicitly if the act would be right or wrong and are thus forced into identifying acts using thin concepts. There is no room for them to consider whether it would be *shameful, inconsiderate, rude, thoughtless,* or *unwise.* For example, participants might reasonably reply that talking in class would still be rude or inconsiderate even if there were not a school rule against it, and this would then fall on the other side of the supposedly sharp distinction between moral and conventional.

Recently, there have been criticisms from other sources of the moral–conventional distinction in Moral Psychology. These criticisms, we believe, gain support from, and lend support to, our claims about thick concepts. Recent experimental evidence and theoretical objections from philosophers throw doubt on the notion that the moral and conventional can be so easily separated along the lines suggested (Kelly & Stich, 2007; Kelly, Stich, Haley, Eng, & Fessler, 2007; Prinz, 2008). Some of these objections make use of cases where different spheres of evaluative discourse connect, such as manners. For example, Jesse Prinz argues that the moral and conventional are two orthogonal dimensions. He gives examples of rules that at first seem to be purely moral or purely conventional yet on further investigation are more complex: "Don't harm a member of your ingroup" seems to be a moral rule, but it has conventional elements once we specify its application, such as saying that we can harm each other in certain sporting events or initiation rites; wearing shoes indoors in Japan is a conventional rule, but if one defies it, this shows disrespect, which is a moral defect (Prinz, 2008, p. 385). Others point to experimental evidence gathered by Shaun Nichols showing that American children and adults respond to some transgressions of norms of etiquette or good manners (not spitting in one's glass in front of others) in some of the ways supposed to be associated with moral transgressions; they find it serious and authority independent (Kelly et al., 2007, p. 121).

Another criticism of the narrowness of the sphere of the moral used in Moral Psychology comes from the social psychologist Jonathan Haidt, who claims that it has focused too much on thin definitions of the moral to do with harm and fairness and that other important aspects of morality have been ignored or dismissed as nonmoral concerns. He argues specifically for five innate bases of morality: (1) harm–care, (2) fairness–reciprocity, (3) authority–respect, (4) purity–sanctity, and (5) ingroup–loyalty (Haidt & Bjorklund, 2008; Haidt & Graham, 2007; Haidt & Joseph, 2004). One does not have to agree with his proposal of the five innate bases to concur with his criticism of the narrow focus of researchers. Using thick concepts in Moral Psychology in addition to thin concepts would be one way of ensuring that theory and investigation do not focus solely on harm and fairness.

The Intersection of Emotional Response and Judgment

Thick concepts are useful objects of study for researchers in Moral Psychology because they help to throw light on the role of emotion in moral psychology and on the connection between emotion and thick concepts. There is wide support in philosophy, psychology, and neuroscience for the idea that emotion is importantly implicated in morality and moral judgment, but just how it is implicated in often misunderstood.

Let us begin with the role of emotion and thick concepts in the phenomenon that Haidt, Björklund, and Murphy labeled *moral dumbfounding* (2000). This phenomenon occurs when participants who have expressed views that certain actions are wrong, such as eating one's pet dog that was killed by a car, find themselves unable to provide reasons why they hold that view. When they do find a reason and the interviewer dismisses it, because no one is harmed by the action, the participants either try to find other reasons or give up trying to justify themselves yet still stick to their original view (Haidt & Björklund, 2008, p. 197). Participants are dumbfounded in this way at least in part because the interviewer uses only thin concepts, such as *wrong*, in the questioning, and interviewees are not encouraged to give their answers in terms of thick concepts, such as *disgusting*, and of emotion, such as *disgust*.[12] If we understand the complexities of the connection between judging something to be disgusting and having the emotion of disgust, we can see that subjects can have a justifying reason for both their emotional response of disgust and their judgment that eating one's pet dog is disgusting.[13]

Emotions are intentional, being directed toward objects in the environment. In the typical case, the experience of responding emotionally to something in the environment will also involve the experience of the emotion as being reasonable or justified. As John Skorupski (2000) put it, "The affective response typically carries with it a normative impulse" (p. 125).[14] An emotion is reasonable or justified because it can be justified by reasons—reasons that justify both the judgment about the object and the emotion that is directed toward that object. So the emotion of disgust at the idea of eating one's pet dog is justified by the very same reasons that justify the judgment that eating one's pet dog is disgusting, and the judgment that it is disgusting in turn justifies the thinner judgment that it would be wrong. Subjects could thus explain their thick and thin evaluative judgments and their emotion: It is wrong because it is disgusting; it is disgusting because what you are eating is the creature—your friend!—that you have loved and cherished for so many years. However, the reason for the wrongness of this action might well not be accessible to subjects at the time, perhaps because they are asked to focus only on a notion of wrongness that is restricted to harm to others. However, if the experimenters had allowed the use of thick concepts when designing this sort of experiment, combined with a broader notion of the moral, it is possible that moral dumbfounding would not have occurred at all.

Thus, emotions have a normative structure that allies them more to reason and to judgment than to mere gut feelings. But the observation just made that one can be unaware of one's reasons at the time one has an emotion and makes a judgment points us toward the epistemology of emotion; in a sense it is right to say that emotions are *intuitive*, or that they are *gut feelings*—not because they are not justifiable (for they are justifiable) but because the grounds of the justification are not accessible to the subject at the time. This is the familiar idea that one's emotions can be a primary source of information about the world—telling one something that reason alone does not pick up on. In such a case, one first feels the emotion, and only later does one become conscious of the reasons that justify one's emotion.

Emotions thus reveal features about our environment that we might not otherwise recognize with the same speed and reliability; for example, we can immediately see that something is frightening or disgusting in a way that we would not be capable of if we were not capable of feeling these emotions.

This epistemic and justificatory role for emotion and judgments involving thick concepts applies in very much the same way when we consider thick concepts such as *promise* and *unfair* that are less thick than *frightening* and *disgusting* and where the connection to emotion is less direct. For example, we might be thinking about the way a young recruit had been treated at work and have a feeling that there was something unfair about it. Without being able to put our finger on just what it was that made it unfair, we still feel angry about the treatment. Only later do we come to see that it was indeed unfair, because she was being singled out for some unpleasant task, so our initial judgment (one might well call it an intuition) and our feelings of anger were indeed justified.[15]

So our emotions, far from being merely irrational gut feelings, attune us to the world around us, enabling us quickly and reliably to see things as they really are and thus to respond as we should. In short, emotions enable us to get things right. And it is, in part, the connection with emotion that makes thick concepts so important; while we acknowledge the rich diversity that these concepts manifest, this connection, more or less direct and immediate, remains a common thread.

Dual-Process Thinking

Roughly, the theory of dual-process thinking holds that we have two different ways of thinking. As Kahneman (2003) puts it, there is the intuitive system 1, which is "fast, automatic, effortless, associative, implicit (not available to introspection), and often emotionally charged," and the deliberative system 2, which is "slower, serial, effortful, more likely to be consciously monitored and deliberatively controlled" (p. 698). In system 1, "an automatic affective evaluation … is the main determinant of many judgments and behaviors" (p. 710), whereas system 2 performs a monitoring role—"one of the functions of system 2 is to monitor the quality of both mental operations and overt behavior" (p. 699). Theorizing in Moral Psychology using thick concepts and emotion lends support to this idea of dual process thinking, but it does so in a way that brings into question some of these ways of marking the distinction between system 1 and system 2, such as the nature of the connection between emotion and reason, and how intuitive thinking can be both fast, automatic, effortless, and emotionally charged, whilst at the same time being available to introspection and justifiable.

For example, in *American Beauty* Mary judges her father's behavior to be shameful, and she does so quickly, automatically, effortlessly, and in an emotionally charged way, without consciously going through any reasoning prior to her judgment. Or, in Haidt's example of eating one's pet dog, with similar speed and facility I judge that it is disgusting and have an immediate feeling of disgust. However, the immediacy and automaticity of the thick judgments in these cases, and of the emotional responses, do not necessarily or even typically make later (system 2) justification for them ad hoc, as is sometimes claimed (cf. Haidt, 2001). As we have seen, the fact that the thinker does not perform a deliberative system 2 calculation before responding does not mean that the response lacks justifying reasons, nor does it mean that the thinker cannot later provide these reasons.

Another way in which considering thick concepts and emotion brings into question some of the ways of marking the distinction between system 1 and system 2 is that system 2 can itself involve emotional responses. Mary might start in system 2 thinking with cool reasoning—deliberatively controlled reasoning—when her friend gives her a description of her father's behavior in a way that puts it in a light that makes her come to see it as shameful for the first time. This deliberative thought process can then lead to her coming to feel shame. Thus, the epistemic route in this case feeds from deliberative system 2 to emotional system 1 rather than the other way around.

System 2 can also involve imagined situations and imagined emotional responses. There are various ways the imagination can be involved in our moral thinking, and we can only briefly touch upon the complex issues that are involved. Consider, for example, how you might imagine your best friend talking about you when you are not there, mocking you and generally making fun of you. When you imagine this, you might imagine it perceptually, imagining seeing and hearing your friend saying those things about you. Or you might imagine something both perceptually and propositionally, merely imagining that your friend did those things. Or you might both imagine it perceptually and propositionally (e.g., you might imagine that all human life on Earth has ceased and also imagine seeing a deserted wasteland of what used to be a teeming city). In these examples, although you are perceptually imagining the scene and you are doing so from a point of view, you are not imagining yourself as part of the imagined scene, as occupying that point of view. In other examples, it might be necessary to imagine yourself as part of the scene. For example, you might imagine yourself gossiping about your best friend when she is not there; here you could imagine experientially, from the inside, imagining how you would feel.

It is possible for the emotions to be involved in these imaginative projects in at least two ways. First, it is possible to imagine having an emotional experience as part of the content of what you imagine—for example, you might imagine feeling smug and superior as you imagine gossiping about your friend behind his back. Second, it is possible to have an actual emotional experience as a response to what you imagine, as you might feel shame in response to imagining yourself gossiping about your friend.[16]

If we return to the example of the hypothetical moral situation of the Moral Psychology participant illustrated earlier, participants are asked what they would think of the action of cutting up an old national flag and using it to clean the bathroom. In light of the previous discussion we can appreciate just how many ways in which the imagination can be involved, with more or less vivacity. A subject might just imagine it propositionally, imagining that someone did such a thing. Or (which we expect would be more likely), a subject might imagine the scenario perceptually, either imagining someone else doing it or imagining doing it herself. A subject might imagine feeling disgust, or she might actually feel disgust as a result of what she imagines. Thus, how the scenario is imagined and with what degree of vivacity will impinge on the way emotion is involved and on how system 1 and system 2 are implicated in the imaginative, the emotional, and the deliberative processes.

Finally, emotions in system 1 can impede and even infect the deliberative, monitoring role of system 2 thinking. For example, a man's feelings of sexual jealousy on seeing his wife talking to another man can easily lead to him finding reasons to support his intuitive judgment that they were flirting. Not only judgment but also perception can be affected. Trifles light as air—the dropped handkerchief—can come to appear as irrefutable evidence with which to justify his jealousy. And evidence the man might otherwise, through deliberative thinking, take to count *against* his emotion he now ignores or even takes to be confirmatory of his suspicions. In this sense, our emotions in system 1 thinking can "skew the epistemic landscape" (Goldie, 2008b, p. 159) and thus undermine the monitoring role of system 2. In these and other ways, consideration in Moral Psychology of thick concepts and their relation to emotion will throw light on the manner of interaction between the two systems in dual-process thinking.

Three Possible Objections

Researchers in Moral Psychology might first object that they need to keep their research simple by avoiding the use of thick concepts, claiming that they can operate only with thin concepts without any significant loss. Matters are complicated enough already, it might be said. We doubt that this is so, for the reasons we have been putting forward. And in fact we would further argue that working just with thin concepts makes Moral Psychology more complicated than it needs be—the phenomenon of moral dumbfounding being a case in point. However, if researchers do think that there are reasons that justify why they must work exclusively with thin concepts and not with thick, reasons that explain why it is necessary to avoid the richness and diversity of the moral phenomena, it behooves them to put forward an argument why this is the case, rather than it remaining an implicit assumption behind their work.

A second possible objection is that our everyday talk of thick concepts can be reduced to talk about thin concepts so that when we talk of someone being generous, this is the same as saying that she "tends to give to others without a thought to herself, and this is evaluated as morally good." However, as we argued earlier, this neglects the variety of connections between thick concept judgments and emotion. Just as Mary's judgment that her father's behavior was shameful cannot be reduced to its descriptive content plus a thin evaluation of wrongness, so the evaluative content in the judgment that eating one's dead pet dog would be disgusting cannot be understood merely as the judgment that it was wrong; what is missing in both instances is the connection with emotion—with shame in one case and with disgust in the other. As we have seen, even with less thick moral concepts such as *unjust* and *promise*, the connection with emotion holds.

A third objection is in roughly the same territory but goes further than the second objection. The objection is, briefly, that we recommend the introduction of thick moral concepts into the theoretic discourse of Moral Psychology in a way that is meant to explain discourse in moral psychology, yet it is far from clear that thick concepts are up to this task; rather, they themselves stand in need of analysis. But this is not our recommendation at all. What we recommend, rather, is that Moral Psychology admits thick concepts as part of its data, given that they are so prevalent in the rich and diverse everyday discourse of moral psychology. This does not entail that this data should remain unanalyzed as part of the theoretical discourse of Moral Psychology; indeed, gaining a better understanding of thick concepts is precisely what Moral Psychology should be attempting to do. The problem, we think, is simply that Moral Psychology at the moment tends, in a variety of ways, simply to exclude thick concepts from its data in spite of their prevalence in what is their object of study and that this omission has a variety of malign influences on Moral Psychology. Perhaps Moral Psychologists have a principled reason for excluding thick concepts in their data, but if so, to repeat what we said earlier, the exclusion should not remain as an implicit assumption underlying the modus operandi without proper argument to support the assumption.

CONCLUSION

If anything, the implicit assumption ought to be in the other direction: The obvious concepts to use as data in theorizing about or empirically researching human moral thinking are those very concepts that we use in moral psychology—thick concepts as well as thin ones. The onus ought to be on the opponent of this assumption to give us reasons we ought not to use thick concepts as data in Moral Psychology and use them in all sorts of ways to help understand and theorize about moral psychology: in finding new ways of opening up the moral–nonmoral distinction; in understanding the connections between emotion and moral judgment; in understanding the connections between emotion and imagination, especially in hypothetical cases; in clarifying the distinction between system 1 and system 2 thinking; in formulating the questions that participants are asked in experiments; and in evaluating and theorizing about the answers that are given by participants. In these and other ways, we believe that Moral Psychology would then more accurately capture the phenomena of our moral psychology and help us to gain a deeper understanding of how and why we make the moral judgments that we do—so many of which are thick moral judgments, connected to emotion in the diverse ways that we have been canvassing.[17]

REFERENCES

Blackburn, S. (2009). The absolute conception: Putnam vs Williams. In D. Callcut (Ed.), *Reading Bernard Williams* (pp. 9–23). London: Routledge.

Blair, R. J. (1995). A cognitive developmental approach to morality: Investigating the psychopath. *Cognition, 57*, 1–29.

Brady, M. S. (2007). Recalcitrant emotions and visual illusions. *American Philosophical Quarterly, 44*, 273–284.

Brooke, H. (2009). Public interest or public curiosity? *BBC News Magazine*, retrieved May 16, 2009 from http://news.bbc.co.uk/2/hi/uk_news/magazine/8051577.stm

D'Arms, J. (2008). Sentimental rules and moral disagreement: Comment on Nichols. In W. Sinnott-Armstrong (Ed.), *Moral psychology, volume 2: The cognitive science of morality: Intuition and diversity* (pp. 279–289). Cambridge, MA: MIT Press.

D'Arms, J., & Jacobson, D. (2010). Demystifying sensibilities: Sentimental values and the instability of affect. In P. Goldie (Ed.), *The Oxford handbook of philosophy of emotion* (pp. 585–613). Oxford, UK: Oxford University Press.

Goldie, P. (2004). Emotion, reason, and virtue. In D. Evans & P. Cruse (Eds.), *Emotion, evolution, and rationality* (pp. 249–267). Oxford, UK: Oxford University Press.

Goldie, P. (2005). Imagination and the distorting power of emotion. *Journal of Consciousness Studies, 12*, 130–142.

Goldie, P. (2006). Wollheim on emotion and imagination. *Philosophical Studies, 127*, 1–17.

Goldie, P. (2008a). Virtues of art and human well-being. *Proceedings of the Aristotelian Society, 82*, 179–195.

Goldie, P. (2008b). Misleading emotions. In D. Kuenzle, G. Brun, & U. Doguoglu (Eds.), *Epistemology and emotions* (pp. 149–165). Aldershot, UK: Ashgate Publishing.

Goldie, P. (2009). Thick concepts and emotion. In D. Callcut (Ed.), *Reading Bernard Williams* (pp. 94–109). London: Routledge.

Haidt, J. (2001). The emotional dog and its rational tail: A social intuitionist approach to moral judgment. *Psychological Review, 108*, 814–834.

Haidt, J., & Bjorklund, F. (2008). Social intuitionists answer six questions about moral psychology. In W. Sinnott-Armstrong (Ed.), *Moral psychology, volume 2: The cognitive science of morality: Intuition and diversity* (pp. 181–217). Cambridge, MA: MIT Press.

Haidt, J., & Graham, J. (2007). When morality opposes justice: Conservatives have moral intuitions that liberals may not recognize. *Social Justice Research, 20*, 98–116.

Haidt, J., & Joseph, C. (2004). Intuitive ethics: How innately prepared intuitions generate culturally variable virtues. *Daedalus, 133*, 55–66.

Haidt, J., Koller, S., & Dias, M. (1993). Affect, culture, and morality, or is it wrong to eat your dog? *Journal of Personality and Social Psychology, 65*, 613–628.

Kahneman, D. (2003). A perspective on judgment and choice: Mapping bounded rationality. *American Psychologist, 58*, 697–720.

Kelly, D., & Stich, S. (2008). Two theories about the cognitive architecture underlying morality. In P. Carruthers, S. Laurence, & S. Stich (Eds.), *The innate mind: 3. Foundations and the future* (pp. 348–366). Oxford, UK: Oxford University Press.

Kelly, D., Stich, S., Haley, K., Eng, S., & Fessler, D. (2007). Harm, affect and the moral/ conventional distinction. *Mind and Language, 22*, 117–131.

Mendes, S. (Director). (2000). *American Beauty* [Film]. Los Angeles: Dreamworks SKG.

Moore, A. (2006). Maxims and thick ethical concepts. *Ratio (new series), 19*, 129–147.

Mulligan, K. (1998). From appropriate emotions to values. *Monist, 81*, 161–188.

Nichols, S. (2004). *Sentimental rules: On the natural foundation of moral judgment*. Oxford, UK: Oxford University Press.

Nucci, L. P. (2001). *Education in the moral domain*. Cambridge, UK: Cambridge University Press.

Nucci, L. P., Turiel, E., & Encarnacion-Gawrych, G. (1983). Children's social interactions and social concepts: Analyses of morality and convention in the Virgin Islands. *Journal of Cross-Cultural Psychology, 14*, 469–487.

Prinz, J. (2007). *The emotional construction of morals*. Oxford, UK: Oxford University Press.

Prinz, J. (2008). Is morality innate? In W. Sinnott-Armstrong (Ed.), *Moral psychology, volume 1: The evolution of morality: Adaptations and innateness* (pp. 367–406). Cambridge, MA: MIT Press.

Rawls, J. (1972). *A theory of justice*. Oxford, UK: Clarendon Press.

Scheffler, S. (1987). Morality through thick and thin: A critical notice of ethics and the limits of philosophy. *Philosophical Review, 96*, 411–434.

Skorupski, J. (2000). Irrealist cognitivism. In J. Dancy (Ed.), *Normativity* (pp. 116–139). Oxford, UK: Blackwell.

Turiel, E. (2002). *The culture of morality: Social development, context, and conflict*. Cambridge, UK: Cambridge University Press.

Williams, B. (1965/1973). Morality and the emotions. In *Problems of the self* (pp. 207–229). Cambridge, UK: Cambridge University Press.

Williams, B. (1985/2007). *Ethics and the limits of philosophy*. London: Routledge.

ENDNOTES

1. Thick concepts are discussed more in recent moral philosophy than they are within the other disciplines in Moral Psychology. For example, the connection for which we argue between judgments involving thick concepts and emotion is at the heart of what is now known as rational sentimentalism. See, for example, D'Arms and Jacobson (2010) and many of the other works discussed therein.

2. This notion of thick concepts is not to be confused with the term *thick descriptions*, introduced by Clifford Geertz to anthropology.

3. These characteristics are discussed by Goldie (2009, pp. 95–97).

4. Our point here is not that thick concept judgments cannot be analyzed into facts and values; we return to this issue in second half of the chapter.

5. This is discussed in detail in Goldie (2009, p. 98). Thanks to Daniel Callcut for help here.

6. Some philosophers, claiming to follow in the footsteps of David Hume, argue that moral judgments are even more closely connected to emotion than we suggest, being in some sense expressive of emotion. This idea is found in emotivism and more recently and in a more sophisticated form in Prinz (2007) and Nichols (2004).

7. We will have more to say later in the chapter about the connections between thick moral judgments and emotion.

8. This extension of thick ethical concepts was proposed by Goldie (2009, p. 95) and the links between the ethical, intellectual, and aesthetic virtues (hence also thick concepts) are discussed in Goldie (2008a).

9. Adrian Moore introduced the notion of grasping a thick concept in an *engaged* or *disengaged* way. He claims that this involves not only being able to apply the concept correctly and being willing to actually do so but also "sharing whatever beliefs, concerns, and values give application of the concept its point" (Moore, 2006, p. 137). Goldie connects Moore's idea of engagement to emotions in his discussion of Bernard Williams's account of emotions and thick concepts (Goldie, 2009, pp. 96–99).

10. Compare here the helpful discussion of his young daughter's use of the concept *not fair* in D'Arms (2008, p. 281) and his reference to Nucci (2001) in regard to this kind of case.

11. It is controversial whether one can learn to apply such a concept accurately without engaging at all at any point with the corresponding emotional responses. The anthropologist has to engage in imaginative role-taking to understand the concept and, if to some degree successful, this imagining could involve real emotional responses. We discuss this in more detail shortly.

12. Haidt recognizes in later work, as we previously mentioned, that the dumbfounding may be partly to do with the narrowness of the sphere of morality used in interviews, which is why he suggests that there are more bases to morality than researchers usually propose (see Haidt & Bjorklund, 2008; Haidt & Graham, 2007; Haidt & Joseph, 2004).

13. This is discussed in more detail in Goldie (2004, 2008b).

14. The nontypical case will be where one realizes at the time that one's emotional response is not reasonable or justified. For example, you feel afraid of the mouse in the corner of the room, yet at the same time you know that your feelings are not justified. In this case the emotion lacks normative impulse.

15. Some thick concepts that are less thick (e.g., fairness, promise, and justice) have related emotions that seem designed to pick up on failures (e.g., unfairness, broken promise, and injustice), and these emotions, in particular resentment and anger, or what Aristotle called righteous indignation, are, in a familiar sense, negative. The positive emotion, when something is found to be just or fair, or where a promise is kept, is less salient. (One might observe that fear and disgust have a similar structure: These negative emotions arise when something is unsafe. Here too the positive emotion—a feeling of safety perhaps—is less salient.)

16. These issues are discussed in detail in Goldie (2005, 2006).

17. Many thanks to Robyn Langdon and Catriona Mackenzie for inviting us to contribute to this volume, and to Catriona, to Ronnie de Sousa, and to an anonymous referee for their helpful and pressing suggestions and comments.

11

Emotions, Reflection, and Moral Agency

CATRIONA MACKENZIE

Macquarie University

Recent work in empirical moral psychology has highlighted the central role of emotions in moral judgment and criticized overly rationalistic models of moral judgment. Although I am sympathetic to the view that emotions are crucial to moral agency, in this chapter I take issue with several prevailing trends in the recent literature. First, I question the prevalent reductive conception of emotions as automatic affective processes and argue that an evaluative appraisal approach yields a better understanding of emotions and their role in moral thinking. Second, moral reflection tends to be characterized in the literature as conscious, effortful, introspective reasoning about moral principles. Although such reasoning does (and should) play some role in moral deliberation and reflection, this conception of moral reasoning is too narrow and pays insufficient attention to the complex emotional and imaginative skills involved in moral reflection and agency. Third, some of the recent empirical research draws conclusions from the analysis of participants' one-off judgments or "intuitions" elicited in response to abstract hypothetical moral dilemmas. However, since moral reflection is both temporally extended and focused on guiding action, it is questionable how much weight should be given to such intuitions for understanding the exercise of moral agency in real-world, everyday situations.

INTRODUCTION

*T*he question of what role emotions play in moral deliberation, judgment, and action has been a central concern of philosophical moral psychology since Plato, Aristotle, and the Stoics. In Aristotle's view, virtuous action is not just a matter of doing the right thing at the right time and in the right manner. It also involves correct perception: being able to discern the morally salient features of the eliciting situation and to respond appropriately (see, e.g., Aristotle, Trans., 1984). This involves both rational and emotional capacities: knowing what principles are relevant to the situation and how they should be applied but also having emotional responses that are appropriate to the situation—feeling anger or compassion or regret when the situation merits such responses. Hume also thought that virtue requires correct perception of the morally salient features of the eliciting situation (see, e.g., Hume, 1739/1978, Book III). For Hume correct moral perception arises from the passions, or sentiments, but not from hot passions; rather, it requires adopting the point of view of what he refers to as the calm passions or the corrected sentiments. Hume compares the corrected, moral sentiments to corrective judgments in sense perception; because we know that sense perception is not always veridical, in our judgments we learn to correct for common sensory illusions. Similarly, the moral sentiments are passions or emotions that have been corrected by reflection. Thus, although Aristotle and Hume recognized that emotions play a key role in alerting us to relevant reason-giving considerations, they were well aware that emotions can also distort moral perception, deliberation, and judgment. This is why, for both, moral agency requires that we reflect on and regulate our emotional responses.

Moral psychologist Pizarro (2000) points to three aspects of emotions that seem to pose a threat to good moral judgment. First, the partiality of emotions seems to conflict with the requirement that moral principles be impartial. Hume was aware of this problem, and although he anticipated the view now widely accepted in developmental and social psychology and in cognitive neuroscience that the capacity for affective empathy (or what Hume called sympathy) is a necessary precondition for moral motivation, he also recognized that the scope of our sympathies is limited. We are more likely to feel compassion for those we care about, or for people more like ourselves, than for distant others. This is why empathy is not sufficient for morality and why the sentiments need to be corrected by general principles. Second, emotions can sometimes latch onto morally irrelevant features of a situation and influence our moral behavior and judgments. Pizarro cites the literature in social psychology showing that something as trivial as finding a dime can have a positive influence on people's motivations to help others. Third, emotions are often conceptualized as mere feelings; passive affective states over which we exercise little voluntary control. This conception of the emotions is reflected in common linguistic usage, for example, when we talk about being overcome by anger, and it is why emotions seem to conflict with the kind of reasoned, principled action that morality is thought to require of us.

It is these features of the emotions that seem to be behind Kant's view that emotions, even beneficent emotions such as sympathy, provide an unreliable foundation for morality (see, e.g., Kant, 1785/1998). Contrary to a common mis-interpretation, Kant does not deny that emotions, such as compassion, might play an important role in motivating actions that accord with moral requirements, but he thinks that what makes an action genuinely moral is that it is guided and moti-vated by a rational universal principle. Kant's influence on Kohlberg's (1969, 1971) account of moral development, and via Kohlberg, on contemporary moral psychol-ogy is well known. Kohlberg understands moral judgment as a process of reason-ing from moral principles to a conclusion about how one ought to act in a specific situation. Moral development is marked by a progress from judgments guided by lower-level egocentric principles to judgments guided by principles based on social conformity to the most mature level of moral judgment guided by impartial, uni-versal principles focused on issues of harm, justice, and rights.

Recently this cognitivist tradition in moral psychology seems to have been challenged on a number of different fronts. Research in cognitive neuroscience on empathy deficits in psychopathy and autism seems to show that empathy is a necessary condition for moral development (see, e.g., Blair, 1995, 2005): Damasio's (1994) work on patients with *acquired sociopathy* arising from damage to the ven-tromedial prefrontal cortex seems to show that while these patients' reasoning abilities are still intact, they suffer affective and emotional deficits, resulting in highly impaired decision-making capacities and moral deficiencies in patients who acquire their injuries at a younger age; neuroimaging studies conducted by Greene and colleagues (see, e.g., Greene, Sommerville, Nystrom, Darley, & Cohen, 2001) seem to show that regions of the brain associated with the emotions are highly active in processing moral judgments (see, e.g., Greene & Haidt, 2002); and Haidt's *social intuitionist model* of moral judgment claims that moral judgments are not the result of effortful, conscious reasoning from principles but of moral intuitions, which Haidt characterizes as automatic, affective responses or gut feelings, akin to perceptions (see, e.g., Haidt, 2001; Haidt & Bjorklund, 2008a).

I am very sympathetic to the view that emotions are crucial to moral agency, and I think that philosophical moral psychology has much to learn from this empirical literature. I also think that moral psychology in the tradition of Kant and Kohlberg has overemphasized the role of rational reflection and principle-based reasoning in moral cognition and has tended to construe emotions as mere feelings, lacking in cognitive content and as at least morally unreliable, if not in conflict with moral-ity. And I agree with Haidt that this tradition has paid insufficient attention to the social dimensions of morality. However, I am troubled by the work of Haidt and Greene for a number of reasons.

First, although Haidt thinks his social intuitionist model of moral judgment poses a serious challenge to the Kantian–Kohlbergian tradition of moral psychol-ogy, the problem with his model is that it upholds, rather than challenges, the tra-dition's impoverished conception of emotions as automatic affects over which we can exercise little reflective and self-regulatory control, just reversing the order of priority given within this tradition to affect and reason; Greene (see, e.g., Greene, 2008) assumes a similarly impoverished conception of emotions. Second, Haidt and Greene also uphold the tradition's conception of moral reasoning as primarily principle-based reasoning and its rationalist conception of moral reflection. While reasoning does and should play a role in moral thinking, I argue that it is a mistake to conceptualize moral reflection so narrowly. The scope of moral reflection is much wider than Haidt and Greene allow, and it involves the exercise of complex emotional, imaginative, and agential capacities. It is also a social process. On this I am in agreement with Haidt (see, e.g., Haidt, 2001; Haidt & Bjorklund, 2008a), although I disagree with Haidt's construal of the social dimensions of morality (more on this later). Third, the empirical work of Haidt and Greene focuses on participants' one-off, snap judgments in response to abstract hypothetical moral dilemmas. But in my view it is not clear how much this research can tell us about a great deal of moral reflection and decision making in everyday contexts, which is extended over time and involves reflection on our responsibilities and commitments to others, our goals and values, our interpretations of and judgments about our own behavior and emotional responses, and so on. To summarize these concerns, I think Haidt and Greene's approaches to moral psychology mischaracterize the moral emotions and moral reflection and present a skewed picture of moral agency.

In the following section of the chapter I outline the central claims of Haidt and Greene and motivate these concerns. In the final section I outline an alternative picture of emotions, reflection, and their role in moral agency that presents an intermediate position between moral intuitionism and rationalism. Just to clarify the parameters of my project here, Haidt and Greene see their work as going beyond their descriptive claims about the role of intuitions and emotions in moral judgment and as having important implications for normative ethics and meta-ethics. Greene, for example, thinks his research provides conclusive proof of the superiority of consequentialism over deontological moral theories (see, e.g., Greene, 2008; see also Singer, 2005)[1], while Haidt's work is sometimes taken to provide support for simple sentimentalist views in meta-ethics (see, e.g., Prinz, 2006; for a critical response, see Jones, 2006). I will not be addressing these claims here, except in passing.

HAIDT AND GREENE ON MORAL JUDGMENT

Despite some important differences between the views of Haidt and Greene, their views converge in many respects, particularly in their conceptions of emotions and moral reasoning. Haidt's social intuitionist model aims to describe the causal processes involved in moral reasoning (see, e.g., Haidt, 2001; Haidt & Bjorklund, 2008a). His thesis, in brief, is that automatic moral intuition precedes and causes moral judgments and that reflective moral reasoning is a process of rationalization—of searching for reasons to support and justify these automatically driven judgments. Not only does this thesis reverse Kohlberg's (1969) account of the relationship between moral reasoning and moral judgment, but the post hoc rationalization claim also debunks Kohlberg's conception of moral reasoning as the search for impartial and universal principles of justification of our moral judgments. Greene and colleagues (see, e.g., Greene et al., 2001; Greene, Nystrom, Engell, Darley, & Cohen, 2004) agree with the claim that moral judgment is mostly driven by intuition. Greene also agrees that much moral reasoning, particularly deontological moral reasoning, which appeals to principles based on rights and duties, is post hoc rationalization. In fact, Greene (2008) suggests that "what deontological moral philosophy really is, what it is *essentially*, is an attempt to produce rational justifications for emotionally driven moral judgments" (p. 39; italics in original).

Moral Intuitions

Haidt claims that moral judgments of rightness or wrongness are automatic, affective responses or gut feelings, akin to perceptions. These automatic, intuitive responses to the actions or character of others are evaluative, but only thinly evaluative, involving judgments of good–bad, like–dislike, approach–avoid, and so on. Haidt compares intuitive moral judgments to aesthetic judgments: Just as we might respond automatically to a landscape, judging it as beautiful, so he claims we make automatic moral judgments about others' actions or characters. In neither case do we make the judgment on the basis of a process of conscious and deliberate reasoning—weighing evidence, using inferential or deductive reasoning to reach a conclusion; in both cases we are often not able to articulate the basis of our judgment—explaining why we find the landscape beautiful or why we regard an action as wrong. In support of this claim, Haidt (2001) cites evidence from social attitude and stereotyping studies, which suggest that many of our judgments about others arise from automatic, affective first impressions. I do not intend to assess whether this evidence does support the social intuition thesis, although Fine (2006) argues that Haidt is very selective in his use of social cognition studies and does not address the literature showing that people can exercise more control over these affective responses than Haidt claims.

Haidt and Greene both claim Hume as a philosophical predecessor for the moral intuitionist thesis. However, note that for Hume although the moral sentiments arise from natural sentiments, such as empathy or the love between parents and children, they are neither partial nor automatic affects; rather, they are detached, impartial, reflective emotional responses developed under the guidance of general principles (see, e.g., Hume 1739/1978, for discussion). For Hume, the education of the moral sentiments is thus a process whereby thinly evaluative, partial, affective responses become more considered, more discriminating, and more thickly evaluative as a result of social interaction and reflection upon our moral experience. Hume therefore has some basis for distinguishing between unreflective affective responses and normatively correct moral perceptions and morally appropriate emotional responses. In contrast, a major limitation of Haidt's social intuitionist model is that it downplays the role of reflection in enabling us to regulate our emotional responses (as I will explain later) and so undercuts the ground for making these kinds of normative distinctions and for explaining the basis on which some moral intuitions are a reliable source of moral knowledge.

This approach also infects Haidt's account of moral development. For example, Haidt and Bjorklund (2008a) propose that moral intuitions arise from innate, distinct moral modules that have become encoded in the brain through the evolutionary process. These modules, they argue, dispose us to be responsive to considerations related to five values: (1) care and the avoidance of harm and suffering, (2) reciprocity and fairness, (3) hierarchy and authority, (4) purity or sanctity, and (5) loyalty to ingroup members. These foundational values underpin all moral systems and conceptions of the virtues, with different cultures constructing specific virtues, such as honesty or kindness, in different, although overlapping, ways. Moral development, according to Haidt and Bjorklund, is a process of the endogenous unfolding, or externalization of the moral modules at different developmental stages, assisted by socialization processes and peer networks that enculturate individuals into culturally specific moral practices and understandings of the virtues. As Jacobson (2008) argues, however, Haidt and Bjorklund's five foundational values are so abstract that they might figure in any moral view, no matter how morally heinous, so it is not clear how they are supposed to provide a basis for moral knowledge (see p. 226). And, despite their denial that their position is a form of moral relativism, their account of moral development suggests that moral intuitions are biological response mechanisms that have been fine-tuned in different ways by cultural practices. To quote Jacobson (2008), "On this view, moral knowledge is simply the habituated ability to see things the way others see them in your parish: to have the same intuitions as others in your society" (p. 228).

Greene is not subject to this same objection because (for reasons that I will explain shortly) he does not think that the kind of moral thought that arises from moral intuitions can provide the basis for genuine moral knowledge. But, like Haidt, he also construes moral emotions as automatic intuitive responses. And, like Haidt, he finds support for this conception of moral intuitions in dual-process models of judgment and problem solving (see, e.g., Greene, 2007, 2008, 2009; Greene et al., 2001). According to dual-process models of the type proposed by Greene and colleagues, information processing involves two parallel systems: (1) a default, hot, affective system that is both phylogenetically and ontogenetically primary and that operates largely automatically; and (2) a cool, controlled cognitive system that is slow and conscious and involves deliberative reasoning. Haidt and Greene apply dual-process models to the domain of moral judgment: Moral intuitions are part of the hot affective system, whereas moral reasoning is a product of the cool cognitive system.

My intention here is not to assess dual-process models of cognition more generally; however, I think that Haidt and Greene's application of dual-process models to the moral domain serves to perpetuate an emotions–reason dualism in moral psychology, which I argue is simplistic. It also perpetuates an impoverished conception of moral emotions as mere feelings or affects. Greene (2008), for example, characterizes moral emotions as "blunt biological instruments" (p. 71), and he describes moral intuitions as alarm-like emotional responses, which are rigid, inflexible, and resistant to reason—the result of "evolutionary adaptations that arose in response to the demands and opportunities created by social life" (p. 60). Because they are automatic, moral intuitions and emotions enable social creatures such as ourselves to respond quickly, efficiently, and reliably to the needs of others. Yet Greene (2008) also claims that because they are the product of evolutionary forces, moral intuitions are suspect sources of moral knowledge that cannot ground adequate moral reasoning. In his view, moral intuitions are fundamentally unreliable because they involve automatic emotional responses and because they "appear to have been shaped by morally irrelevant factors having to do with the constraints and circumstances of our evolutionary history" (p. 75). As Levy (2007) argues, however, the fact that some of our basic moral intuitions might have evolved under nonmoral selection pressures does not show, in and of itself, that these intuitions are suspect or that moral reasoning that is responsive to them ought to be distrusted (see pp. 300–306).

Greene (2008) cites neuroimaging studies (see, e.g., Green et al., 2001) involving what he calls personal and impersonal dilemmas, as evidence both for his evolutionary claims about moral intuitions and for the dual-process view of moral judgment. These dilemmas involve variants of Judith Jarvis Thomson's (1976) famous Trolley and Footbridge Dilemmas. In the Trolley Dilemma, a runaway trolley is headed for a section of the track on which five men are working. The only way to prevent the trolley from killing these men is to pull a lever, which will divert the trolley onto a side track on which one man is working, resulting in his death. In the Footbridge Dilemma the only way to stop the runaway trolley from killing the five men is to push a fat stranger off a footbridge spanning the tracks. This will result in his death, but it will save the five men. (For further discussion, see, e.g., Langdon & Delmas, Chapter 5, this volume; McIlwain, Chapter 6, this volume). In experimental studies, participants judge these cases as morally different without necessarily being able to articulate why. Typically, they judge the act of pushing the fat stranger off the footbridge to be more morally wrong than the act of diverting the trolley.[2]

Greene argues that there is no moral justification for drawing any distinction between the cases since both involve the death of one person to save five others, so the act of causing the death of the one person can be justified morally on consequentialist grounds. His hypothesis is that people respond differently to these cases because the footbridge case involves a personal moral violation, which involves directly bringing about bodily harm to another person. Such personal violations trigger strong negative emotional responses to the causing of direct harm that conflict with the more sophisticated cognitive reasoning required to make a consequentialist judgment. On the other hand, the trolley case involves an impersonal moral violation. In this case, because the harm is brought about by indirect means it does not trigger such strong negative emotional responses, so people find it easier to reason logically to a consequentialist judgment. Greene argues that our negative emotional responses to personal moral violations are the result of innate but evolutionarily primitive responses to interpersonal violence that predate the development of our rational capacities. And he claims that neuroimaging studies of participants' brains as they responded to a range of personal and impersonal dilemmas provide support for this hypothesis in two ways.

First, neuroimaging showed increased neural activity in regions of the brain associated with emotional response and social cognition when participants were responding to moral dilemmas involving personal harm, whereas when they were responding to moral dilemmas involving impersonal harm there was greater activity in brain regions associated with higher cognitive functions. There has been considerable discussion in the cognitive neuroscience literature about whether neuroimaging studies of this type do support the dual-process theory of moral judgment. For example, Moll and de Oliveira-Souza (2007; Moll et al., 2008) dispute the dual-process theory and argue that neuroimaging data shows that moral appraisals involve a complex interaction of cognitive and emotional mechanisms.

Second, Greene et al. (2001) reported that the reaction time required to reach a consequentialist judgment in cases involving personal harm was greater than the reaction time required to reach a nonconsequentialist judgment (i.e., to judge the act as "not okay"). There was no such difference in reaction time in cases involving impersonal harm. Greene and colleagues argued that the differences in reaction time supports the view that reasoning to a consequentialist conclusion in personal cases requires overriding strong negative emotional responses and thus takes longer. However, McGuire, Langdon, Coltheart, and Mackenzie (2009) recently reanalyzed Greene et al.'s data and conducted a detailed reanalysis of participants' reaction times to so-called personal and impersonal dilemmas. This reanalysis shows that Greene et al.'s results showing differential reaction times were driven primarily by a small subset of personal dilemmas, to which participants reacted very quickly and which they almost universally judged to be impermissible (e.g., not rescuing someone who has been involved in an accident because you don't want to ruin the upholstery in your car). Once the data from this subset of items were excluded from the analysis, there was no significant difference between reaction times to personal and impersonal dilemmas. Greene (2008, 2009) has recently conceded that the personal–impersonal distinction is problematic, but he thinks the imaging studies still provide support for a dual-process model of moral judgment.[3]

From the foregoing it should be clear that Haidt and Greene both construe moral emotions as automatic affective responses and that Greene in particular thinks of them as primitive biological mechanisms that give rise to unreliable moral thinking. Just to clarify my argument at this point, I am not disputing that intuitions play a role in moral cognition. What I want to dispute is the way Haidt and Greene narrowly conceptualize the emotions and their role in moral thought.

Moral Reasoning

If moral judgments are just automatic affective responses, what is moral reasoning, and what role does it play in moral cognition? Haidt distinguishes four different kinds of moral reasoning: (1) *post hoc rationalization,* (2) *reasoned social persuasion,* (3) *reasoned judgment,* and (4) *private reflection* (see, e.g., Haidt, 2001; Haidt & Bjorklund, 2008a). He argues that reasoned judgment and private reflection are rare species of moral reasoning; most moral reasoning takes the form either of post hoc rationalization or reasoned social persuasion. In Haidt's view most moral reasoning is post hoc rationalization—it is moral intuitions that do the real causal work in explaining people's moral judgments. It is only when pressed to provide reasons for our moral judgments that we appeal to moral principles. Haidt claims that philosophers and psychologists like Kohlberg emphasize the role of principled reasoning in moral judgment because they assume that reasoning aims to track the truth. However, in Haidt's view, the goal of reasoning—and here what he seems to mean by goal is an evolutionary goal—is not to track the truth but to achieve social integration and harmony and to influence and persuade others. This conception of the goal of moral reasoning underpins Haidt's account of reasoned social persuasion. Haidt thinks that we do sometimes engage in reasoned moral discussion and debate with other people, sometimes with the aim of reaching a community consensus. But he does not see this as a process of collective reasoning that is driven by concerns about moral justification or truth. It is rather a process of trying to persuade others to our partial and interested perspectives, a process of using rhetoric to trigger the desired affectively valenced intuitive responses in others. When it comes to moral judgments, he claims, our interest in reasons is not the disinterested interest of the scientist but the partial interest of the lawyer. In other words, most activities of reason giving are nothing more than exercises in rhetorical persuasion.

Haidt (2001) does concede that sometimes people can engage in genuine moral reasoning, or reasoned judgment, which he characterizes as systematic, step-by-step, conscious reasoning from first principles to reach consistent moral conclusions that may override our initial intuitions (see also Haidt & Björklund, 2008a). Like Greene, he seems to think that consequentialist reasoning, as discussed already, is the best exemplar of this kind of reasoning, citing Singer's (1979) work as an example and suggesting that most objections to Singer's conclusions arise from the recalcitrance of people's moral intuitions. Haidt (2001; see also Haidt & Bjorklund, 2008a) also concedes that sometimes—for example, when we have no clear intuitions, or when our intuitions conflict—we can engage in a process of private reflection or inner moral dialogue. He suggests that moral perspective taking—imaginatively putting oneself in another person's place—is one of the chief means of doing so. However, he thinks such reflection plays very little role in moral cognition (see, e.g., Haidt, 2001; Haidt & Björklund, 2008a).

Haidt (2001) cites a range of different studies as evidence for his claims about moral reasoning, such as studies purporting to show that when people are not aware of the cognitive processes causing their behavior (e.g., because they have acted under posthypnotic suggestion or subliminal priming) they search for plausible-sounding reasons to explain that behavior; defensive motivation studies showing that people adjust their beliefs and thinking to preserve coherence with self-definitional attitudes, such as their values and moral commitments; and biasing studies showing that people are not very good at understanding and assessing evidence or providing evidence for their views and that their assessment of evidence is biased—in other words they put greater weight on evidence that supports their beliefs while discounting other evidence that seems to question those beliefs.

One study (Haidt, Koller, & Dias, 1993) aimed to resolve a debate about whether the moral domain is universally limited to issues of harm, justice, and rights or whether in some cultures it extends to issues more typically regarded as matters of social convention, such as practices concerning food and sex roles. Participants from different socioeconomic status (SES) groups in Brazil and the United States were presented with a series of vignettes involving what Haidt stipulates to be harmless taboo violations, such as a family who eats its pet dog after it has been killed by a car or a man who masturbates with a chicken carcass and then cooks and eats it. The researchers found that high and low SES groups in both Brazil and the United States expressed disgust at these actions or at the least found them strange, but high SES groups did not regard them as morally wrong. On the other hand, low SES groups, while acknowledging that these actions did not cause harm to anyone, nevertheless regarded them as moral violations and as universally wrong. Some participants from both groups, while quick to make judgments, were often at a loss to explain why and became puzzled and confused when pressed for their reasons. Haidt and colleagues refer to this inability to provide reasons for one's moral judgment as *moral dumbfounding*. In a later study (Haidt, Bjorklund, & Murphy, 2000, reported in Haidt, 2001; Haidt & Björklund, 2008a) participants seem to have been particularly dumbfounded when pressed to provide reasons for their judgments in cases involving other taboo violations that Haidt and colleagues characterize as harmless—such as consensual adult incest or cannibalism of an unclaimed corpse in a pathology lab—and in cases designed to elicit strong disgust reactions (taking a sip from a drink in which a dead, sterilized cockroach had just been dipped). Haidt and Björklund (2008a) also cite a study (Wheatley & Haidt, 2005) in which participants were hypnotized to experience disgust in response to reading completely neutral words (e.g., *take* or *often*) and then asked to read moral judgment stories containing these words. Participants primed to experience disgust expressed more severe moral judgments.

Haidt (2001) thinks moral dumbfounding provides evidence that, because we are not aware of the processes that give rise to our moral judgments, when pressed to justify them we engage in a post hoc confabulatory search for possible reasons to bolster these judgments. Dumbfounding occurs when we are unable to find any such reasons. In other cases we appeal to prior moral theories to rationalize our judgments. Haidt (2001) defines moral theories as "a pool of culturally supplied norms for evaluating and criticizing the behavior of others" (p. 16). As a descriptive claim, Haidt might be correct that people may not be very good at providing good reasons for their judgments. He is undoubtedly also correct that moral reasoning can be biased, defensively motivated, and sometimes a matter of post hoc rationalization of prejudice. However, that people can be bad reasoners or dumbfounded when it comes to explaining the reasons for their judgments, is not sufficient to show that moral reasoning reduces to a matter of post hoc rationalization.

I argue that there are several limitations of Haidt's views about moral reasoning. First, Haidt conflates a causal claim about the origin of evaluative judgments with a justificatory claim about what justifies those judgments (for related critiques see, e.g., Jacobson, 2008; Saltzstein & Kasachkoff, 2004). Haidt thinks that so-called rationalists are making the causal claim that our moral judgments arise from reasoning, to which his response is that they arise from moral intuitions and that reasoning is just post hoc rationalization. However, rationalism is a justificatory claim to the effect that moral judgments can be justified only by rational principles. So one can hold this view about justification while also acknowledging that people can be bad reasoners or not able to articulate the principles on which their judgments are implicitly based. As I have already indicated, Greene's view is not subject to this objection because he does think that moral judgments must be rationally justified and that consequentialist reasons can provide such justification.

Second, although Haidt does concede that sometimes a process of giving and exchanging reasons with others will yield better understanding and judgment, it is not clear on what grounds he can in fact distinguish good or justified moral reasons from mere rationalization or rhetorical persuasion—this is because Haidt does not explain what constitutes moral knowledge, as distinct from socially agreed norms, as I explained earlier.

Third, while I agree with Haidt that moral reflection and reasoning is a social process, I disagree with his debunking characterization of this process as primarily rhetorical persuasion aimed at influencing other people to one's point of view. In my view, Levy (2007) provides a much better characterization of the sense in which moral reasoning is social—namely, that moral knowledge, like all knowledge, is an ongoing, distributed, community-wide enterprise in which, through moral debate and under the pressure of objection and argument, our judgments are tested and revised (see pp. 308–316).

I now want to press a more general objection to Haidt's and Greene's claims about moral judgment and moral reasoning. While their work in moral psychology is focused on judgments about the rightness or wrongness of particular actions in hypothetical moral dilemma situations, it is far from evident that participants' one-off responses to such hypothetical dilemmas can tell us much about ordinary moral reasoning and reflection, for a number of reasons. First, many of the scenarios describe situations that people are likely to regard as unrealistic, abstract, and underspecified, because they are far removed from everyday moral concerns and lack the kind of contextual information that typically feeds into our decision making and judgments. This includes information about the surrounding circumstances of an action such as the events leading up to it, about people's characters and patterns of behavior over time, and about the possible effects of an action on people's relationships and self-concepts. In the absence of such information, it is not particularly surprising that people might be dumbfounded when asked whether it is morally right for adult siblings to have allegedly harmless consensual sex or to cannibalize an unclaimed corpse in a mortuary (for further discussion, see Kennett, Chapter 12, this volume). It is noteworthy that participants in Haidt and colleagues' (2000) study were not similarly dumbfounded when presented with Kohlberg's Heinz dilemma (should Heinz steal a drug he cannot afford to buy to save his wife's life?), which presents a scenario that most people can relate fairly easily to their moral experience.

Second, given the inevitable limitations of most experimental paradigms, the scope of our everyday moral reasoning and reflection is much broader than these experimental situations allow. Because moral decision making and action usually have significant repercussions for ourselves and others, deliberation will often take account of multiple factors as relevant to the specific situation in question: moral intuitions and principles certainly, but also responsibilities and commitments to others, our own and others' needs, our short and long-term goals, our values, the ideals we want to live up to, our understanding of our own characters—our virtues and limitations—and so on. Take a familiar example. Let's say I have a pressing deadline to meet and I work out a timetable for meeting it consistent with meeting my obligations to my students and my family. But then a colleague becomes ill and some arrangement needs to be made for his lectures next week. I feel an obligation to help out and I could teach the material, but I am feeling under pressure already.

One course of action that is open to me is to say to the head of the department that I cannot take on the extra load and that the lectures should be canceled or that he needs to find someone else to take them. But I find that decision hard to square with my self-conception as a reliable and responsible colleague. On the other hand, I know that agreeing to do this is going to require me to work extra on the weekend and that I may not be able to go to my son's cricket match as I had promised. I am worried that either way I am going to let somebody down. The kind of moral reflection required to respond to this rather mundane moral dilemma involves emotional, imaginative, agential, and reasoning skills that are more complex than those tapped by the experimental paradigms typically used by Greene and Haidt (I will say more about these skills shortly). Here I want to point out that in response to a similar objection raised by Narvaez (2008), Haidt and Bjorklund (2008b) have recently conceded that moral decision making and deliberation do require this kind of broad-ranging moral reflection. However, they claim that the social intuitionist model was originally designed to describe only the causal processes involved in moral judgment, not moral decision making, and that moral judgment and moral decision making are quite different processes that are not closely related functionally. Without further argument to support this claim, I can see no good reason for supposing that moral judgment and moral decision making are functionally quite distinct. I suggest that moral judgment and moral deliberation recruit the same emotional, imaginative, reasoning, and reflective capacities—so in my view, the objection still stands.

Third, in real-world moral contexts, as this example shows, moral deliberation, reflection, decision making, and judgment are usually not one-off, single decisions but processes that are extended over time and are shaped by prior histories (for related discussion, see Kennett, Chapter 12, this volume). My decision to take the lectures is likely to be shaped to some extent by my relationship with my colleague and the patterns of our prior interactions. If I suspect the genuineness of his illness and see it as yet another instance of a common pattern of reneging on his obligations and expecting other people to pick up the slack, then my response to the head of the department's request is likely to be quite different than if I know him to be a highly responsible person who would cancel his classes only if he is really ill. If I feel resentful toward my colleagues because I think they regard me as the departmental dogsbody, then again my thinking about the reasonableness of the request will be quite different from if I think that everyone in the department shares the load. Further, any decision I make will be nested in a complex set of interconnected decisions and judgments, both my own and that of other people, so that the process of reflection, deliberation, and decision making will be an iterative one, involving ongoing moral interaction and negotiation with others (see, e.g., McGeer, Chapter 14, this volume, for a related account of moral agency as co-reactive). For this reason, it is not clear to what extent neuroimaging or moral judgment studies of one-off responses to abstract hypothetical dilemmas can illuminate the cognitive processes involved in such temporally extended, iterative, real-world moral decision-making situations.

To recap, I have argued that Haidt and Greene assume an impoverished conception of moral intuitions and emotions as automatic affective processes and promote an overly narrow conception of moral reasoning that does not do full justice to the complexity of moral reflection. I have also objected to the post hoc rationalization claims and to Haidt's construal of the social dimensions of moral cognition. However, I haven not yet outlined an alternative picture of the role of emotions and reflection in moral agency—this is what I aim to do in the final section of the chapter. What I hope to do is to find a way of acknowledging Haidt's insights that intuitions, emotions, affects, and social interaction play a far more central role in moral cognition than rationalist models of reasoning and reflection recognize, without simply reversing the rationalist view, as I think he does, or embracing his debunking conclusions about morality.

EMOTIONS, REFLECTION, AND MORAL AGENCY

Much contemporary philosophical emotions theory rejects the view that emotions are merely blunt biological instruments, or nonrational affective responses, mere feelings. This is not to deny that emotions involve characteristic affective and physiological components and give rise to characteristic action tendencies, some of which involve biological response mechanisms—for example, the fight-or-flight responses characteristic of fear. But the prevailing view is that emotions also have cognitive content. There is a debate in the literature about how the cognitive dimensions of emotions should be understood. Judgmentalist theories (see, e.g., Solomon, 1977) construe the cognitions involved in emotions as beliefs or judgments. In this view, the cognition central to my fear of a snake is a belief that the snake is dangerous; the cognition central to my love of my children is a judgment that they possess qualities and characteristics that are lovable. Judgmentalist theories have been criticized on a number of grounds, in particular that they cannot account for recalcitrant emotions—emotions that conflict with our considered judgments, such as my continuing to feel frightened of a snake even though I know it is harmless (see, e.g., Greenspan, 1980, for further discussion of this criticism). For this reason, many contemporary emotions theorists argue that the cognitive component of an emotion should not be construed as a belief or a judgment but as an evaluative perspective, attitude, or appraisal that frames the way we perceive and interpret the eliciting situation (for different variants of this view, see, e.g., de Sousa, 1987; Goldie, 2000; Greenspan, 2003; Jones, 2003). In this view, jealousy, for example, is an affect that might involve certain bodily and psychic feelings, but it also involves an evaluation of the eliciting situation that picks out certain features of the situation as salient, others as less salient. So a person who is feeling jealous is likely to notice and attach significance to aspects of his partner's behavior that he might otherwise not pay attention to at all—such as her making a phone call or wearing a new piece of clothing. And he might appraise her behavior through the lens of jealousy while at the same time not believing that she is unfaithful. Or, in the example I gave earlier, construing my colleague's illness as part of a pattern of reneging on his commitments is likely to be an evaluative appraisal bound up with the emotion of resentment.

Evaluative appraisal theories can accommodate many of the insights that seem to underlie Haidt's moral intuitionism. Appraisal theories can accommodate the insight that emotions are quasi-perceptual in the sense that they are ways of seeing or construing a situation from a particular point of view or perspective. They can also accept that these appraisals are often quick responses to the eliciting situation that are not always amenable to deliberative control (Greenspan, 2003, p. 117). And they can allow for affective dissonance—namely, that our emotional responses do not always cohere with our all-things-considered judgments. Sometimes, this may be because this dissonance is an expression of deep-seated implicit evaluative attitudes that we do not endorse and that conflict with our more considered, conscious judgments (e.g., racial stereotyping). These are the kinds of cases that appear to drive Haidt's approach to moral intuitions. However, as Jones (2003) argues, sometimes affective dissonance—recalcitrant or outlaw emotions—can be important for practical rationality, alerting us to reasons, including moral reasons, that we may not be consciously aware of or able to articulate. Compassion, for example, or friendship can help unseat racist convictions that agents might consciously endorse, as the example of Huck Finn attests. Because recalcitrant emotions, which may be no more than gut feelings, can attune us in this way to reasons to which we ought to attend, it need not be irrational to act on the basis of these emotions rather than on the basis of our all-things-considered judgments.

Evaluative appraisal theories thus hold that emotions can be rational, not just in the strategic sense that they can aid decision making but also in the normative sense that they can attune us to relevant reason-giving considerations. To say that emotions are rational in this sense is to say that they are responsive to features of the situation to which we ought to be responsive. It is also to say that the evaluation expressed in the emotion is correct in the sense that the emotion is an appropriate, or fitting, response to the situation. Grief is an appropriate or fitting response to the death of a loved one; compassion is an appropriate response to another's suffering; remorse is an appropriate response to wrongdoing. By the same token, emotions can be assessed as unreasonable or disproportionate, which is to say that the evaluations expressed in the emotion are not warranted by the situation. Road rage is a good example of an irrational emotional response, a response that is not fitting or warranted and that blinds us to the relevant reason-giving considerations.

A central focus of the moral socialization of children is to train their capacities for recognizing the specific emotional responses that are appropriate or fitting to the eliciting situation. De Sousa (1987) has developed an influential analysis of how this kind of socialization works. He argues that we learn our emotional repertoires—our emotional vocabulary and our emotional responses—through what he calls paradigm scenarios. Paradigm scenarios involve two aspects: "first, a situation type providing the characteristic objects of the specific emotion-type … and second, a set of characteristic or 'normal' responses to the situation" (de Sousa, 1987, p. 182). In de Sousa's view, we learn which properties are relevantly motivating for particular emotions and which situation types should elicit a particular emotional response partly as a function of in-built biological mechanisms but largely through the learning of sociocultural norms. Emotional education involves teaching children to identify and name particular emotional responses, teaching them which objects characteristically warrant those responses in which typical situations, and also teaching them how to respond, that is, which action tendencies are appropriate.

So the basis for our emotional understanding is developed in childhood, through the paradigm scenarios that taught us the meaning of particular emotions. However, this understanding is layered by our subsequent encounters with a range of emotional paradigms. As a result, our emotional responses sometimes incorporate extended and complex scenarios, which may not be accessible to conscious introspection. This complexity explains both the degree to which emotions are intelligible and communicable to ourselves and others and the degree to which they are opaque. Their intelligibility and communicability derives from the biological basis of many emotions but also from the sociocultural norms they come to implicitly embody. Their opacity derives from the fact these norms are interpreted and played out in a variety of subtly or significantly different scenarios, reflecting the complex individual and familial biological and psychic histories that generated them.

Evaluative appraisal theories are thus quite consistent with a naturalistic outlook, with recognition of the social dimensions of the emotions and with acknowledging that we may be unaware of the processes that give rise to our emotions. But they are also responsive to the normative dimensions of emotional evaluations, to the fact that we do not just regard emotions as biological responses or outbursts of feeling. Our moral practices and norms and our expectations of our own and other people's behavior assume a normative conception of the emotions—that some emotional responses are appropriate or fitting and provide accurate evaluations of the eliciting situation and others do not. And our conception of moral agency assumes that people are responsible for reflecting upon and regulating their emotional responses. Appraisal theories thus provide an intermediate position between the kind of rationalism that discounts the capacity of emotions to attune us to relevant moral reasons (and I think Greene is actually a rationalist in this sense) and views like Haidt's that focus on gut responses and discount our capacities to reflect upon and regulate our emotional responses.

I want to conclude by saying something about the conception of moral agency and reflection that I think is assumed, and reasonably so, by our moral practices. My claim is that our moral practices operate under the assumption that as moral agents we regard ourselves and other moral agents as what Jones (2003, 2006) calls *reason responders*. To be a reason responder is to be the kind of creature who is capable of rationally guiding her actions in light of her best reasons, reasons that she regards as providing a justification for those actions. This involves a capacity to conceive of reasons as reasons, as distinct, say, from mere desires, automatic emotional responses, or rationalizations. And this in turn requires complex second-order capacities to reflect on our desires, automatic emotional responses, and reasoning processes and to consider whether they do provide us with genuine reasons for action, reasons that we should regard as authoritative in determining what we do. Say I find myself feeling enraged by the poor driving skills of another motorist and experience a very strong desire to shout at him abusively and make rude gestures. To think of myself as a reason responder is to think of myself as an agent who is capable of reflecting on this desire, considering whether I have good reasons to act on it and regulating my actions accordingly. It is also to regard myself as committed to what Jones describes as "the on-going cultivation and exercise of habits of reflective self-monitoring" (Jones, 2003, p. 194).

Now this second-order capacity for reflective self-monitoring is sometimes understood in highly intellectualist terms, as requiring some kind of conscious, reflective endorsement of our desires and emotional responses. Sometimes reflective self-monitoring does take this form; however, we engage in this kind of self-monitoring in a range of other ways, deploying emotional and imaginative as well as rational skills. For example, what I call reactive emotions (psychologists refer to these as meta-emotions) are second-order emotional evaluations of our first-order emotional responses. Let us imagine a young mother of a toddler who is being particularly trying as the mother is doing the grocery shopping in a supermarket. She finds herself growing increasingly irritable and impatient and more and more inclined to lose her temper and shout. Regulating this first-order emotional response need not be a matter of consciously reflecting on whether she endorses this response; it might take the form of experiencing reactive emotions of distress or shame about this response, prompting her to reframe her perspective on her child's behavior. Or, she might take up her child's perspective, perhaps self-consciously, but perhaps not, coming to see the shopping trip from the child's perspective as boring and interminably long when all that the child wants to do is to go to the playground. This reframing of the situation might then prompt her to be more patient. Let us also imagine that the mother begins to notice a common pattern in her emotional responses to her child on shopping trips. She might then deliberately take steps to try to ensure that she is not required to take her child with her when she does the grocery shopping. This might be because she knows that she cannot rely on herself to control her emotional responses once the child starts nagging about lollipops. In the same way, an alcoholic might try to ensure that she avoids social situations in which alcohol is going to be consumed. These are all very ordinary ways we regulate our emotional responses, either by reappraising the situation emotionally or imaginatively or by trying to exercise control over the circumstances we put ourselves in. There is a significant empirical literature demonstrating that people do employ such strategies to exercise second-order control over their emotional reactions (for discussion of this literature see, e.g., Fine, 2006; Pizarro & Bloom, 2003), so what I am saying here is not new. However, my point is also that the conception of moral agency embodied in our norms and practices not only assumes that we regard ourselves and others as reason responders capable of this kind of reflective self-monitoring, but also rightly holds us responsible for cultivating habits and skills of reflective self-monitoring and for exercising these skills. This does not mean that we always succeed—quite evidently we don't always do so.

I want to make two final points. First, cultivating and exercising the skills of reflective self-monitoring requires extensive social scaffolding, not just when we are learning these skills but also to maintain them. To give just a few examples: We often need the assistance and encouragement of others to devise and maintain strategies for exercising regulative self-control; we rely on others' responses and on broader social norms, values, and institutions to gauge whether our emotional evaluations are reasonable and appropriate; we engage in social debate and discussion concerning the adequacy of norms of appropriateness for particular emotions; and through art, literature, film, or interaction with people from other social, ethnic, or racial groups, we can expand our emotional repertoires and imaginative horizons and challenge automatic or habitual patterns of emotional response, such as racist attitudes.

Second, reflective self-monitoring as I have characterized it is quite different from the kind of conscious reasoning from universal principles that Haidt and Greene think of as paradigmatic moral reasoning. I agree with them that this kind of conscious reasoning plays a less central role in moral agency than some rationalist models suggest. However, reflective self-monitoring and moral deliberation more generally may implicitly be guided by principles and is implicitly or explicitly guided by our values, ideals, and self-concepts, as I hope to have made clear through my examples. Haidt (see, e.g., Haidt, 2001; Haidt & Bjorklund, 2008a) seems to think that trying to bring our emotional responses and behavior into line with our self-concepts, values, and moral commitments is a species of rationalization. However, I argue that this quest for normative coherence is evidence of the reflective capacities that are necessary for moral agency.

REFERENCES

Aristotle. (1984). Nicomachean ethics. (W. D. Ross & J. O Urmson, Trans.). In J. Barnes (Ed.), *The complete works of Aristotle. Revised Oxford translation*. Princeton, NJ: Princeton University Press.

Berker, S. (2009). The normative insignificance of neuroscience. *Philosophy and Public Affairs*, 37, 293–329.

Blair, R. J. R. (1995). A cognitive developmental approach to morality: Investigating the psychopath. *Cognition*, 57, 1–29.

Blair, R. J. R. (2005). Responding to the emotions of others: Dissociating forms of empathy through the study of typical and psychiatric populations. *Consciousness and Cognition*, 14, 698–718.Damasio, A. (1994). *Descartes' error: Emotion, reason and the human brain*. New York: Putnam.

Damasio, A. R. (1994). *Descartes' error: Emotion, reason, and the human brain*, New York: Putnam.

de Sousa, R. (1987). *The rationality of emotion*. Cambridge, MA: MIT Press.

Fine, C. (2006). Is the emotional dog wagging its rational tail, or chasing it? *Philosophical Explorations*, 9, 83–98.

Goldie, P. (2000). *The emotions*. Oxford, UK: Clarendon Press.

Greene, J. D. (2003). From neural "is" to moral "ought": What are the moral implications of neuroscientific moral psychology? *Nature Reviews: Neuroscience*, 4, 847–850.

Greene, J. D. (2007). Why are VMPFC patients more utilitarian?: A dual-process theory of moral judgment explains. *Trends in Cognitive Sciences*, 11, 322–323.

Greene, J. D. (2008). The secret joke of Kant's soul. In W. Sinnott-Armstrong (Ed.), *Moral psychology, volume 3: The neuroscience of morality: Emotion, brain disorders, and development* (pp. 35–79). Cambridge, MA: MIT Press.

Greene, J. D. (2009). Dual-process morality and the personal/impersonal distinction: A reply to McGuire, Langdon, Coltheart, and Mackenzie. *Journal of Experimental Social Psychology*, 45, 581–584.

Greene, J., & Haidt, J. (2002). How (and where) does moral judgment work? *Trends in Cognitive Sciences*, 6, 517–523.

Greene, J., Morelli, S., Lowenberg, K., Nystrom, L., & Cohen, J. (2008). Cognitive load selectively interferes with utilitarian moral judgment. *Cognition*, 107, 1144–1154.

Greene, J. D., Nystrom, L. E., Engell, A. D., Darley, J. M., & Cohen, J.D. (2004). The neural bases of cognitive conflict and control in moral judgment. *Neuron, 44*, 389–400.

Greene, J., Sommerville, R. B., Nystrom, L. E., Darley, J. M., & Cohen, J. D. (2001). An fMRI investigation of emotional engagement in moral judgment. *Science, 293*, 2105–2108.

Greenspan, P. (1980). A case of mixed feelings: Ambivalence and the logic of emotions. In A. O. Rorty (Ed.), *Explaining emotions* (pp. 223–250). Berkeley: University of California Press.

Greenspan, P. (2003). Emotions, rationality and mind/body. In A. Hatzimoysis (Ed.), *Philosophy and the emotions* (pp. 113–125). Cambridge, UK: Cambridge University Press.

Haidt, J. (2001). The emotional dog and its rational tail: A social intuitionist approach to moral judgment. *Psychological Review, 108*, 814–834.

Haidt, J., & Björklund, F. (2008a). Social intuitionists answer six questions about moral psychology. In W. Sinnott-Armstrong (Ed.), *Moral psychology, volume 2: The cognitive science of morality: Intuition and diversity* (pp. 181–217). Cambridge, MA: MIT Press.

Haidt, J., & Björklund, F. (2008b). Social intuitionists reason, in conversation: Reply to Jacobson and Narvaez. In W. Sinnott-Armstrong (Ed.), *Moral psychology, volume 2: The cognitive science of morality: Intuition and diversity* (pp. 241–254). Cambridge, MA: MIT Press.

Haidt, J. Bjorklund, F., & Murphy, S. (2000). *Moral dumbfounding: When intuition finds no reason*. Unpublished manuscript.

Haidt, J., Koller, S., & Dias, M. (1993). Affect, culture, and morality, or is it wrong to eat your dog? *Journal of Personality and Social Psychology, 65*, 613–628.

Hume, D. (1739/1978). *A treatise of human nature* (L. A. Selby-Bigge, Ed.), 2d ed. with text revised and notes by P. H. Nidditch. Oxford, UK: Clarendon Press.

Jacobson, D. (2008). Does social intuitionism flatter morality or challenge it? In W. Sinnott-Armstrong (Ed.), *Moral psychology, volume 2: The cognitive science of morality: Intuition and diversity* (pp. 219–232). Cambridge, MA: MIT Press.

Jones, K. (2003). Emotion, weakness of will, and the normative conception of agency. In A. Hatzimoysis (Ed.), *Philosophy and the emotions* (pp. 181–200). Cambridge, UK: Cambridge University Press.

Jones, K. (2006). Metaethics and emotions research: A response to Prinz. *Philosophical Explorations, 9*, 45–54.

Kant, I. (1785/1998). *Groundwork of the metaphysics of morals* (M. Gregor, Trans.). Cambridge, UK: Cambridge University Press.

Kohlberg, L. (1969). Stage and sequence: The cognitive-developmental approach to socialization. In D. A. Goslin (Ed.), *Handbook of socialization theory and research* (pp. 347–480). Chicago: Rand McNally.

Kohlberg, L. (1971). From is to ought: How to commit the naturalistic fallacy and get away with it in the study of moral development. In T. Mischel (Ed.), *Cognitive development and epistemology* (pp. 151–235). New York: Academic Press.

Levy, N. (2007). *Neuroethics*. Cambridge, UK: Cambridge University Press.

McGuire, J., Langdon, R., Coltheart, M., & Mackenzie, C. (2009). A reanalysis of the personal/impersonal distinction in moral psychology research. *Journal of Experimental Social Psychology, 45*, 577–580.

Moll, J., & de Oliviera-Souza, R. (2007). Moral judgments, emotions and the utilitarian brain. *Trends in Cognitive Sciences, 11*, 319–321.

Moll, J., de Oliviera-Souza, R., Zahn, R., & Grafman, J. (2008). The cognitive neuroscience of moral emotions. In W. Sinnott-Armstrong (Ed.), *Moral psychology, volume 3: The neurocience of morality: Emotion, brain disorders, and development* (pp. 1–17). Cambridge, MA: MIT Press.

Narvaez, D. (2008). The social intuitionist model: Some counter-intuitions. In W. Sinnott-Armstrong (Ed.) *Moral psychology, volume 2: The cognitive science of morality: Intuition and diversity* (pp. 233–240). Cambridge, MA: MIT Press.

Pizarro, D. A. (2000). Nothing more than feelings? The role of emotions in moral judgment. *Journal for the Theory of Social Behavior, 30*, 355–375.

Pizarro, D. A., & Bloom, P. (2003). The intelligence of the moral intuitions: Comment on Haidt (2001). *Psychological Review, 110*(1), 193–196.

Prinz, J. (2006). The emotional basis of moral judgments. *Philosophical Explorations, 9*, 29–43.

Saltzstein, H., & Kasachkoff, T. (2004). Haidt's moral intuitionist theory: A psychological and philosophical critique. *Review of General Psychology, 8*, 273–282.

Singer, P. (1979). *Practical ethics*. Cambridge, UK: Cambridge University Press.

Singer, P. (2005). Ethics and intuitions. *Journal of Ethics, 9*, 331–352.

Solomon, R. (1977). *The passions*. New York: Doubleday-Anchor Books.

Thomson, J. J. (1976). Killing, letting die, and the trolley problem. *Monist, 59*, 204–217.

Wheatley, T., & Haidt, J. (2005). Hypnotic disgust makes moral judgments more severe. *Psychological Science, 16*, 780–784.

ENDNOTES

1. For a devastating critique of Greene's and Singer's arguments from the neuroscientific data to this normative claim see Berker (2009).
2. Many philosophers would argue that the intention–foresight distinction seems to provide the most plausible principled basis for explaining the intuition that there is an important moral difference between these cases, namely, that in the Trolley Case you foresee that by pulling the lever you will bring about the worker's death but you are not intentionally aiming to harm him, whereas in the Footbridge Case you are intentionally aiming to cause the death of the fat stranger.
3. Greene and colleagues (Greene et al., 2008) have recently reported new data which they claim shows that a different pattern of response times for personal and impersonal moral dilemmas is not always reducible to a subset of items; in other words, they argue that this is a general effect. It is beyond the scope of my concerns in this chapter to assess this claim, but for doubts about whether the data in the 2008 paper do support the claim that this is a general effect see Berker (2009).

12

Living With One's Choices
Moral Reasoning In Vitro *and* In Vivo

JEANETTE KENNETT

Macquarie University

Much of the recent research on moral judgment in the social and cognitive sciences focuses on subjects' responses to vignettes that impose a forced choice (e.g., approve–disapprove, appropriate–inappropriate) on them or that present them with highly unusual or disgusting scenarios—for example, various versions of the trolley problem or sex with animals. No doubt many useful things can be learned from such studies—such as the ways moral opinions covary with socioeconomic status. However, it is not clear that they shed as much light as is claimed on the cognitive processes involved in moral reasoning, in part because they do not, and perhaps cannot, take account of the cross-temporal aspects of moral reasoning in everyday life. The moral verdicts subjects give in response to these vignettes are not decisions they must live with and for which they are accountable. Our moral choices have histories as well as consequences, and many of the most important moral decisions we make are not the work of a moment. I explore some representative cases of moral reasoning and revision across time and consider the implications for meta-ethics and conceptions of moral agency.

INTRODUCTION: MORAL JUDGMENT IN VIVO

D uring the 2008 election campaign, Barack Obama and John McCain were asked what they regarded as their greatest moral failure. What was it that they most regretted in their lives? Obama named his teenage drug and alcohol use, which he felt showed a disregard for others. I was more taken, however, with McCain's response: He named the failure of his first marriage.

It was 11 years ago that my then-husband and I separated after a long marriage. It was not an easy thing to do—we had four children—but by the time we reached that point, my defense for what I did indeed regard as a morally freighted course of action was one of necessity. I simply couldn't go on. The separation was a blessed relief, and for a number of years I marveled at the fact that I never for one moment missed the company of the man with whom I had spent over 20 years of my life.

Readers will be relieved to find that I have no intention of regaling them with the detailed story of my marriage, but it is true to say that when we split, despite publicly paying a bit of lip service to the mantra that there were faults on both sides, we were each much more keenly aware of the other's deficiencies than we were of our own. I laid the blame for the breakdown of the marriage with him (i.e., "If only he had...") while angrily rejecting his complaints about me. The failure of the marriage was a moral disaster certainly, but he was largely responsible for it. I was right; he was wrong. And it wasn't hard to find evidence to support my view. I replayed countless examples of his insensitivity, selfishness, unavailability. Meanwhile, we each set about convincing ourselves that though the end of the marriage was not ideal for our children, it was better than if we had remained unhappily married. In the course of time we each repartnered with people much better suited to us in interests and dispositions, and our children appear to have forgiven us. We now have a very cordial relationship—over the last few years we have even spent Christmas Day together to save the kids (now adults) from having to divide their time between celebrations. So you might say there has been a happy ending and my original decision has been vindicated.

But that is not how it seems to me. Over the years I have revisited the scene of my marriage countless times, and I now view many of the events I have reflected on quite differently. Now that the anger and resentment have dissipated, I see the justice of many of my husband's criticisms of me and the reasonableness of his aspirations for our relationship (I am not suggesting, mind you, that he is off the hook completely—just that I now appreciate what I then paid lip service to). By the time the marriage ended it was beyond saving, but I cannot comfort myself now, as I did then, that the split was always inevitable—because it wasn't. If we had addressed our problems—problems we were well aware of—earlier, and with greater commitment, goodwill, humility, and intelligence, we would probably still be together. And I have no doubt that that would have been better for our children and would have avoided or ameliorated some of the difficulties they have faced in their lives. They bore the brunt of decisions they had no say in. I cannot unequivocally say that I wish we had worked harder at our marriage—that would mean wishing away my present relationship and the person I have become within it—but I can say that we should have. It is a part of what we owed to our children. Our failure to do so was a significant moral failure and is a source of guilt and regret, to me at least.

I take it this story is not unusual, though others may arrive at different moral conclusions about their particular situation. Whether to end or stay in a marriage, whether to give a child diagnosed with attention deficit/hyperactivity disorder (ADHD) Ritalin, whether to put an elderly parent into a nursing home or care for him or her oneself, whether to accept a job offer in another city and move children away from their school and their friends—these are decisions with significant moral dimensions, and they are the kinds of decisions most of us will face. They are not usually snap decisions. We tend to spend a lot of time thinking about them and canvassing the options before deciding what to do, and we often engage in a process of reevaluation and revision after they are made. The past is a country we often return to, and on each visit we find something new.

I tell this rather ordinary tale and suggest other equally ordinary tales as a backdrop to an examination of some well-known recent empirical work on moral judgment. I urge you to keep cases like this in mind as we proceed.

HAIDT AND SOCIAL INTUITIONISM

Recent research into moral judgment in the cognitive and social sciences has focused largely on subjects' responses to hypothetical third-personal moral dilemmas or morally charged situations and has sought by this means to elucidate the cognitive processes engaged in moral judgment. Examples of this research include Hauser's Moral Sense Test (Hauser, Cushman, Young, Jin, & Mikhail, 2007), Greene and colleagues' work on moral dilemmas (Greene, 2007; Greene, Nystrom, Engell, Darley, & Cohen, 2004), and Haidt and colleagues' work on disgust and moral dumbfounding (Haidt, 2001; Haidt & Bjorklund, 2008a; Haidt, Bjorklund, & Murphy, 2000). Most of this research proceeds by providing subjects with a short vignette and then asks them to render a moral verdict. They are asked if it would be OK (permissible or appropriate) for the person in the story to perform a certain action, for example, killing one person to save five others. The results gained from these studies are claimed not only to reveal the nature of moral cognition but also thereby to support or question various theses in meta-ethics[1] about the nature and status of moral judgment, to illuminate differences between political liberals and conservatives, and even to argue for the rational superiority of utilitarianism over duty-based morality. My focus here is primarily on Haidt's work and his meta-ethical conclusions, but I shall also provide a more general critique of the methodology used in much of the moral judgment research. Haidt has argued on the basis of a number of studies that "moral judgment is caused by quick moral intuitions and is followed (when needed) by slow, ex post facto moral reasoning" (Haidt, 2001, p. 817; see also Haidt & Bjorklund, 2008a, p. 181). Haidt (2001) defines moral "judgments" as "evaluations (good vs. bad) of the actions or character of a person that are made with respect to a set of virtues held to be obligatory by a culture or subculture" (p. 817) and moral "reasoning" as "conscious mental activity that consists of transforming given information about people in order to reach a moral judgment …. [T]he process is intentional, effortful, and controllable" (p. 817).

The words *intuition* and *reasoning* are intended to capture the contrast between two kinds of cognition—fast, automatic, affectively charged processes versus slow, effortful, controlled, conscious processing. Haidt's work assumes this dual-process model of cognition and is concerned to reject the "causal role of reflective conscious reasoning" in moral judgment (Haidt, 2001, p. 817). He argues that reasoning is rarely the cause of moral judgment; rather, "most of the action is in the intuitive process" (Haidt, 2001, p. 819). Haidt and Bjorklund (2008a) note a variety of evidence that suggests our everyday reasoning is a biased search "only for reasons that support one's already favored hypothesis" (p. 190). Their argument is that we are misled by the facility with which people generate justifications for their moral judgments into thinking that the reasoning process is a cause of the judgment itself (for a related discussion of Haidt, see Mackenzie, Chapter 11, this volume).

Haidt's work has been of great interest to philosophers working in meta-ethics and moral psychology and has usually been taken to support emotivist or simple sentimentalist accounts of moral judgment, which hold that moral judgments express or report one's feelings of approval or disapproval about an action or event, over their rationalist counterparts. As has been pointed out however (e.g., Jacobson, 2008; Kennett & Fine, 2009), simply demonstrating that many or even most moral judgments are the product of automatic processing, or that reasoning processes themselves are subject to systematic biases, does not undermine rationalist claims about the role of reason in moral judgment. Haidt's project is descriptive—he aims to reveal the cognitive processes that produce moral judgment and claims that his results support sentimentalist claims. But rationalist claims are conceptual and normative rather than descriptive. For rationalists, moral judgments are constitutively concerned with what we have reason to do and reasoning is often required to determine what that is. Moral judgments must meet certain standards of rational justification if they are to so count.[2] A consequence of this view is that not every utterance of the form "x is wrong (or right)" will meet rationalist criteria for moral judgment. Nevertheless, it would be a blow to rationalism if no moral utterances met or could meet the rationalist criteria. It would undermine any account of moral judgment that stresses a conceptual connection between moral judgment and justification if reason *could not* play the role assigned to it in the theory—if our particular moral judgments and the moral intuitions on which they often rely were cognitively impenetrable and thus not subject to rational shaping and revision.

Haidt does not go so far as to suggest that reason never plays a role in moral judgment. Three of the six links in his *social intuitionist model* involve conscious processing (Figure 12.1).

Link 3, the *reasoned persuasion* link, focuses on social striving to reach consensus on normative issues. In this link people offer each other reasons, but notably Haidt and Bjorklund (2008a) claim that these "are best seen as attempts to trigger the right intuitions in others" (p. 191). In a piece of rhetoric against female circumcision they cite as an example, "each argument is really an attempt to frame the issue so as to push an emotional button.... Rhetoric is the art of pushing the ever-evaluating mind over to the side the speaker wants it to be on and affective flashes do most of the pushing" (Haidt & Bjorklund, 2008a, p. 192). The so-called reasoned persuasion link is thus readily analyzable in terms of the early emotivist position put by Ayer (1936) and Stevenson (1937), which held that the twin functions of moral judgment/discourse were to express one's feelings and influence the feelings of others. Links 5 and 6 of the model offer a little more to the empirically minded rationalist. Link 5, the *reasoned judgment* link, acknowledges that "people may at times reason their way to a judgment by sheer force of logic, overriding their

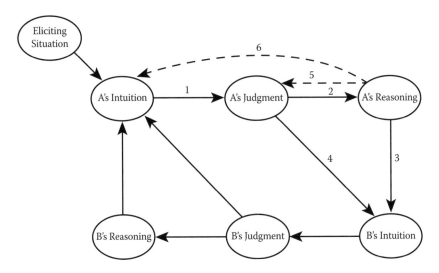

Figure 12.1   Social intuitionist model. (From Haidt, J., *Psychological Review*, 108, 814–834, 2001. With permission.)

initial intuition" and acknowledges that "…in such cases reasoning truly is causal… however such reasoning is hypothesized to be rare, occurring primarily in cases in which the initial intuition is weak and processing capacity is high" and the intuitive judgment persists below the surface (Haidt & Björklund, 2008a, pp. 193–194). Link 6, the *private reflection* link, occurs when a person spontaneously generates a new intuition that conflicts with their initial intuitive judgment. The reflective process then, according to Haidt and Björklund, may involve weighing pros and cons or applying a rule or principle to the situation. However, they insist that "all cases of moral reasoning probably involve a great deal of intuitive processing" (Haidt & Björklund, 2008a, p. 195) by which they appear to mean processing that is opaque to, and largely impenetrable by, reason. In moral dilemmas the person ultimately decides based on "a feeling of rightness, rather than a deduction of some kind" (Haidt & Björklund, 2008a, p. 195). Haidt suggests that only psychopaths and philosophers are honestly able to examine emotive issues dispassionately, and this may not be cause for celebration since there is plenty of evidence (e.g., Damasio, 1994) to suggest that "reasoning stripped of affective input becomes inept" (Haidt & Björklund, 2008a, p. 195).

The most general claim of the social intuitionist model then is that "the action in morality is in the intuitions, not in reasoning" (Haidt & Björklund, 2008a, p. 196). This is the claim we will probe. In the next section I examine the strategy adopted by Haidt and colleagues to reveal, as they see it, the post hoc nature of (most) moral reasoning and focus on their interpretations of their own data. I will suggest that their interpretations are not well supported by the data they present and that part of the problem is generated by the nature of the experimental situation, which does not model real-life moral judgment and decision making. I will then provide an alternative account of the role reasoning may play in governing our particular moral judgments, including many, and perhaps most, of our fast intuitive judgments. If I am right then the meta-ethical conclusions that Haidt and others have drawn from his work will not stand, even by their own lights.

MORAL DUMBFOUNDING AND MORAL JUDGMENT

Haidt (2001) argued that standard moral judgment interviews give a misleading impression of the role of reason in moral judgment because "they create an unnaturally reasoned form of moral judgment" (p. 820). While according to the social intuitionist model most of the action in moral judgment is to be found in links 1–4 (intuitive judgment, post hoc reasoning, reasoned persuasion, and social persuasion), "...if the person talking to you is a stranger (a research psychologist) who challenges your judgment at every turn ... then you will be forced to engage in extensive, effortful, verbal central processing ... leading to the erroneous conclusion that moral judgment is primarily a reasoning process" (Haidt, 2001, p. 820). Haidt, Björklund, and Murphy (2000) found that Kohlberg's (1981) Heinz dilemma (should Heinz steal the expensive drug to save his wife's life?) did indeed elicit moral reasoning and that people confronted with the dilemma were somewhat responsive to counter arguments. However, this was not the case when people were presented with harmless taboo violations designed to cause an immediate, strong, affective reaction, such as consensual adult sibling incest and harmless cannibalism of an unclaimed corpse. In the case of the taboo violations, subjects' incapacity to justify their initial judgments did not cause them to change their minds even though they confessed they could not explain the reasons for those judgments—a phenomenon Haidt and Hersh (2001) labeled *moral dumbfounding*. Thus, Haidt and colleagues (Haidt & Björklund, 2008a; Haidt & Hersh, 2001) conclude that the dumbfounding evidence supports the social intuitionist model: Reasoning is effective only when the initial intuition is weak (link 5).

Haidt's criticisms of Kohlberg's methodology show that he is alive to the fact that work done in the laboratory might not accurately model what goes on in more naturalistic settings and thus might not provide a guide to people's everyday moral judgments or standard modes of reasoning. Curiously, he does not apply the same level of critical scrutiny to his own experimental methods. I too am concerned that research in the laboratory on moral judgment gives a misleading picture of ordinary moral judgment and the role of reasoning. I also agree with Haidt that in some cases formal moral judgment interviews elicit more in the way of explicit reasoning than we would find from the same persons in vivo. But before airing some concerns about Haidt's own research methods, let's consider what there is to be said for the moral dumbfounding method used by Haidt, which he claims vindicates the social intuitionist model and in turn supports a Humean sentimentalist picture of moral psychology and moral judgment over rationalist alternatives. To do so let us look more closely at one of the examples presented to subjects—that of consensual adult sibling incest:

> Julie and Mark are brother and sister. They are travelling together in France on a summer vacation from college. One night they are staying alone in a cabin near the beach. They decide it would be interesting and fun if they tried

making love. At the very least it would be a new experience for each of them. Julie was already taking birth control pills but Mark uses a condom just to be safe. They both enjoy making love but decide not to do it again. They keep that night as a special secret, which makes them feel even closer to each other. What do you think about that? Was it OK for them to make love? (Haidt, 2001, p. 814, cited in Haidt et al., 2000)

Subjects confronted with this story immediately said that it was not OK for Mark and Julie to make love. When asked to justify their responses they cited the possibility of deformed children or harm to Mark and Julie's relationship. When it was pointed out to them that these bad consequences were ruled out by the story they showed no disposition to withdraw their initial assessment even though they admitted they could not explain it. This is the state Haidt dubs moral dumbfounding. Haidt thus concludes that moral reasoning is largely idle:

> Moral reasoning is usually an ex post facto process used to influence the intuitions (and hence judgment) of *other* people. In the social intuitionist model one feels a quick flash of revulsion at the thought of incest and one knows intuitively that something is wrong. Then when faced with a social demand for a verbal justification, one becomes a lawyer trying to build a case rather than a judge searching for truth. One outs forward argument after argument never wavering in the conviction that Julie and Mark were wrong even after one's last argument has been shot down. (Haidt, 2001, p. 814; emphasis added)

Why use such confronting and unusual cases as incest, cannibalism, or masturbation with chicken carcasses to test the causal powers of moral reasoning? First, the experimenter needs to elicit strong unopposed intuitions since Haidt thinks these will provide the clearest test case of the causal powers of explicit moral reasoning. Haidt allows that in rare cases where initial intuitions are weak reasoning may be genuinely causal. Moreover, where there are conflicting intuitions (as may be the case in the Heinz dilemma) it will not be clear that reason alone is playing a role in overcoming the initial judgment. Second, if we provide familiar or straightforward cases (e.g., killing a relative for personal gain, sexual predation on young children, gambling away the rent) then it is highly likely that the reasons subjects provide for their judgments would in fact support and justify those judgments, even if they have played no causal role.[3] We need extreme examples from which the standard justifications have been cleverly removed. If subjects were found to change their views and override their initial intuitions in cases of these harmless taboo violations, this would be evidence of the causal power of reasoning. That Haidt's subjects did not change their views when their justifications were removed allegedly exposes the ex post facto nature of most moral reasoning. But, is Haidt's conclusion supported by the moral dumbfounding studies, or are there other, better explanations of the subjects' responses?

Let us accept Haidt's claims that (1) much moral judgment is fast, automatic, intuitive, and not directly preceded or caused by explicit reflection; and (2) that we often engage in ex post facto rationalization of our judgments or actions. If all that is claimed by the social intuitionist model is that moral reasoning is most often not the proximate cause of individual moral judgments, then this is very likely true. However, this does not provide a sufficient basis for the meta-ethical conclusions that Haidt and others wish to draw from his data. In particular it does not vindicate simple sentimentalist or emotivist accounts of moral judgment over rationalist or neo-sentimentalist accounts, which require reflective endorsement of the deliverances of affect and intuition.

My claim is that even if the majority of our particular judgments are not preceded by a bout of explicit effortful reasoning, it doesn't follow that moral reasoning is mostly window dressing undertaken out of social motives. Much of what we see in the lab—both in the dumbfounding experiments and in work by Hauser and colleagues, and Greene and colleagues, testing responses to Trolley Problems and other moral dilemmas—doesn't give an accurate picture of the role of reason and reflection in everyday moral judgment and decision making (for other discussions of the Trolley Problem, see Langdon & Delmas, Chapter 5; McIlwain, et al., Chapter 6). I argue that these sorts of experiments are not capable of measuring the role of reflection in the exercise of moral agency in judgment and decision: in significant part because they only seek and thus can only measure the proximate and not the distal causes of moral judgment. Before turning to this general methodological point about moral judgment research, I will highlight some other factors that should be taken into account in interpreting the data.

MORAL JUDGMENT IN VITRO: REASONS FOR CAUTION

What experimental artifacts might affect the results of research into moral judgment and so the conclusions drawn from them? My focus here is on research that proceeds by presenting subjects with short vignettes and asks either for a moral verdict on the behavior described or a judgment on the options presented in the vignette. As well as the moral dumbfounding experiments previously described, other researchers (Greene et al., 2004; Hauser et al., 2007) have presented subjects with a variety of dilemmatic situations in which they must decide whether it is right or permissible to sacrifice one life to save several others. The best known of these are the many variants on the Trolley Problem. In the original version a bystander may pull the lever to direct a runaway trolley that is hurtling toward five workers on a railway track down a disused side track instead, where it will certainly kill one person who is walking along it. In another version the bystander may push a heavy man off a footbridge into the path of the trolley, the heavy man will die, but the trolley will be stopped before it reaches the five workers. What should the bystander do? I will highlight some shared features of these and other vignettes used in moral judgment studies that suggest that we should be cautious in drawing meta-ethical conclusions from them. I also draw attention to a particular feature of the moral dumbfounding studies that may also limit the usefulness of the results.

Third-Personal, Hypothetical Judgments

A first limitation of the approach is that the vignettes elicit only a subset of moral judgments—those that require verdicts on the actions of (unknown) third parties in hypothetical situations. They do not probe first-personal moral judgments or verdicts about one's own moral choices. While we do regularly make judgments about other parties, it is not altogether clear that we can generalize from evidence about the cognitive underpinnings of those judgments—especially those made in response to highly artificial or unlikely scenarios (to be addressed next)—to first-personal online moral judgments and decisions, which will inevitably be subject to a much more extensive and subtle range of informational inputs, as well as a range of practical constraints.[4] What we say in the lab in response to a vignette might not match what we would judge or do if placed in the situation described.

Haidt and Björklund (2008b) acknowledge this limitation in their response to commentators. There they distinguish between moral *judgments*, which are "about whether *another person* did something right versus wrong" (Haidt & Björklund, 2008b, p. 243; emphasis added), and moral *decision making*, and they stipulate that the social intuitionist model describes the phenomenology and causal processes of (third-personal) moral judgment only. They argue that moral judgment is functionally distinct from moral decision making and adopt the suggestion that it would have been shaped by different selection pressures. As they see it, moral judgment and moral decision making differ insofar as, in the former, there is very little at stake for the self: "We can make a hundred judgments each day and experience them as little more than a few words of praise or blame, linked to flashes of feeling that dart through consciousness. But moral ... decisions are different: they have real consequences for the self and others" (Haidt & Bjorklund, 2008b, p. 243). They concede that moral decisions must take into account many factors besides the initial intuitive response.

Haidt and Bjorklund may be correct in making a functional distinction between third-personal judgments and practical decisions in this way,[5] but they seem not to notice that such a distinction, and the consequent restriction of the scope of the social intuitionist model to third-personal moral judgment, limits both the interest and explanatory power of their model and seriously undercuts the Humean meta-ethical conclusions they and others wish to draw from their work. It is surprising that first-personal moral judgments—those concerning what I have done or should do—are here excluded from the model, although they would ordinarily be considered to be primary instances of moral judgment and are particularly salient to moral decision making. Moreover, two important conceptual features of moral judgments—their universality and their authority—which are used in both philosophical and social psychology to distinguish them from nonmoral judgments are ignored by Haidt and Bjorklund. Yet these features help to explain the link between third-personal moral judgment and decision making. The universality of moral judgment means that it applies to me too on pain of hypocrisy. Arguably, if I think that my judgment that a certain kind of action is impermissible doesn't apply to me in relevant circumstances, then I am not making a moral judgment at all.

Our moral judgments, both third personal and first personal, are supposed to underwrite our moral decisions. If we find, at the moment of decision, that we cannot choose in accordance with our prior judgment, we are either straight-forwardly weak willed, or we will have reason to revisit the judgment itself in the light of the additional inputs (and gut responses) experienced in the context of the decision. So if Huck Finn finds that he cannot bring himself to turn Jim in to the authorities, he might berate himself as weak, or he might be prompted by his sympathies to revise his views on the morality of slavery.[6] On rationalist accounts of the process he could treat his reluctance as a kind of data that alerts him to the possibility of error in his original judgment. There is thus an internal process by which principles, intuition, judgment, and choice are brought into reflective equilibrium.[7] For sentimentalist accounts too, the functional dissociation between moral judgment and moral decision making now posited by Haidt and Björklund is significant, for it means that their evidence about the nature of third-personal moral judgments, even if unchallenged, can provide little support for the Humean position they have claimed to vindicate. Sentimentalists hold that moral judgment is internally connected with motivation to act, and this connection is established by the affective dispositions of approval and disapproval that constitute the judgment. Mere "flashes of feeling" that dart through consciousness cannot explain what contemporary sentimentalist Jesse Prinz (2006) calls "the rapid move from thinking an action is wrong to thinking I ought to prevent or avoid that action" (p. 36). Moral judgments are apparently now not posited by Haidt to be the kind of thing that "vie for control of the will" such that "[w]hen they occur we are thereby motivated to act" (Prinz, 2006, p. 36). If anything, Haidt and Bjorklund now assume a version of externalism[8] that claims a merely contingent connection among moral judgment, decision, and action, mediated perhaps by social pressures.

Extreme or Fantastic Examples

The second limitation of the studies is their use of highly unusual, decontextualized, or artificial examples. Subjects must consider situations that they are unlikely ever to encounter in real life and choose among options that would probably never occur to them if they did. Take the footbridge version of the trolley problem outlined earlier. How likely is it, as you become aware of the impending tragedy below you, that the option of using the stranger next to you to stop the train would occur to you? How likely is it, at the moment of decision, that you would know all the consequences of your action? The experimental scenarios stipulate what in real life may be very unclear and then impose a forced choice on the subject, and subjects may resist either the scenario or the choices offered (for a discussion of the problems concerning forced-choice questionnaires, see Malle & Guglielmo, Chapter 13, this volume).

I suspect that what I will call *cognitive resistance* plays a role in responses to many of the highly artificial, stylized scenarios and dilemmas beloved by both philosophers and moral judgment researchers. Consider the Mark and Julie incest case: A quick Internet search indicates that even sibling incest overwhelmingly occurs in circumstances of significant family dysfunction and abuse and involves power imbalances and long-term damage to relationships and individuals (I exclude here exploratory play between young children). This fits with what I take to be the lay understanding of incest, yet the story presented to the subjects implicitly invites them to think of Mark and Julie as normal, functioning, happy siblings from a well-off family (they are college students holidaying in France). But how then did the subject of having sex with each other even arise for them, let alone seem like a feasible and inviting option for passing the evening together? What is the context that could possibly explain such a conversation? Why would they engage in behavior that anyone could reasonably suspect would be damaging to that relationship and possibly harmful in other ways as well? At the very least having sex with one's sibling, given the taboo on incest, seems like a profoundly morally risky thing to do, and their decision to do so was not justified by any other considerations (boredom, perhaps) that were available to them. On these grounds alone they would be well advised not to proceed. How could Mark and Julie be so sure they would not feel shame and disgust when reflecting on what they did? What kind of people would casually contemplate a one-night stand with their sibling as providing "at the very least a new experience" and remain unaffected by engaging in it? The story of Mark and Julie just does not ring true.

Is there any evidence that these scenarios encounter cognitive resistance? Anecdotally there is, at least in the philosophy classroom. Those of us who teach philosophy find plenty of resistance to the use of fanciful or impossible examples; it can take years to get students to see their methodological usefulness—a usefulness that is increasingly questioned in the field of moral philosophy. Students frequently challenge the supposed omniscience of the protagonist in the moral examples and seem to think that this matters for moral decision making. They say things like, "But you couldn't know that." They try to fill out thin stories, reject bits they find unbelievable, ask for more detail, and look for third options if they don't like those on offer. But does this carry over to the lab? Interestingly, Haidt (2001) tells us that his subjects continued to argue "that Julie and Mark will be hurt, even though the story makes it clear that no harm befell them" (Haidt, 2001, p. 814). This is taken by them as further evidence for the post hoc reasoning thesis. I think it is, rather, evidence that the participants don't buy the story (or don't buy the very limited account of harm assumed by the experimenters, or don't buy the assumption implicit in the study design that utility is all that matters morally). Their clear resistance to the claim of harmlessness suggests that their responses and justifications might be tracking their estimation of the probable impact of incest on siblings in the actual world rather than in the scenario as given. For these nearby cases their responses may be justified. When their responses are disallowed by the experimenter, rather than explored, they are unsurprisingly left with nothing to say. Haidt et al. (2000) may have succeeded at inducing a state of dumbfounding in their subjects, but, given that it is likely engendered at least in part by disbelief, it does not unambiguously support the post hoc reasoning hypothesis.

Experimenter Effects

Third, it is also likely that Haidt's subjects are at least somewhat disempowered by the experimental situation. For one, they lack the skill to play the game and the ability to see the point of it—a skill we do indeed often find in philosophers where we play the game for certain theoretical purposes (e.g., to reveal the structure of normative theories). For example, they almost certainly lack the skill to identify and challenge the utilitarian assumptions embedded in the study design with which they may inchoately be disagreeing. Utilitarians think that the only thing that matters morally is the utility of an action. The assumption is that if you remove the ordinary bad consequences of the suspect action, as these scenarios do, then you thereby undercut reason-based moral objections to it—this is what Haidt and Björklund take themselves to have done. But nonutilitarians will say that, since utility is not all that matters morally, one can still rationally condemn the action. So an action might be judged wrong because it is a lie (and lies are wrong because they fail to show proper respect for the autonomy of the person lied to) whether it has negative utility or not. Or an action might betray a poor character whether, in particular circumstances, it had bad consequences.

Subjects may lack either the confidence or motivation to outright reject the scenario and say to the experimenter, "But it wouldn't be like that." How could their relationship not be affected? What about when they meet and fall in love with other people? The secret could become a terrible burden. It is surprising that Haidt and Björklund (2008a), who cite Milgram's studies (see, e.g., Milgram, 1963) as an example of the power of the situation to induce "obedience without persuasion" (p. 192), do not acknowledge the possible influence of the experimental situation—including the authority of the experimenter and the desire of the subject to cooperate with the experimenter, not to appear rude or even to get course credit for participation—on their results. Jonathan McGuire (personal communication, 2008) reports that subjects he has tested on the Greene and Haidt style dilemmas often later make remarks such as, "That wouldn't happen." If subjects don't find the scenarios credible, their responses may not give us much information on how they make moral judgments in vivo.

Bias Toward the Proximate Cause of Judgment

Fourth, the speed and automaticity of moral responses to many (but not all) of the vignettes given in the laboratory and also to many moral situations encountered in daily life can show only that reflective processes were not engaged at that time but do not and cannot show that moral reflection is idle since the research does not distinguish between proximate and more distant causes of moral judgment. Work in the laboratory will tend to pick up on the proximate cause so the results will be biased against both rationalist accounts of morality and neo-sentimentalist accounts that also emphasize the process of reasoned reflection and justification in refining and expanding our moral sensibilities and schooling our intuitions.

Recovering the role of reflection in a manner consistent with data on the automaticity of much moral judgment requires at least four things:

1. An understanding of the processes by which reasoned judgments become automatized over time
2. Attention to the subject matter of moral thought
3. Attention to the history of moral judgments and their cross-temporal aspect
4. Acknowledgment of the full range of inputs to reflection

It is to these issues that I now turn.

MORAL REASONING AND CROSS-TEMPORAL MORAL GUIDANCE

My claim is that it does not follow from the fact that the majority of our particular judgments are not immediately preceded by a bout of explicit effortful reasoning that moral reasoning is mostly window dressing. To see this we need to distinguish between clear-cut, core moral judgments and the ways they guide us and more difficult, nuanced, and complex judgments (such as those with which we began).

Reasoning and Core Moral Judgments

Core moral judgments include those based on simple, straightforward, and uncontentious rules about physical harm, cheating, and fairness, which we learn as children and in general do come to reflectively endorse. As evidence from social psychology suggests, moral education involves both empathy induction (Hoffman, 2000) and reason giving. The child must come to see the point of core moral rules, and indeed the reason-giving practices of children indicate that they are active participants in this process, providing increasingly differentiated evaluations of various violations (Pool, Shweder, & Much, 1983; see also Smetana, 1993). However, as others have pointed out, while the acquisition of any skill (e.g., driving) may initially require a lot of cognitive effort, once a skill is mastered it becomes largely automatized (Saltzstein & Kasachkoff, 2004; implicitly acknowledged in Haidt & Björklund, 2008a). Many of our moral judgments could be like this. In support of this idea, Fine (2006) reviews a variety of studies indicating that "at least some automatic processes reflect the action of prior controlled processes" (p. 93). She argues that the repeated explicit selection of a goal leads to its being triggered automatically by eliciting situations. For example, Fishbach, Friedman, and Kruglanski (2003) found that for successful dieters temptation stimuli led to automatic activation of their goal of staying slim, and Moskowitz, Gollwitzer, Wasel, and Schaal (1999) found that subjects with egalitarian goals exerted preconscious control over stereotype activation. Fine concludes that "the [social intuitionist model] overlooks some of the important subtlety of how ... some automatic processes arise" (Fine, 2006, p. 93).

In the realm of moral judgment it is surely true that we don't waste time wondering whether and how core moral rules and principles apply in straightforward cases. Experienced moral agents don't need to expend conscious effort to judge that it is impermissible to hit someone over the head and steal their wallet, just as experienced drivers don't need to expend conscious effort on turning the steering wheel in the direction they want to go. Ingrained moral rules or principles can give rise to fast automatic responses in situations where they apply. These responses can present themselves as strong intuitions that may be resistant to challenge. Does this tell us anything deep about moral reasoning? In particular does it tell us, as Haidt and colleagues argue, that reasoning is almost always post hoc and plays no role in the formation of moral judgment itself? Surely not. At best it indicates that in easy cases or where we are required to make a quick decision, our decision will be governed by automated responses— hardly a surprise.

It is not difficult for those who endorse rationalist views of moral judgment and agency to offer an alternative explanation of such ingrained moral responses that is consistent with an account in which reason plays a significant causal role. To do so one needs to acknowledge the cross-temporal aspects of reasoning that are substantially ignored by moral judgment research. Consider this summary of Michael Bratman's account of the relation between planning and decision:

> A rational intentional action … is one which is part of a plan … that is rational for an agent to adopt and not irrational for her to fail to reconsider. In that way, first-order desires that are not reflectively considered at the time of action are nevertheless rational … ongoing or recurring reflection is not a plausible requirement for rational action. Most action involves habit and automatic response that not only fails to involve reflection, it sometimes precludes it. (Christman, 2008, p. 153)

In this kind of account, reason may guide action at a distance via the reflectively endorsed establishment of habit and automatic response in accordance with our principles, plans, and goals.

Moral Revision and Unusual or Difficult Cases

Haidt and colleagues might protest at this point that the moral dumbfounding cases they present challenge the subject to reconsider their automatic moral responses, but it is rare for subjects to do so even when the justifications on which they rely have been shown not to apply to the case at hand. These are cases where it *is* irrational, by the subjects' own lights, to fail to reconsider and so the cases demonstrate that reason has precious little to do with driving moral judgment.

There are two responses available to the defender of the role of reason in moral judgment here. Consider, first, the sort of response the indirect utilitarian makes to the objection that her utilitarianism is compromised by her endorsement of the following of rules or policies even in situations where following those rules or policies may not maximize utility. This response accepts that there may be extreme and unusual circumstances, such as those presented in experimental vignettes, where actions that are normally very wrong might be justified. Still, given our human limitations, we may regard it as a good thing to be averse to such actions, even in exceptional circumstances. Similarly, it might not be irrational for someone to resist revising their core moral judgments, considered as policy, with respect to, for example, the killing of innocent strangers, incest, or torture, in the face of an exceptional or fantastic scenario. Overall, we will do better by adopting policies through which we fashion ourselves into the kinds of people for whom committing incest, pushing people off bridges, or cutting up healthy people for spare parts are not even options.

The second response connects with the previous discussion of the Mark and Julie scenario, which identified reasons for concern over Mark and Julie's conduct that were not neutralized within the story. Karen Jones (2006) argues that ordinary subjects tacitly take their intuitive moral responses to be "tracking reasons" that once articulated would justify their moral judgments. That they cannot presently "put their finger" on the reason may not rationally compel them to the view that no such reason exists, for, as Jones points out, experience teaches us that sometimes "emotions can key us to the presence of real and important reason-giving considerations" (Jones, 2006, p. 50) even though it is only later that we can reflectively access and articulate those reasons.

Of course we are sometimes mistaken in our tacit assumption that our intuitive responses are reason tracking; there is certainly evidence that a person's incidental mood or emotional state can "contaminate" her moral judgments (e.g., Forgas & Moylan, 1987; Wheatley & Haidt, 2005). However, there is also evidence that this bias can be corrected more or less accurately (see Wilson & Brekke, 1994) when individuals' attention is drawn to their mood as a possible source of bias (e.g., Schwarz & Clore, 1983).[9] Data such as this suggest that not only do we tacitly assume that our moral judgments are responsive to reasons—something Haidt could concede—the fact is that often enough they are so responsive: We will revise our judgments if and when we become convinced that our gut reactions are, in a particular case, irrelevant to the issue at hand or, though relevant, not decisive. According to the social intuitionist model, revision of a moral judgment will usually involve developing a competing intuition as a result of social pressure (and this is certainly one path to changing one's mind). Haidt thinks private reasoning only rarely plays a role in this process. However, the social intuitionist model's prediction that private moral reasoning is rare and that in the absence of social pressure people simply engage in post hoc justification of automatic moral attitudes, does not sit well with other findings—for instance, in stereotype research. Such research has found consistent discrepancies between subjects' consciously held nonprejudiced beliefs and their automatic prejudiced responses (e.g., Monteith & Voils, 1998). Indeed, Fine (2006) points out, "the vast majority of individuals (over 90 percent) report discrepancies between their privately experienced 'should' and 'would' responses to stereotyped groups" (p. 94). If moral intuitions lead directly to moral judgment, or constitute the moral judgment, we would not expect such discrepancy between gut reactions to, for example, homosexual practices or racial minorities and one's judgments about how one should respond. Evidence cited by Kennett and Fine (2009) of individuals explicitly discounting their intuitive or gut responses to homosexuality further suggests that reasoning, both privately and with others, may often enough override intuition.[10]

But what do we mean by *reasoning* here? The dual-processing model of cognition characterizes reasoning in terms of "abstract thinking and high level cognitive control" (Greene, 2007, p. 398). As we have seen, this is the model presupposed by the social intuitionist model: As Haidt (2001) put it, controlled processing is "a tool used by the mind to obtain and process information about events in the world or relations among objects" (p. 816). This view of reason is clear in Greene's interpretation of subjects' responses to The Crying Baby Dilemma (Greene et al., 2004):

> It's war time, and you are hiding in a basement with several other people. The enemy soldiers are outside. Your baby starts to cry loudly, and if nothing is done the soldiers will find you and kill you, your baby, and everyone else in the basement. The only way to prevent this from happening is to cover your baby's mouth, but if you do this the baby will smother to death. Is it morally permissible to do this?[11]

In this dilemma participants "answer slowly and exhibit no consensus," indicating, according to Greene, that negative social-emotional responses compete with a strong *cognitive* case. The cognitive case involves explicit reasoning about the consequences: It involves the processing of information about the world to reach the utilitarian conclusion, whereas the nonutilitarian conclusion on this account is driven by affect.

I rather doubt that this interpretation does justice to the case. Greene's couching of the dilemma as a simple competition between the two processes with one eventually proving dominant sells the reflective process short. Much of moral reflection involves an interplay between reason and emotion, with our emotional responses treated as possible markers of reason-giving considerations (for further discussion see FitzGerald & Goldie, Chapter 10; Mackenzie, Chapter 11, this volume). It involves at least something like the process of reflective equilibrium. Greene does not consider the implications of such interplay for accounts of moral cognition. But I suggest that moral reflection involves even more than this: What is notable about the Crying Baby case and what distinguishes it from many other dilemmas used in moral judgment research is that it invites genuine moral reflection. It is instructive to consider why it does so:

1. *It is first personal.* The subjects are not being asked to make a judgment on the actions of an unknown third party. They are being asked to consider what they should do.
2. *It is a morally difficult case.* It is no small thing to contemplate killing your innocent and defenseless infant even if the child will almost certainly die anyway. Considerations of utility are weighty, but they are not the only moral considerations at stake.[12] It matters, for example, whether it is I rather than a stranger who kills the very person I have the most stringent duty to protect.[13] And while Greene has suggested that the "up close and personal" factor pushes the social-emotional response in many moral dilemmas I doubt that this plays a big role here. Killing one's child remotely by flicking a switch is not obviously less morally difficult than killing her by smothering her.
3. *The scenario is realistic.* Finally, and crucially, the dilemma, while not one that most people are likely to personally encounter, is realistic. Participants are unlikely to experience cognitive resistance to the vignette. Rather,

they are able to imaginatively occupy the scenario and use this to inform their responses.

MENTAL TIME TRAVEL, IMAGINATION, AND MORAL REASONING

Reflection on the Crying Baby case and the resources we bring to it reveals a lacuna in the accounts of moral judgment made available by dual-processing models and drawn upon in interpreting moral cognition research—namely, consideration of what makes for a moral agent and thereby secures the derivative capacity for moral judgment. The role of the moral agent, the one who makes the judgment, is left out of the picture by dual-processing accounts. This decoupling of moral judgment from agency is, I suggest, a mistake. The reflective self-awareness that makes us agents capable of moral judgment, and of the regulation of our moral responses, requires the exercise of additional capacities not explicitly encompassed by dual-processing theory or recognized by the social intuitionist model.

Real-life moral choices often, as Haidt now acknowledges, engage our sense of self. A crucial aspect of this sense of self is given by what is known as autonoetic awareness. This is awareness of oneself as a continuous entity across time (Tulving, 1985). Such temporally extended self-awareness seems to be a necessary condition of the kind of reflection—on the worth of possible goals, activities, and the type of person we want to be—that provides us with normative reasons, including moral reasons, and so establishes us as agents capable of moral judgment. More generally, any kind of agential planning requires the capacity to imaginatively project ourselves forward and backward in personal time, a capacity that has been dubbed *mental time travel* (Suddendorf & Corballis, 1997).

Mental time travel is a controlled activity we undertake for the purpose of evaluating the past, choosing for the present, or planning for the future. In mental time travel the agent recalls, reexperiences, and reimagines episodes involving his or her past self or imagines himself as taking part in some future episode. Mental time travel, then, includes episodic or personal memories in the backward-looking cases and what is called prospection in the forward-looking cases. Episodic remembering is the category of memory in which a person recalls a past experience in which she was personally involved (Tulving, 1972, 1983). Prospection involves the simulation of future events in which we mentally rehearse a situation. As Suddendorf, Addis, and Corballis (2009) stressed, conceiving of both past and future events involves conscious acts of construction. Both memory and prospection are essential to agency and are intimately connected with imagination, planning, and reflection and so, I claim, with the capacity for genuine moral judgment.

For example, in planning for this year's family Christmas dinner I might recall last year's disaster when the turkey took too long to cook, with the result that the children got overtired and irritable and Uncle Ray got drunk and argued with Granddad. On the basis of my trip to the past, I judge that things will go better this year if we eat earlier and limit alcohol, so I plan to get the turkey in the oven by 8:00 a.m. and to serve no alcohol until everyone is seated for dinner. Coming to this conclusion requires not just accurate recollection but also imagination and reconstruction of the past (how things might have gone if), background knowledge of various kinds, and judgment. Or I might upon reflecting how my life is going decide that living up to my principles and becoming the person I want to be requires that I do more to help the needy. As a result I might commit my future self in various ways: arranging for automatic donations to charity from my pay or volunteering my time at a charity for the homeless and making the required forward-looking revisions to my busy schedule.

Because I see myself as a diachronic agent and my choices as interconnected, events that occur now can also prompt reflection on past choices and behavior leading to reinterpretation of the past and revision of relevant judgments and principles.[14] The examples given herein and at the outset of this chapter suggest that this kind of private reflection is not limited to an exotic minority of professional philosophers and the like or provoked only by unusual circumstances. It is the constant companion of many, if not most, of us as we move through our lives. Such reflection may be prompted directly by some consequence of past decisions but also by other trigger events such as illness, the birth of a child, or the aging and death of a parent. Who has not revised their view of their parents and of their own behavior as, say, a teenager, in the light of their own parenting experiences? To be sure, such reflection might not often meet ideal standards of deliberation. Imagination may fall short, we may not adequately discount for cognitive biases, and the quality of our moral judgments may reflect these shortcomings in reasoning. But if we significantly lack these capacities for reflection, our very status as moral agents is called into question.

The ongoing activities of planning, monitoring, judging good or bad, moral reflection, and moral revision all require memory, imagination, and prospection. They all require a diachronic conception of self and others. Without such cognitive resources an individual's verbal judgments of right and wrong would be so impoverished and unsupported as to seriously undermine any claim to be even minimally competent moral judges and interlocutors. Severe amnesiacs who lack autonoetic awareness and the capacity for both forward and backward mental time travel may retain some capacity for synchronic moral judgment. Provided that their semantic memory is normal they will be able to apply a learned rule to a situation and may have normal affective responses to present pleasant or unpleasant stimuli. But insofar as they cannot reflect upon their behavior, imagine how things might have gone if they had acted differently, or revise their moral judgments and principles, it seems clear that they do not count as full moral agents and do not meet the conditions for responsibility. Their concept of a reason and their capacity to both track and respond to reasons is minimal. To the extent that they could count as unimpaired moral judges on dual-processing accounts of the cognitive foundations of moral judgment this will surely be a problem for such accounts and for meta-ethical positions that claim support from this picture of moral cognition (Gerrans & Kennett, 2010; Kennett & Matthews, 2009).

CONCLUSION

Christine Korsgaard (1992) claims that it is "from the standpoint of practical reason that moral thought and moral concept ... are generated" (p. 132). That is the conclusion to which this discussion has led. The processes of memory, imagination, projection, and rehearsal described here can take as their objects our gut reactions, our more abstract moral principles, conflicts between them, and much more besides. These processes can deliver justifications that are neither mere rationalizations of gut intuitions nor effortful rule application. They enable us to respond to our reasons as reasons and so vindicate a rational reflective conception of moral agency. While we do not need to invoke these processes in many easy cases in which we are required to render a moral verdict we commonly do so in the more complex and ambiguous situations with which we began. Moral judgments can be made prospectively, synchronically, or retrospectively, and plausibly they require an agent who can see things diachronically. Perhaps the social intuitionist model could be even further revised to incorporate a role for mental time travel and the reflection made possible by it. However, I suggest that the distinctiveness of the model will then be lost, since it will be an impossible task to show that a mature agent's moral judgments, many of which will have been revisited and modified over a prolonged period, are the product solely or primarily of intuitive processes as Haidt wishes to understand them. This is why the thin, decontextualized, encapsulated scenarios and the restricted, time-limited choices presented to subjects in moral judgment research may not tell us very much about the processes underlying our more interesting real-life, interconnected moral judgments and choices—choices with which we must live.

REFERENCES

Ayer, A. J. (1936). *Language, truth, and logic,* 2d ed. London: Gollancz.

Bennett, J. (1974). The conscience of Huckleberry Finn. *Philosophy, 49,* 123–134.

Bratman, M. (2000). Reflection, planning, and temporally extended agency. *Philosophical Review, 109,* 35–61.

Christman, J. (2008). Why search for lost time? Memory, autonomy and practical reason. In K. Atkins & C. MacKenzie (Eds.), *Practical identity and narrative agency* (pp. 146–166). New York: Routledge,

Damasio, A. (1994). *Descartes' error: Emotion, reason, and the human brain.* New York: Putnam.

Daniels, N. (2008, Fall). Reflective equilibrium. In E. N. Zalta (Ed.), *The Stanford encyclopedia of philosophy.* Retrieved September, 2008 from http://plato.stanford.edu/archives/fall2008/entries/reflective-equilibrium/

Fine, C. (2006). Is the emotional dog wagging its rational tail, or chasing it? *Philosophical Explorations, 9,* 83–98.

Fishbach, A., Friedman, R. S., & Kruglanski, A. W. (2003). Leading us not into temptation: Momentary allurements elicit overriding goal activation. *Journal of Personality and Social Psychology, 84,* 296–309.

Forgas, J. P., & Moylan, S. J. (1987). After the movies: The effects of transient mood states on social judgments. *Personality and Social Psychology Bulletin, 13,* 478–489.

Gerrans, P., & Kennett, J. (2010). Neurosentimentalism and moral agency. *Mind, 119,* 585–614.

Greene, J. D. (2007). Why are VMPFC patients more utilitarian?: A dual-process theory of moral judgment explains. *Trends in Cognitive Sciences, 11,* 322–323.

Greene, J. D., Nystrom, L. E., Engell, A. D., Darley, J. M., & Cohen, J. D. (2004). The neural bases of cognitive conflict and control in moral judgment. *Neuron, 44,* 389–400.

Haidt, J. (2001). The emotional dog and its rational tail: A social intuitionist approach to moral judgment. *Psychological Review, 108,* 814–834.

Haidt, J., & Björkland, F. (2008a). Social intuitionists answer six questions about moral psychology. In W. Sinnott-Armstrong (Ed.), *Moral psychology, volume 2: The cognitive science of morality: Intuition and diversity* (pp. 181–217). Cambridge, MA: MIT Press.

Haidt, J., & Björkland, F. (2008b). Social intuitionists reason, in conversation. In W. Sinnott-Armstrong (Ed.), *Moral psychology, volume 2: The cognitive science of morality: Intuition and diversity* (pp. 241–254). Cambridge, MA: MIT Press.

Haidt, J., Björklund, F., & Murphy, S. (2000). *Moral dumbfounding: When intuition finds no reason.* Unpublished manuscript.

Haidt, J., & Hersh, M. A. (2001). Sexual morality: The cultures and emotions of conservatives and liberals. *Journal of Applied Social Psychology, 31,* 191–221.

Hare, R. M. (1981). *Moral thinking.* Oxford, UK: Oxford University Press.

Hauser, M., Cushman, F., Young, L., Jin, R. K., & Mikhail, J. A. (2007). A dissociation between moral judgments and justifications. *Mind and Language, 22,* 1–21.

Hoffman, M. (2000). *Empathy and moral development.* Cambridge, UK: Cambridge University Press.

Jacobson, D. (2008). Does social intuitionism flatter morality or challenge it? In W. Sinnott-Armstrong (Ed.), *Moral psychology, volume 2: The cognitive science of morality: Intuition and diversity* (pp. 219–232). Cambridge, MA: MIT Press.

Jones, K. (2006). Meta-ethics and emotions research: A response to Prinz. *Philosophical Explorations, 9,* 45–54.

Jones, K. (2008). How to change the past. In K. Atkins & C. Mackenzie (Eds.), *Practical identity and narrative agency* (pp. 269–288). New York: Routledge.

Kennett, J., & Fine, C. (2008). Internalism and the evidence from psychopathy and acquired sociopathy. In W. Sinnott-Armstrong (Ed.), *Moral psychology, vol. 3: The neuroscience of morality: Emotion, disease, and development.* Cambridge, MA: MIT Press.

Kennett, J., & Fine, C. (2009). Would the real moral judgment please stand up? The implications of social intuitionist models of cognition for meta-ethics and moral psychology. *Ethical Theory and Moral Practice, 12,* 77–96.

Kennett, J., & Matthews, S. (2009). Mental time travel, agency, and responsibility. In M. Broome & L. Bortolotti (Eds.), *Psychiatry as cognitive neuroscience: Philosophical perspectives* (pp. 327–349). Oxford: Oxford University Press.

Kohlberg, L. (1981). *Essays on moral development, vol. 1: The philosophy of moral development.* San Francisco: Harper & Row.

Levine, B., Black, S. E., Cabeza, R., Sinden, M., Mcintosh, A. R., Toth, J. P., et al. (1998). Episodic memory and the self in a case of isolated retrograde amnesia. *Brain, 121,* 1951–1973.

McGuire, J. (2008). Personal communication, Macquarie University.

Milgram, S. (1963). Behavioral study of obedience. *Journal of Abnormal and Social Psychology, 67*(4), 371–378.

Monteith, M. J., & Voils, C. I. (1998). Proneness to prejudiced responses: Toward understanding the authenticity of self-reported discrepancies. *Journal of Personality & Social Psychology, 75,* 901–916.

Moskowitz, G. B., Gollwitzer, P. M., Wasel, W., & Schaal, B. (1999). Preconscious control of stereotype activation through chronic egalitarian goals. *Journal of Personality and Social Psychology, 77,* 167–184.

Pool, D. L., Shweder, R. A., & Much, N. C. (1983). Culture as a cognitive system: Differentiated rule understandings in children and other savages. In E. T. Higgins, D. N. Ruble, & W. W. Hartup (Eds.), *Social cognition and social development: A socio-cultural perspective* (pp. 193–213). Cambridge, UK: Cambridge University Press.

Prinz, J. (2006). The emotional basis of moral judgments. *Philosophical Explorations, 9,* 29–43.

Saltzstein, H. D., & Kasachkoff, T. (2004). Haidt's moral intuitionist theory: A psychological and philosophical critique. *Review of General Psychology, 8,* 273–282.

Schwarz, N., & Clore, G. L. (1983). Mood, misattribution, and judgments of well-being: Informative and directive functions of affective states. *Journal of Personality & Social Psychology, 45,* 513–523.

Smetana, J. G. (1993). Understanding of social rules. In M. Bennett (Ed.), *The child as psychologist: An introduction to the development of social cognition* (pp. 111–141). New York: Harvester Wheatsheaf.

Stevenson, C. L. (1937). The emotive meaning of ethical terms. *Mind, 46,* 14–31.

Suddendorf, T., Addis, D. R., & Corballis, M. C. (2009). Mental time travel and the shaping of the human mind. *Philosophical Transactions of the Royal Society: B, 364,* 1317–1324.

Suddendorf, T., & Corballis, M. C. (1997). Mental time travel and the evolution of the human mind. *Genetic, Social, & General Psychology Monographs, 123,* 133–167.

Tulving, E. (1972). Episodic and semantic memory. In E. Tulving & W. Donaldson (Eds.), *Organization of memory* (pp. 381–403). New York: Academic.

Tulving, E. (1983). *Elements of episodic memory.* Oxford, UK: Clarendon.

Tulving, E. (1985). Memory and consciousness. *Canadian Journal of Psychology, 26,* 1–12.

Wheatley, T., & Haidt, J. (2005). Hypnotic disgust makes moral judgments more severe. *Psychological Science, 16,* 780–784.

Williams, B. (1973). A critique of utilitarianism. In J. J. C. Smart & B. Williams (Eds.), *Utilitarianism: For and against* (pp. 75–150). Cambridge, UK: Cambridge University Press.

Wilson, T. D., & Brekke, N. (1994). Mental contamination and mental correction: Unwanted influences on judgments and evaluations. *Psychological Bulletin, 116,* 117–142.

ENDNOTES

1. Meta-ethics is the branch of philosophy that examines questions about the nature and status of our moral judgments. Can our moral judgments be objectively true, and if so what makes them so? Do our moral judgments express our beliefs about the world or our feelings about actions and events? Relatedly, are moral judgments based on reason or on sentiment? Cognitivists hold that moral judgments express beliefs. Noncognitivists hold that they express or report emotional responses. Simple sentimentalism holds that the judgment "X is wrong" just means "I disapprove of X." Emotivism holds that in making a moral judgment one is expressing one's feelings and attempting to influence the feelings of others. Rationalists, on the other hand, hold that moral judgments require justification and are essentially subject to rational revision in the face of evidence or argument.

2. For example, many writers (Hare, 1981) argue that moral judgments must pass the test of universalizability. If you would make an exception for yourself or your group on the basis of some morally arbitrary characteristic, such as skin color, you are not making a moral judgment at all.

3. Subjects would have access to these reasons by social processes of distributed reasoning.

4. For a discussion see Kennett and Fine (2008).

5. For a discussion of the differences between third-personal moral judgment and online moral decision making see Kennett and Fine (2008). Clearly there is slippage between what one might judge for a third party in a hypothetical situation and what one might judge and do if faced with those circumstances. Individuals might be weak-willed in changing their mind, or they might be responding to the additional information the situation provides in a rationally appropriate way. A conscientious moral agent will revise her judgment in light of new information, but if the new judgment is to count as moral she must be prepared to apply it to others in like circumstances. That is, she must regard her previous judgment, perhaps her condemnation of a course of action, as mistaken.

6. As Bennett (1974) persuasively argued, Huck is appropriately described as weak willed in giving into his sympathies. This is an interesting case for Haidt's account in a variety of ways, including his relativist account of virtue. Huck's action in helping a slave escape could not be considered virtuous by the standards of his culture even if Huck had taken it for explicitly moral considerations and there is no other cultural standard available to him.

7. The *Stanford Encyclopedia of Philosophy* defines the method of reflective equilibrium as follows: "The method of reflective equilibrium consists in working back and forth among our considered judgments (some say our 'intuitions') about particular instances or cases, the principles or rules that we believe govern them, and the theoretical consid- erations that we believe bear on accepting these considered judgments, principles, or rules, revising any of these elements wherever necessary in order to achieve an accept- able coherence among them. The method succeeds and we achieve reflective equilib- rium when we arrive at an acceptable coherence among these beliefs" (Daniels, 2008).

8. Externalists say that the connection between moral judgment and action is forged by motives external to (i.e., not necessarily implied by or required for) the judgment itself. They claim that moral judgments are beliefs and that beliefs alone cannot motivate action. They can do so only in conjunction with an appropriate desire that we might fail to have.

9. All cited in Kennett and Fine (2009).

10. Note that Haidt's own studies produce evidence in line with this. Haidt found that the capacity to discount or override one's gut reactions in reaching a judgment on so- called harmless disgust scenarios is correlated with higher socioeconomic status and lack of religious belief.

11. Version taken from Greene's webpage, http://www.wjh.harvard.edu/~jgreene/ (accessed August 10, 2010).

12. Williams (1973) canvasses some of these in his discussion of negative responsibility and integrity.

13. Greene is a consequentialist and is dismissive of deontological considerations as antirational. Most of his dilemmas are set up to pit consequentialist considerations against deontological ones. But it seems possible to construct dilemmas with compet- ing deontological demands or demands of virtue, which would also elicit slower and more conflicted responses. The demands of justice and loyalty, truth and generosity, autonomy and community can also conflict.

14. See Jones (2008) on a related issue. Jones claims that whether certain properties (e.g., love) obtain at a time can depend on events subsequent to that time. Some properties are trajectory dependent.

13

Are Intentionality Judgments Fundamentally Moral?

BERTRAM F. MALLE and STEVE GUGLIELMO

Brown University

Considerable evidence documents the foundational role that judgments of intentionality play in human social cognition. Even before their first birthday, children distinguish intentional from unintentional behavior and soon learn to recognize the goals and beliefs that motivate intentional action. Adults' judgments of intentionality are grounded in a sophisticated concept in which they consider five distinct components (the agent's belief, desire, intention, skill, and awareness); nonetheless, they typically make these judgments extremely quickly. Several recent studies suggest, however, that intentionality judgments are also heavily influenced by moral concerns. Specifically, if a behavior is morally blameworthy, people appear to judge the behavior as intentional even when critical components of intentionality are missing (e.g., intention or skill). When the same behavior lacks moral valence, virtually nobody considers it intentional. If true, these claims would cast serious doubts on the assumed foundational status of intentionality judgments. In a series of studies we examined these challenging findings, hoping to identify the psychological processes that drive them and carefully assessing whether blameworthiness truly guides intentionality judgments.

INTRODUCTION

*P*eople's capacity to recognize a behavior as intentional is a central component of human social cognition. This capacity has evolved for its adaptive value in social interaction, and it develops rapidly in the early years of life (Malle, Moses, & Baldwin, 2001; Zelazo, Astington, & Olson, 1999). Furthermore, the intentionality concept is part of folk psychology, the larger conceptual and cognitive system that allows people to make sense of human behavior in terms of mental states. In this system, intentionality plays a pivotal role because it directly connects behavior with mind, classifying actions as intentional when they are caused by certain characteristic mental states such as belief, intention, and awareness.

Much of the research on intentionality judgments has focused on their conceptual structure (Kashima, McKintyre, & Clifford, 1998; Malle & Knobe, 1997), their underlying cognitive and neural processes (Baldwin & Baird, 2001; Davis, 2005; Saxe, Xiao, Kovacs, Perrett, & Kanwisher, 2004), and their essential role in behavior explanations (Malle, 2004). Recently, however, a flurry of research and vigorous debates has drawn attention to the relationship between judgments of intentionality and moral judgments, especially blame.

INTENTIONALITY AND MORAL JUDGMENT

We can distinguish two opposing models of the relationship between judgments of intentionality and moral judgments. The first assumes that intentionality judgments are one of the important inputs to perceptions of moral valence. According to this model, a social perceiver first assesses an observed behavior's intentionality (a cognitive judgment) and then, in light of this judgment, assigns blame or praise to the agent of that behavior. Schematically, the model claims *intentionality* → *blame/praise*. This model has dominated the literature (Darley & Shultz, 1990; Fincham & Jaspars, 1980; Ohtsubo, 2007; Shaver, 1985; Weiner, 1995) and has received considerable empirical support. We call it the *standard model*.

The second model assumes that social perceivers have immediate moral intuitions in response to a negative outcome or behavior and that these intuitions influence and direct subsequent judgments of the behavior's intentionality. As a general account of how moral judgments arise from intuitions and emotions, such models have been promoted for some time (Alicke, 2000; Greene, Sommerville, Nystrom, Darley, & Cohen, 2001; Haidt, 2001; for a review, see Haidt & Kesebir, 2010). Recently, however, a specific account of the purported influence of moral valence on intentionality judgments in particular has emerged (Knobe, 2010, 2003a, 2003b). In contrast to the standard model, this model reverses the schematic relationship between intentionality judgments and moral perception: *blame/praise* → *intentionality*.[1] We call it the *challenger model*.

In this chapter we will briefly review the evidence for each model and then introduce our own studies that have pitted the two models against each other. To set up the comparison between the two models, we highlight at the outset two related claims that distinguish the models. The first claim concerns information processing. The standard model assumes that whatever information is processed in making intentionality judgments, the moral valence of the behavior is not critically considered; the challenger model assumes exactly such consideration. What is at issue here is a direct influence of moral valence by virtue of its morality (e.g., by a simple rule "if bad, then likely intentional"), not by virtue of factors concomitant with moral valence (e.g., rarity or difficulty of the action; see Guglielmo & Malle, 2010b). The challenger model assumes that even if all concomitant factors were controlled for, moral valence would still influence judgments of intentionality.

The second claim concerns the timing of judgments. The standard model assumes that intentionality judgments are made before genuine moral judgments, whereas the challenger model assumes that moral judgments are made before intentionality judgments. For example, Nadelhoffer (2006) argued that "our judgments about the blameworthiness of an action may come before our determination of whether the action was performed intentionally" (p. 583).[2]

THE STANDARD MODEL: EVIDENCE FOR INTENTIONALITY JUDGMENTS GUIDING BLAME

To understand exactly how judgments of intentionality relate to moral judgments, we must first clarify what we mean by "intentionality." Malle and Knobe (1997) examined the ordinary conception of this term and found that people require the presence of five components to deem an action intentional: (1) the agent's desire for an outcome, (2) beliefs about the action leading to the outcome, (3) the intention to perform the action, (4) awareness of the action while performing it, and (5) a sufficient degree of skill to reliably perform the action. Only when all five conditions are met do people call an action intentional (Malle & Knobe, 1997).

A great deal of evidence demonstrates that variations in a behavior's intentionality produce substantial variations in people's moral judgments about the behavior.[3] In his model of responsibility and blame, Weiner (1995) argued that blame is maximal when an agent could have done otherwise but nonetheless intentionally performs a negative behavior. Similarly, Darley and Shultz (1990) reviewed evidence demonstrating that agents receive some blame when they foresee but fail to prevent harm (e.g., through negligence or recklessness) but much more blame when they intentionally bring about the harm. More recently, Cushman (2008), Lagnado and Channon (2008), and Ohtsubo (2007) showed that a given negative behavior (e.g., cutting off a pedestrian, burning a stranger's hand) elicits substantially more blame when performed intentionally than when performed unintentionally. Mikhail (2007, 2008) proposed that assessments of intentionality—along with those of causality and physical harm—may constitute an essential part of people's *moral grammar.* In this model, the fundamental representational structure that people use when judging the morality of behavior contains a node that tracks the intentions of the agents in question. Solan (2003, 2006), too, assigns considerations of the agent's intentionality a fundamental role in moral blame; once causality, harm, and intentionality are taken into account, a judgment of blame comes essentially for free.

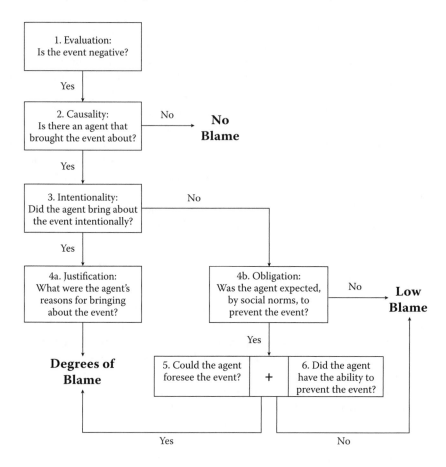

Figure 13.1   A step model of blame and the central role of intentionality. (Reprinted from Guglielmo, S., Monroe, A. E., & Malle, B. F., *Inquiry*, 52, pp. 449–466, 2009. With permission.)

Integrating the extant research on intentionality and blame, our step model of blame (Figure 13.1; Guglielmo, Monroe, & Malle, 2009) maps the major cognitive antecedents to blame judgments and specifically localizes the role of intentionality judgments. We argue that once social perceivers decide that an agent caused a negative event, they assess intentionality. People will tend to strongly blame the agent if they regard the negative behavior as intentional (though they may reduce that blame if the agent can offer a justification for the behavior; Quigley & Tedeschi, 1996). However, even an unintentional behavior warrants substantial blame if two conditions are met: The agent had an obligation to prevent the negative event (should have prevented it), and the agent had the capacity to prevent the event (could have prevented it). Thus, judgments of intentionality guide people's paths of arriving at blame and are normally causal and temporal antecedents to blame.

THE CHALLENGER MODEL: EVIDENCE FOR BLAME GUIDING INTENTIONALITY JUDGMENTS

Despite the evidence in support of the standard model of intentionality and blame, a number of findings appear to suggest the opposite model, according to which blame precedes and influences judgments of intentionality. Alicke (1992, 2000, 2008) documented ways in which *spontaneous evaluations* (e.g., regarding an agent's negative motives or an outcome's undesirability) may influence a variety of judgments leading up to the agent's culpability. Alicke proposed that "observers may engage in a biased information search to support a desired blame attribution" (2000, p. 567) and, even more strongly, that "everyday blamers are capable of violating virtually every rational prescription that moral philosophers, legal scholars, and rational decision theorists hold dear" (Alicke, 2008, p. 179).

In one study, Alicke (1992) demonstrated that a character who was speeding to hide a vial of cocaine was judged more blameworthy and more causally responsible for his ensuing car accident than was a character who was speeding to hide an anniversary gift for his parents. Alicke, Davis, and Pezzo (1994) showed that a character who shot and killed an intruder in an act of self-defense was seen as both more blameworthy and more negligent when the victim happened to be innocent than when the victim happened to be a dangerous criminal. In general, Alicke's findings show that spontaneous evaluations either directly increase blame or indirectly increase blame by influencing one of the steps in our blame model (see Figure 13.1), such as assuming a stronger causal link (step 2), an unjustified motive (step 4a), or the ability to prevent the bad outcome (step 6). Thus, although Alicke's findings suggest that spontaneous evaluations may influence certain steps of our blame model, they do not appear to threaten the basic structure of the model. In addition, Alicke's studies have not, at least so far, examined whether people's judgments of intentionality (step 3 in our blame model) are biased by spontaneous evaluations.

Recent work by Knobe (2003a, 2003b), however, claimed just that: Judgments of intentionality are often guided by moral evaluations. Knobe found that, under some circumstances, people appear to judge negative actions intentional but corresponding neutral or positive actions unintentional. In particular, even if an agent (1) does not intend to perform a particular action (Knobe, 2003a), or (2) does not have the requisite skill to perform the action (Knobe, 2003b), people deem the action intentional so long as it is negative. We refer to the first pattern as the *side effect effect* (Leslie, Knobe, & Cohen, 2006), as it suggests that people view negative side effects as intentional. We refer to the second pattern as the *skill effect*, as it suggests that people view negative unskilled actions as intentional.

These findings pose a challenge for two reasons. First, they suggest that certain criteria of the folk concept of intentionality (Malle & Knobe, 1997), such as intention and skill, may not be necessary conditions for judging the intentionality of negative actions. Second, they suggest that an action's immorality or blameworthiness may influence judgments of its intentionality, a claim that contradicts extant models of intentionality as well as the legal process of assessing intent to decide on guilt and punishment (Malle, 2006).

NEW EVIDENCE ON THE COMPETING MODELS

In a series of recent and ongoing studies, we analyzed Knobe's findings to assess whether the standard model of the intentionality–blame relationship should be abandoned in favor of Knobe's challenger model. To do so we took the experimental conditions in Knobe's original studies as a starting point and manipulated a variety of critical elements. These were Knobe's (2003a) original conditions demonstrating the side effect effect (with the relevant differences indicated by italics):

> HARM: The vice president of a company went to the chairman of the board[4] and said, "We are thinking of starting a new program. It will help us increase profits, but it will also *harm* the environment." The chairman answered, "I don't care at all about *harming* the environment. I just want to make as much profit as I can. Let's start the new program." They started the new program. Sure enough, the environment was *harmed*.
>
> Did the chairman intentionally *harm* the environment? (yes or no)
>
> HELP: The vice president of a company went to the chairman of the board and said, "We are thinking of starting a new program. It will help us increase profits, and it will also *help* the environment." The chairman answered, "I don't care at all about *helping* the environment. I just want to make as much profit as I can. Let's start the new program." They started the new program. Sure enough, the environment was *helped*.
>
> Did the chairman intentionally *help* the environment? (yes or no)

People's intentionality judgments varied greatly depending on the moral valence of the outcome: Whereas only 23% said the helping was intentional, 82% said the harming was intentional (Knobe, 2003a). Moreover, blame ratings in HARM were higher than praise ratings in HELP, and these ratings were correlated with judgments of intentionality—the more blame people assigned, the more likely they were to view the harming as intentional.

The conditions demonstrating the original skill effect (Knobe, 2003b) were as follows:

> AUNT: Jake desperately wants to *have more money*. He knows that he will *inherit a lot of money when his aunt dies. One day, he sees his aunt walking by the window.* He raises his rifle, gets *her* in the sights, and presses the trigger. But Jake isn't very good at using his rifle. His hand slips on the barrel of the gun, and the shot goes wild.... Nonetheless, the bullet *hits her directly in the heart. She dies instantly.*
>
> Did Jake intentionally kill his aunt? (yes or no)
>
> CONTEST: Jake desperately wants to *win the rifle contest*. He knows that he will *only win the contest if he hits the bull's-eye*. He raises the rifle, gets the *bull's-eye* in the sights, and presses the trigger. But Jake isn't very good at using his rifle. His hand slips on the barrel of the gun, and the shot goes wild.... Nonetheless, the bullet *lands directly on the bull's-eye. Jake wins the contest.* Did Jake intentionally hit the bull's-eye? (yes or no)

Again, people's intentionality judgments varied greatly depending on moral valence: Whereas only 28% said that Jake hit the bull's-eye intentionally, 76% said he killed his aunt intentionally (Knobe, 2003b).

The side effect and skill results speak directly to the first of the two differences between the contrasting intentionality–blame models: information processing. They show that manipulating the moral valence of an action (negative vs. positive or neutral) influences intentionality judgments. The important question is, however, whether moral valence or concomitant nonmoral factors drive the effect on intentionality. We now examine this question.

WHAT REALLY GUIDES WHAT?

The Side Effect Effect

In a series of studies (Guglielmo & Malle, 2010a, 2010b), we tested the hypothesis that Knobe's scenarios differ with respect not only to moral valence but also to other information about intentionality. In the side effect vignettes, the agent's desire (or pro-attitude; Davidson, 1963) toward the outcome varies systematically between HARM and HELP. People (and the law) expect others to foster positive outcomes and to prevent negative outcomes (Pizarro, Uhlmann, & Salovey, 2003). The protagonists in HARM and HELP both defy this expectation, but with different implications. The helping chief executive officer (CEO) fails to welcome the benefit ("I don't care at all about helping the environment") and thus displays no evidence of desire or pro-attitude toward the environment. The harming CEO fails to prevent the harm to the environment, which shows some degree of pro-attitude toward the harm—he may tolerate, embrace, or even welcome it. Therefore, the harming CEO seems to show greater pro-attitude toward the outcome than does the helping CEO, which may account for the difference in intentionality judgments between the two conditions.

Our findings supported this claim. We found that pro-attitude judgments (i.e., "how much the CEO wanted to harm or help the environment") were significantly higher in HARM than in HELP and that these judgments strongly predicted intentionality judgments: The more the CEO was seen as wanting the harmful or helpful outcome, the more likely the harming or helping was seen as intentional (Guglielmo & Malle, 2010a). It was therefore more appropriate to judge the negative case intentional, not because it was negative but because it contained intentionality-supporting information (about desire) that was clearly absent in the positive case.

We further showed that reducing the evidence of the CEO's desire for the harm led to a reduction in intentionality judgments. In this study, the CEO gave a more socially normative response when learning about the harmfulness of the program: "It would be unfortunate if the environment got harmed. But my primary concern is to increase profits. Let's start the new program." Results showed that judgments of both pro-attitude and intentionality were lower for this regretful CEO than for the original uncaring CEO, and inferred pro-attitude again strongly predicted intentionality judgments. Finally, we manipulated the pro-attitude of the helping CEO, who said, "I'm thrilled about helping the environment! And it's crucial that we increase profits. Let's start the new program." In this condition, inferred pro-attitude toward environmental benefits significantly increased, and so did people's intentionality judgments. According to our results, therefore, Knobe's (2003a) side effect may have arisen not from moral differences but rather from differences in desire or pro-attitude, which happened to be confounded with the moral differences in Knobe's study.

However, differences in pro-attitude only partially account for the side effect findings. In the help condition, desire is clearly absent, so no intentionality judgment is made; in the harm condition, desire is present but intention is still absent—and most people recognize this absence (Knobe, 2004; McCann, 2005). So why do people say that the CEO intentionally harmed the environment even though he lacked an intention to harm the environment?

Our answer is that people don't actually want to say that the CEO intentionally harmed the environment. To show this, we have to take a step back and consider the typical method of measuring intentionality judgments: the dichotomous forced choice between saying "yes, it was intentional" and "no, it was not intentional." If people have a very clear representation of whether a given behavior is intentional, such a forced choice is unproblematic. However, there is good reason to believe that people did not have such a clear representation when facing the typical side effect vignettes. Overall, information about the scenarios was sparse, and manipulation of intentionality components (e.g., desire, intention) created ambiguity by design. In such a situation we should mistrust responses to a two-option forced choice. This is especially true because in the HARM scenario the intentional option and the unintentional option were differentially attractive. The intentional option was linguistically attractive because of the frequent co-occurrence (and thus semantic association) of the English word intentional and morally negative events (Malle, 2006). Conversely, the unintentional option was conversationally unattractive because to say that somebody unintentionally harmed the environment would normally relieve the person of blame, which participants certainly did not want to imply (Adams & Steadman, 2004; Wright & Bengson, 2009). In this situation, therefore, choosing the intentional option might reflect either a genuine intentionality judgment or a semantic association or the rejection of an unacceptable option. Importantly, if people had doubts about the intentionality of the harm, they could not properly express those doubts because only two very different options to characterize the situation were available.

In our studies, we therefore offered multiple response options to capture more precisely how people represent the relevant scenarios and to determine how often they would freely characterize a negative side effect as intentional (Guglielmo & Malle, 2010a). Participants read the HARM scenario and considered a list of five descriptions, selecting which was the most accurate and which one was the second-most accurate description of the CEO's behavior. In one study, the options were as follows:

1. The CEO intentionally harmed the environment.
2. The CEO intentionally put profits before the environment.
3. The CEO intentionally adopted a program he knew would harm the environment.

4. The CEO intentionally disregarded the environment when adopting the program.
5. The CEO intentionally started an environment-harming program.

After pondering these options, just 2% of participants selected the first statement as either most accurate or second-most accurate—even though 71% of those same participants had endorsed this description when given the usual two-option (yes or no) forced-choice question. A strong majority (68%) favored the third statement as most accurate, in which the CEO "intentionally adopted a profit-raising program that he knew would harm the environment." People do not appear to think that the agent brought about the side effect intentionally. Instead, they feel that the agent performed his primary action of adopting the program (intentionally, of course) while knowing that harm would result from the action. This is a choice, and it is blameworthy—but when given a chance, people distinguish between *intentionally* doing something and *knowingly* doing something, making a distinction that even some legal systems confound (Malle & Nelson, 2003).

To directly demonstrate that people make this distinction we conducted a study in which people indicated whether it was most accurate to say that the CEO *intentionally harmed, knowingly harmed, willingly harmed,* or *purposefully harmed* the environment. Nearly everyone (86%) said the CEO knowingly harmed the environment. Just 2% said that the CEO either intentionally or purposefully harmed the environment (Guglielmo & Malle, 2010a).

But perhaps our measurement method was restrictive in its own way, because people had to commit to only one (most accurate) or two (most and second-most accurate) behavior descriptions. Thus, in a follow-up study we asked people to endorse all descriptions they believed were correct. Even with this lenient endorsement criterion, just 46% said the *intentionally harmed* description was correct, whereas 82% said the *knowingly harmed* description was correct.

In this same study, we integrated the two factors we argue are responsible for the illusory side effect effect: the influence of pro-attitude and the influence of response options. That is, besides offering multiple behavior descriptions, we also attempted to equate the HARM and HELP scenarios with respect to the agent's expressed pro-attitude toward the side effect. To do so, we compared the standard HARM scenario with the variant of the HELP scenario described earlier, in which the CEO expresses a pro-attitude toward the side effect: "I'm thrilled about helping the environment! And it's crucial that we increase profits. Let's start the new program." In this modified HELP condition, 45% of participants said it was correct that "the CEO intentionally helped the environment," a rate that was essentially identical to the 46% of people in the standard HARM condition who said it was correct that "the CEO intentionally harmed the environment." These data further support the contention that intentionality judgments vary as a function of pro-attitude, not as a function of moral valence.

Together, our studies on the side effect effect (Guglielmo & Malle, 2010a) contradict the information processing claim of the challenger model of the intentionality–blame relationship. Our results showed that Knobe's (2003a) original HARM and HELP scenarios differed in the agent's pro-attitude toward the respective side effects and that pro-attitude strongly predicts intentionality judgments. Once the pro-attitude was lowered in the HARM scenario, intentionality judgments decreased; once pro-attitude was raised in the HELP scenario, intentionality judgments increased. Thus, the side effect effect was, to a considerable extent, a pro-attitude effect, not a moral-valence effect. In addition, we showed that, even leaving the agent's pro-attitude toward HARM in place, most people do not view the negative side effect as intentional once they are given multiple options of describing the scenario. They prefer to describe the negative side effects as being brought about knowingly, not intentionally. In sum, people's systematic sensitivity to variations in pro-attitude and their consistent distinction between subtle alternatives of behavior descriptions suggest a careful process of judging intentionality even when considering highly immoral actions.

The Skill Effect

The second packet of evidence for the challenger model of intentionality and blame comes from studies on the skill effect (Knobe, 2003b). In the absence of the agent's skill of performing a behavior, the standard model of intentionality predicts infrequent intentionality judgments (Malle & Knobe, 1997). Knobe (2003b) confirmed this prediction for a neutral action of shooting at and hitting the bull's-eye intentionally (28%). However, the prediction was violated for an immoral act of shooting at and killing another person (76%). Do we have here decisive evidence for an impact of moral valence on intentionality judgments?

Our analysis of this effect, too, casts doubt on such a possibility. The first nonmoral element that helps account for the skill effect is an important basic action performed by the protagonist in Knobe's (2003b) original AUNT vignette: pulling the trigger. In the original scenario, Jake first pulls the trigger, then slips, and the shot goes wild. Consider an amateur photographer who presses the shutter but then slides off and shakes the camera. Arguably, she intentionally took the photo. Consider further that her shaking actually caught a moving target so perfectly that the target was in focus. Arguably, she did not intentionally take that shot. Our reasoning was that, just as the pressing of a shutter is a sufficient basic action that counts as taking a picture, so is the pulling of a trigger a sufficient basic action that counts as killing. If this reasoning is correct, then people's intentionality judgments should decline once the intentionality of the basic action is called into question.

Our results supported this hypothesis. Whereas nearly everyone said the killing was intentional when Jake slipped after pulling the trigger (93%), fewer said it was intentional when he slipped before pulling the trigger (71%), and even fewer said it was intentional when he slipped but there was no mention of the trigger being pulled (42%). But if pulling the trigger counted as killing—thus leading people in Knobe's (2003b) original AUNT case to judge the act of killing intentional—why did it not also count as hitting the bull's-eye intentionally in the CONTEST case?

Here we need to consider whether the two actions described in Knobe's (2003b) study were truly of equal scope—which refers to the ease and number of ways the action can be accomplished (cf. Goldman, 1970; Wegner & Vallacher, 1986). And it appears they were not. One description referred to the general action of killing

("Did Jake intentionally kill his aunt? [yes or no]), whereas the other referred to the specific action of hitting the bull's-eye ("Did Jake intentionally hit the bull's-eye? [yes or no]). We hypothesized that wide-scope actions such as killing get called intentional more easily than narrow-scope actions such as hitting the bull's-eye and that this confounding of moral valence and scope helps account for the skill effect.

Wide-scope actions are so general that many variations allow for successful performance (e.g., there are all kinds of ways of killing somebody). Narrow-scope actions, by contrast, are so specific that few variations allow for successful performance (e.g., there are only a few ways of hitting the bull's-eye). Thus, an agent with a given level of skill has a greater chance of intentionally performing a wide-scope action than a narrow-scope action because there are many more paths of reaching the goal. And that is particularly important for a person with low levels of skill, for whom there may be some ways of reaching a wide-scope goal but few to no ways of reaching a narrow-scope goal.

We can illustrate this principle with an example from an entirely nonmoral domain—geometry. Consider someone who is told to draw a line that either intersects or bifurcates an existing line drawn on a sheet of paper. To accomplish the action of intersecting, the person may draw the second line anywhere it crosses the first. To accomplish the action of bifurcating, the person must draw the second line precisely at the midpoint of the first line on the paper. Thus, the verb *intersect* has wider scope than the verb *bifurcate*—that is, there are many ways to successfully intersect but only one way to successfully bifurcate. Imagine now two people who have very limited fine-motor skills. One is told to draw a line that bifurcates the first line. He clumsily and erratically draws a line—and it exactly bifurcates the first. We expect that most people would say that he did not do that intentionally (it was luck). The second person is told to draw a line that intersects the first. He clumsily and erratically draws a line—and it intersects the first. We expect that most people would say he did that intentionally. Given a limited amount of skill, an action that can be accomplished in many ways is easier and therefore more likely to be performed intentionally than an action that can be accomplished in only very few specific ways.

Returning to Knobe's (2003b) example, two predictions follow. First, if the act of killing is of wider scope than the act of hitting the bull's-eye, killing should be seen as easier than hitting the bull's-eye. Indeed, this is what we found: The two actions differed not only in moral valence but also in difficulty (Guglielmo & Malle, 2010b). Second, if Jake's immoral action were to be described with a verb of narrower scope, people's intentionality judgments should become infrequent. Once more, the prediction was borne out. Whereas 98% of participants said that Jake intentionally killed his aunt, only 27% said he intentionally hit his aunt's heart, a percentage as low as the percentage of people who said that Jake intentionally hit the bull's-eye. So even though Knobe's (2003b) original vignettes attempted to hold skill constant across the conditions, it was not. Whereas Jake did not have enough skill to hit the bull's-eye (and did not have enough skill to hit his aunt's heart), he did have enough skill to kill. And that is why people say that he killed intentionally.

The skill effect—people's apparent tendency to view unskilled immoral actions (but not positive or neutral ones) as intentional—can thus be explained by two factors. First, the agent in the original studies intentionally performed a basic action (pulling the trigger) that counts as the broader act of killing. Once we removed this basic action, intentionality judgments fell below 50%, even though the highly immoral outcome remained constant. Second, the act of killing—as described in the judgment choice, "Did Jake intentionally kill his aunt? (yes or no)"—is of wider scope and is therefore easier to accomplish than the act of hitting the bull's-eye. Once we equated the immoral and the neutral action for scope—comparing hitting the aunt's heart to hitting the bull's-eye—there was no longer a difference in intentionality judgments, even though the actions continued to differ in valence.

A further study combined these two factors into a single manipulation. Focusing on the puzzling AUNT case, (1) we told participants that the agent slipped but we did not mention that the trigger was pressed, and (2) we asked participants to judge the intentionality of the specific action (hitting the aunt's heart). Under these conditions, just 10% of participants deemed the action intentional even though they assigned a great deal of blame to the agent.

Finally, we designed a study in which there was no separation between a basic action (such as pressing the trigger) and a focal action (such as killing) and in which the difficulty and scope of the focal action was equal across conditions. In the story, the protagonist and his sister were playing darts, and he attempted a final shot in the game that was either mean spirited (to beat his sister, who has already had a very rough time and would be even more unhappy if she lost) or benevolent (to let his sister win and thus make her happy). In addition to this valence factor, the actor's skill was manipulated in the action performance (high skill: "He sets up his shot and … the dart lands in" vs. low skill: "As he sets up his shot, he loses his balance, the dart slips out of his hand"). The results of this 2×2 design were decisive: People's intentionality judgments were highly sensitive to the skill manipulation (85% for high skill and 27% for low skill) but unaffected by valence.

THE EVIDENCE SO FAR

Initial tests of the challenger model of blame and intentionality followed this logic: Remove a component of intentionality (such as intention or skill) from a behavior that is either negative or neutral/positive, and measure people's intentionality judgments for each behavior. Initial evidence suggested that, in the absence of those components, people still consider the negative behavior intentional but do not consider the neutral to positive behavior intentional. These studies, however suffered from serious problems.

First, critical pieces of information were not held constant across the two behavior conditions. In the side effect studies, the agent's pro-attitude toward the negative side effect was stronger than the agent's pro-attitude toward the positive side effect. In the skill studies, the negative behavior's scope (killing) was wider and its difficulty lower than the neutral behavior's scope (hitting the bull's-eye), making a low level of skill sufficient for intentionally performing the negative behavior but not the neutral behavior. Once the CEO's pro-attitude toward the negative side-effect was reduced by restricting the evidence of his desire for harm, intentionality ascriptions dropped markedly; likewise, once scope was restricted in the skill studies, intentionality ascriptions dropped markedly.

Second, people identified a core action in each case that was clearly intentional, but when they were asked about a different action, they were inclined to mark this different action as intentional—rather like a proxy for the clearly intentional one. In the side effect studies, the core action was adopting a program that the agent knew would harm the environment. That is, the agent intentionally decided not to take the knowledge about harmful consequences into account, flouting the norm of preventing harm. Both the more concrete action of adopting the program and the more abstract action of flouting a norm were undoubtedly intentional actions, making it difficult for people to deny that the agent's overall behavior was intentional when asked about harming the environment. In the skill studies, the core action was pulling the trigger, which counted as killing because it occurred before the bullet entered its wayward flight and thus constituted the agent's performed action, followed by the world not operating quite as anticipated. When the act of pulling the trigger was removed in our revised studies, intentionality judgments dropped notably.

Third, people were typically forced to choose between two descriptions of the behavior in question, neither of which properly captured how people conceptualized those behaviors. Of the two options, saying that the agent "did not intentionally harm the environment" may have connoted impunity, so most people went with the option that he "intentionally harmed the environment" but did so only in a two-option forced-choice assessment. Once a variety of descriptions was available, people least often chose a characterization of the (negative) side effect as intentional and most often chose a description of the agent knowingly bringing about the outcome.

IT'S TIME FOR TIMING

The findings we have reviewed thus far cast doubt on the challenger model of the relationship between blame and judgments of intentionality. In particular, these findings contradict the challenger model's first major claim, which concerns information processing. According to this claim, genuinely moral considerations exert a direct influence on the formation of intentionality judgments, and this influence should persist even if concomitant factors are controlled for. But when we controlled for various concomitant factors—such as the agent's pro-attitude toward a side effect or the scope or difficulty of an unskilled action—intentionality judgments no longer seemed influenced by moral valence.

We now turn to the second claim: the timing of blame and intentionality judgments. The standard model and the challenger model of the relationship between intentionality and blame make distinct predictions about two aspects of the timing of these judgments.[5] The first concerns latency. The challenger model entails that blame judgments precede intentionality judgments—that is, it should take people less time to assess blame than to assess intentionality. In contrast, the standard model entails that intentionality judgments precede blame judgments, so it should take people less time to assess intentionality than to assess blame.

The second aspect of timing concerns facilitation. The challenger model claims that blame should facilitate intentionality judgments because blame guides, directs, and informs intentionality judgments. Thus, people should be faster to assess intentionality if they have first assessed blame than if they have not first assessed blame. In contrast, the standard model claims that because intentionality guides, directs, and informs blame judgments, intentionality judgments should facilitate blame. Thus, people should be faster to assess blame if they have first assessed intentionality than if they have not first assessed intentionality.

Our ongoing research examines these contrasting sets of predictions (Guglielmo & Malle, 2009). In one study, participants read a series of sentences, each describing a negative behavior that was performed either intentionally (e.g., shoving a stranger while in line at an ATM) or unintentionally (e.g., knocking over a vase, breaking it into pieces). Following each sentence, participants provided a yes or no button-press response to one of several questions, which were indicated by a single-word question cue. For example, the cue "Intentional?" stood for "Did the main character intentionally perform the behavior?" and the cue "To blame?" stood for "Does the main character deserve to be blamed for how he behaved?"

As we described earlier, the challenger model predicts that blame judgments should be faster than intentionality judgments, whereas the standard model predicts the reverse pattern. Our results contradicted the predictions of the challenger model, as people were faster to judge intentionality than to judge blame. In fact, this latency difference was strongest for the behaviors that were the most blameworthy, namely, the intentional ones.

In a second study (Guglielmo & Malle, 2009) we examined moral judgments that are more basic than blame. Rather than asking whether the main character deserved to be blamed, we simply asked people whether the main character's behavior was bad. Even these basic moral judgments were no faster than judgments about intentionality. In fact, badness judgments tended to be slower than intentionality judgments, but this pattern was not statistically significant in this sample. Thus, our studies on the latency predictions contradict the challenger model and support the standard model, showing that people take longer to assess blame (and, to a lesser extent, badness) than to assess intentionality.

We have also completed one study (Guglielmo & Malle, 2009) that assessed the contrasting predictions regarding facilitation. According to the challenger model, assessing blame should speed up subsequent assessments of intentionality; according to the standard model, assessing intentionality should speed up subsequent assessments of blame. Participants read several side effect scenarios, similar to those used in Knobe's (2003a) original study and its many replications. After reading each scenario, participants answered two questions—one about blame and one about intentionality, whereby the order was randomized for each trial. We examined facilitation by comparing the latency of each judgment in the first position (i.e., when it could guide the other judgment) with the latency of the same judgment in the second position (when it could be guided by the other judgment). For example, blame would facilitate intentionality if the intentionality response latency was faster in the second position (when guided by blame) than in the first position (when guiding blame).

Contradicting the challenger model, blame did not facilitate intentionality. People's intentionality judgments were actually slightly slower (although not significantly so) when made after a prior blame judgment than when made first. Supporting the standard model, intentionality facilitated blame. People's blame judgments were much faster (by an average of 800 ms) when made after a prior intentionality judgment than when made without a prior intentionality judgment.

In sum, our initial studies on the timing of blame and intentionality judgments contradict the predictions of the challenger model. We found that people are slower to judge blame (and, to a lesser extent, badness) than they are to judge intentionality. Moreover, we found that intentionality judgments facilitated subsequent blame judgments but that blame did not facilitate subsequent intentionality judgments. These results—in combination with those discussed earlier regarding information processing—are highly problematic for the challenger model. All in all, our findings consistently support the standard model, according to which intentionality judgments both precede and guide moral judgments.

FUTURE RESEARCH

Studies on the timing of judgments of intentionality and moral judgments are a first important step in studying the actual psychological processes implied by recent claims that intentionality judgments are infused with moral considerations (Doris, Knobe, & Woolfolk, 2007; Knobe, 2004; Nadelhoffer, 2006). In our research so far, we have measured the access speed of various judgments—that is, the time it takes people to report a judgment. However, we do not know whether people actually make the judgment when they see the question cue (e.g., "Intentional?") or whether they have already made the judgment beforehand and then retrieve this judgment when presented with the cue. In the case of sentences as stimuli, some people may engage heavily in semantic processing and not make the relevant judgment until they see the question cue. For these people, response latencies (from the time the cue appears to the time of response) represent the time it takes to *make* the relevant judgment. However, for people who made the judgments even before the question cue appeared, the latencies represent the time it takes to *retrieve* the relevant judgment when cued. We are currently planning studies that address this ambiguity by presenting video stimuli and asking people to stop the video as soon as they have made a particular judgment. For example, the participant is asked to determine whether the upcoming behavior is intentional, begins to watch the video, and stops it as soon as the intentionality of the behavior is apparent. This stopping latency may be a better indicator of the time it truly takes to make the relevant judgment.

In future research, we need to explore the conditions under which certain judgments are slow or fast, not only which judgments are in general faster than others. We can expect to slow down both moral and intentionality judgments by making the behavior (or its context) ambiguous. Also, holding people accountable for their judgments—especially their moral ones—is likely to induce a deliberative process that slows down final judgments, but it would be interesting to see whether potential early flashes of evaluation are influenced by accountability as well. One might also expect that inducing affect just before people observe the stimuli could influence subsequent judgments (Goldberg, Lerner, & Tetlock, 1999). An angry, impatient, vindictive state of mind might lower the threshold for blame, and the question is whether it also influences judgments of intentionality.

Additional methodologies are needed to resolve another ambiguity in extant studies. Moral judgments, and in particular blame, are sometimes considered full-blown, deliberated assessments and sometimes flashes of approving or disapproving affect. An important, albeit difficult, question is whether such early affective flashes respond only to outcome information or whether they already take into account information about the behavior's intentionality. Physiological measures, such as skin conductance responses, will be too slow to investigate the timing of such flashes, but electrophysiological measures of brain activity may well be able to handle the tight timing windows. Previous work suggests that there may be electrophysiological markers for fast negative affect (Tucker, Luu, Desmond, Hartry-Speiser, Davey, & Flaisch, 2003); it remains to be seen whether any such markers can be found for intentionality judgments.

Most empirical research on morality and intentionality has focused on judgments of blame or responsibility (Shaver, 1985; Weiner, 1995), whereas far fewer studies have looked at the logic of praise, which appears to be distinct, not the mirror image of the logic of blame (Guglielmo & Malle, 2010a; Ohtsubo, 2007; Solan, 2010). Moreover, judgments of intentionality and related social inferences may relate in interesting ways to other, infrequently studied moral sentiments, such as resentment, indignation, pride, and forgiveness.

The broader context of all this work is a deeper understanding of what it means to be human, to be a participant in social communities. Emotions, social cognition, and morality—as well as the capacities for language and complex relationships—are intertwined in ways that we are only beginning to understand (e.g., Malle, 2002; Tomasello, 1998). In light of this network of interrelated capacities, it may seem a somewhat narrow issue to probe the primacy of blame over intentionality or intentionality over blame. But we must know whether people's judgments of mind and action are irrevocably moral or whether people can distinguish between descriptive and normative assessments of human behavior. For if they cannot, our trust in juries, our hope for fairness, and the confidence in our own judgments may be shattered. The research reported here encourages us to maintain that trust, that hope, and that confidence.

REFERENCES

Adams, F., & Steadman, A. (2004). Intentional action in ordinary language: Core concept or pragmatic understanding? *Analysis, 64,* 173–181.

Alicke, M. D. (1992). Culpable causation. *Journal of Personality and Social Psychology, 63,* 368–378.

Alicke, M. D. (2000). Culpable control and the psychology of blame. *Psychological Bulletin, 126*, 556–574.

Alicke, M. D. (2008). Blaming badly. *Journal of Cognition and Culture, 8*, 179–186.

Alicke, M. D., Davis, T. L., & Pezzo, M. V. (1994). A posteriori adjustment of a priori decision criteria. *Social Cognition, 12*, 281–308.

Alicke, M. D., Weigold, M. F., & Rogers, S. L. (1990). Inferring intentions and responsibility from motives and outcomes: Evidential and extra-evidential judgments. *Social Cognition, 8*, 286–305.

Baldwin, D. A., & Baird, J. A. (2001). Discerning intentions in dynamic human action. *Trends in Cognitive Sciences, 5*, 171–178.

Cushman, F. (2008). Crime and punishment: Distinguishing the roles of causal and intentional analyses in moral judgment. *Cognition, 108*, 353–380.

Darley, J. M., & Shultz, T. R. (1990). Moral rules: Their content and acquisition. *Annual Review of Psychology, 41*, 525–556.

Davidson, D. (1963). Actions, reasons, and causes. *Journal of Philosophy, 60*, 685–700.

Davis, M. H. (2005). A "constituent" approach to the study of perspective taking: What are its fundamental elements? In B. F. Malle & S. D. Hodges (Eds.), *Other minds* (pp. 44–55). New York: Guilford Press.

Doris, J. M., Knobe, J., & Woolfolk, R. L. (2007). Variantism about moral responsibility. *Philosophical Perspectives, 21*, 183–214.

Fincham, F. D., & Jaspars, J. M. F. (1980). Attribution of responsibility: From man the scientist to man as lawyer. In L. Berkowitz (Ed.), *Advances in experimental social psychology, Volume 13* (pp. 82–120). New York: Academic Press.

Goldberg, J. H., Lerner, J. S., & Tetlock, P. E. (1999). Rage and reason: The psychology of the intuitive prosecutor. *European Journal of Social Psychology, 29*, 781–795.

Goldman, A. (1970). *A theory of human action.* Englewood Cliffs, NJ: Prentice Hall.

Greene, J. D., Sommerville, R. B., Nystrom, L. E., Darley, J. M., & Cohen, J. D. (2001). An fMRI investigation of emotional engagement in moral judgment. *Science, 293*, 2105–2108.

Guglielmo, S., & Malle, B. F. (2009). *The timing of blame and intentionality: Testing the moral bias hypothesis.* Poster presented at the annual meeting of the Society for Philosophy and Psychology, Bloomington, IN.

Guglielmo, S., & Malle, B. F. (2010a). Can unintended side effects be intentional? Resolving a controversy over intentionality and morality. *Personality & Social Psychology Bulletin, 36*, 1635–1647.

Guglielmo, S., & Malle, B. F. (2010b). Enough skill to kill: Intentionality judgments and the moral valence of action. *Cognition, 117*, 139–150.

Guglielmo, S., Monroe, A. E., & Malle, B. F. (2009). At the heart of morality lies folk psychology. *Inquiry, 52*, 449–466.

Haidt, J. (2001). The emotional dog and its rational tail: A social intuitionist approach to moral judgment. *Psychological Review, 108*, 814–834.

Haidt, J., & Kesebir, S. (2010). Morality. In S. T. Fiske, D. Gilbert, and G. Lindzey, (Eds.), *The handbook of social psychology* (5th ed., vol. 2, pp. 797–832). Hoboken, NJ: McGraw-Hill.

Higgins, E. T. (Ed.). (1996). *Handbook of motivation and cognition: Foundations of social behavior* (pp. 550–582). New York: Guilford.

Kashima, Y., McKintyre, A., & Clifford, P. (1998). The category of the mind: Folk psychology of belief, desire, and intention. *Asian Journal of Social Psychology, 1*, 289–313.

Knobe, J. (2003a). Intentional action and side effects in ordinary language. *Analysis, 63*, 190–194.

Knobe, J. (2003b). Intentional action in folk psychology: An experimental investigation. *Philosophical Psychology, 16*, 309–324.

Knobe, J. (2004). Intention, intentional action and moral considerations. *Analysis, 64,* 181–187.

Knobe, J. (2010). Person as scientist, person as moralist. *Behavioral and Brain Sciences, 33,* 315–329.

Lagnado, D. A., & Channon, S. (2008). Judgments of cause and blame: The effects of intentionality and foreseeability. *Cognition, 108,* 754–770.

Leslie, A. M., Knobe, J., & Cohen, A. (2006). Acting intentionally and the side-effect effect: "Theory of mind" and moral judgment. *Psychological Science, 17,* 421–427.

Malle, B. F. (2002). The relation between language and theory of mind in development and evolution. In T. Givón & B. F. Malle (Eds.), *The evolution of language out of prelanguage* (pp. 265–284). Amsterdam: John Benjamins.

Malle, B. F. (2004). *How the mind explains behavior: Folk explanations, meaning, and social interaction.* Cambridge, MA: MIT Press.

Malle, B. F. (2006). Intentionality, morality, and their relationship in human judgment. *Journal of Cognition and Culture, 6,* 61–86.

Malle, B. F., & Knobe, J. (1997). The folk concept of intentionality. *Journal of Experimental Social Psychology, 33,* 101–121.

Malle, B. F., Moses, L. J., & Baldwin, D. A. (Eds.). (2001). *Intentions and intentionality: Foundations of social cognition.* Cambridge, MA: MIT Press.

Malle, B. F., & Nelson, S. E. (2003). Judging *mens rea*: The tension between folk concepts and legal concepts of intentionality. *Behavioral Sciences and the Law, 21,* 563–580.

McCann, H. J. (2005). Intentional action and intending: Recent empirical studies. *Philosophical Psychology, 18,* 737–748.

Mikhail, J. (2007). Universal moral grammar: Theory, evidence and the future. *Trends in Cognitive Sciences, 11,* 143–152.

Mikhail, J. (2008). Moral cognition and computational theory. In W. Sinnott-Armstrong (Ed.), *Moral psychology, vol. 3: The neuroscience of morality: Emotion, brain disorders, and development* (pp. 81–92). Cambridge, MA: MIT Press.

Nadelhoffer, T. (2006). On trying to save the simple view. *Mind and Language, 21,* 565–586.

Ohtsubo, Y. (2007). Perceiver intentionality intensifies blameworthiness of negative behaviors: Blame–praise asymmetry in intensification effect. *Japanese Psychological Research, 49,* 100–110.

Pettit, P., & Knobe, J. (2009). The pervasive impact of moral judgment. *Mind and Language, 24,* 586–604.

Pizarro, D., Uhlmann, E., & Salovey, P. (2003). Asymmetry in judgments of moral blame and praise: The role of perceived metadesires. *Psychological Science, 14,* 267–272.

Quigley, B. M., & Tedeschi, J. T. (1996). Mediating effects of blame attributions on feelings of anger. *Personality and Social Psychology Bulletin, 22,* 1280–1288.

Saxe, R., Xiao, D. K., Kovacs, G., Perrett, D. I., & Kanwisher, N. (2004). A region of right posterior superior temporal sulcus responds to observed intentional actions. *Neuropsychologia, 42,* 1435–1446.

Shaver, K. G. (1985). *The attribution of blame: Causality, responsibility, and blameworthiness.* New York: Springer.

Solan, L. (2003). Cognitive foundations of the impulse to blame. *Brooklyn Law Review, 68,* 1003–1029.

Solan, L. (2006). Where does blaming come from? *Brooklyn Law Review, 71,* 941–945.

Solan, L. (2010). Blame, praise, and the structure of legal rules. *Brooklyn Law Review, 75.*

Tomasello, M. (1998). Social cognition and the evolution of culture. In J. Langer & M. Killen (Eds.), *Piaget, evolution, and development* (pp. 221–245). Mahwah, NJ: Erlbaum.

Tucker, D., Luu, P., Desmond, R., Hartry-Speiser, A., Davey, C., & Flaisch, T. (2003). Corticolimbic mechanisms in emotional decisions. *Emotion, 3,* 127–149.

Wegner, D. M., & Vallacher, R. R. (1986). Action identification. In R. M. Sorrentino & E. T. Higgins (Eds.), *Handbook of motivation and cognition: Foundations of social behavior* (pp. 550–582). New York: Guilford.

Weiner, B. (1995). *Judgments of responsibility: A foundation for a theory of social conduct.* New York: Guilford.

Wright, J. C., & Bengson, J. (2009). Asymmetries in judgments of responsibility and intentional action. *Mind and Language, 24,* 24–50.

Zelazo, P. D., Astington, J. W., & Olson, D. R. (Eds.). (1999). *Developing theories of intention: Social understanding and self-control.* Mahwah, NJ: Erlbaum.

ENDNOTES

1. More recently, Knobe (2010; Pettit & Knobe, 2009) has argued that people's intentionality judgments are influenced by their assessments of badness–goodness rather than by their blame/praise. Regardless of which particular moral sentiment is implicated by Knobe's model, our discussion is relevant to the general claim that morality influences judgments of intentionality.

2. The models disagree here about people's genuine moral judgments of the specific agent's action, not about people's assessment that something desirable or undesirable happened, which any model places early in the processing chain (see Figure 13.1).

3. Extant studies have manipulated intentionality in a variety of ways. Some studies manipulated the overall intentionality of the behavior (e.g., by telling participants that the behavior was performed "on purpose" or "by mistake"). Others manipulated specific features of intentionality (e.g., by telling participants that the agent knew about or wanted the bad outcome to occur). Regardless of the experimental approach, results have consistently shown that stronger evidence for a negative behavior to be intentional leads to stronger perceived blameworthiness.

4. In all our replications and variations of this scenario, we introduced, for brevity, a chief executive officer (CEO) instead of a chairman of the board. We will therefore refer to the protagonist of the side effect studies as a CEO from here on out.

5. The challenger model does not make clear predictions about the relationship between praise and intentionality. Alicke's (2000, 2008) model does not incorporate praise, and Knobe's proposals have been inconsistent regarding praise. Knobe (2003b) suggested that the skill effect holds for both blameworthy negative actions (killing) and praiseworthy positive actions (saving lives). At the same time, Knobe's (2003a) side effect demonstration contrasted a negative action (harming) with a positive action (helping). Pettit and Knobe (2009) do not mention praise and support their general claim that moral considerations influence folk-psychological judgments only with respect to negative moral valence. Thus, we focus here on predictions about negative moral judgments and use the term blame as a shortcut for any judgment about the immorality or blameworthiness of an action or the agent performing the action.

14

Co-reactive Attitudes and the Making of Moral Community

VICTORIA McGEER

Princeton University

According to P. F. Strawson, the concepts and practices of holding responsible, as animated by reactive attitudes and emotions, presuppose not libertarian free will but what I call *co-reactivity*: a sensitivity to the scaffolding
structure of reactive emotions that is displayed by most human beings most
of the time. Many contemporary cognitive theorists, while paying deference
to Strawson, have reverted to the idea that a presumption of libertarian free
will is essential to reactive practice. Some treat this presumption as a hopeless error, others as a necessary illusion. This divide between Strawsonians
and non-Strawsonians has important research implications for cognitive psychology, but, more important still, it has great significance for the theory and
practice of corrective justice. The *hopeless error* theorists will be drawn to a
crude consequentialist view of punishment purged of individual blame; the
necessary illusion theorists to an equally crude retributivist view. By contrast, those of a Strawsonian bent should find themselves drawn to a novel
restorative vision that pays due deference to the natural kinematics of reactive emotions.

INTRODUCTION

*T*he term *reactive attitudes* was introduced by P. F. Strawson (1974) in his
paper "Freedom and Resentment," rightly viewed as one of the most important and revolutionary contributions to the free will debate in contemporary

philosophical discourse. Reactive attitudes, in Strawson's terminology, are special emotion-laden responses to which human beings are naturally prone in their inter-actions with one another. They encompass emotions such as (this is Strawson's list): gratitude and resentment, hurt feelings, indignation and approbation, shame and guilt, remorse and forgiveness, certain kinds of pride, and certain kinds of love. What makes reactive attitudes special is that they express both a sensitivity to how people are regarded and treated by one another in the context of their interactions and a normative demand that such treatment and regard reflect a basic stance of good will, modulated to suit the kinds of interactions in question (e.g., between family members, friends, relative strangers). As Strawson says, we care enormously whether people manifest good will, affection, or esteem in their interactions with others or if they express contempt, indifference, or malevolence. And we care whether we are the recipients of such treatment or whether others are (e.g., we might feel indignation when someone else is treated badly). We even care when others are the recipients and we are the perpetrators, actual or prospective (i.e., we are prone to feel shame and guilt).

Reactive attitudes form an important subset of our moral emotions, but even given their rich variety they do not encompass the entire range of our moral sen-timents. For instance, we might feel compassion or pity for those we take to be appropriate targets of moral regard. But the reactive emotions—Strawson men-tions gratitude and resentment as exemplary instances—are felt only toward those who we think meet more stringent conditions. Such individuals must be appropri-ate targets of moral regard to be sure, but they must also be capable of showing moral regard in return. It is this capacity of showing moral regard that we take to be critical for responsible agency. So reactive emotions are emotions we think it appropriate to feel only toward *responsible agents*—agents we consequently hold responsible for their actions and attitudes, not just by responding to them with reactive emotions but also by engaging in activities that we take to be fitting in light of our reactive emotions, activities such as praising and blaming, punishing and rewarding.

Strawson does a masterful job of laying bare the shape and structure of our reactive attitudes: reminding us of their variety, of the significance they have for us, of the sorts of conditions that lead us to modify or suspend such attitudes, and of their critical role in making and sustaining moral community. But Strawson's purpose in doing this rich forensic work is ostensively a rather arcane philosophical one: to show that metaphysical discussions about whether human beings possess a contra-causal or libertarian free will are simply irrelevant to the justification of our concepts and practices of holding responsible—concepts and practices that are embodied in the complex web of our reactive exchanges.

In light of this, it is worth asking whether Strawson is rightly viewed as a staunch *compatibilist*: Is he committed to the view that our concepts and practices of holding responsible are compatible with the metaphysical thesis of determinism, according to which every event, including every human action, is entirely deter-mined by the prior physical state of the universe in accordance with natural law? In a sense, yes, but this characterization is also misleading. Certainly Strawson rejects *incompatibilism*—the view that our concepts and practices of holding responsible cannot be justified if determinism is true. In other words, he rejects the thesis that maintaining such concepts and practices requires a belief in libertarian (contra-causal) free will. So if the rejection of incompatibilism entails the acceptance of compatibilism, Strawson is a compatibilist. But his is not a justificatory compatibilism. That is to say, he does not regard the concepts and practices of holding responsible as being justified only if they can be squared with the metaphysical thesis of determinism. Strawson's view, once again, is that any such metaphysical justificatory project (whether incompatibilist or compatibilist) is deeply misguided. As he says:

> Inside the general structure or web of [reactive] attitudes and feelings ... there is endless room for modification, redirection, criticism and justification. But questions of justification are internal to the structure or relate to modifications internal to it. The existence of the general framework of attitudes itself is something we are given with the fact of human society. As a whole, it neither calls for, nor *permits*, an external "rational" justification [i.e., in terms of either a libertarian or a deterministic metaphysics]. (Strawson, 1974, p. 23, emphasis added)

Why is this issue of justification so important? One answer—perhaps Strawson's own—flows from a disinterested concern with the philosophical enterprise: If philosophers could only get this right, they could liberate themselves from the deep and tired grooves of a pointless metaphysical debate, with compatibilists on one side urging that causal determinism is no threat to our ordinary practices of holding responsible and incompatibilists on the other side arguing that it is. But, to my mind, there is a far more significant worry lurking in the shadows of various remarks that Strawson makes—one he never explicitly develops but that ought to command more attention. It is that certain practical dangers are likely to flow from falling prey to a mistaken belief that metaphysical theses are relevant to the justification of our practices of holding responsible—dangers that threaten the very practices themselves. Of course, there is a bit of irony here. The free will debate is generally motivated by the thought that we cannot hold on to our ordinary concepts and practices of holding responsible without making them metaphysically acceptable: without squaring them with one or another metaphysical picture of human choice. But, in my view, the deeper significance of Strawson's work is to show that these concepts and practices may be vulnerable to damage and distortion precisely as a consequence of seeking to square them with a metaphysical picture of human choice; hence, such metaphysical inclinations are important to nip in the bud before they can flower into noxious, though possibly seductive, practical recommendations.

In this chapter, I aim to build on Strawson's insights in a novel context and to novel purpose. In the first philosophical section, I lay out two distinctive theses I derive from Strawson's work indicating why I think they are attractive. In the second more interdisciplinary section, I show that both of these theses have been rejected by a new wave of moral psychological research that otherwise takes its cue from Strawson in focusing on reactive attitudes as the key to understanding our folk concepts and practices of holding responsible. And then in the third (brief and schematic) criminal justice section, I explore the practical implications of these rival approaches (Strawsonian and non-Strawsonian) for thinking about our institutions of corrective justice. My aim in this final section is to show that, while the new wave of moral psychological research leaves us with the old dichotomy under which *just punishment* is cast either as strategic conditioning or rigorist retribution, Strawson's approach points us in a quite novel direction, one that I associate with the relatively new movement of restorative justice.

TWO STRAWSONIAN THESES

The thesis that has attracted most philosophical attention in Strawson's work is one he explicitly defends. I will call it the *metaphysical non-commitment thesis*. According to this thesis, the concepts and practices of responsibility, as embodied in our reactive exchanges, do not presuppose anything so metaphysically demanding as libertarian (or contra-causal) free will. Hence, the truth or falsity of determinism is simply irrelevant to the coherence of these concepts and practices. The metaphysical non-commitment thesis is thus a thesis about what sort of property we must be tracking in one another for our reactive attitudes to be properly targeted—that is, targeted on agents who are not justly exempted (as Strawson says) from our practices of holding responsible.[1] And Strawson's claim is that this property has nothing whatsoever to do with the metaphysical underpinnings of human choice. So what then is this property? Strawson's discussion suggests both a negative and a positive point.

The negative point is that this property cannot consist in having or exercising a libertarian free will. Libertarians defend the view that people are only appropriately held responsible for what they do, if they could have done otherwise right up to the moment they acted. But the only way that they could have done otherwise in this extreme sense is if their choice was not determined by any prior events but proceeded instead from the free exercise of their own will, where this implies an ability to intervene in the causal order and select from genuinely open options. But apart from the spooky (Strawson says "panicky") metaphysics involved in this libertarian story, it just doesn't serve any useful function. After all, if the story were true, our reactive attitudes would be appropriately targeted only by detecting when people possess or exercise their contra-causal free will. But how do we detect this? As everyone must agree, we cannot do so directly; we have no "free-will-o-meters" to do this tricky job. So, this means we can do so only indirectly, i.e., we must rely on some other property that attests (indirectly) to when someone has or exercises their contra-causal free will by way of attesting (more directly) to whether they are fit to be held responsible. In other words, we need to be tracking some other property that attests (more directly) to whether or not they are fit to be held responsible. Hence, the capacity for exercising a libertarian free will is just an idle metaphysical wheel; it does no real work in underpinning our reactive practices.

That is Strawson's negative point. Now to the positive point. What makes people fit to be held responsible? What makes them an appropriate kind of target for our reactive attitudes? What property must they possess—and which we must be tracking—to make it appropriate for us to treat them as responsible agents?

First, we need to remind ourselves that, in Strawson's view, not all individuals are proper targets of the reactive attitudes. There are people who are cognitively and affectively abnormal in various ways (perhaps they are psychotic, deeply neurotic, or brain damaged in certain critical respects), and though these people may injure or even benefit us we don't think there is any point in responding reactively to them (e.g., with resentment or gratitude, indignation, or hurt feelings). Their handicap makes them incapable either of understanding the kind of demand expressed in our reactive attitudes (a demand, as Strawson says, for appropriate moral regard) or of responding appropriately to that demand. They are unfit to be treated as *participants* in our shared moral practice, so it makes no sense to respond to them reactively.[2] Of course, we might respond to them in all sorts of other ways: We may think it right to manage them, or restrain them, or provide them with some kind of treatment. And naturally this does not mean that they fall outside the scope of our moral regard. The point is just that we reserve our reactive responses for those whom we take to be capable of understanding what we are communicating through our reactive attitudes and capable of responding appropriately.

But just what are we communicating though our reactive attitudes? It is certainly part of our message that we expect, and indeed demand, that individuals show one another an appropriate degree of moral regard. But given that our reactive attitudes are sensitive to judgments that we make about whether someone is a fitting recipient of these attitudes, the fact that we express them in effect communicates a good deal more. It says to the recipients of our reactive attitudes that we do not despair of them as moral agents; that we don't view them objectively—that is, as individuals to be managed or treated or somehow worked around; indeed, that we hold them accountable to an ideal of moral agency because we think them capable of living up to that ideal. So reactive attitudes communicate a positive message even in their most negative guise—even in the guise of anger, resentment, or indignation. The fact that we express them says to the recipients that we see them as individuals who are capable of understanding and living up to the norms that make for moral community.

Our reactive attitudes will be well targeted, I have said, if the recipients can understand this message and have a capacity to respond in ways that show normative awareness of the demands being made of them. What will such a response involve? It may reflect some prior understanding of why their behavior prompted the reactive attitude in question. But I don't think this is the essential thing. What is more essential is that the recipients of such attitudes understand—or can be brought to understand—that their behavior has been subjected to normative review, a review that now calls on them to make a normatively fitting response. Of course, such responses may still be many and varied. They will depend, for instance, on whether the recipient agrees with the judgment implied in the reactive attitude. For instance, in the case of anger or resentment, a recipient can show basic normative sensitivity in my sense by getting defensively indignant in return, thereby refusing (initially at any rate) to accept the moral judgment implied in the reactive attitude. However, such defensive indignation is rarely very satisfying to either party in the exchange. The reason, I suspect, is that morally capable agents have a basic human need to reach agreement on the normative significance of what they do to one another. Thus, in optimal cases, a fitting normative response to anger or resentment involves parties on both sides working to understand why the offender's behavior prompted the reactive attitude and for the offender to make amends, if amends are really due.

In sum, reactively responsive agents are the kind of agents who care, or can be brought to care, about living up to the demands of responsible agency that we express through our reactive attitudes. And by *living up to the demands* I simply mean that, however they have failed before, such agents will at least behave reactively in ways commensurate with treating them as responsible agents, including justifying or reviewing their actions, negotiating about their meaning, and (in cases of genuine offense) coming to terms with what they might owe others by way of contrition, apology, and commitment to reform. Hence, the kind of responsiveness we look for in responsible agents (i.e., agents who we take to be appropriate targets of the reactive attitudes) can now be summed up in a single word: *co-reactivity*. They are co-reactive agents: *co*, because their own attitudes and responses will be normatively sensitive reactions (some better, some worse) to the reactive attitudes of others. This is the property that Strawson takes to be critical for responsible agency.

Identifying this property puts the reactive attitudes themselves in a different light—and here I elaborate on Strawson's work with two further observations. First, there is a tendency (no doubt encouraged by the name Strawson gave them) to focus on the fact that reactive attitudes are backward-looking responses to the actions and attitudes of others. Yet, because they are themselves attitudes expressing the good or ill will of others, they will naturally prompt reactive responses in turn. After all, as Strawson points out, reactive responses reflect the fact that we care enormously about what attitudes others manifest toward us, and this will be true—perhaps even more true—when the attitudes in questions are themselves reactive attitudes: attitudes that in their nature have commented on the quality of our moral agency. So while reactive attitudes are backward-looking responses to the actions and attitudes of others, they have, more importantly, a forward-looking dimension, serving to elicit some further reactive response from the individuals to whom they are directed. It is this forward-looking dimension that is critical for understanding the power they have to scaffold the moral agency of others.

This leads to the second important observation. Reactive attitudes will function successfully in this scaffolding role, so far as they prompt normatively appropriate reactive responses in others. But since part of their aim is to elicit such responses when that aim is accomplished, these reactive attitudes are naturally answered and transformed, replaced by new reactive attitudes that are themselves appropriate responses to the reactive responses prompted by the original reactive attitudes. In other words, reactive attitudes perform their scaffolding role so far as they are normally embedded in dynamic trajectories of reactive exchange (see Figure 14.1). These trajectories are actually what give the reactive attitudes that constitute them the meaning and power they have. Forgiveness is a good example. Forgiveness is a reactive attitude that serves to reaffirm the moral competence of the individual to whom it is directed. But it only makes sense as a reactive attitude—and only has

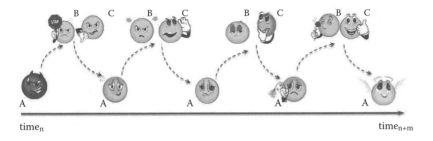

Figure 14.1   A sample trajectory of co-reactive exchange: forgiveness.

the power it does—so far as it comes at the end of a trajectory of reactive exchanges occurring principally between a victim and a wrongdoer, but often involving the reactive responses of bystanders as well. Hence, if we want to understand how reactive attitudes play a constructive role in making and sustaining moral community, we need to understand the trajectories of reactive exchange in which they are naturally embedded (this point will become important in my final section).

So where have we got to so far? The philosophically important thesis that Strawson defends in his work is the metaphysical noncommitment thesis. According to this thesis, individuals must possess a certain property if they are to be appropriate targets of the reactive attitudes, if they are fit to be held responsible. However, this property has nothing to do with the metaphysics of human choice and so presupposes no commitment to the falsity of determinism (and no commitment to its truth either). It is simply the property of co-reactivity, or of being susceptible to the scaffolding dynamics of reactive exchange. To put this another way, individuals who are appropriate targets of reactive attitudes (i.e., who are fit to be held responsible) have a certain kind of character from which their actions flow—that is, the kind of character that is reactively responsive to, and so shaped under, the scaffolding influence of others' reactive attitudes.

I put the point this way for an important reason. A central plank of the libertarian metaphysician's argument is that our ordinary concept of responsibility is essentially connected to the following thought: Responsible agents are agents who "could have done otherwise." They say that the only sensible interpretation we can give to this thought is metaphysical—that is, it is a thought that makes sense only if we impute to agents special (nondeterministic) causal powers. Call this the *causal reading* of "could have done otherwise." Yet if Strawson is right, there is another far more sensible interpretation we can and should give to this commonplace thought. Call it the *character reading* of "could have done otherwise." On this reading, the thought is that responsible agents have the kind of character such that they could have done otherwise. That is to say, their character is not cut in stone, leading inevitably to the behavior in question; it is rather living and breathing, as George Eliot says, open to being formed and reformed under the regimen of reactive scaffolding. Thus, to say that responsible agents are agents who "could have done otherwise" simply expresses the commonplace view that though we certainly do not expect moral perfection from such agents on every occasion, we do expect them to have an ever-present moral sensitivity, where such sensitivity is operationalized as having a disposition to respond appropriately—that is, co-reactively—to reactive attitudes.

The last point I want to make in this section is the following. While the metaphysical non-commitment thesis constitutes the philosophical core of Strawson's work, there is a second pragmatic thesis that I think is suggested by his view. I'll call it the *metaphysical corruption thesis.*

The concepts and practices of holding responsible embodied in our reactive attitudes make no metaphysical presuppositions. But, according to the metaphysical corruption thesis, these attitudes and practices may be vulnerable to the mistaken belief that particular metaphysical views are relevant to their coherence and sustainability of such attitudes and practices. That is to say, if people become convinced that such concepts and practices rest on embracing a libertarian conception of free will, and if they also accept the truth of determinism, then this can have a negative impact on the concepts and practices themselves. Hence, according to the metaphysical corruption thesis, specific practical dangers flow from failing to embrace the metaphysical non-commitment thesis.

These practical dangers might arise at two levels. At the first level, the threat is quite direct. The worry is that if ordinary folk believe that the concepts and practices of holding responsible make sense only if people have libertarian free will, and if they become convinced that free will in this sense is an illusion, then they might lose faith in the idea that there is any real distinction to be made between individuals who are appropriate targets of their reactive attitudes and those who are not, leading to substantial changes in the ways they conduct their interpersonal affairs. For reasons I won't go into here, Strawson was not particularly concerned with this possibility, and I think rightly so (I discuss this issue further in the appendix to this chapter, where I also consider Strawson's view in relation to some recent empirical studies conducted by Nichols & Knobe, 2007).

But there is another kind of threat operating at a higher-order level of social policy and institutional design. This threat could be put like this: Suppose that we, now as *theorists* of reactive practice, form the mistaken belief that such attitudes embody a concept of responsibility that depends for its coherence on a libertarian conception of free will. Then we, as theorists, are likely to misunderstand the internal dynamics of ordinary reactive practices and how they function to make and sustain moral community. And if we, as theorists, do misunderstand this, then we'll have little chance of designing institutions that capitalize on, and so enhance, the best features of these practices; in fact, we may end up designing institutions that distort and disfigure them, to everyone's loss.

Although Strawson may not have paid too much mind to this possibility, I think the concern is real, having significant practical import in the field of corrective justice. I come to this issue in the third and final section of my chapter. In the next section, I prepare the ground for this discussion by briefly reviewing some recent work at the confluence of philosophy, cognitive psychology, neuroscience, and the law that raises this concern most directly.

A NEW WAVE OF MORAL-PSYCHOLOGICAL RESEARCH: A CAUTIONARY TALE

In this section, the focus of my concern is a recent debate that emphasizes the significance of empirical work for long-standing philosophical disputes about the nature of criminal responsibility and the justification for punishment. While I do not dispute the general claim that empirical work can shed new light on these concerns, I worry that theorists engaged in this work are sometimes so focused on the empirical results that they pay insufficient attention to the grounding philosophical assumptions on which they base their arguments. It may be that they think these assumptions are so secure they do not require further interrogation. However, with regard to this debate, I think such confidence is deeply misplaced.

The debate involves two papers published in a special issue of *The Philosophical Transactions of the Royal Society* on law and neuroscience: one by Joshua Greene and Jonathan Cohen (2004), and the other by Oliver Goodenough (2004). (Goodenough's paper is, in fact, a direct response to Greene & Cohen's.) These papers make radically different normative recommendations for systems of corrective justice, based on the authors' opposing views of how we should think of our reactive emotions. Nevertheless, despite the obvious ways in which these authors disagree, they embrace a common framework that utterly fails to take on board Strawson's central philosophical insight concerning the reactive attitudes. My aim in this section is, first, to show how these authors arrive at their opposing views within this common framework, and then to argue that their views do not exhaust the field of possibilities. In fact, if what I have argued in the previous section is correct, the framework reflects a deeply impoverished understanding of the reactive attitudes and their role in supporting moral agency and moral community.

So what is the shape of this common framework? Both sets of authors are heirs to a Strawsonian tradition in the following sense: They share the view that reactive emotions (or attitudes) are intimately tied to folk concepts and practices of responsibility. Hence, like Strawson, these authors are jointly concerned with understanding how such reactive attitudes contribute to shaping our interpersonal lives. Moreover, since they embrace the thesis of determinism, they are jointly preoccupied with Strawson's issue; they too are concerned with what impact the truth of determinism might—and perhaps should—have on our reactive emotions and reactive practices. Here, however, these theorists depart radically from Strawson's own line, raising the specter of the metaphysical corruption thesis. For they jointly reject, albeit without argument, Strawson's main philosophical insight: the metaphysical non-commitment thesis. That is, these authors simply assume that the folk concept of responsibility, as embodied in reactive emotions, *is* metaphysically committed to libertarian free will.

Greene and Cohen's primary aim is to argue that discoveries in cognitive neuroscience have tremendous potential to effect reform in the law, by way of undermining the (metaphysically loaded) folk view of criminal responsibility and just deserts. This may seem surprising, as Greene and Cohen endorse the claim (defended, e.g., by Morse, 2004) that the law makes no heavy metaphysical presuppositions about human agency in its assessment of criminal responsibility. All that matters in the eyes of the law is that individuals have a general capacity for *rational choice,* which is understood minimally as the capacity to act rationally in light of one's beliefs and desires. Hence, the legal determination of responsibility is in no way threatened by the thesis of determinism.

However, while Greene and Cohen agree that the law "as written" is essentially compatible with the truth of determinism, they insist that this is simply not true of ordinary folk intuitions of responsibility, which are deeply libertarian. As they say, "In modern criminal law, there has been a long tense marriage of convenience between compatibilist legal principles and libertarian moral principles" (p. 1778). In their view, the reason the relationship has lasted so long is that ordinary folk have felt no pressure to engage in the kind of "esoteric theorizing" that tortuously reconciles current legal practices with a compatibilist doctrine of agential control. The folk simply assume that the law reflects their libertarian moral intuitions. However, Greene and Cohen predict that if push ever came to shove and ordinary folk were forced to choose between rejecting or accepting a compatibilist defense current legal practices, they would reject current legal practices—or at least the retributive elements of those practices. In Greene and Cohen's view, this is where contemporary neuroscience can play a major role—by making push come to shove. As they say, "the legitimacy of the law depends on its adequately reflecting the moral intuitions and commitments of society. If neuroscience can change those intuitions, then neuroscience can change the law" (p. 1778).

So how is contemporary neuroscience to achieve this transformation? According to Greene and Cohen, the first thing it will do is to demonstrate beyond a shadow of a doubt that behind all the neural firings that constitute brain activity there is no *self* that is in charge of our actions. And if there is no self, there is no source of libertarian free will: What human beings do is just a matter of how their neurons fire, and how their neurons fire is completely determined by complex biological and environmental factors. As they say, "Neuroscience can help people appreciate the mechanical nature of human action in a way that bypasses complicated arguments" (p. 1780). Once this happens, Greene and Cohen predict that ordinary folk will experience conflict in their moral intuitions: This is because the ordinary notion of responsibility embodied in reactive attitudes embeds a commitment to libertarian free will. And since the folk will come to see this commitment as a hopeless error, they will come to regard our own reactive attitudes as deeply misguided and unfair.

Will this change the shape of everyday reactive practices? Alas, probably not, according to Greene and Cohen. They suggest that the reactive affective system is part of our evolved biological heritage: that it is likely driven "by phylogenetically old mechanisms in the brain" and, hence, very unlikely to be cognitively penetrable (p. 1784). In other words, though we may come to regard our reactive attitudes (e.g., resentment, indignation, retributive anger) as embedding a hopeless error in the way we think about human agency, we may be stuck with such attitudes in the hurly-burly of everyday life.

In Greene and Cohen's view, this is very bad news. Unlike Strawson, who for quite different reasons agrees that our everyday practices are no doubt immune to metaphysical revision (see the appendix), Greene and Cohen regard such a change as normatively mandated. How then do we ordinary folk, handicapped by our evolutionary heritage, cope with this predicament? The way is not easy, in Greene and Cohen's view, but cognitively mediated processes may still come to our rescue. Although we may not be able to suppress our reactive attitudes in day-to-day life, we can at least bracket these attitudes—that is, not be guided by them and not cater to them—when it comes to designing or evaluating social institutions, especially those concerned with criminal justice. Indeed, since ought implies can, this is where our normative obligations must lie. I return to this point in the next section.

Greene and Cohen represent one strand in this new wave of moral psychological research. Goodenough (2004) represents a different strand, which nevertheless shares many of the same elements. As mentioned already, Goodenough acknowledges the basic Strawsonian point that reactive attitudes and practices embody our folk notion of responsibility. But, like Greene and Cohen, he rejects Strawson's metaphysical non-commitment thesis out of hand; that is, he does not argue the point but simply accepts that the folk notion of responsibility presupposes a commitment to libertarian free will. Furthermore, since Goodenough accepts the truth of determinism, he agrees with Greene and Cohen that this folk commitment to libertarian free will is an error. He also agrees with Greene and Cohen that this error "may be deeply lodged in human cognitive and emotional psychology" and hence will not be abandoned through deeper reflection on metaphysical issues (p. 1807). He thus arrives at Greene and Cohen's conclusion that good institutional design requires theorists to come to grips with how reactive practices depend on a libertarian metaphysics of free will—contrary to what the metaphysical corruption thesis explicitly warns against.

Now comes the interesting twist. Whereas Greene and Cohen (2004) see the commitment to libertarian free will as a hopeless error, showing the rot (as it were) at the heart of our reactive attitudes, Goodenough (2004) regards it as a useful fiction, playing a critical strategic role in regulating human interactions. Reactive attitudes, and more precisely punitive attitudes, with their in-built commitment to libertarian free will, have a strategic evolutionary rationale. Moreover, this rationale not only explains why they are such a deep feature of human psychology but also demonstrates, *contra* Greene and Cohen, why we would be foolish to bracket them in designing or evaluating our social institutions.

Here is a brief summary of Goodenough's argument explaining the evolutionary rationale for our commitment to the free will illusion: As psychologists have shown, punishment, especially by a third party (i.e., someone not directly involved in the offensive transaction), is effective at "stabilizing cooperative social structures" (Bendor & Swistak, 2001; Fehr & Fischbacher, 2004). However, to be effective, threats of punishment must be credible and must involve a commitment to punish in the face of transgression (Dixit & Skeath, 2004). Yet punishment is typically not without cost—think of how much we pay for prisons, protracted criminal trials, appeals, and so forth. Moreover, since there is often no direct material gain to punishers, especially third-party punishers, this cost must be borne altruistically (Fehr & Gachter, 2002). Strategically, this means that punishers will not want to waste punishment on those for whom punishment has no effect—that is, on those who truly cannot be changed or deterred through punishment. Yet this introduces an incentive for transgressors to make it seem to would-be punishers as if they could not be influenced through punishment, making those punishers less likely to inflict punishment on the transgressors. Now Goodenough asks: How could such feigned indifference to punishment be guarded against? One plausible evolutionary solution to this strategic problem is to build a *commitment* into human psychology—i.e., to "design" human beings in such a way that they are cognitively programmed to see one another as having greater powers of rational agency and behavioral control than they actually have. Goodenough describes this default assumption as follows:

> The commitment is to treating the other agent as if he/she had the capacity to fully integrate the threat of punishment into its decision-making calculus, and to act accordingly, i.e., as if she/he had a kind of free will. Declaring this committed position both neutralizes attempts at deception by the transgressor and to some degree forces the role of a considering agent on the other player. (p. 1807)

In other words, by grace of natural selection, we are committed to punishing would-be transgressors because we inevitably default to viewing human beings in a certain light—that is, as self-directed agents possessed of a libertarian free will that gives them ultimate control of anything they do. Our reactive attitudes, especially our punitive attitudes, may be an ineradicable of human psychology, resting on a total fiction, but this is a good thing, according to Goodenough, something to be honored in the context of social policy and institutional design. In short, theorists would do well to accommodate the following esoteric truth:

> However counter-factual the free will proposition may be in a deterministic world, it is a strategic fiction that underlies the productivity of a punishment rule.... Our free will intuitions may be false in the world of deterministic science and yet nonetheless effective in the world of strategic interaction [presumably the world in which we human beings, as social animals, have to survive, and indeed thrive]. (p. 1807)

In sum, the theorists whose work I have reviewed in this section come to radically opposed conclusions concerning the stance we should take toward our ordinary reactive attitudes: whether we should regard them, on one hand, as embodying a hopeless atavistic error to be bracketed as much as possible in the context of social policy and institutional design or, on the other hand, as embodying a strategically useful fiction that should be maintained as far as possible. This difference has profound relevance for their views on corrective justice, the topic to which I now turn in the final section of my chapter. As we shall see, these authors embrace the standard opposing views in that domain: an enlightened welfarist approach focused on deterrence and rehabilitation (traditionally associated with consequentialism) versus a strict retributive approach focused on giving offenders their just deserts (traditionally associated with deontology). However, my aim in the next section is to insist that these views are not exhaustive but depend instead on endorsing a shared view of the reactive attitudes that we have good reasons to reject. Once that common assumption is rejected and we adopt a properly Strawsonian view of reactive attitudes, it is interesting to see what new theoretical terrain is made available for critical exploration.

INSTITUTIONAL SIGNIFICANCE OF OUR THEORETICAL COMMITMENTS

Let me sum up the state of play so far. There is a big divide among theorists who maintain that our reactive attitudes both express our ordinary intuitions and judgments of responsibility and underpin our ordinary practices of holding responsible: On one side, including Strawson himself, are those who think that these reactive attitudes and practices are metaphysically modest so far as they merely presuppose coreactivity on the part of responsible agents (the metaphysical noncommitment thesis). On the other side, representing a new research program in moral psychology (Goodenough; Greene & Cohen), are those who think that such attitudes and practices depend for their coherence on viewing responsible agents as possessing a metaphysically expensive, libertarian (or contra-causal) free will. These two sides also differ on a related pragmatic issue: Strawsonians worry that theorists will do a poor job of institutional design if they fail to come to grips with the fact that ordinary concepts and practice of responsibility make no metaphysical commitments; they will fail to understand—and so will not properly exploit—the real internal dynamics of reactive attitudes and practices, thus undermining their power to make and sustain moral community (the metaphysical corruption thesis). The opposition, by contrast, thinks that theorists will do a poor job of institutional design if they fail to come to grips with the fact that reactive attitudes and practices depend on a libertarian metaphysics, whether this means compensating for a hopeless atavistic error or exploiting a strategically useful fiction.

In the first section of this chapter, I argued in support of Strawson's metaphysical noncommitment thesis on the following grounds: Even if ordinary folk have a cognitive tendency to buy into a metaphysical belief in libertarian free will at a quasi-reflective level, this belief cannot really be driving day-to-day judgments of responsibility as these are embodied in reactive attitudes and practices.[4] After all, even if individuals exercised this libertarian power of free will, there is no direct way of detecting when they have done so. So when we judge that people are responsible—and fit to be held responsible—it must be on the basis of some other evidence—evidence, as I argued, for their being co-reactive agents, agents who are sensitive to the scaffolding dynamics of ordinary reactive attitudes. If this is right, we have good reason to reject the opposing views about how to conceptualize reactive attitudes when it comes to institutional design.

In this section, I want to explore why it matters. What is the practical significance of this debate for institutional design, specifically in relation to the issue of criminal justice? At this point, I can offer only a brief sketch of the directions in which the different theories lead.

First of all, where would Greene and Cohen's hopeless error view of reactive attitudes and practices lead? Greene and Cohen are explicitly reformist in their policy recommendations. They argue that, since ordinary folk ideas of responsibility are deeply mistaken, policy makers have an obligation to put these ideas aside in thinking about crime and punishment. But what does this leave? Appealing to a well-developed consequentialist line of argument (e.g., Smart, 1961), Greene and Cohen propose that the only just and equitable legal institutions are those that maximize overall social welfare. Of course, as they point out, there is nothing in the truth of determinism that suggests people cannot be conditioned by their external environment. Hence, if punishment, or the threat of punishment, serves to regulate behavior in socially desirable ways, then to that extent it is all to the good. Furthermore, with this welfarist agenda in mind, incarceration in one form or another is a legitimate way to protect others in society, especially against those who cannot be deterred by the threat of punishment.

As advocates of consequentialist legal reform, Greene and Cohen (2004) say they are promulgating a view that will "radically transform … our approach to criminal justice" (p. 1784). But how radical are their suggestions? For instance, in response to standard complaints leveled against this consequentialist approach, they insist that their view justifies neither "extreme over-punishment" nor "extreme under-punishment" (p. 1783), presumably relative to current norms. Moreover, they argue that their view leaves intact a number of distinctions currently recognized in the law, underpinning a variety of defenses that diminish or undermine criminal responsibility (e.g. duress, diminished capacity). More importantly, they argue that their view leaves intact the very notion of criminal responsibility officially recognized in the law, which, as Morse (2004) points out, already presupposes just the general and minimal capacity for rational agency that compatibilists favor. Given all this conservatism, one wonders just how radically transforming Greene and Cohen's consequentialist legal reforms would actually be.

Against such pessimism, Greene and Cohen remain convinced that there is much room for improvement. In their view, retributivism is the source of a number of ills in this domain: the idea that when we punish criminals we are giving them their *just deserts* or what they truly deserve for the crimes they have (willfully) committed. As they say, "Our penal system is highly counter-productive from a consequentialist perspective, especially in the USA, and yet it remains in place because retributivist principles have a powerful moral and political appeal" (p. 1783). Of course, with regard to certain consequences, Greene and Cohen should insist that people's motivations are not relevant when it comes to assessing the pros and cons of a given penal system. If retributive impulses deliver the appropriate amount of punishment from the perspective of maximizing overall social welfare, then those impulses may well be serving a useful societal function (as we shall see, this is Goodenough's view, discussed following). So, by "counter-productive" they could mean only that such retributive impulses do not deliver the best outcome from a social welfarist perspective after all.

Naturally, this is an empirical issue, and as such I do not have much to say about it. But, surprisingly, nor do Greene and Cohen. They do suggest that, absent retributivism, people might be less keen on the death penalty (see, e.g., p. 1784), and perhaps that would conduce to overall social welfare (although they nowhere argue for this point explicitly). Another potential gain (which they also don't discuss) is that people might be more prone to support efforts at rehabilitating offenders, where presumably those efforts would be stripped of any taint of moral blame and focus instead on the kinds of conditions that debilitate individuals from acting in law-abiding ways (e.g., poverty, ignorance, social maladjustment) and doing what they can to address those conditions, both in the particular case and in society at large.

However, against these gains must surely be set an overall cost—one that Greene and Cohen do explicitly discuss yet seem not to factor into their consequentialist calculations. Recall that, in their view, retributive feelings (with their implicit commitment to free will) are likely to be an ineradicable feature of the human psyche, "driven by phylogenetically old mechanisms in the brain" (p. 1784). Indeed, this is why Greene and Cohen think that the best we can hope to achieve is to bracket these feelings when it comes to policy making and institutional design. We will still experience these feelings in day-to-day life, but in "special situations" we can put them aside, adopting the more "detached" and "humane" perspective on criminal behavior mandated by the truth of determinism. Perhaps this dual perspective is genuinely possible for us—sufficient even for achieving the sort of reforms in our criminal justice system that Greene and Cohen would like to see. But at what psychic cost to individuals in society? Stuck as we are with our atavistic tendencies to "see one another as free agents who deserve to be rewarded and punished for our past behaviours" (ibid), how stable could our endorsement of these consequentialist reforms really be? We might continually remind ourselves of the neuroscientific findings that "graphically illustrate" how things "really are" (p. 1784), but when faced with the next hideous crime in the morning news our retributive impulses, in Greene and Cohen's own view, will come screaming to the fore. Moreover, just consider how much stronger such feelings would be if we, or our friends or loved ones, were the actually victims of the crime. Naturally, we need not—and often do not—act on all the feelings we experience. But to envision a situation in which we are so continuously at war with ourselves, with all of the likely social and political instability that portends, is surely a cost to be reckoned in any consequentialist assessment of the overall social welfare that would result from the reforms Greene and Cohen advocate.

In sum, Greene and Cohen's recommendations are both vague and problematic. On one hand, they insist that once ordinary folk understand the importance of bracketing reactive attitudes (especially retributive impulses) in designing a genuinely fair and humane criminal justice system they will naturally endorse a reformist agenda that is guided exclusively by consequentialist considerations of what produces the best societal outcome overall. On the other hand, even on Greene and Cohen's own consequentialist terms, it is unclear how radical such a reformist agenda would—or should—be. In the first place, empirical arguments are needed to support the claim that a punishment system designed on strict retributivist guidelines does not in fact deliver the best results from the point of view of deterring crime, keeping criminals off the street, and so on. And, second, even if those arguments were to fail, Greene and Cohen forget to take account of the psychic and, ultimately, social costs of designing a criminal justice system that runs counter to what, in their view, are ineradicable reactive attitudes that we will continue to experience in our day-to-day lives. In effect, what Greene and Cohen propose is a new and far less happy marriage of convenience between an intellectually sanctioned criminal justice system and persistent atavistic retributive feelings that will need to be continually policed and contained if the marriage is to survive. Perhaps in Greene and Cohen's utopia there are no personal, social, or political costs to this ongoing domination of detached objective reason over interpersonal affect, but that is rather a lot to hope for. A better empirical bet is that such envisioned reforms will come at considerable cost to overall social welfare, thereby undermining their consequentialist rationale. Hence, at the end of the day, it is not clear that their enlightened welfarist agenda, with its hopeless error view of reactive attitudes, has much to recommend it.

Goodenough is likewise skeptical of Greene and Cohen's reformist aspirations. Although he agrees with them that reactive attitudes embed a mistaken view of individual responsibility, he argues that consequentialists in particular should embrace the strategic advantages that flow from this illusion. In his estimation, evolutionary considerations and game-theoretic studies strongly suggest that the erroneous belief in libertarian free will ensures that punishment practices will be as effectively deterrent as possible, signaling to would-be transgressors that exempting conditions are hardly available and thereby creating a big enough stick that most individuals would be hard-pressed to ignore. This argues for a criminal justice system that is organized around staunch retributive principles: holding people responsible and blaming them for their actions, even if, in some deeper causal sense, they are determined to do what they do. Goodenough agrees with Greene and Cohen that this is effectively how our current penal system is organized, so his policy recommendation is to leave well enough alone. In the strategic fiction view of reactive attitudes, a retributive approach to criminal justice is bound to deliver the best societal outcome overall.

What of Greene and Cohen's concern that a retributive system is hardly "fair" or "humane" in its treatment of individual offenders? Goodenough can certainly allow that committed consequentialists should be concerned with questions of individual fairness. However, it is hard to see how or why this should be a trumping concern. Deontologists may insist that it should be, but consequentialists are bound to reject such a move, keeping their eye on considerations of overall social welfare. Hence, if a concern with individual fairness is outweighed by other legitimate concerns, such as those connected with the psychic or social tolerability of various types of penal systems, then consequentialists will just have to bite the bullet on questions of individual fairness. As Goodenough says:

> ...Sadly, the efficacy of a punishment system may rest on a willingness to punish people who really could not help it. For better or worse, the Anglo-American approach to the law of responsibility ... is consistent with an in built commitment [to libertarian free will]. (p. 1808)

The upshot of this new wave of empirical-driven theorizing is that it does not take us very far in the field of criminal justice. In effect, we are left to choose between an old dichotomy of policy recommendations: on one hand, an explicitly reformist, enlightened welfarist approach that refuses to endorse any deep notion of criminal responsibility and focuses instead on using the justice system to maximize deterrence and rehabilitation; and, on the other hand, a traditional retributive approach that embraces a deep notion of criminal responsibility and insists on using the justice system, not primarily for deterrence but rather to deliver merited punishment to individuals who willfully engage in criminal behavior. The only difference between these new wave discussions and the more traditional views is the change that is rung on the retributive approach. While retributivism is traditionally associated with the deontological concern of giving just deserts no matter what the consequences for overall social welfare—hence, with what deontologists view as trumping considerations of individual fairness—Goodenough shows, perhaps surprisingly, that this approach may also recommend itself to welfare-maximizing, deterrence-oriented consequentialists. Indeed, if Goodenough is right, clear-eyed consequentialists *ought* to endorse retributivism, even if considerations of individual fairness (on their reckoning) speak against the approach rather than in favor of it. This is a bitter pill for consequentialists like Greene and Cohen to swallow. After all, their primary motivation is to advocate for a more humane and progressive criminal justice system. But now it seems as if they can maintain their consequentialism only at the cost of following in Goodenough's enlightened retributive footsteps, a dire option for those with a reformist agenda. Is there no way out of this dilemma?

An obvious suggestion is to give up on the consequentialism, but in my view this is the wrong course to follow. The root of these thinkers' problem is not in fact their consequentialism but rather what Strawson (1974) identified as an "incomplete empiricism, a one-eyed utilitarianism" that distorts their consequentialist reasoning (p. 23). In the final telling paragraph of "Freedom and Resentment," Strawson writes:

> It is far from wrong to emphasize the efficacy of all those practices which express or manifest our moral attitudes, in regulating behaviour in ways considered desirable; or to add that when certain of our beliefs about the efficacy of some of these practices turn out to be false, then we may have good reason for dropping or modifying those practices. What *is* wrong is to forget that these practices, and their reception, the reactions to them, really *are* expressions of our moral attitudes and not merely devices we calculatingly employ for regulative purposes. Our practices do not merely exploit our natures, they express them. Indeed the very understanding of the kind of efficacy these expressions of our attitudes have turns on our remembering this. (p. 25)

As I read Strawson, his main complaint against one-eyed consequentialists is their impoverished understanding of reactive attitudes and practices. In particular, because they are transfixed by the supposed metaphysical error they discern at the root of these attitudes and practices, they are concerned merely to bracket them or to exploit them in the crudest possible way (as devices calculatingly used for regulative purposes). Thus, they fail, each in their own way, to come to grips with how these attitudes and practices constitute a complex interconnected system of moral address. Indeed, as I argued in the first section, it is precisely because these attitudes and practices constitute a system of moral address that they are efficacious in scaffolding moral behavior. To recap that argument: (1) certain normative demands are expressed in and through reactive attitudes; (2) reactive attitudes are properly directed only toward agents who are sensitive to those demands and have a capacity to live up to them; (3) such sensitivity is shown through an agent's coreactivity—the disposition to respond reactively to others' reactive attitudes; (4) this disposition to co-reactivity means that reactive attitudes are naturally situated in dynamic trajectories of reactive exchange, where reactive attitudes serve to elicit some further response as much as they react to what has gone before; and, (5) while trajectories of reactive exchange can be more or less productive, they are psychologically and normatively most satisfying when they serve to restore, maintain, or even generate a commitment to uphold the normative demands expressed in the reactive attitudes. Hence, well-directed and well-supported trajectories of reactive exchange serve the normatively critical function of scaffolding moral community. With this in mind, we can now turn to the criminal justice system, arguing that a Strawsonian approach to these matters would aim to make corrective practices co-reactive, helping to mimic in an institutional way the dynamics of co-reactive scaffolding.

From a theoretical perspective, it is important to see how this approach departs significantly from those previously discussed. Consider, first, the differences with Greene and Cohen's enlightened welfarism. A Strawsonian approach would not suggest that in punishment we simply look to the future good we can do by imposing deterrent penalties. It would vindicate a focus on the offender and on the wrong that was done. It would take the person as someone to be addressed in a properly reactive way—that is, as a moral agent—and would not treat the person just as an instrument of social policy. To this extent it jibes more nearly with our intuitive understanding of what it means to treat an individual fairly—as deserving of an appropriate reactive response. Next, consider the contrast with Goodenough's enlightened retributivism: While endorsing the need to indict the offender in the manner just mentioned, a Strawsonian practice of corrective justice would embody a very different telos. Its aim would not be that of brutely imposing punishment simply to achieve maximum deterrent effect; rather it would strive to treat the offender as an appropriate target of moral address, holding up an ideal of responsible agency to the offender while at the same time ascribing a capacity to live up to that ideal. In this way, it would treat offenders respectfully, recognizing their capacity for co-reactivity and thereby scaffolding them in their efforts of restitution and reform. To this extent, it jibes more nearly with reformist ideals of what it means to treat an individual humanely—that is, as potentially always reclaimable in the context of moral community.

Among existing practices of corrective justice, is there any that would answer to this Strawsonian approach? Let me, in conclusion, mention one that looks to be on the right lines from the point of view of this chapter. I cannot explore the approach here in any detail, but even a brief mention will help to support the claim that the considerations rehearsed here have a positive lesson in institutional design. The approach I have in mind is usually described as one of restorative justice. As an explicit movement it began from Mennonite-led initiatives in the 1970s, but one of the claims among supporters is that it represents a return to a type of community practice often found in traditional societies. Indeed, many restorative programs are being trialed in these societies, e.g., among the first nations of Canada and the Maori of New Zealand. Indeed, in New Zealand things have progressed to the point that these practices now dominate the juvenile justice system.

There is a great deal of variation in restorative justice programs, but certain features are particularly noteworthy. They have been highlighted explicitly in connection with one of the more extensive empirical studies comparing such practices with more standard criminal justice procedures. This is the Reintegrative Shaming Experiment (RISE) conducted in Canberra, Australia, from 1995 to 2000. RISE dealt with four different categories of offense: (1) youth violent crimes (offenders under the age of 30), (2) juvenile property offenses with personal victims (offenders under 18), (3) juvenile shoplifting (offenders under 18), and (4) drunk driving (offenders all ages). Here are the main elements in the restorative justice practice, as practiced in the Canberra RISE (discussed in Strang, 2002; see also Ahmed, Harris, Braithwaite, & Braithwaite, 2001):

1. Offenders admit guilt before agreeing to take part.
2. They are then invited to participate in a conference to determine how their admitted offense should be rectified.
3. The offender can bring a number of supporters (family members, friends) to the conference, as can the victim, assuming that the victim is willing to take part. Community representatives may also be present. The conference is chaired by a police officer.
4. The formal purpose of the conference is to determine what offenders should do to make up for their offense, but a crucial by-product is often that the offenders come to recognize the harm caused to the victim, and the victim comes to appreciate that recognition and, as often happens, the contrition offenders display.
5. Restorative justice supports the natural trajectory of reactive exchanges, discussed in the first section, and thereby provides the scaffolding that reactive attitudes can provide. This is good for the offender and good for the victim.
6. In support of (5), the Canberra experiment revealed that restorative justice practices gave both greater offender and greater victim satisfaction than court proceedings—victims in particular felt justice was done. In addition, there was some reduction in recidivism rates, more for those involved in violent crime.[5]

The elements of restorative justice as summarized here reflect central points that have been argued for in this chapter. Under restorative justice initiatives, offenders are not treated in a crude consequentialist way as nonresponsible targets of rehabilitation or deterrence; they are assumed to be fully responsible agents. Yet, in contrast with a traditional retributive approach, this presumption of responsibility is not focused simply on the crime, justifying a punitive response ensuring that offenders receive appropriate payback for the wrong they have willfully done. Instead, offenders are encouraged to *take* responsibility for their wrongdoing by coming to see themselves not only as agents of crime but more importantly as agents both of restitution and of recommitment to the standards of moral community. While such restitution may be legally required and enforced, what cannot be required are the reactive emotions that victims, offenders, and other stakeholders often feel in the context of a restorative justice conference as they try to come to grips with their own experiences of the crime and the meaning it should have in their shared community. Yet it is this reactive dynamic—in particular, specific trajectories of reactive exchange—that seems to correlate most nearly with genuine recommitment to the standards of moral community, at least as this recommitment is measured in terms of recidivism rates as well as a general feeling among all the stakeholders that justice was served. But this fact is not well theorized or even recognized in the context of criminal justice. As Braithwaite and Braithwaite (2001, p. 59) observe:

> The genius of restorative circles is their collective emotional dynamics. At the moment, the research literature on restorative justice has not risen to the challenge of capturing these dynamics in research reports.... The result of this failing is that even the most literate of criminologists and criminal lawyers understand restorative justice in terms of material reparation to victims, rather than in terms of symbolic reparation which all evidence to date suggests is more important.

This chapter is the beginning of an attempt to fill that theoretical gap. It suggests that a broadly Strawsonian perspective on the importance of reactive dynamics for scaffolding moral agency and moral community can have significant institutional implications. It indicates why restorative justice holds out real promise as a just, humane, and effective innovation in criminal justice. And it even gives some theoretical guidance to practitioners of various restorative justice initiatives, accounting for at least one factor that explains why some of these initiatives may be more successful than others. More work must be done to defend these claims, both empirical and philosophical. But I hope there is sufficient promise in what I have argued here to make that work worth undertaking.

APPENDIX 14.1: METAPHYSICAL NON-CORRUPTION AT THE PRACTICAL LEVEL

The metaphysical corruption thesis holds that mistaken beliefs about the relevance of metaphysical views to our ordinary concepts and practices of holding responsible can have a corrosive effect on those concepts and practices themselves. Philosophers familiar with Strawson's (1974) paper may find it surprising that I would find such a thesis compatible with his views on the following grounds: In

"Freedom and Resentment," Strawson explicitly takes up this issue, asking both a predictive and a normative question:

> What effect would, or should, the acceptance of the truth of a general thesis of determinism have upon … [our] reactive attitudes? More specifically, would, or should, the acceptance of the truth of the thesis lead to the decay or the repudiation of all such attitudes? Would, or should, it mean the end of gratitude, resentment, and forgiveness; of all reciprocated adult loves; of all the essentially *personal* antagonisms? (p. 10, emphasis in original)

Unsurprisingly, his response to the normative question is a decided no. This just follows from his endorsement of the metaphysical noncommitment thesis: since reactive attitudes and practices do not presuppose any metaphysical commitments—in particular, a commitment to libertarian free will—accepting the truth of determinism generates no rational obligation to abandon them.[6]

More interesting, for present purposes, is Strawson's response to the predictive question. In a famous passage he remarks:

> The human commitment to participation in ordinary inter-personal relationships is, I think, too thoroughgoing and deeply rooted for us to take seriously the thought that a general theoretical conviction might so change our world that, in it, there were no longer any such things as inter-personal relationships as we normally understand them; and being involved in inter-personal relationships as we normally understand them precisely is being exposed to the range of reactive attitudes and feelings that is in question.
>
> This, then, is a part of the reply to our question. A *sustained* objectivity of inter-personal attitude—[i.e., of treating others as mere objects of manipulation or management], and the human isolation which that would entail, does not seem to be something of which human beings *would* be capable, even if some general truth were a theoretical ground for it. (pp. 11–12, emphasis added)

Of course, given the metaphysical noncommitment thesis, Strawson does not think that the truth of determinism really provides any such theoretical ground. But here the question is: What if we thought that it did? And his answer seems to indicate that he endorses something closer to a metaphysical noncorruption thesis: Our theoretical commitments just wouldn't make much of a difference to our reactive attitudes and practices, no matter how relevant in more reflective moments we might (mistakenly) take such commitments to be.

Interestingly, recent empirical work seems to support this Strawsonian prediction. Nichols and Knobe (2007) describe a series of studies they conducted to test how people's judgments about moral responsibility might vary under different conditions. Specifically, their studies indicate that (1) under abstract conditions, an overwhelming majority of people (86%) are inclined to judge that a person cannot be fully morally responsible for their actions in a deterministic universe;[7] but (2) under more concrete affect-inducing conditions, where a specific protagonist does something morally wrong (e.g., "Bill stabs his wife and children"), people are much more inclined to judge that the protagonist can be fully morally responsible, even in a deterministic universe. Overall, Nichols and Knobe conclude that the more people's reactive emotions are stimulated by a scenario, the more prepared they are to view the protagonist as fully morally responsible, even in a deterministic universe.[8]

It is worth pointing out that Nichols and Knobe take these studies to support something like a dual-process account of how people make judgments about moral responsibility: Under emotionally neutral conditions, people's judgments are subserved by a "more abstract, theoretical sort of cognition" (p. 664), guided by a particular quasi-reflective understanding of how moral responsibility is linked to the metaphysics of human choice (and here it appears that ordinary folk tend to be overwhelmingly incompatibilist in their intuitions).[9] But, under conditions that trigger reactive emotions, people are more likely to make judgments about moral responsibility that are in line with compatibilism (i.e., that are unaffected by the thesis of determinism). Nichols and Knobe suggest that such compatibilist judgments are generated by affect-involving processes that constitute a quite distinct psychological subsystem.[10] Since this subsystem is presumed to be relatively impenetrable to reflective cognition, any consciously held beliefs (e.g., that the universe is deterministic and that full moral responsibility is not possible in such a universe) would have little impact on its workings. In other words, though they don't use this word, Nichols and Knobe would explain Strawson's metaphysical noncorruption thesis by appeal to the modular nature of an affect-involving psychological subsystem that willy-nilly generates judgments of moral responsibility under concrete, affect-inducing conditions.[11]

While a current trend in moral psychology is toward such dual-process models, the Nichols and Knobe account does not do justice to the point Strawson is trying to make. The key idea behind Nichols and Knobe's proposed model is that our affective reactions are driving (in a causal sense) our assessments of moral responsibility. But, in Strawson's view, this gets the causal order the wrong way around: With regard to our reactive attitudes, our reactive attitudes do not *cause* our judgments of moral responsibility; instead, they are *expressions* of those judgments in particular concrete situations, namely, situations that reveal the quality of a person's good or ill will toward us or toward other individuals. Hence, they are expressions of a basic moral stance we take toward others, namely, a stance that assumes they are fit to be held responsible. Of course, this implies that reactive emotions will be sensitive to considerations that bear on whether we think it appropriate to treat others as responsible for what they do. And this is just what we find: If we come to realize that it is inappropriate to blame someone for a harm they did, then we cease to be resentful. Strawson emphasizes this point in arguing that *excusing* and *exempting* considerations trigger an end to resentment and the like. Excusing considerations go to the question of whether a responsible agent bears responsibility for a particular act (maybe she was coerced or did what she did accidentally), whereas exempting considerations go to the question of whether an agent is indeed a responsible agent—that is, fit to be held responsible (maybe she suffers from a serious psychological disorder). Strawson's point is that, in the context of our everyday interactions, our reactive attitudes are deeply (though, perhaps, imperfectly) sensitive to a wide variety of such excusing and exempting considerations. With respect to exempting considerations, Strawson simply adds that these will have nothing to do with abstract and perfectly general metaphysical beliefs, but only with more pedestrian and individually specific signs of moral incompetence.

Does the Strawsonian reading of reactive attitudes, and the considerations to which they are sensitive, provide an alternative explanation of the experimental results that Nichols and Knobe (2007) review? Well, certainly the Strawsonian interpretation is not ruled out. The toy concrete scenarios, unlike the more abstract question, do at least provide a little snapshot of real interpersonal engagement; hence, it is no surprise that respondents are more prepared to fall back on their ordinary ways of assessing moral responsibility in these contexts, as opposed to being guided by abstract (and likely ill-understood) metaphysical doctrine. Of course, the toy scenarios provide no information about the protagonists' capacity to operate as morally competent agents in Strawson's sense. Still, the default assumption of ordinary interpersonal interaction is that such competence exists unless and until proven otherwise (this is the force of Strawson's claim that exempting conditions are not the norm). Hence, it is no surprise that, in the absence of more specific indications of moral incompetence, respondents will view the protagonists as responsible agents (by responding to them reactively), especially when the stakes are high—especially when the protagonists have manifested the kind of significant disrespect or ill will toward particular others who would normally demand a moral response from those in the surrounding community.[12] In effect, such high-stakes situations make it morally problematic for putatively disinterested bystanders (e.g., respondents to questionnaires) to stand idly by, not even offering so much as a breath of moral condemnation just because exemption is claimed for the protagonist on abstract and unfamiliar grounds.

In light of these observations, let us now return to Strawson's explanation of his metaphysical noncorruption thesis. The reason reactive attitudes are relatively immune—in everyday contexts—to abstract theoretical considerations about determinism and human freedom is that these attitudes express our expectations of, and respect for, one another as morally responsive and responsible agents; hence, reactive attitudes presuppose a view of others on which many of our ordinary interpersonal relationships depend. To suppress or distance ourselves from these attitudes is to take a view of others—an objective view—that is deeply inimical to this interpersonal view. As Strawson says:

> [These views] are not altogether *exclusive* of each other; but they are, profoundly, *opposed* to each other. To adopt the objective attitude to another human being is to see him, perhaps, as an object of social policy; as a subject for what, in a wide range of sense, might be called treatment; as something certainly to be taken account, perhaps precautionary account, of; to be managed or handled or cured or trained; perhaps simply to be avoided…. The objective attitude may be emotionally toned in many ways, but not in all ways: it may include repulsion or fear, it may include pity or even love, though not all kinds of love. But it cannot include the range of reactive feelings and attitudes which belong to involvement or participation with others in inter-personal human relationships; it cannot include resentment, gratitude, forgiveness, anger, or the sort of love that two adults can sometimes be said to feel reciprocally for each other. (p. 9)

I quote at length to emphasize that, for Strawson (1974), what differentiates these two views is not the level of affect we experience toward others—we might be deeply afraid of someone toward whom we think it right or appropriate to take an objective attitude (e.g., the murderous psychopath running loose at night in our city). Rather, what differentiates these two views is the stance we take toward others, which stance will determine the *kind* of affect it is possible to experience in relation to them. That is, do we treat them as appropriate subjects for moral address (exposing them to the range of our reactive attitudes)? Or do we treat them as individuals to be managed, whether for our good, for society's good, or even for their own good?

Both stances are available to us. Indeed, as Strawson says again and again, the objective stance is one we *ought* to adopt toward those who are not fit to be held responsible, and adopted to varying degrees depending on moral capacity. Furthermore, it is a stance we can take toward others for various reasons, having nothing to do with the practical assessment of another's moral competence. As Strawson points out, "We *have* this resource and can sometimes use it: as a refuge, say, from the strains of involvement; or as an aid to policy; or simply out of intellectual curiosity" (pp. 9–10, emphasis in original). But—and this is the essence of Strawson's metaphysical non-corruption thesis—resorting to the objective stance can hardly be the norm, since it precludes the kinds of interpersonal relationships that are absolutely central to our human way of life. Thus, practically speaking, the option of systematically suppressing or distancing ourselves from reactive attitudes is simply not available to us, no matter what we might come to believe about the propriety of our moral concepts in more benighted philosophical moments.

Now we come to the nub of the point I want to make in this appendix. It is clear that Strawson endorses a metaphysical noncorruption thesis at the practical level, at the level of day-to-day human interactions, but his thesis has nothing to do with the cognitive impenetrability of some intuitive affective processes, as some cognitive scientists might be tempted to suppose. Rather, his thesis depends on the fact that there are certain kinds of interpersonal relationships we cannot do without if we are to live a recognizably human form of life. Thus, his thesis is perfectly consistent with the idea of our removing ourselves from these relationships to some degree, some of the time. And in fact, we may think it rationally desirable to do so for certain constrained purposes; Strawson explicitly mentions assuming the objective attitude as an aid to social policy. But however valuable this resource may be, it is clearly a double-edged sword. In particular, from the objective stance, it's easy to lose sight of—or at any rate discount—certain key features of our ordinary concepts and practices of holding responsible, leading to their systematic mischaracterization.

Why is this important? Because it suggests that there is another, higher-order level at which our ordinary concepts and practices of responsibility, as embodied in reactive attitudes, can be threatened by failing to grasp the import of Strawson's metaphysical noncommitment thesis. This is what I am calling the metaphysical corruption thesis. Once again, it goes like this. Suppose we, in our cooler theoretical moments, come mistakenly to believe that our ordinary concepts and practices of responsibility depend for their coherence on a libertarian conception of free will. Then we, as theorists, are likely to misunderstand the internal dynamics of ordinary reactive practices and how they function to make and sustain moral community. And if we, as theorists, misunderstand this, then we'll have little chance of designing institutions that are well suited to actual reactive practices. This chapter has been an attempt to show why this concern is real.

REFERENCES

Ahmed, E., Harris, N., Braithwaite, J., & Braithwaite, V. (2001). *Shame management through reintegration*. Cambridge, UK: Cambridge University Press.

Bendor, J., & Swistak, P. (2001). The evolution of norms. *American Journal of Sociology, 106*, 1493–1545.

Braithwaite, J., & Braithwaite, V. (2001). Shame, shame management and regulation. In E. Ahmed, N. Harris, J. Braithwaite, & V. Braithwaite (Eds.), *Shame management through reintegration* (pp. 3–70). Cambridge, UK: Cambridge University Press.

Dixit, A., & Skeath, S. (2004). *Games of strategy*. New York: W. W. Norton.

Fehr, E., & Fischbacher, U. (2004). Third-party punishment and social norms. *Evolution and Human Behavior, 25*, 63–87.

Fehr, E., & Gachter, S. (2002). Altruistic punishment in humans. *Nature, 415*, 137–140.

Goodenough, O. R. (2004). Responsibility and punishment: whose mind? A response. *Philosophical Transactions of the Royal Society of London B: Biological Sciences, 359*, 1805–1809.

Greene, J., & Cohen, J. (2004). For the law, neuroscience changes nothing and everything. *Philosophical Transactions of the Royal Society of London. Series B, Biological Sciences, 359*, 1775–1785.

Morse, S. J. (2004). New neuroscience, old problems. In B. Garland (Ed.), *Neuroscience and the law: Brain, mind, and the scales of justice* (pp. 157–198). New York: Dana Press.

Nichols, S. (2004). The folk psychology of free will: Fits and starts. *Mind and Language, 19*, 473–502.

Nichols, S., & Knobe, J. (2007). Moral responsibility and determinism: The cognitive science of folk intuitions. *Noûs, 41*, 663–685.

Sherman, L. W., Strang, H., & Woods, D. J. (2000). *Recidivism Patterns in the Canberra Reintegrative Shaming Experiments (RISE)*. Canberra: Australian National University.

Smart, J. J. C. (1961). Free-will, praise and blame. *Mind, 70*, 291–306.

Strang, H. (2002). *Repair or revenge: Victims and restorative justice*. Oxford, UK: Clarendon Press.

Strawson, P. F. (1974). Freedom and resentment. In *Freedom and resentment and other essays* (pp. 1–25). London: Methuen.

ENDNOTES

1. Strawson mentions two sorts of conditions that might cause us to withhold or moderate our reactive responses to perceived injury: *exempting* conditions and *excusing* conditions. Exempting conditions (which I discuss here) concern the moral capacity of the offending agent: Is she someone who is genuinely fit to be held responsible? Excusing conditions concern whether a responsible agent (i.e., a nonexempted individual) is indeed responsible for a given act—perhaps she was coerced or perhaps the act in question was an accident. I say a bit more about the difference between exempting and excusing conditions in the appendix to this chapter.

2. In one sense, this paragraph may be highly misleading. As Strawson emphasizes, the distinction between those who are fit to be held responsible and those who are not is hardly black and white. This, indeed, is one important consequence of shifting from a metaphysical account of responsible agency, focusing on whether an agent possesses a libertarian free will, to a more naturalistic account of the sort Strawson favors. Responsible agency involves capacities that can be more or less well developed and developed in part (at least on Strawson's account) by how we engage with one another—for instance, to what degree and with what purpose we respond reactively to one another. Hence, I do not read Strawson as suggesting that our reactive responses are limited to those who are "fully capable" moral agents, whatever that might mean. On the contrary, although he does not say much on this topic, it is a strength of his account that it allows for (limited) reactive responsiveness to those less able, precisely as a means of developing whatever capacity for responsible agency these individuals might possess (see, e.g., Strawson's discussion of young children, or therapeutic interactions of various sorts). Nevertheless, Strawson certainly thinks it possible that some individuals will be so disabled that ordinary, or even limited, reactive responsiveness is inappropriate. The point is to understand what sort of disability this might be—not from a biological perspective but rather from a functional one. This is the question I am currently addressing.

3. It seems clear from various studies (e.g., Nichols & Knobe, 2007) that ordinary people (at least in North America, and I presume other Western countries) have an overwhelming *theoretical* tendency to cash out the intuition that responsible agents "could have done otherwise" in terms of their possessing something like a contra-causal free will. This is an interesting datum that deserves explanation. However, I stress that this is a theoretical tendency—meaning, it is the explanation that people are most naturally drawn to in giving a reflective account of what makes for responsible agency. Similarly, when people give a reflective account of the behavior of physical objects (e.g., how an object will fall when thrown from a speeding train), they do so most naturally in Aristotelian terms. So here is my conjecture: Folk theoretical proclivities do reveal something interesting about the way human beings are cognitively structured. Certain theories for various natural phenomena are simply more intuitively appealing than others. However, the theories people are attracted to in their more reflective moments may have very little to do with what is guiding their behavior in day-to-day life (e.g., catching balls that are thrown to them, or discerning when someone is fit to be held responsible). This hypothesis is not ruled out by Nichols and Knobe, discussed at greater length in the appendix.

4. For more detailed analysis of how recidivism rates appear to depend on the offense category (at least partially), see Sherman, Strang, and Woods (2000).

5. Strawson's answer to the normative question is, in fact, more nuanced than I indicate here. Specifically, he argues first that the question is fundamentally absurd since there are no realistic conditions under which it could ever arise in such a comprehensive form. But second, and more importantly, since such a choice would not be mandated by the truth of determinism—again, this is the import of the metaphysical noncommitment thesis—then the only rational grounds on which we could ever abandon such concept and practices must hinge on "an assessment of the gains and losses to human life, its enrichment or impoverishment"—an assessment that is quite independent of accepting (or rejecting) the truth of determinism (Strawson, 1974, p. 13).

6. The exact form of their question was: "In [deterministic] Universe A, is it possible for a person to be fully morally responsible for their actions?"

7. The follow-up study involved presenting participants with a "high-affect" and "low-affect" scenario, each of which was presented in a deterministic universe and a nondeterministic universe with respect to human choice. In the high-affect condition,

participants were presented with the following question: "As he has done many times in the past, Bill stalks and rapes a stranger. Is it possible that Bill is fully morally responsible for raping the stranger?" In the low-affect conditions, participants were presented with the following question: "As he has done many times in the past, Mark arranges to cheat on his taxes. Is it possible that Mark is fully morally responsible for cheating on his taxes?" Findings were as follows: Assuming a deterministic universe, 64% of participants said Bill could be fully morally responsible, whereas only 23% of participants said that Mark could be fully morally responsible. In the nondeterministic universe, 95% thought Bill could be fully morally responsible, and 89% thought Mark could be (Nichols & Knobe 2007, pp. 675–677).

8. I say quasi-reflective understanding because I don't mean to suggest that this view is arrived at through any deep reflection, only that it represents the natural folk way of theorizing about what makes us responsible agents.

9. Nichols and Knobe (2007) describe this subsystem as generating compatibilist intuitions. I presume all they mean by this is "intuitions or judgments in line with a compatibilist theory of moral responsibility." After all, if they are right to posit such a subsystem, the *implicit* theory of moral responsibility according to which this subsystem operates has yet to be determined. For all their studies show, the implicit theory might be libertarian, with agential action automatically coded as produced by a *sui generis* act of will (no matter what views of agential action may be held at the level of conscious belief). This seems to be Greene and Cohen's (2004) view, discussed in the second section. Alternatively, the implicit theory might make no such metaphysical presuppositions, simply coding agential action as action produced by appropriate psychological antecedents (beliefs, desires, intentions), which psychological states are themselves sufficient to trigger an affective response. Perhaps this is Nichols and Knobe's own view, although they do not discuss this issue explicitly.

10. In a more puzzling part of their paper, Nichols and Knobe (2007) raise the question of whether such affective processes should properly be viewed as delivering "more reliable" judgments about moral responsibility than the consciously endorsed theory (an *affect competence model*) or whether the consciously endorsed theory should be viewed as delivering more reliable judgments about moral responsibility, with affective processes skewing these judgments whenever they are brought into play (a *performance error model* of affective processes). I say this is puzzling, because it is not quite clear what they mean by more reliable in this context: more reliable in the sense that the judgments so delivered better conform to people's (possibly benighted) underlying ideas about moral responsibility, or more reliable in the sense that the judgments so delivered conform to the true view of moral responsibility? I assume Nichols and Knobe cannot mean the latter—otherwise their stated reason for preferring the performance error model does not make much sense (viz., that it better captures the patterns of judgment observed in participant responses). However, if Nichols and Knobe mean the former, the whole question of *reliability* seems off base, since their data may be indicating that people do not have any consistent underlying view of moral responsibility for such judgments to track (reliably or unreliably).

11. In this context, it is worth noting that someone's cheating on their taxes does not demand the same kind of moral redress from morally responsible bystanders. No ill will has been manifested, or harm done, to particular identifiable others. So, respondents can afford to relax their moral vigilance and let idler metaphysical speculations weigh in on (relatively inconsequential) responsibility judgments.

15

Reflections on Emotions, Imagination, and Moral Reasoning
Toward an Integrated, Multidisciplinary Approach to Moral Cognition

WAYNE CHRISTENSEN
Konrad Lorenz Institute for Evolution and Cognition Research

JOHN SUTTON
Macquarie University

Beginning with the problem of integrating diverse disciplinary perspectives on moral cognition, we argue that the various disciplines have an interest in developing a common conceptual framework for moral cognition research. We discuss issues arising in the other chapters in this volume that might serve as focal points for future investigation and as the basis for the eventual development of such a framework. These include the role of theory in binding together diverse phenomena and the role of philosophy in the construction of moral theory. We discuss the problem of distinguishing descriptive and normative issues and the importance of systematic normative analysis for empirical research. We argue that theories of cognitive architecture should play an important role as a backdrop for investigation into specific aspects of moral cognition, and we consider some of the taxonomic issues that will arise for moral cognition research, including types of moral agents, forms of moral cognition, and the nature of morality itself. Finally, we discuss some key issues in moral development, including the importance of understanding the fine-grained structure of moral motivation and emerging conceptual schemas and the role of active interpretation and problem-solving as children acquire moral skill.

INTRODUCTION

R ecently, one of us (Christensen) was visiting a friend, and the discussion turned to the friend's oldest child, a 9-year-old boy with some behavioral difficulties. The boy is visiting a psychologist regularly, and the diagnosis is that he might have mild Asperger's. The father was considering buying a pop psychology book that provides techniques for teaching empathy to children in the hope that this would help. And after all, he said, you cannot have too much empathy. Christensen agreed that the book might help but wasn't so sure that you "cannot have too much empathy." He has a relative with schizophrenia who experiences powerful empathic responses when in more acute phases of her illness. These empathic responses are often inappropriate—responses to perceiving others' distress and unhappiness when there is none—but, more importantly, for this person the strength of these empathic responses is disabling. Fortunately, most of us do not experience such strong empathic responses to the emotional states of others, because it would be difficult to live our own lives coherently if we did.

Clearly, emotions and empathy play a fundamental role in mediating our relations to others. Normal, fluid interaction with others depends on nuanced responsiveness: Based on mutual expressiveness and sensitivity, we can enjoy a conversation, gain trust, and over time develop intimacy with a friend or partner. When social emotions go awry—as they do in individuals with schizophrenia, Asperger's, and psychopathy—social interaction can be difficult or even dangerous. This book, and the workshop on which it is based, explores these issues, and here we reflect on some of the contributions and themes.

INTEGRATING MULTIPLE PERSPECTIVES ON MORAL COGNITION

A central concern of philosophy from its beginnings, moral cognition is now an important subject of investigation for a number of empirical disciplines, and this volume reflects the vibrancy of contemporary research. This is an exciting new phase, but it also presents new problems. At a basic level, there is a problem of mutual understanding: The various disciplines employ diverse methods, concepts, and research questions. Those from a philosophical background may struggle to understand, for instance, how a psychometric instrument like the Psychopathy Checklist Revised (PCL-R) is devised and employed (see, e.g., Langdon & Delmas, Chapter 5; McIlwain et al., Chapter 6). Equally, those from a psychological or neuroscience background may have difficulty following the nuances of theoretical discussion of the *metaphysical noncommitment thesis* and its relation to moral responsibility (McGeer, Chapter 14). The greatest difficulty may lie not with the immediate content of what is written—authors have generally done well in writing for an interdisciplinary audience and are admirably clear—as with grasping the deeper "logic" of the research: the background context and reasoning that go into conceptualizing the issues in just this particular kind of way. It can take a long immersion in the activities of a neighboring discipline, along with some luck finding the right colleagues and informants, to begin to operate successfully within an alien system of concepts and assumptions. Many of the chapters provide substantial introductory discussions that helpfully present some of the relevant context; however, such discussions can go only so far, and it's notable that the conceptual landscape differs greatly across chapters.

Mutual understanding arises from and contributes to mutual engagement, and there is a substantial amount of cross-disciplinary engagement on show here. In addition to the fact that the volume as a whole is interdisciplinary, many chapters straddle disciplinary boundaries. Many of the moral problems used as stimuli in empirical studies discussed here are sourced from philosophy: Malle and Guglielmo (contributors to this volume from psychology) respond to work by philosopher Knobe (e.g., 2003); Ravenscroft (a contributor to this volume from philosophy) draws on findings from a range of empirical fields to buttress a view of the role of fiction in moral thought developed in philosophy by Nussbaum (1995, 1997); Mackenzie and Kennett (both philosophers contributing to this volume) respond (critically) to psychological research and theory by Haidt and Greene; while Levy (a contributor to this volume from philosophy) makes use of Haidt's theory to address questions in neuroethics concerning cognitive enhancement. Over time, such interaction will surely increase cross-disciplinary understanding, so what then is there to worry about?

In service of imagining how things might be, we suggest the following ideal for mutual engagement. The various disciplines might work in a complementary fashion within a common framework of issues and concepts. Important results in a particular field would quickly propagate to related areas across disciplinary boundaries. Interdisciplinary collaboration would be common.

While the cross-disciplinary interaction displayed in this volume is promising, there is as yet not much in the way of such a common framework. Nor is it clear that the various disciplines involved will inevitably develop a stronger cross-disciplinary focus since there are many pressures favoring within-discipline orientation, not the least of which are publication, grant, and career prospects. It may therefore need special effort if moral cognition research is to become a single coherent multidisciplinary project. We aim in this chapter to identify some questions and issues that might be the focus of further research and out of which a common framework might be developed.

It will help to initially focus on philosophy in particular, both because it has a special concern with integration and the big picture and because its relationship to empirical disciplines is especially problematic. Philosophy is often viewed suspiciously by empirical scientists, who can find its methods obscure and seemingly antiquated. It thus has, if nothing else, a crucial public relations problem, because if philosophy is to participate effectively in the aforementioned cooperative disciplinary matrix envisaged then respect for its methods and contributions is important. Broadly speaking, we see three possibilities for the relation between philosophy and the sciences: *replacement, engagement*, and *separatism*. In the replacement model, the expansion of empirical science wrests from philosophy its traditional subject matter; progress in (rigorous) empirical science will sweep aside (merely speculative) philosophical theory.[1] In the engagement model—which we will defend—philosophy becomes a full-fledged member of a cooperative disciplinary matrix, taking information from the empirical disciplines and contributing to them. In the separatism model, philosophy has fundamentally different methods and subject matter to the sciences and operates autonomously.

Separatism has been dominant in English-speaking analytic philosophy, which has conceived of the division between philosophy and the sciences in terms of a distinction between conceptual and empirical questions. Philosophy is properly concerned with conceptual questions, using *conceptual analysis* as its method, where conceptual analysis involves the formulation of theories concerning the meaning of particular concepts, like *knowledge, intentional action*, or *responsibility*. Such theories are evaluated by their success against counterexamples—that is, cases that fit the definition but are not instances of the concept. The method is notoriously dependent on intuitions: The judgment that a particular case is or is not an instance of the concept in question is based on the intuitions of the philosophical community, and the invention of counterexamples is also left to the imagination of the philosopher.[2] Philosophers, it turns out, have very fertile imaginations, with examples sometimes taking the form of esoteric science fiction–like scenarios. One problem is that it is not clear whether we can trust our intuitions for such strange cases. Another problem is that it is not clear whether the intuitions of highly trained philosophers are representative of the broader community, with some reason to think that they are not. This leads directly to the problem that, since psychologists can and do use empirical methods to investigate concepts, it seems hard to justify the claim that philosophers do not need to. The field of *experimental philosophy* was developed in response to these kinds of problems and uses experimental methods to investigate the interpretations that laypeople have of the conceptual problems that philosophers have been grappling with. Knobe (see, e.g., 2003) is an exponent of experimental philosophy, and Malle and Guglielmo's (Chapter 13) critical response to Knobe here is a fascinating example in which a traditional philosophical problem (the nature of intentionality judgments) has first been tackled by experimental philosophy, and then been taken up by psychology proper.

But philosophical theories are not always about the meaning of concepts; sometimes they are in ontological mode, concerned with the nature of something, albeit often something quite general or abstract. A salient example here is the nature of reflective agency. Philosophers are interested in concepts of reflective agency, but they also think it is a capacity that people really have (or in some cases lack), and theoretical investigation is particularly concerned with capturing the capacity that people have or lack. No matter how abstract such theories may be, to the extent they concern something real they must make some empirical assumptions. In the past, philosophers have thought that they could safely take as their empirical data common-sense facts that are obvious to any intelligent member of society and hence do not require any special scientific support. Basic common sense and introspection tell us that humans make decisions and often use reasoning to make these decisions. Philosophical theories have been built on such mundane facts, tracing out their more subtle implications. However, empirical cognitive research, including notably the seminal work of Nisbett and Wilson (1977), has shown that common sense and introspection can be very wrong about how our minds work (see also Schwitzgebel, 2008): This leaves philosophical theory potentially vulnerable.

Haidt's (2001) social intuitionist model of moral judgment taps into this structural weakness. It challenges the standard philosophical view of moral agency, which assigns an important role to reasoning, by drawing on contemporary cognitive research that has tended to emphasize the role of automatic emotional processes in moral judgment and action. The social intuitionist model is truly radical and would require philosophers to rethink many fundamental issues. For instance, Mackenzie (Chapter 11) argues toward the end of her chapter that our moral practices assume that we are *reason responders*, and philosophical conceptions of moral agency tend to place considerable weight on this (it is, for example, assumed in McGeer's concept of *coreactivity*; Chapter 14, this volume). If the social intuitionist model is correct, then our capacity for reason responding is far more limited than folk practice and philosophical theory have assumed, and substantial practical implications would follow from this. Because the standard philosophical view of moral agency has not been provided with clear, rigorous, empirical support, the challenge from social intuitionism has a great deal of plausibility. For comparison, Camerer, Loewenstein, and Prelec (2005) argue on similar grounds for much the same kind of intuitionist revolution in economics.

We find Mackenzie's (Chapter 11) and Kennett's (Chapter 12) criticisms of the social intuitionist model convincing: They argue that moral judgment and reasoning usually take place in a meaningful personal context and that as an important and not infrequent part of our lives we face major moral decisions that have significant and often complex consequences and that tend to provoke extended bouts of moral reflection. The examples they discuss include whether to end or stay in a marriage, whether to give Ritalin to a child diagnosed with attention deficit/hyperactivity disorder (ADHD), and whether to put an elderly parent in a nursing home. The experiments used to support the social intuitionist model, in contrast, typically involve artificial third-personal judgments, and there is good reason to worry that the results will not generalize to the kinds of major moral decisions that Mackenzie and Kennett describe. It is plausible that the bouts of moral reflection that accompany these kinds of decisions do indeed play a causal role in shaping the decisions made, even if the mechanism by which they do so is not straightforward. However, although these defenses of reflective reasoning are successful, in our view they are also incomplete. A more comprehensive, systematic empirical validation of the nature and role of reflective reasoning is needed. Ravenscroft's (Chapter 4) approach here is instructive: He begins with an intuitively plausible philosophical theory of the role of fiction in the development of moral capacities and surveys relevant empirical research, concluding that the findings do indeed support the theory. The empirical foundations of philosophical theories of moral agency need similar buttressing.

So, in our view, the separatism model cannot work for philosophy because it needs engagement with the sciences if it is to place its theories on a defensible footing against empirical challenges; however, the basic problem for philosophy also applies to some extent to all disciplines. That is, each discipline, and indeed each field, makes assumptions that might in principle be disproved by results in other fields and disciplines. Philosophy's structural weakness has been that it has had no systematic mechanisms for checking its empirical assumptions, but equally there are few systematic mechanisms for ensuring that research within any particular empirical field is compatible with results in other fields and disciplines. Thus, interdisciplinary engagement is an appropriate model to strive for, not simply because it would be nice but also because it is mandated by basic scholarly principles. It is important to have systematic mechanisms for checking assumptions.

Some may wonder, however, whether replacement is not the more or less inevitable fate of philosophy. The previously described case of psychological research on intentionality judgments, where we see psychology intruding into a traditional field of philosophy, is grist for such a view. And the issue of testability provides further motivation for the replacement view. The idea that important claims should be testable is a core value for scientists, one that philosophers do not always appear to take very seriously. A comment we have overheard (we name no names) is, "I don't mind working with philosophers as long as they're talking about things that are testable." Experimental philosophy applies empirical methods to philosophical questions, but if one is thinking of doing experimental philosophy the question arises, why not go all the way and become a full-fledged psychologist? After all, just what is the primary distinction between experimental philosophy and psychology?

One reason replacement might not be the inevitable fate of philosophy is that the remorseless drive to testability and experimentation may carry with it crucial limitations that are balanced by distinctive philosophical strengths. Testability as a goal can take different forms: We can distinguish *narrow* and *broad* testability. Narrow testability is the idea that every important claim should be testable and, if it is to be taken seriously, actually tested. Broad testability is the idea that theories should be assessed against available evidence, with theories that provide the best overall account of the evidence being preferred. Experimental scientists focus on narrow testability: Their mode of operation is the experiment, in which the manipulated phenomena are carefully shielded from uncontrolled contextual influences, and their primary academic currency is the experimental journal article. However, philosophers of science long ago gave up on the idea that narrow testability is an appropriate goal for science as a whole, and with good reason. Scientific theories can be complex and abstract; consequently, to arrive at a specific prediction it may be necessary to take into account multiple aspects of a theory (in some cases multiple theories) and use a complex chain of inferences that bridge between the theory and the shielded experimental situation. If an experimental result is not as predicted, the fault may lie with bridging inferences and methodological limitations rather than the theory (see, e.g., Levy & McGuire, Chapter 8). And, if the fault lies with the theory, it may be difficult to isolate where in the structure of the theory the mistake lies. Narrow experimental testing of all the individual ideas that go into a theory can be not merely impractical but also logically impossible. Hence, broad theory assessment must also focus on internal coherence and predictive and explanatory success in relation to the overall body of evidence. Darwin's theory of natural selection is a good example: It is strongly supported by the evidence, but there are no decisive individual tests.

Theories get their value because they can unite a variety of seemingly disparate cases into a coherent picture, draw subtle distinctions between superficially similar phenomena, and provide deep explanations. They make difficult phenomena tractable. In the case of moral cognition, we are in urgent need of theory because the phenomena are very complex. The issues that arise in the investigation of moral cognition include many that are fundamental to human cognition and agency in general and hence span all of the cognitive disciplines. Many of the issues are very abstract and conceptually difficult—for instance, the question of what it is to be a morally accountable agent appropriately held responsible for one's actions. As it happens, philosophy has a rich and sophisticated body of theory on exactly these issues (see, e.g., McGeer, Chapter 14). In fact, it is no accident that philosophy has this body of theory: It is constitutionally interested in high-level, synoptic issues and conceptually difficult questions. Thus, philosophy has distinctive strengths that can make a valuable contribution to the investigation of moral cognition, and these strengths are linked to the fact that it is *not* focused on narrow testability.

For this reason, although we think that experimental philosophy is a valuable addition to the philosophical toolkit, we do not think it is the right general model for conducting philosophy. Philosophy is concerned with more than just concepts; it has a broader role in theory construction on fundamental issues, such as the nature of moral agency, for instance. Indeed, the theoretical orientation of philosophy means that there can be problems translating philosophical thought experiments and counterexamples into experiments that investigate how laypeople think. Philosophical thought experiments and counterexamples are often designed to probe theoretical issues that are relatively distant from everyday problems, and the reactions of laypeople to such problems may not be particularly relevant to the theoretical questions being posed by philosophers. For comparison, there is little reason physicists should care about the responses of layfolk to the Schrödinger's cat thought experiment, which is an analytic tool for investigating the structure of a theory that only a competent physicist can properly understand. The problem of translating from a theoretical context to the investigation of ordinary thinking is compounded when the theory is normative because relations between normative theory and the descriptive nature of lay responses to moral problems are complex, as discussed in the next section. Philosophical thought experiments such as the Trolley Problem may prove useful tools for empirical researchers, (as, e.g., employed by Langdon & Delmas, Chapter 5; McIlwain et al., Chapter 6), but results should be interpreted with caution because the original thought experiments were framed with abstract theoretical concerns in mind. They were *not* originally designed to probe how people actually think about moral issues, and while they might nevertheless provide useful insights in the longer run it may be better to devise moral stimuli that specifically target real-world moral cognition.

One of the ways that high-level synoptic theory is valuable is that it can provide a carefully framed context within which more specific empirical questions can be posed and results interpreted. Other things being equal, the fact that a particular set of experimental results are consistent with the experimenter's hypothesis is only weakly informative because they might be consistent with other hypotheses. Theory can help to identify plausible or interesting alternative hypotheses; conversely, if these have not been carefully identified the experimenter's interpretation of the results is vulnerable. This is the weakness targeted by Mackenzie (Chapter 11) and Kennett (Chapter 12) in their critiques of the social intuitionist model. The latter is itself a relatively complex theory (confirming that philosophers are not alone in engaging in theory construction), but its specific analysis of moral agency is simplistic. This is because it gives relatively little thought to the real-world circumstances in which moral cognition usually occurs, overlooking important aspects of those circumstances, and it uses a limited conception of moral reasoning as solely principle-based reasoning. These limitations affect the generalizability of findings that are interpreted to support the theory. Although the results on *moral dumbfounding* (see, e.g., Haidt, 2001) are consistent with expectations derived from social intuitionist theory, the experiments are not representative of real-world circumstances of moral judgment and reasoning, so we cannot safely generalize from these results to real-world moral judgment and reasoning. The attention that philosophy has given to the high-level analysis of moral agency pays off here, helping us identify aspects of moral agency in the unshielded, contextually influenced, natural human situation that may not be apparent in a narrow, laboratory-based context. In this case, qualitative analyses of data on real-world moral agency may reveal personal situatedness, skill learning, and a far more complex suite of cognitive processes than engaged by snapshot moral judgments in response to peculiar third-personal vignettes.

Thus, in our view, replacement is an unlikely scenario because moral cognition research needs theory, and philosophy has distinctive strengths in theory construction. It will not be the only locus of theory, but philosophy is well suited to the development of abstract, conceptually difficult theory. In this respect, the proneness of philosophy to the use of bizarre science-fiction examples makes some sense: If one is being very careful about the logical structure of a theory then logically possible examples and counterexamples matter, even if they are well outside the range of normal experience. On the other hand, theory must also capture the actual cases, and it is a problem that philosophy has not had a structured approach to the use of empirical examples. Philosophy cannot levitate: It needs firm empirical grounding, and it should strive for broad testability. To achieve this it needs engagement. But the empirical disciplines also need cross-disciplinary engagement for assumption checking, the framing of questions, and the interpretation of results. Ideally, we might hope for a rich flow of information between fields and disciplines and a virtuous feedback cycle in which current empirical findings revise the conceptualization of high-level theory, which feeds back to the framing of empirical questions.

One of the most important ways for interdisciplinary engagement to occur is organically through ad hoc connections and by means of workshops and books such as this. Ongoing engagement should lead to better mutual understanding and better use of complementary skills and knowledge across disciplines. Considering the pressure for within-discipline focus across the cognitive sciences as a whole, piecemeal interactions in the context of a mostly mosaic field and discipline structure might be the more probable future of moral cognition research. However, as we have noted, it is not clear that organic interactions will be enough to promote sustained cooperative engagement. Thus far, we have tried to make the case that closer forms of engagement would be better, but the question then is how this might be achieved. A strongly top-down approach is unlikely to succeed, among other reasons because it is hard to anticipate the directions that future research will take. However, some core issues of enduring interest are relevant to all of the disciplines involved in moral cognition research, including (1) relations between descriptive and normative issues; (2) the nature of core cognitive architecture, as applied to the question of the various forms of moral cognition and the ways that they shape action; (3) taxonomies of moral types; and (4) moral development. Topics such as these could serve as cross-disciplinary focal points, and if the conceptualization of core topics becomes more standardized it would become easier to relate research in one field to others. Even the identification of areas of dispute, as we seek to do in each of the following cases briefly, may help to clarify the kind of work that needs to be done.

RELATIONS BETWEEN DESCRIPTIVE AND NORMATIVE ISSUES

Philosophical moral theory is more normatively than descriptively oriented, though as discussed already it does aim to capture the capacities of real agents, and philosophers need no reminding of the significance of normative issues. Empirical researchers, on the other hand, have a strong descriptive orientation. Close connections between empirical and normative questions will be an ongoing challenge for moral cognition research because they present difficult conceptual and practical problems. To begin with, it is important to clearly distinguish between descriptive and normative questions. For instance, Mackenzie (Chapter 11) claims that Haidt (e.g., 2001) has failed to grasp the normative nature of cognitivist moral theory, misunderstanding it as descriptive. Criticisms appropriate to descriptive theory do not necessarily apply to normative theory; thus, even if the evidence indicated that people do not commonly employ reflective reasoning to causally influence their decisions, this wouldn't show that they should not. Descriptive and normative issues are linked, however. Thus, if people cannot shape their decisions using reflective reasoning then we should abandon normative models that suggest they ought to.

Empirical research tends to take *normal* (e.g., normal subjects, healthy subjects, normal development) as the baseline for comparison in defining pathological conditions. This is a reasonable starting point. However, it will be important to clarify distinct descriptive and normative issues, and as empirical research makes progress it will be increasingly necessary for it to directly address normative issues. As a basic point we should not confuse *normal* with *normative*: Normal moral cognition may differ substantially between cultures and across times, and, moreover, the most morally admirable individuals may be fairly rare. It is even possible that we might come to decide that statistically normal forms of moral cognition are morally objectionable. There are thus two quite distinct projects: (1) identify the statistical distribution of forms of moral cognition in the population, and (2) develop normative classifications of forms of moral cognition. Psychopathy is both statistically abnormal and morally objectionable, and the classification of psychopathy as morally objectionable is part of the normative project.

We have already said that philosophical conceptual analysis is notorious for relying on intuitions, but empirical researchers are also relying on some combination of intuitions and community attitudes for their normative classifications. Philosophy at least has the advantage that it subjects such intuitions to sustained critical scrutiny; it will be a problem if a veneer of objectivity obscures the role of normative intuitions in empirical research. In the case of psychopathy, the appropriate normative classification (that it is morally objectionable and should be prevented) seems obvious and unproblematic, but in other cases things won't be so easy. As empirical classifications become more fine-grained and interventions more powerful, the normative issues will become less obvious and in some cases more consequential. For example, it may be possible to prevent a psychopathic or Machiavellian developmental pathway with empathy-enhancing treatment in early childhood but at the expense of later career success for the individual. As powerful intervention techniques become available, parents, with varied knowledge and goals, will want to take them up. Some parents may try to promote empathy to a degree that is unbalanced and dysfunctional. Others may attempt to deliberately reduce the empathy of their child in the hope that this will help them succeed in a career such as business or law.[3] Entrepreneurial figures of the Dr. Phil variety will promulgate advice widely.

In such a context, careful, systematic, normative analysis will be a vital input for all aspects of empirical research, including the classification of pathologies and the construction of intervention techniques. Normative models of moral cognition will be important both as a contrast for classifying pathologies and as a goal for interventions. Again, these are reasons for close engagement between philosophy and the empirical disciplines studying moral cognition.

MORAL COGNITION AND COGNITIVE ARCHITECTURE

Separatism is not a good model also because larger theories of cognition can have important implications for moral cognition, including the form that moral knowledge takes and the way that it shapes behavior. Part of understanding moral cognition is the task of embedding moral cognition in a larger account of cognitive architecture, and no individual field can adequately tackle this alone. By *cognitive architecture* we mean the major structure of the cognitive system. Is there one main system or multiple interacting systems? If the latter, how are the systems related? What are the representational and processing characteristics of each system?

Haidt's appeal to dual-process accounts (see, e.g., 2001) is an example of how broader conceptions of cognitive architecture can shape and constrain proposals on the nature of moral cognition. According to dual-process theorizing, there is a fast, high-capacity automatic system and a slow, low-capacity conscious system (see Evans, 2008, for a review). Mackenzie (Chapter 11) and Kennett (Chapter 12) argue that major moral decisions induce moral reasoning that plausibly influences decisions and that even when moral judgments or actions are fast and automatic they will often have been shaped by a prior history of moral learning that involved rational reflection. But, if all rapid moral judgments, and the actions thus instigated, are purely automatic, as dual-process theory suggests, our rational moral agency is still very limited and somewhat robotic—for instance, we can review and plan ahead rationally, and rationally learn new response dispositions, but in the heat of the moment we operate on autopilot.

It is arguable, however, that an important class of cognitive processes does not fit into either pole of the dual-process taxonomy. Specifically, these processes are controlled but relatively low effort, rapid, and relatively high capacity. These characteristics might allow effective cognitive control of proximal action in time-pressured situations, contrary to dual-process theory. If such cognitive processes exist, they might support controlled moral judgment in proximal action control. The question then is what reasons there are to think these processes exist. To begin with, consider controlled cognition. Although the paradigm form of controlled cognition is reasoning—extended linguistic deliberation—there are a variety of kinds of controlled cognition. Mental rotation is a nonlinguistic example (e.g., imagine a red Volkswagen Beetle; now rotate the mental image 180 degrees in the horizontal plane), as is visual search (e.g., scanning the room for your keys). Controlled cognitive processes can be used to make rapid explicit judgments (e.g., a visual comparison to decide which of two objects is larger), and controlled judgment processes can also tap into implicit knowledge systems. Consider, for instance, estimating whether a box containing books will be too heavy to pick up or whether you will be able to jump between two rocks when crossing a stream. These judgment processes tap into motor emulation mechanisms that are not directly consciously accessible but that provide input to conscious judgment.

The next issue to consider is working memory. Famously, Miller (1956) argued that working memory capacity is about seven items, though Broadbent (1975) estimated that for active reasoning processes capacity was significantly less: three to four items. This is reflected in the dual-process theory claim that system 2 is capacity limited. Miller, however, noted a mechanism for circumventing the capacity limitation of working memory, namely, chunking. The number of representations that can be actively maintained is limited, but each representation may itself contain a lot of information. Using representations with high information content is thus a way of extending the capacity of working memory without violating the basic capacity limit. Ericsson and Kintsch's (1995) theory of long-term working memory built on this idea to show how experts can rapidly encode and retrieve large amounts of information by using familiar conceptual structures as a framework for encoding and retrieval. Because experts can rapidly access large amounts of information, they can make rapid controlled judgments. Consider a pilot coming in to land, whose airspeed is high and who must decide whether he can lose enough speed to land safely or should abort the landing and go around. The pilot must make the decision under time pressure, but the decision is likely to involve practiced controlled evaluation employing a rich situation model of the aircraft and circumstances (Endsley, 1995).

With these pieces in place we can now tease out the connection to moral cognition. Just as Mackenzie (Chapter 11) and Kennett (Chapter 12) point out, we are all morally skilled: Through childhood and as adults we gain extensive moral training. Not only has this furnished us with a stock of prelearned judgments and responses—we do not need to think through whether stealing is wrong every time we go to the shops—but it also provides us with a body of moral knowledge we can draw on to make controlled moral judgments on the fly. For instance, we rightly blame people for being tactless, but being tactful is a complex skill that must at times draw on rich situational information, including personality, the mood of the person we are talking to, and their recent experiences. We are often tactless because we are thoughtless, and conversely being tactful requires thought (i.e., paying attention, anticipating, choosing our words carefully). Just like the pilot, we can shape our actions using controlled evaluation that draws on a rich understanding of the situation. Thus, we suggest, it is possible to make considered moral judgments in the heat of the moment and to use them in proximal control of action.

In this case we should reject the apparent limitation on moral reasoning implied by dual-process theory because, we have argued, dual-process theory is oversimplistic in neglecting the possibility of pervasive decision making that is fast and relatively effortless but controlled and relatively unencapsulated. Generalizing from this case, the nature of cognitive architecture will impose strong constraints on many aspects of moral cognition, and consequently it will be important to relate moral cognition to global theories of cognition. At this point, it may be worth returning to the question of the relation between philosophy and the sciences. Before, we claimed that philosophical theories of agency need buttressing against empirical challenges like that of Haidt (e.g., 2001), and we cited Ravenscroft's (Chapter 4) survey of empirical evidence pertaining to Nussbaum's (1995, 1997) theory of the role of fiction in moral cognition as an example of how such buttressing might occur. The critique we have just given of dual-process theory is another example, and conceptually the issue of cognitive architecture is an appropriate intermediate level for theory bridging between more specific forms of cognitive research and theories of agency. Theories of cognitive architecture and theories of agency should be closely meshed, both because facts about cognitive architecture will be constraints on theories of agency and because theories of agency provide a higher-level understanding of the role that cognitive architecture performs. If they are meshed it will be easier to relate theories of agency to empirical findings about cognition, and challenges like that of Haidt can be assessed on a systematic basis.

MORAL TAXONOMIES

All of the fields investigating moral cognition have an interest in reaching a shared conceptualization of core moral phenomena. Key taxonomies include kinds of moral agents, kinds of moral cognitive states, and kinds of moral cognitive processes. More fundamentally, there is the question of how the domain of the moral itself is to be characterized. Still more fundamentally, there are questions concerning the basic structure of the taxonomies.

With regard to the last issue we will distinguish between *clean* and *messy* taxonomies: Clean taxonomies partition neatly, whereas messy taxonomies do not. One reason messy taxonomies can arise is because the categories are the product of complex underlying causal factors that overlap across categories. Some work in moral cognition research appears to assume a fairly clean taxonomy for the domain of the moral—for instance, the idea that moral cognition is domain specific (see, e.g., de Rosnay & Fink, Chapter 2) and the idea that the moral can be neatly delineated in terms of the moral–conventional distinction (Blair, 1995). FitzGerald and Goldie (Chapter 10) are skeptical that the scope of the moral is so clear-cut, and we tend to agree. As they point out, a given thick concept such as *moral disgust* can integrate ethical, prudential, and aesthetic considerations. Case, Oaten, and Stevenson (Chapter 9) similarly argue that moral disgust is rich and distinct from *core disgust*. They find that there is little evidence to support a causal link between judgments of moral violations and core disgust. FitzGerald and Goldie also note that supposedly conventional rule violations may involve causing offense or other kinds of harms. They cite Prinz's (2008) example of wearing shoes indoors in Japan: Although the rule is nominally conventional, violating it can cause great offense (a harm). De Rosnay and Fink (Chapter 2) list not putting toys away properly as an example of a conventional violation, but not putting toys away properly might be seen as a harm to Mummy. When Mummy is explaining to the child why she must put her toys away properly she may emphasize just this point.

The idea that moral rules are obligatory and universal whereas conventional rules are alterable and contextual also seems open to challenge. Moral rules are also indexed to context—for example, the rule "do not kill" is suspended in war and for self-defense (a point that exerts considerable imaginative pull for young boys)—and on the other hand, within a context, supposedly conventional rules may be treated as obligatory. The way that harm is caused may be context sensitive, meaning that some kinds of harm avoidance or prevention may not be easily captured by universal rules. Tact, which we used already as an example of on-the-fly moral judgment, shows this kind of context sensitivity. "Be tactful" is a good rule of thumb, but being tactful is very context specific. Tact also shows higher-level context sensitivity: Being tactful is not always the right thing to do, for sometimes plain speaking is more appropriate.

The general point is that the nature and scope of the domain of the moral is itself a difficult issue. Even the idea that morality should be understood in terms of rules and moral action understood as rule following is contested. This view is known in philosophy as *ethical generalism* and contrasts with the position known as *moral particularism* (Dancy, 2009). It is problematic that many researchers in the interdisciplinary field of moral cognition seem to be favoring ethical generalism without much critical analysis or awareness that there are plausible alternative views. It is important to consider moral particularism as a normative theory because it provides a very different vision of ideal moral cognition to that suggested by ethical generalism. It is also worth examining actual forms of moral cognition from a particularist standpoint. For instance, some forms of cognition that are not moral from a generalist point of view will count as moral from a particularist point of view; the normative distinction thus affecting the descriptive scope of the phenomena to be investigated. An emphasis on moral rules and obligation, for instance, may obscure nuanced situational judgment. De Rosnay and Fink (Chapter 2) describe the mind-set of older children as "increasingly deontic"; this may be right, but only part of the story. That is, older children may have greater awareness of moral obligation and the emotional consequences of moral violations but also can be more fluid and context sensitive in their moral judgments and reasoning. They become not crude rule followers but sophisticated moral interpreters able to weigh up multiple morally relevant factors in a situation and make a context-sensitive judgment (compare Churchland, 2000; Clark 1996, 2000). Is it okay to lie sometimes, for instance, to protect someone else's feelings? Was the hungry, deprived child wrong to steal food from the local store? Maybe not so much. It is also possible that there are individual differences in styles of moral cognition, with some individuals tending toward a universal, rule-oriented style and others to a particularist style that emphasizes contextual judgment.

If it is hard to even define the scope of the domain, more specific taxonomic issues in moral cognition research are not likely to be much easier. The nature of the moral emotions will be one of the key taxonomic issues, and empathy is a particular focus of attention in this volume. As noted in Langdon and Mackenzie's introduction, definitions of empathy vary across chapters. To briefly recapitulate, Hawes and Dadds (Chapter 3) define empathy as encompassing both *affective empathy* (the sharing of another's emotional state), and *cognitive empathy* (the understanding of another's mental state). McIlwain et al. (Chapter 6) adopt a similar distinction between *hot* and *cold* empathy. In contrast, de Rosnay and Fink (Chapter 2) distinguish empathy from psychological *perspective taking*, claiming that perspective taking need not involve empathy. They see empathy as taking two forms: as experienced responsive emotions (typically sadness or concern), and a more active *empathic role-taking* (distinct from perspective taking). Ravenscroft (Chapter 4) similarly conceives empathy as involving the experience of the emotion of the other; simply understanding the emotional state of the other is not sufficient and indeed not necessary, according to Ravenscroft.

One point to note in assessing these various usages of the term *empathy* is that there is some degree of leeway in how we frame our definitions. Thus, if we want to define the term empathy so that it encompasses all ways of knowing about the emotional states of others, we can stipulate that it does. On the other hand, we might prefer definitions that are finer-honed to avoid conflation of distinctive content. According to the *New Oxford American Dictionary*, empathy is "the ability to understand and share the feelings of another." To our sensibilities, simple emotion contagion does not count as sufficient for empathy on this definition because emotion contagion lacks the understanding component (so we disagree with Ravenscroft [Chapter 4] on this point). And, on the other hand, we agree with de Rosnay and Fink (Chapter 2) that empathy is not reducible to perspective taking or theory of mind. We think the most natural interpretation is to conceive empathy as having two components that are jointly required: emotion mirroring and emotion knowledge. Empathy involves emotion mirroring, with cognitive understanding that the experienced emotion is that of the other. In effect, this way of defining empathy limits it to de Rosnay and Fink's second form, in which case their first form is better understood as sympathy rather than empathy. Sympathy is distinct from empathy in that the emotion may complement rather than mirror the other; feeling concerned for someone else is not necessarily sharing their emotion, for example (see Goldie, 2000, Chapter 7, for a similar view).

This way of defining empathy is consistent with the appraisal view of emotions advocated by Mackenzie and the picture articulated by de Oliveira-Souza and Moll, which see moral emotions and other morally relevant cognitive states as involving the coordination of multiple systems and processes. They suggest that moral behavior involves the engagement of *event-structured complexes*, which are procedures evoked by specific contexts, and they define psychological states as *event-feature-emotion complexes*, which involve the coordinated activation of social knowledge, emotions, and motivations. One way that the involvement of cognition in the emotional response is significant is that it can permit higher-order regulation. For example, consider a hypothetical case involving a man who, to punish his wife, seems to forget her birthday. In the definition of empathy proposed here, if he simply knows she will be hurt and unhappy then he is using emotion knowledge and this is not a case of empathy. On the other hand, if he thinks about what it will be like from her point of view and senses how she will feel, then he is using empathy. But *he* is *happy* that she will be hurt: He can empathically mirror her emotional state but maintain his own distinct (contrary) emotional attitude. Call this unsympathetic empathy. The emotion here has a complex higher-order psychological structure that includes high-order regulation (the simultaneous maintenance of two distinct emotional attitudes). Such high-order regulation may be a key part of skilled social emotional engagement of both pathological and good kinds. Of the various discussions of empathy in this volume, only McIlwain et al. (Chapter 6) consider strategic control of empathy, and their focus is on its role in Machiavellian moral psychology. But the strategic control of emotion may be integral to healthy emotional responsiveness (Lambie & Marcel, 2002; Ochsner & Gross, 2005).

The three models of moral judgment canvassed by Langdon and Delmas (Chapter 5) emphasize bottom-up processes. In the Humean model, an act triggers an emotional response, which triggers an intuitive judgment as to the moral properties of the act. In the Humean–Kantian model, an act triggers parallel emotional and conscious reflective responses, which may cohere or conflict. In the Rawlsian model, an act triggers unconscious analysis of causal and intentional properties of the act, which produces a moral judgment, which in turn induces emotional responses and conscious reasoning. Of these models, only the Rawlsian identifies a clear directive role for cognition, though confined to unconscious cognitive processes. This may underestimate the role of conscious cognitive processes in situational interpretation and the sensitivity of emotional responses to interpretation. Consider a case in which someone you meet at a conference tells you about problems they are having in their department. Colleagues are being unkind, are undermining the person, and so on. You respond empathically and sympathetically. As the conversation goes on, though, you find out that this is only the latest in a long series of troubled work situations: The person had unhappy relations at the previous place they worked, and the place before that; in fact, in a long series of positions the person does not seem to have ever had decent, considerate colleagues. You start to notice that this person's manner is socially odd, and you begin to wonder if he might not be at least partly responsible for his problems. Your initial empathic response declines.

From a normative point of view the cognitive formation of interpretations is crucial: It is important to make a reasonable effort to form an accurate interpretation before arriving at a moral judgment, especially if the judgment will be acted upon. In other words, *rushing to judgment* is a moral failure. For instance, if you were to repeat to others as true, or as likely to be true, the accusations of your unhappy conversation partner concerning his colleagues and they turn out to be false, you would be participating in slander. Malle and Guglielmo (Chapter 13) find that intentionality judgments are not driven by moral judgments, which is as it should be. Normatively, we want moral judgments to depend on analysis of intentionality. In some cases the analysis of intentionality is likely to be very rapid and largely unconscious, but in other more difficult cases we may need to employ controlled cognition. In this example, your initial moral interpretation follows that of the person telling you their story: You believe there has been injustice, and you feel angry on their behalf; however, as the conversation unfolds you begin to suspect this interpretation. Musing reflectively, you assemble clues to a different interpretation: the person's hunched and somewhat mechanical demeanor, wooden voice and prolix monologue-style of conversation, the improbability of having uniformly bad colleagues, and so on. Your moral assessment of the situation changes—you are no longer confident that the person's colleagues are being unfair to him—and flowing from this revised interpretation your emotional responses also change.

In addition to highlighting the role of cognitive processes in reaching moral judgments, this example also supports another point made by Mackenzie (Chapter 11), namely, that conceptualizing moral evaluations in terms of *acts* and *judgments* may give an overly static sense of what is going on. Moral evaluations may sometimes concern complex situations that unfold over time rather than individual acts and may involve more or less continuously developing interpretations rather than one-shot judgments.

A general conclusion to draw from these points is that our moral taxonomy will tend to be somewhat messy. It is hard to neatly characterize the domain of the moral; emotion and cognition are entangled, and moral judgments sometimes involve thick concepts and rich cognitive processes, making it both difficult and unnecessary to strictly distinguish moral cognition from cognition more broadly. As noted already, the integrative account of moral psychology given by de Oliveira-Souza and Moll (Chapter 7) is consistent with—and helps to explain—this messiness. The multidimensional trait view of personality espoused by McIlwain et al. (Chapter 6) and by Langdon and Delmas (Chapter 5) also fits this picture, as does the continuity view of psychopathy that Langdon and Delmas argue for. In their view, the traits of clinically identified psychopaths are continuous with personality traits present in the general population. Broadly speaking, the messiness of moral taxonomies will count in favor of cross-disciplinary engagement because many issues and phenomena are closely linked and will tend to cut across field specializations.

MORAL DEVELOPMENT

Different theoretical perspectives will regard development differently; a nativist perspective diminishes the importance of specific experience and learning in favor of maturational processes, whereas perspectives that emphasize cognitive learning will emphasize social experience as a driver of learning, as considered by de Rosnay and Fink (Chapter 2). Skill learning emerges as an important feature of moral development for Mackenzie (Chapter 11) and Kennett (Chapter 12), underwriting their claims that many unreflective intuitions and response dispositions in the adult are both rationally acquired and rational in execution, despite the absence of concurrent reflection. The account of controlled moral judgment sketched herein similarly appeals to moral development as involving expertise and skill acquisition. In light of these kinds of claims, the literature on skill and expertise may have interesting implications for research on moral development. For example, expertise research indicates that high levels of deliberate practice are needed to reach elite levels, as opposed to more informal performance and exposure (Ericsson, Krampe, & Tesch-Römer, 1993). In contrast, although instruction and "coaching" play an important role in early moral development, most moral learning is informal.

The *shunting* view of moral development advocated by McIlwain et al. (Chapter 6) suggestively depicts what moral development might be like from a multidimensional trait perspective. Traits show parametric variation and are linked. Consequently, extreme scores on some traits restrict later variation in other traits. Some trajectory-dependent multidimensional trait constellations become more likely than others. This is congenial to the integrative account of de Oliveira-Souza and Moll (Chapter 7), and indeed their integrative picture is a necessary complement to the multidimensional trait picture because we need to understand the process interactions (e.g., McIlwain et al.'s *cascading constraints*) that underlie changes in trait values.

For this kind of analysis it will be important to characterize the fine-grained structure of the shunting forces. McIlwain et al. (Chapter 6) suggest that early distrust and fearlessness might combine to reduce the kind of experience of others' emotions required for the full development of emotion perception. Cognitive control and interpretation, which we suggested already as being important to emotions such as empathy, may also play an important role in developmental shunting. For instance, it may be that children learn interpretive schemas that help to organize their behaviors, to enhance their reward experience, and to justify those behaviors. Abnormal affective responsiveness produces unusual reward structure and unusual behavior patterns. We might expect that the interpretive schemas that develop will tend to support these behaviors and to incorporate defensive and justificatory mechanisms that support a coherent self-concept in the face of dissonance with socially normative schemas and values. The cynical worldview and blame shifting that McIlwain et al. (Chapter 6) report in Machiavellian people are consistent with this picture. Thus, as well as a broad understanding of the role of empathy in moral development, it will be important to look at the nature of children's conceptual learning in relation to the role of interpretive schemas in both moral evaluation and in self-control. De Rosnay and Fink's (Chapter 2) findings concerning conscience point in this direction; they show that higher levels of moral self-concept are associated with more mature social behavior.

The issue of conscience, however, raises questions about the nature of moral motivation. The conception of the moral domain in terms of obligations and the restriction of self-interest[4] tends to put the emphasis on the negative side of things: Moral agents avoid actions they would otherwise want to perform. De Rosnay and Finks's (Chapter 2) discussion of conscience in terms of awareness of the negative psychological consequences of moral violations is consistent with this, suggesting a negative view of moral motivation: Moral agents seek to avoid morally bad actions. But some moral agents, at least some of the time, may be seekers of good, actively pursuing morally worthy outcomes because they value them. In relation to learning, we may need to consider learning in which children discover the benefits of being good, as well as learning in which they come to appreciate the negative consequences of being bad.

Another way we may need to take an active view of moral agency relates back to the role of interpretation discussed already. Our emphasis on the controlled use of mental models is consistent with a strong role for imagination in cognition, and we agree with Mackenzie (Chapter 11) that imaginative engagement with situations will be an important form of moral reasoning. We also agree with Ravenscroft (Chapter 4) and Nussbaum (1995, 1997) that fiction will play a strong role in cultivating imaginative capacity. But Ravenscroft's view of the response to fiction strikes us as too passive, in that he doesn't allow enough of a role for control and interpretation. Ravenscroft's view of the dangers of violence in fiction seems still to regard the consumers of fiction as passive, noninterpretive imitators. The empirical evidence on the impact of fictive violence on real-world violence may be more mixed than his survey indicates, with Ferguson (2008) casting doubt on a link between violent computer games and violent behavior in boys—for example, youth violence has declined substantially even as sales of violent computer games have been increasing. From a theoretical standpoint, we would expect that children with sophisticated interpretive schemas will be skilled at distinguishing fictive from real violence and able to enjoy the former relatively safely. Young boys may fantasize about being Batman or a Jedi Knight, but most of them realize that, unfortunately, the world they actually live in operates on different rules.

Fiction provides children with conceptual schemas, and it probably also teaches them to be sophisticated navigators of conceptual schemas, distinguishing different perspectives and actively interpreting and evaluating, along the way cultivating their own point of view. The right kind of parental encouragement may promote active interpretation and facilitate the development of reflective skills. Active interpretation is a double-edged sword, however, and in some cases children may become resistant to the moral messages that parents and other members of society are sending them. The general point is that it will be important to understand the specific conceptual structures that emerge in moral development and the active processes of engagement and interpretation employed by the child.

The final point we make here concerns the nature of moral reasoning. The conception of moral reasoning employed by Piaget (1932/1997), Haidt (2001), and many others is one based on ethical generalism: Moral reasoning is concerned with abstract principles. A different conception, more consistent with the personal, situated point of view of moral agency, is that moral reasoning tends to take the form of relatively concrete problem-solving, employing conceptual resources derived from situations encountered. Consider a young child trying to build a bridge with wooden blocks: A good part of the problem-solving process will involve direct manipulation, rearranging the blocks, comparing one block with another. It will also involve the formation of mental models of the blocks and their bridge-relevant possibilities. These mental models guide controlled exploration of the physical problem, and controlled manipulation of the mental models themselves can be used to explore the structure of the problem and generate insight. But the child almost certainly will not form an abstract geometric representation of the bridge construction problem and arrive at a solution through formal geometric analysis. Moral reasoning in general may be more like the child's problem solving, involving situationally acquired mental models rather than deep theoretical analysis. Piaget (e.g., 1970) thought that problem solving leads to the formation of abstract formal representations, but we can reject that aspect of his theory while retaining the insight that problem solving plays a key role in psychological development (cf. Hooker, 1994).

CONCLUSIONS

A large part of our purpose in this chapter has been to tease out higher-level issues that arise out of the other chapters in the pursuit of elements of a framework that might eventually help to coordinate research across the fields and disciplines that study moral cognition. To reiterate the point we made at the end of the second section, all of the disciplines have an interest in the development of shared conceptualizations of core issues, and such conceptualizations could serve as cross-disciplinary focal points. Some of the more fundamental issues include relations between descriptive and normative issues, moral cognition and cognitive architecture, key moral taxonomies such as normative and pathological forms of moral cognition, the nature of morality itself, and the nature of moral development. Our discussion of these issues here can do little more than gesture at some of the problems that will need to be addressed in the development of a common framework, and no doubt many will disagree with our take on some of these issues. The more important point, however, is that, in general, multilevel theorizing will be helpful—that is, approaching particular issues in moral cognition with an explicit account of how these issues are embedded in a picture of moral cognition as a whole, and (in turn) of cognition as a whole. The big picture will be heavily contested, but even the recognition of disputed ground will help in the development of a more coordinated multidisciplinary approach. In terms of content, many of the chapters here have supported a more cognitive view of moral cognition than the intuitionist account while nevertheless recognizing that emotion plays an integral role. As such, they challenge the principle-based picture of moral reasoning and support an active, situated picture of moral agency.[5]

REFERENCES

Blair, R. J. R. (1995). A cognitive developmental approach to morality: Investigating the psychopath. *Cognition, 57,* 1–29.

Broadbent, D. E. (1975). The magic number seven after fifteen years. In A. Kennedy & A. Wilkes (Eds.), *Studies in long-term memory* (pp. 3–18). London: Wiley.

Brooks, D. (2009). The end of philosophy. *New York Times.* Retrieved December 21, 2010 from http://www.nytimes.com/2009/04/07/opinion/07Brooks.html

Camerer, C., Loewenstein, G., & Prelec, D. (2005). Neuroeconomics: How neuroscience can inform economics. *Journal of Economic Literature, 43*(1), 9–64.

Churchland, P. M. (2000). Rules, know-how, and the future of moral cognition. *Canadian Journal of Philosophy, S26,* 291–306.

Clark, A. (1996). Connectionism, moral cognition, and collaborative problem-solving. In L. May, M. Friedman, & A. Clark (Eds.), *Mind and morals: Essays on ethics and cognitive science* (pp. 109–127). Cambridge, MA: MIT Press.

Clark, A. (2000). Word and action: Reconciling rules and know-how in moral cognition. *Canadian Journal of Philosophy, S26,* 267–289.

Dancy, J. (2009, Spring). Moral particularism. In E. N. Zalta (Ed.), *The Stanford encyclopedia of philosophy.* Retrieved March 2009 from http://plato.stanford.edu/entries/moral-particularism/

Endsley, M. R. (1995). Toward a theory of situation awareness in dynamic systems. *Human Factors, 37,* 32–64.

Ericsson, K. A., & Kintsch, W. (1995). Long-term working memory. *Psychological Review, 102,* 211–245.

Ericsson, K. A., Krampe, R. T., & Tesch-Römer, C. (1993). The role of deliberate practice in the acquisition of expert performance. *Psychological Review, 100,* 363–406.

Evans, J. S. B. T. (2008). Dual-processing accounts of reasoning, judgment, and social cognition. *The Annual Review of Psychology, 59,* 255–278.

Ferguson, C. J. (2008). The school shooting/violent video game link: Causal relationship or moral panic? *Journal of Investigative Psychology and Offender Profiling,* 5, pp. 25–37.

Goldie, P. (2000). *The emotions: A philosophical exploration.* Oxford, UK: Oxford University Press.

Goldman, A. (2007). Philosophical intuitions: Their target, their source, and their epistemic status. *Grazer Philosophische Studien, 74,* 1–26.

Haidt, J. (2001). The emotional dog and its rational tail: A social intuitionist approach to moral judgment. *Psychological Review, 108,* 814–834.

Haidt, J., Björklund, F., & Murphy, S. (2000). *Moral dumbfounding: When intuition finds no reason.* Unpublished manuscript, University of Virginia.

Hooker, C. A. (1994). Regulatory constructivism: On the relation between evolutionary epistemology and Piaget's genetic epistemology. *Biology and Philosophy, 9,* 197–244.

Knobe, J. (2003). Intentional action in folk psychology: An experimental investigation. *Philosophical Psychology, 16,* 309–324.

Lambie, J. A., & Marcel, A. J. (2002). Consciousness and the varieties of emotion experience: A theoretical framework. *Psychological Review, 109,* 219–259.

Miller, G. A. (1956). The magical number seven, plus or minus two: Some limits on our capacity for processing information. *Psychological Review, 63,* 81–97.

Nisbett, R. E., & Wilson, T. (1977). Telling more than we can know: Verbal reports on mental processes. *Psychological Review, 84,* 231–259.

Nussbaum, M. (1995). *Poetic justice: The literary imagination and public life.* Boston: Beacon Press.

Nussbaum, M. (1997). *Cultivating humanity: A classical defense of reform in liberal education.* Cambridge, MA: Harvard University Press.

Ochsner, K. N., & Gross, J. J. (2005). The cognitive control of emotion. *Trends in Cognitive Sciences, 9*(5), 242–249.

Piaget, J. (1932/1997). *The moral judgment of the child.* Oxford, UK: Harcourt, Brace.

Piaget, J. (1970). *The principles of genetic epistemology* (W. Mays, Trans.). London: Routledge & Kegan Paul.

Prinz, J. (2008). Is morality innate? In W. Sinnott-Armstrong (Ed.), *Moral psychology, volume 1: The evolution of morality: adaptations and innateness* (pp. 367–406). Cambridge, MA: MIT Press.

Schwitzgebel, E. (2008). The unreliability of naïve introspection. *Philosophical Review, 117,* 245–273.

Sosa, E. (2007). Experimental philosophy and philosophical intuition. *Philosophical Studies, 132,* 99–107.

ENDNOTES

1. The idea that science will replace philosophy is a not uncommon trope (see, e.g., a *New York Times* article discussing Haidt's research; Brooks, 2009).
2. The nature of the intuitions involved in philosophical theorizing is controversial, but they are arguably not in general the gut feelings posited by Haidt's social intuitionist model. According to Sosa (2007) intuitions are cognitive competencies, while Goldman (2007) sees intuitions as associated with the content of concepts: Possessing a concept gives rise to beliefs in accord with the concept.
3. Toughening up a child for the rigors of life is not an uncommon parental strategy. Sending the child to military school is a traditional method, whereas the song "A Boy Named Sue" poignantly describes a more unconventional approach.
4. For example, de Oliveira-Souza and Moll (Chapter 7) say that "the key for defining ... motivations as 'moral' is their ability to overcome the (proximate) interests of the self or agent."
5. Our thanks to Catriona Mackenzie for helpful comments on an earlier draft of this chapter and to Andrew Geeves and Doris McIlwain for many discussions on skill and emotion.

Author Index

Subject Index